DATE DUE

PERSPECTIVES IN SOCIOLOGY

PERSPECTIVES IN SOCIOLOGY

Herman R. Lantz, *General Editor*

Forty Years of Pioneer Life

MEMOIR OF

JOHN MASON PECK D.D.

Edited from His Journals and

Correspondence by **Rufus Babcock**

Introduction by Paul M. Harrison

Foreword by Herman R. Lantz

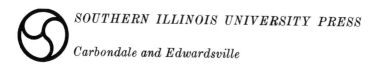

SOUTHERN ILLINOIS UNIVERSITY PRESS

Carbondale and Edwardsville

FOREWORD

IN THE BROADEST SENSE THE REPUBLICATION OF THE PRESENT
work represents an addition to our knowledge and understanding of the frontier in American Society. Yet the rele-
vance of writing about the frontier has to be examined. A
good deal of writing is purely of antiquarian interest and
must be justified primarily on the basis of such interest.
Often such literature is largely descriptive, deficient in ori-
enting the scholar and reader to further avenues of exploration.

Other writings on the frontier transcend the antiquarian
and descriptive characteristics and offer the exciting possibility of adding to our understanding in regard to the formation of social institutions, the conflicts inherent in this emer-
gence, and the conditions under which social change occurs.
Within this socio-historic context it becomes possible to re-
examine the generalizations of social science and formulate
relevant hypotheses about the many facets of social organization. The *Memoir of John Mason Peck* falls clearly within
this category. John Mason Peck was an unusually shrewd,
careful, and astute observer who was sensitive to the theological, social, and ideological issues which surrounded him.
As a member of the clergy who traveled through the early
Illinois country, he was able to report and comment on the
people, their social institutions, and the communities in
which they lived.

John Mason Peck's *Memoir* is significant primarily from
a sociological and historical point of view. Indeed, as Paul

Harrison suggests in his Introduction to this work, Peck was not a theological innovator in any major sense.

With regard to sociology, however, Peck's important observations are several. First in the area of general methodology Peck was unusually astute. He was aware of how social data ought to be collected; he could distinguish between primary and secondary sources; and he was sensitive to the necessity for objectivity in dealing with social data. He developed a typology of religious and moral people with distinguishing characteristics based on empirical observations. Considering the period and setting in which he worked, his astuteness was most unusual.

A second significant sociological observation which Peck makes lies in the stress he places on the need for continuous social contact with the socialization process; the failure to do so results in the degeneration of the human community. What is commonplace in every introductory textbook in sociology today was observed and reported by Peck over a century ago.

A third significant sociological observation has to do with Peck's observations on the phenomenon of collective behavior as demonstrated in revivals. Here he notes the differences between emotional contagion, the impact of persons upon one another in crowd type collectivities, and what he depicts as a genuine religious experience. The former is a social product, the latter spiritual; the two are separate experiences.

A fourth significant sociological observation concerns Peck's comment on the relation between social deviation and normlessness in the community. Indeed, while Peck belonged to a different age with no formal training in sociology, his observations were in the mainstream of the concern for anomie and alienation, a concern so prevalent in the literature today. Yet while this concern in the present has been focused on the urban industrial milieu, Peck was concerned with small, rural communities in which collective roots and identifications were difficult to find.

A fifth significant sociological observation concerns Peck's comments on the problems of organizational structures. These problems were observed within the context of the antimissionary controversy. Viewed superficially this may be seen as a theological issue. Looked at more closely, the controversy takes on added dimensions. As Professor Harrison suggests, it is in part an expression of fear from antimissionary adherents; a fear regarding replacement and loss of status by the better educated, class-elevated missionaries. As such it represented also an effort on the part of the antimissionaries to assert their own identity against the older, elite elements of the East. If there is any truth to the assertion that many who inhabited the frontier were also those who were unable to adapt to eastern settlements, then it is also true that the norms and values of the society embodied in the missionaries came back to haunt them.

Clearly the problems associated with order and stability in the human community were of major concern to Peck. Yet he saw no simple solutions. While starting with the assumption that the ethics and morality of human existence had religious roots, he saw also the need for civil controls through government; both of these could help nurture the growth of the individual in order that the individual become ultimately responsible to himself and those around him.

From the historical point of view, it is noted by Paul Harrison, editor of this volume, that Frederick Jackson Turner was influenced by Peck's observations on the frontier. In both lectures and writings Peck's comments were employed to develop Turner's thesis on the significance of the frontier in American society.

The introduction was prepared by Professor Paul M. Harrison of Pennsylvania State University, a man well versed in theology, history, and sociology. Professor Harrison's contribution is particularly important and significant because he treats John Mason Peck in terms of his major writings and concerns rather than limiting his exposition to the *Memoir*. As such the reader is presented with the ideological setting of the period in which Peck was writing. It is within this perspective that Harrison examines Peck's writings. Scholars and researchers interested in John Mason Peck and the role of religion on the frontier in America will find this work and Professor Harrison's comments a most fruitful base from which to extend their investigations.

Herman R. Lantz

Southern Illinois University
January, 1965

CONTENTS

INTRODUCTION

RUFUS BABCOCK, the original editor of the *Memoir of John Mason Peck*, wrote for an audience that was for the most part familiar with its subject. Peck had become a minor legend in his time so that virtually every reader had heard of him and knew something of his character. They knew he was a man of astonishing endurance—"indefatigable" being the word most often used to describe him—that he was a religious and social pioneer who possessed an unusual combination of gifts. He had an unshakeable personal faith and a powerful sense of destiny and mission accompanied by a driving conviction that the West was the New Zion, the instrument of God's salvation for the world.

Modern readers do not share the advantage of his contemporaries and have to dig more deeply into Peck's published writings in order to develop a portrait of this missionary, teacher, administrator, founder of uncounted religious and educational institutions, and active participant in the political affairs of the emerging frontier. Peck as a man with foibles as well as energy and ability does not fully appear until the closing pages of the *Memoir*. One purpose of this essay is to fill some of the vacuums in Babcock's commentary and partially to remedy the insufficiency of selection he made from Peck's Journals.

Babcock was a younger friend of Peck's. He was born in 1798, graduated from Brown University in 1821, was ordained in 1823 in Poughkeepsie, served several pastorates, and became a popular Baptist preacher. He was President of

Waterville College (Colby) from 1833 to 1837, served as President of the American Baptist Publication Society, as Corresponding Secretary of the American and Foreign Bible Society, and as an agent of the American Sunday School Union. He died in 1875.

Peck had left fifty-three volumes of handwritten diaries and journals with the request that Babcock edit them and seek a publisher. The task was enormous, given the limitations always set upon this kind of work by the publisher. Babcock fulfilled the petition, but the contemporary reader may wish that Peck had chosen an editor whose catholic interests corresponded more closely with his own. Babcock's pious opinions and observations which are interspersed between Peck's entries were undoubtedly fondly cherished by the religious readers of his time, but by present-day religious standards they add nothing to the text and might cause many readers to lose sight of the important elements in this volume. More serious, Babcock harbored prejudice against "secular" events and affairs which played a significant part in Peck's life. After an important session with the Illinois legislature in which Peck's role was crucial in the antislavery controversy, Babcock comments cryptically that Peck had only been "mingling from necessity with politicians and legislators," and that he was happy to return again to his religious work. Whether he enjoyed it or not, however, Peck obviously believed that the full religious life necessarily demanded participation in secular affairs.

Peck's journals have been lost so it is impossible to know precisely what was included in them, but it is apparent that Babcock's exclusive ecclesiastical and educational interests led him to neglect Peck's comments on several of his various activities. We shall seek to remedy this by referring to other books and addresses by Peck and by quoting from them extensively since they are not readily available in our libraries and have been out-of-print for about a century. Limitations upon this particular project, however, do not permit a search for the hundreds of refugee articles written by Peck for numerous papers and journals. But his books and several public addresses provide sufficient information about his activities and interests and his analysis of frontier society to provide an adequate introduction to the work of this man. The selections included in this essay have been chosen on the basis of criteria that are generally considered more traditionally sociological than historical, although increasingly members of both disciplines are recognizing the essential affinity of their interests and methods. This fact is reflected in the nature of this general project, "Perspectives in Sociology."

Rufus Babcock, following Peck's prior request, turned the journals over to the Mercantile Library in St. Louis. "It proved to be their grave. . . . By and by the library moved into new quarters, and in the bustle the box and its contents went with other rubbish to the Graham paper-mill, and the precious diaries were turned into wrapping paper."[1]

Peck's Character, Beliefs, Presuppositions, and Life Purpose

John Mason Peck was born in Litchfield, Connecticut, in 1789, where he received his training in the schools of the latter-day Puritan tradition. His conversion experience occurred in 1807, and he became a full member of the Congregational church. He moved to Green County, New York, in 1811 and in the same year was convinced that Baptist doctrine was truer to the Scripture. He was re-baptized and ordained into the Baptist ministry in 1813. He spent one year in Philadelphia under the tutelage of William Staughton, later President of Columbian College (George Washington University). This was the only formal educational training that Peck received beyond the "secondary" level. In 1817 he was appointed a missionary to the West by the Triennial Baptist Missionary Convention and moved to St. Louis in that year, where he established a small school and co-operated

in pastoral duties with James Welch. He moved to Rock
Spring, Illinois in 1822. It was from this homestead, eighteen
miles from St. Louis, that he spent the rest of his life engaging in innumerable missionary activities. Among other things
he was the founder of Shurtleff College, the first institution
of higher learning in the Illinois Territory; he was an officer
and executive in various denominational and inter-denomi-
national societies and with Jonathan Going the co-founder
of the Baptist Home Mission Society. In an era when traveling forty miles a day was an excellent achievement, he
traveled thousands of miles every year. He wrote uncounted
letters, sermons, addresses for public occasions, and articles
for various journals, such as the *Western Pioneer and Baptist Standard Bearer,* the *Western Baptist, The Sunday
School Banner,* and the *Western Watchman.* Of those mentioned he was editor or associate editor for several years.[2] His
books, with their various revisions and editions, included
Guide for Emigrants, 1831; *New Gude for Emigrants to the
West,* 1836, 1837, 1843; *Life of Daniel Boone, the Pioneer of
Kentucky,* 1847; *Life of John B. Meachum,* 1854; *Traveler's
Guide for Illinois,* 1839; *A Gazeteer of Illinois,* 1834, 1837;
"Father Clark," or, *The Pioneer Preacher,* 1855; *Annals of
the West,* with J. H. Perkins, revised and expanded by Peck,
1850; and *Dupuy's Hymns and Spiritual Songs,* revised,
corrected, and enlarged by Peck, 1843. In addition, as Babcock said, he wrote enough "letters, circulars, reports, or
communications for the press to fill up the entire time of an
ordinary man."

Peck has been described in several places as a man of
pleasant and gentle but firm disposition, as one who could
calm the fury or fear of others during moments of critical
dispute or danger. There is ample evidence for this in the
Memoir, for example, when a boat is torn to pieces in a storm
on the Mississippi. Peck was a man of extraordinary mental
and moral capacity and beneath the visible composure and
serenity there was a furnace of religious devotion and intellectual passion. His energy and devotion to the missionary
endeavor and settling of the West can be illustrated by

enumerating some of his activities during a seven month
period when he served as executive secretary of the Baptist
Publication Society. He preached seventy-eight times, gave
thirty-eight public addresses, visited forty-five churches, four
associations, five state conventions, six ministerial meetings,
one camp meeting, and one college commencement. He
traveled 3310 miles and did his administrative work by correspondence. The rigorous routine of pioneer missionary life
is described by two itinerant preachers from New York;
John Lawton and John Peck—not the John Mason Peck of
this volume. However, the entire piece, especially the reference to the family problems of the missionary, could have
been written by the Illinois pioneer. These ideas were often
expressed by him.

We will now proceed to take a brief view of the labors and privations of these pious men and worthy champions of the cross. . . .
The frequent calls, "Come over, and help us," from the little clusters
of saints here and there in the wilderness, subjected them to frequent journeys, in which they had to encounter many obstacles and
endure many hardships and various sufferings. They toiled in the
cold and in the heat, by day and by night, traversing the wilderness
from one solitary dwelling to another, by marked trees and half-
made roads, fording dangerous rivers, and rapid streams, often
without a guide, and at the hazard of their lives. They suffered
much from hunger and thirst, and frequently had to pursue their
journeys through bleak winds and storms both of rain and snow, to
meet their appointments and administer to the perishing the bread
of life. The afflictions of some of them were greatly increased, and
their tenderest sympathies often excited, by the privations and
sufferings in respect even to the necessaries of life to which their
families were subjected. Sometimes, in their journeys, on sitting
down at the tables of their brethren, to enjoy their hospitality, a
recollection of the sufferings of their families at home, would destroy their appetite, and fill them with grief. They could receive
little earthly reward, the country being new, the churches small,
and the people hardly able to support themselves, much less to
expend a large amount on the preachers.[3]

The techniques of the woodsmen were well-known by Peck
and other missionaries.[4] On the deepest frontier they hunted
and fished like the earliest pioneers. Peck often slept with his

saddle bags as a pillow. During these periods of isolation he accomplished his work by reading and writing on horseback. He was described as a man of great physical stamina, but he was apparently incapable of pacing himself. Throughout his life he worked to the point of exhaustion, and then he would collapse, completely overcome by illness and high fever. His profound sense of purpose and fanatic discipline enabled him to schedule everything except rest and recreation. He worked ten to sixteen hours a day, six days a week, and on "the day of rest" Peck was more heavily burdened than on the weekdays. Babcock's description in the *Memoir* of Peck's activities during his periods of recuperation from illness and following "retirement" from the Publication Society are indicative of the inordinate drive which impelled this man. In one of his rare critical observations, Babcock says that Peck's mind was "ever eager, enterprising, and almost too grasping in its conceptions of the possibilities of success."

The inner impulses which drove Peck to an excess of activity and contributed to his achievement are not reflected in his theological formulations. He was not an imaginative or creative theologian and made no significant contribution in this area. On the contrary, he played the role of religious mediator between the staid and respectable Puritan moralism of the eastern states and the frantic revivalism of the frontier.[5] Most historians emphasize the dramatics of the revival technique in the early West and minimize the powerful modifying influence of sensitive and cultivated preachers. Tyler says, "a militant evangelical Protestantism preached by itinerant ministers often as illiterate as those who listened to them was the force that exhilarated, united, and at the same time tamed the frontier."[6] This is partially correct, but Peck's life demonstrates that the radical evangelical and revivalist gospel was also a part of the frontier that had to be tamed.

Many historical accounts of missionary endeavors on the frontier concentrate upon the theology of the outstanding pioneer preachers, the sermons of the ministers, the liturgy of the various churches, the revival techniques of the churches and sects, the theological conflicts, the competition between denominations, and the increase in the religious population. But Peck, while never ignoring these aspects of the evangelizing crusade, was more interested in the infinitely complex organizational procedures and political conduct that was necessary to initiate and support these endeavors, and he participated in the institutional roles requisite for the maintenance of these societies. At various times he acted as financial, recording, or executive secretary; as missionary, minister, itinerate and supply preacher; as board member, officer of the board, and trustee; and much of his time was spent as fund-raiser, promotional worker, and editor and writer for various organizational papers.

On the frontier, bondage to sin and conversion to freedom were the chief doctrinal tenets of evangelical religion; its method was a violent emotional conversion stimulated by the sympathetic and contagious power of crowd revivals. Peck was in general agreement with the theology, in disagreement with the method. Although he sought for a "revival" religion and repeatedly used that word to describe his efforts, he was not a revivalist in the common sense of the term. He was not repelled by what modern preachers consider excessive emotion in religious exercises, but the crude techniques used to stimulate masses of people, in which there was no emphasis upon doctrine or logic, which discarded theology for dramatics, and which tended to divide rather than unite the denominations on the frontier, were repugnant to Peck.

He had been reared in Litchfield, one of the few towns in Connecticut that had not been swept by the revivals of Edwards and Whitefield. This was the town of Ethan Allen, Aaron Burr, Horace Bushnell, and the home of the Wolcott and Beecher families. It was a respectable village that had no taste for the religious excesses that were moving in successive waves through the state and even through the country of Litchfield from the time of Peck's birth until his own quiet conversion experience in 1807. Of this he reports: "I was brought to see myself a guilty sinner before God, deserving his wrath. . . . When I was delivered and found a peace of mind and a joy in God which I had never felt before." His Calvinism was not of the radical predistinarian type, but he shared the emphasis of the Calvinists upon the providence of God. After his conversion he saw the finger of God moving every personal and historical event. Through disaster and suffering, of which he saw and experienced a great deal, his faith in providence was never severely threatened. All things worked for good. Catastrophe which caused apparently meaningless suffering was God's means to inform men of their depravation and to demonstrate how they could conquer natural evil. Thus the doctrine of providence was combined with a practical inclination so that following the accident on the river in which lives were lost he appealed to Congress for removal of snags and development of a safe channel.

Peck's doctrine of providence and the vestiges of predistinarian theology that remained in his theology were amended by his internal compulsion for engaging in benevolent enterprises. "I am somehow pressed forward in a great work," he wrote in his journal, so in a most characteristically American Puritan fashion, every idle thought was deplored, every moment taken from his work to devote even to the necessary business of survival for himself and his family was regretted, and every instance of religious doubt was profoundly lamented. "Amidst a multiplicity of business, which though not chiefly of a worldly character, yet proves a temptation for relaxation in more spiritual and heavenly engagement, I find myself prone to depart from the living God." His congenital good humor, wit, and ability to entertain with anecdotes drawn from his reading and broad experience were regretted by him as some sort of superficial and distracting tendency toward levity. "There is a consitutational tendency in me to hilarity of spirits which is frequently indulged beyond the bounds of propriety, and on reflection induces me to exclaim, 'Who shall deliver me from this dead body?' " Peck was obviously disturbed by the ambiguities which plague every man who is both deeply human and profoundly religious. He was proud of his work and the achievements he believed to be so important, but also experienced an oppressive guilt for gaining satisfaction from his successes. After recording an impressive list of achievements in the journal, he says, "Lord, give me both gratitude and humility, that I may praise thee for all my success, and seeing my own weakness and insignificance may sink into the dust of self-abasement, that I may never be proud or vain!"

He possessed an open and tolerant disposition toward other denominations which once had led him to remark that "there is much trash cleaving to us all." He became a leader in the development of many undenominational agencies—Sunday school unions, temperance societies, and Bible societies at the local, state, and national level. His attitude toward the Roman Catholic church placed him far ahead of most men of his time. While he shared the general fear and prejudice of the evangelicals toward the Catholics and viewed that church as a competitor and antagonist, he viewed positive evangelical work as the only legitimate competitive instrument and deplored the nativist movements. In his time anti-Catholic prejudice was current in the highest intellectual circles of the nation. Lyman Beecher set the tone for thousands of Protestant clergy. "The ministers of no Protestant sect," he wrote, "could or would dare to attempt to regulate the votes of their people as the Catholic priests can do, who at the confessional learn all the private concerns of their people, and have almost unlimited power over the conscience as it respects the performance of every civil or social duty. . . . A tenth part of the suffrage of the nation, thus condensed and wielded by the Catholic powers of Europe, might decide our elections, perplex our policy, inflame and divide the nation, break the bond of our union, and throw down our free institutions." Beecher wrote several more pages in which he said he opposed attempts "to cast odium upon Catholics," and concluded that they would be far more acceptable to the nation if they would accept Protestant principles of politics and religion and assimilate the American spirit of democracy and freedom.[7]

Peck's strongest prejudice, if it may be called that in academic circles, was directed against ignorance, lack of sophisticated social organization, and forms of immorality that tended to disrupt society. This is reflected in his comments on the Indians. He did not, however, harbor a predilection against those who lacked educational advantage. "Indolence and imbecility," he wrote, "never produced a Simon Kenton, a Tecumthè, or a Daniel Boone. To gain the skill of an accomplished hunter requires talents."[8] Peck's powers of social observation and his view of human nature derived from Calvinism led him to refute the current romantic theories of the noble savage.

That the Indian character has deteriorated, and the numbers of each tribe greatly lessened by contact with Europeans and their descendants, is not questioned; but many of the descriptions of the comforts and happiness of savage life and manners, before their country was possessed by the latter, are the exaggerated and glowing descriptions of poetic fancy. Evidence enough can be had to show that they were degraded and wretched, engaged in petty exterminating wars with each other, often times in a state of starvation, and leading a roving, indolent and miserable existence. Their government was anarchy. Properly speaking, civil government had never existed among them. They had no executive, or judiciary power, and their legislation was the result of their councils held by aged and experienced men. It had no stronger claim upon the obedience of the people than advice.[9]

The condition of depraved man, unimproved by habits of civilization, and unblest with the influences and consolations of the gospel, is pitiable in the extreme. Such was the condition of the 'Red Skin,' before his land was visited by the 'Pale faces.' I have often seen the aboriginal man in all his primeval wilderness, when he first came in contact with the evils and benefits of civilization,—have admired his noble form and lofty bearing,—listened to his untutored and yet powerful eloquence, and yet have found in him the same humbling and melancholy proofs of his wretchedness and want, as is found in the remnants on our borders.

The introduction of ardent spirits, and of several diseases, are the evils furnished the Indian race, by contact with whites, while in other respects their condition has been improved.[10]

One of Peck's most striking characteristics, because most unusual in a minister of the gospel in any age, was his highly developed interest in and sensitivity to the machinery of secular politics. Had Peck lived in the present century Reinhold Niebuhr might have had a close competitor as a theological and political analyst. Fortunately, Babcock included Peck's comments on the election of William Henry Harrison and his questions: ''Who are the children of light? Who are the children of this world? In what sense are the children of this world the wiser?'' The answer to these questions bears a remarkable similarity to the work of Niebuhr.[11] Peck's political views and activities are discussed more fully in the final section of this essay.

The best description of Peck that is available was written by Jeremiah B. Jeter, the first president of the Foreign Mission Board of the Southern Baptist Convention. Babcock located it in an extensive footnote in the closing pages of the *Memoir*. It seems more appropriate and advantageous for the reader to include it here.

I had known Dr. Peck several years before I went to St. Louis in 1849, but not intimately, and my estimate of his worth was considerably increased by my intimacy with him for nearly three years. He was a true, earnest, laborious, faithful servant of the Lord Jesus. I was particularly struck with his *disinterestedness*. He was willing to labor anywhere, in any department, and with anybody, if he might be useful. He engaged with equal readiness in the labors of a pastorate, an agency, an editorship, or authorship, with little regard to the exposure and fatigue involved in the enterprise, or the meagerness of its pecuniary reward. He was not a man to wait for important and honored posts of usefulness to be opened to him; but he entered promptly the fields of service before him, and cultivated them diligently, with the assurance that he would not fail of his reward. Though he was a man of strong will, and loved, as earnest and energetic men are apt to do, to have his own way, yet I never discovered in him the signs of envy or of mortified ambition. He thought, of course, his own plans right, and struggled manfully to carry them out; but accorded to brethren differing from him sincerity and worthy motives. In all his plans for extending the kingdom of Christ—and they were numerous—and in all his warm controversies in supporting them, there was an almost perfect self-abnegation.

The most remarkable trait in the character of Dr. Peck, that arrested my attention, was *volubility*. Brother Peck was both a full and ready man. He was well informed on almost all subjects; and on matters relating to the West, his knowledge was various, general, and minute. He might be called a Western Gazetteer, and poured forth an incessant stream of conversation on any subject—religious, scientific or political, grave or ludicrous—that might be broached in his presence. His resources in conversation were perfectly inexhaustible. When once he was fairly enlisted in conversation, the most resolute hearer could do nothing more than ask a question, suggest a doubt or difficulty, or give some direction to the current of discourse. Being somewhat fond of talking myself, when I first became acquainted with him I made frequent attempts to participate in the conversation; but soon I resigned myself, as did others, a mute auditor of his ceaseless and interesting remarks. Let it not be supposed that he was rude or overbearing in his manner. He was a courteous man. His manners, however, were eminently Western. In most social circles he was the acknowledged autocrat. He talked because all wished him to talk, and all chose to be silent in his presence. When he associated with those whose age, culture, and position gave them a title to a full share in conversation, he still engrossed it, partly from habit, and partly from the gushing fulness of his thoughts which would admit of no restraint. You might as well roll a ball down the mountain side, and attempt to stop it in its mid-career, as to arrest, or hold in check the impetuous thought and bounding words of the old pioneer.

Much has been said, and foolishly said, of Western character. Most people in the West formed their characters before they emigrated thither; and they have been slightly or not at all modified by their change of residence. But Mr. Peck was a *Western man*. He removed to the West while young; and his tastes, manners, habits, and modes of thinking and speaking were formed there. No intelligent and observant man could be in his presence five minutes without perceiving unmistakable evidence of this truth. The pioneers were a hardy, self-denying, courageous, and independent class of men. For forms, etiquette, and pretensions they had no respect. They were practical, not theoretic. Mr. Peck was not only a pioneer, but a master-spirit among the pioneers. Perhaps no man of the class did more than he to guide the thoughts, mould the manners, and form the institutions of the West. He was an embodiment of Western character—plain, frank, self-reliant, fearless, indomitable, with all his powers, physical and intellectual, subordinated by grace to the service of Christ.

I will mention an anecdote as illustrative of the peculiar character of Dr. Peck. When he resided in Philadelphia—so the story runs—as Secretary of the American Baptist Publication Society, after having been absent some months, he reached home by the stage in the morning, and, unobserved by any of his family, went into his study, and finding a great accumulation of letters and papers during his absence, soon became absorbed in the examination of them. Late in the afternoon some member of his family, to his great surprise, found him in his study, peering over his papers. I do not vouch for the accuracy of the story—indeed, I do not wholly believe it; but it is significant that such a story should be circulated concerning him. Of all the men I have ever known, it was most likely to be true of him. He was not without social affections—had, no doubt, a fair measure of them. His wife held him in the highest reverence. He was never charged with the slightest neglect of his family. But so completely had he subordinated all his social affections, and all his habits, to duty and usefulness, that if any man could have been innocently oblivious of his family under the circumstances indicated in the anecdote, that man was John M. Peck.

In a high sense of the terms, I did not consider Dr. Peck either a great or a learned man, or an eminent preacher; but a man of sound sense—of various attainments—of earnest piety—of good preaching gifts—of extensive labors—of much usefulness, and as deserving a name among the benefactors of his race, and the lasting gratitude of the inhabitants of the Mississippi Valley, and of the Baptist denomination.[12]

This description will help to answer many questions as one progresses through the pages of the *Memoir*. Above all Peck was a Western man. The vast region in which he chose to be a missionary shared its youth and its destiny with him. In this virgin wilderness a new hope for humanity was being born. The settlers had brought much from Europe and from New England, but all of these ideas, traditions, customs, and procedures had to be reformed in the crucible of practical need in a unique historical situation. Peck fully recognized

that the inherited institutions were the greatest asset possessed by the settlers, but whether they were political, economic, philosophical, or religious, they had to be transformed
within the new situation. The forces for adjustment had to
be no less powerful and no less legitimate than those of
tradition. Peck had the perception to recognize that blending
of the traditional and the new would be guided primarily
by the fundamental needs of the people in this unprecedented
situation. For the first time in history hundreds of thousands
of civilized people were moving into the wilderness; their
guiding purpose being to alter the unimpeded course of
nature and to form out of that wilderness a new earth, a New
Jerusalem, to be a light to all the nations. In his introduction
to the *Guide to the West,* Peck quoted from Isaiah 66:8.
''Who hath heard such a thing? Who hath seen such things?
Shall the earth be made to bring forth in one day? or shall
a nation be born at once?''

George H. Williams in his fascinating interpretation of
Wilderness and Paradise in Christian Thought relates a
story that is often repeated. A Presbyterian minister ''making his way over the lonely prairies . . . was arrested by the
sound of an ax. Upon observing a woodman near by, he
called to him, 'What are you doing here, stranger?' 'I am
building a theological seminary,' was the reply. 'What, in
these barrens?' 'Yes,' responded the woodman, 'I am planting the seed.' The planter in the wilderness was John M.
Peck.''[13] Williams argues that in religious thought the
wilderness is viewed in contrasting ways. Positively it is as a
refuge, a place for protection, contemplation and retreat, or
''again as one's inner nature or ground of being, and at
length as the ground itself of the divine being.'' Negatively,
the wilderness is understood as the world of the unrepentant,
as the wasteland where the sinner retreats to be purged in
preparation for salvation.[14] Both themes can be detected in
Peck's interpretation of the western wilderness.

The two primary needs of man on the frontier as understood by Peck were simple survival and maintenance of the

cultural and religious heritage. Under the primitive conditions presented by the wilderness the threat to both of these
was severely accentuated. But a remedial antidote operated
in the concept of American destiny. God's new Israel was to
be carved out of the western forests. Peck shared this vision
which was drawn in part from Puritan theocratic ideals, in
part from the rising sense of national destiny. God was
bringing forth a new nation of servants for his purposes.
"Home mission needs caused many clerical promoters to
give renewed emphasis to America's great destiny under
God. 'If the Gospel is to form our character, and guide our
power, we shall be a fountain of life to all nations,' Charles
Hodge declared in 1829."[15] The reverberations of this religio-
political hope are periodically resurrected, most recently in
the 1964 presidential campaign. The words of the historian-
theologian, Philip Schaff, who died in 1893, have a familiar
cadence. "The Anglo-Saxon and Anglo-American, of all
modern races, possess the strongest national character and
the one best fitted for universal dominion, and that, too, not
a dominion of despotism but one, which makes its subjects
free citizens."[16]

Peck observed at every opportunity this sense of destiny
stimulated by the acts of God. Daniel Boone, he says, "spoke
feelingly, and with solemnity, of being a creature of Providence, ordained by heaven as a pioneer in the wilderness, to
advance the civilization and extension of his country."[17]
Again, in his preface to the *Guide for Emigrants* he quotes
Lyman Beecher: "The West is a young empire of mind, and
power, and wealth, and free institutions rushing up to a
giant manhood, with a rapidity and power never before
witnessed under the sun. And if she carried with her the
elements of her preservation, the experiment will be glorious—the joy of the nation—the joy of the whole earth, as
she rises in the majesty of her intelligence and benevolence,
and enterprise, for the emancipation of the world."

Peck recognized that "vast and important benefits for
future generations seem to hang on present efforts."[18] Re-

ligion, of course, was one of the foundation blocks for the building of the future, although by no means the only one.

Amongst the causes that have awakened the attention of the community in the Atlantic States, to this Great Valley, and excited the desires of multitudes to remove hither, may be reckoned the efforts of the liberal and benevolent to aid the West in the immediate supply of her population with the Bible, with Sunday Schools, with religious tracts, with the gospel ministry, and to lay the foundation for Colleges and other literary institutions. . . .

The author's first book, "A guide for Emigrants," &c. was written in the winter and spring of 1831. . . . Since that period, brief as it has been, wide and rapid changes have been made, population has rapidly augmented, beyond that of any former period of the same extent—millions of acres of the public domain, then wild and hardly explored, have been brought into market; settlements and counties have been formed, and populous towns have sprung up where, at that time, the Indian and wild beast had possession; facilities for intercommunication have been greatly extended, and distant places have been brought comparatively near; the desire to emigrate to the West has increased, and everybody in the Atlantic States has become interested and inquires about the Great Valley. That respectable place, so much the theme of declamation and inquiry abroad, "The Far West," has gone from this region toward the setting sun. Its exact locality has not yet been settled, but probably it may soon be found along the gulf of California, or near Nootka Sound. And if distance is to be measured by time, and the facility of intercourse, we are now several hundred miles nearer the Atlantic coast than twenty years since. Ten years more, and the facilities of railways and improved machinery will place the Mississippi within seven day's travel of Boston."[19]

Peck was fully aware of the unique character of this vast movement of people and the unprecedented character of the social change which was occurring.

These States have been unparalleled in their growth, both in the increase of population and property, and in the advance of intellectual and moral improvement. Such an extent of forest was never before cleared—such a vast field of prairie was never before subdued and cultivated by the hand of man, in the same short period time.

And, as in many portions of his writings, he was inclined to social and moral prophecy.

> The general improvement of the country, and the development of its physical, intellectual and moral resources have kept pace with the extension of settlements. And such are its admirable facilities for commerce, by its numerous navigable rivers, and its productions—such the genial nature of its climate—the enterprise of its population—and the influence it must soon wield in directing the destinies of the whole United States, as to render the Great West an object of the deepest interest to the American patriot. To the philanthropist and christian, the character and manners—the institutions, literature, and religion of so wide a portion of the country, whose mighty energies are soon to exert a controlling influence over the character of the whole nation, and in some measure, of the world, are not less matters of momentous concern.[20]

In all of these things Peck merely reflected the dominant spirit of his time which was characterized by a naive confidence in the goodness of man and the assurance that with the help of God the moral beatitudes of Protestant evangelical moralism would pervade the world. Horace Bushnell, the greatest American theologian of his day, believed that "we have the future in our charge, and we mean to see the trust faithfully fulfilled. . . . To present mankind the spectacle of . . . a religious nation, blooming in all the Christian virtues; the protector of the poor; the scourge of oppression; the dispenser of light; and the symbol to mankind of the ennobling genial power of righteous laws and a simple Christian faith— this is the charge God lays upon us; this we accept, and this by God's blessing we mean to perform."[21]

Most of Peck's prophecies, however, were not based on idle speculation or religious yearnings but upon careful social observation. Noting that the population of the Mississippi Valley had increased from 229,368 in 1790 to 3,951,466 in 1830 and had increased to an estimated 5,400,000 in 1835, he suggests why "the population of this Valley must increase in the future in far greater ratio than in the past"— the elimination of the Indian threat; a greater market outlet

due to population increase and density; transport facilities
which already exceed the best in most countries of the world;
the increasing emigration from the East and Europe; the
availability of land, much of it at $1.25 per acre; the con-
quest over the health problem which is present in all pioneer
settlements; and the Valley is no longer an intellectual and
moral desert populated by squatters and trappers because
schools, colleges, churches and libraries have increased
rapidly.[22]

Peck's Method of Scholarship

President Patterson of Lake Forest College, in an historical
review of the early literature of Illinois, estimated that Peck
was "the most telling and widely influential" of "several
men of respectable attainments." "He was not a classical
scholar; but he was a man of keen observation, a careful
reader, a bold and independent thinker, amazingly industrious and enterprising, and a pioneer in the advocacy of
liberty, temperance, education, Sunday schools, and evangelical Christianity. Our State probably owes more to him
than to any other one man."[23] In 1852 he was awarded the
degree of Doctor of Systematic Theology by Harvard University, together with Andrew P. Peabody and Horace
Bushnell. In the same ceremony the Doctor of Laws was
awarded Alexis de Tocqueville, François Guizot, Francis
Wayland, Caleb Cushing and Benjamin R. Curtis.[24]

Peck's acute powers of social observation were augmented
in his scholarship by a rough distinction he drew between
"truth and fiction." Unlike many of his contemporary
preacher-commentators he understood the difference between
primary and secondary sources and first and second-hand
observation. There is a difference in tone and approach,
however, between his "secular" histories and social com-
mentaries, and his journal entries and religious writings. In
the former he does not evaluate or offer opinions on the
validity of sectarian theologies. He understood the differ-

ence between scholarship and proselytizing and fully recognized that the purpose of both would be lost by carelessly blending them.

The care with which he worked and the method he used can be roughly illustrated. A report was published in 1854 that Peck had been commissioned by the legislature to write a history, of Illinois. He responded as follows:

All the promises the writer made was to do his best *to collect materials* for such a work; leaving it to Providence and future contingencies whether he would write out and publish them. In gathering materials, the writer soon found he could compile a *Book* that might pass as a *History of Illinois;* but like similar works, gotten up from second hand authorities, and in customary haste, it would be a mixture of truth and fiction, of facts and fables. . . ."

It is not the business of the historian to hold controversies, or presume to judge disputes between the religious sects, but to give the facts as accurately as possible, and leave the reader to deduce his own inferences, and do his own moralizing. . . . But it will be his province to judge of the legitimate tendencies of customs, institutions, and social organizations, whether as a whole they have been beneficial or injurious to the moral progress of the population of this Valley.[25]

The last sentence is a primitive statement of functional theory. Peck was a social historian who was acutely aware of the necessity of what we have come to call structural and functional imperatives. He wrote thus of hunters and trappers who became isolated from society:

Some become so enamored with this wandering and exposed life as to lose all desire of returning to the abodes of civilization, and remain for the rest of their lives in the American deserts. There are individuals, who are graduates of colleges, and who once stood high in the circles of refinement and taste, that have passed more than twenty years amongst the roaming tribes of the Rocky mountains, or on the western slope, till they have apparently lost all feelings toward civilized life. They have afforded an interesting but melancholy example of the tendencies of human nature towards the degraded state of savages. The improvement of the species is a slow and laborious process—the deterioration is rapid, and requires only to be divested of restraint, and left to its own unaided tendencies.[26]

On the other hand, he did not equate civilization in any of its forms with perfect human harmony. He wrote of Rock Spring, his own little community in Illinois:

> It offered no claim to rank as a village or town. It is in the midst of a tract of barrens, with only a few families within two miles. . . . It possesses the advantage of being removed from the contaminating influences of a village, is unquestionably healthy, has an abundance of excellent water, and a back country range for stock.[27]

It is very difficult to know precisely what attitude Peck held toward towns and cities because in all of his work he was disinterested and critical in the highest sense of those terms.

> Chicago will eventually become the greatest place for business and commerce in all the north west. Already it is a great thoroughfare for so new a location. Merchants through the northern portion of Indiana, as far south as Terre Haute, and throughout the northern portion of Illinois, obtain their goods through the medium of Chicago. Schooners are the principal vessels that navigate Lake Michigan. When the harbor is made, Steam boats will take their place. . . .

> The population in 1832 did not exceed 150:—now it is estimated at 1000. More than 100 dwelling houses, stores, and shops, with three churches, were erected last summer. There are about 30 stores, some of which do extensive business. A respectable academy is established, and taught by a gentleman and lady. In time, I have no doubt but Chicago will greatly exceed any other place in Illinois.[28]

The kind of knowledge which is displayed in this letter was acquired through methods of research used today. Where Peck found the time and energy is another question.

> It is an easy task to a belles-lettre scholar, sitting at his desk, in an easy chair, and by a pleasant fire, to write "Histories," and "Geographies," and "Sketches," and "Recollections," and "Views," and "Tours" of the Western Valley—but it is quite another concern to explore these regions, examine public documents, reconcile contradictory statements, correspond with hundreds of persons in public and private life, read all the histories, geographies, tours, sketches, and recollections that have been published, and correct

their numerous errors—than collate, arrange, digest, and condense the facts of the country.[29]

Thus Peck was sensitive to the advantages and necessity as well as the costs of advances in knowledge of civilization and technical development. Whenever possible he supported his observations with statistical information.

> There were throughout the country in this year 1854, one hundred and ninety-three railroad accidents, killing one hundred and eighty-six persons, and wounding five hundred and eighty-nine; there were forty-eight steamboat accidents, in which five hundred and eighty-seven persons were killed and two hundred and twenty-five wounded; being an increase of two hundred and sixty-eight killed, over the previous year. There were also one hundred and seventy-one lives lost, by means of eighty-three fires, and the total loss of property by fire was twenty-five millions of dollars. Of all these accidents and losses, and particularly of the two first named, *the West* bore a very large proportion. Crime, too, this year footed up a fearful catalogue. There were six hundred and eighty-two murders committed; and eighty-four executions took place throughout the Union.[30]

All of Peck's scholarly work, whatever else we observe concerning it, was directed toward a paramount goal, the evangelization and civilizing of the West. His social criticism was directed to this end because he firmly believed the Christian man, equipped with full knowledge of the true social and moral situation, could bring into being a new and creatively free society. But he was also a moral and political realist who shared the simple hope of his day that a more perfect union of mankind would be established "with justice for all and malice toward none," to borrow words from an Illinois congressman with whom Peck had some correspondence.[31]

Peck's View of the Frontier: Social Classes and Social Organization

Peck was capable of developing systematic generalizations on the basis of minute and painstaking observations. At

the time of the birth of sociology on the continent—
Peck was almost the precise contemporary of August
Comte (1798–1857)—he was developing primitive sociological methods on the American frontier. His procedures and
views were more in accord with Durkheim, who was born
the year of Peck's death, than with Comte. For example, his
inclination to relate patterns of antisocial response to the
phenomenon of social discord was not dissimilar to Durkheim's theory in *Suicide* which has been described as an
analysis of deviance that may occur when institutional
patterns fail to provide norms for the guidance of individuals. It was Durkheim and not Peck who developed the
theoretical concept of *anomie,* but the Illinois pioneer was
sensitive to the disruptive power of normlessness and gave
expression to this observation in many of his writings.

Peck was a moralist who believed that social harmony and
viable, mature religion were inseparable, each being an expression of God's will for mankind. The immorality of the
early pioneers disturbed him mightily. The American Uni-
tarian Association had wryly noted, ''those who are pioneers
in a new country, are not infrequently more engaged in beginning the world anew, than in preparing to leave it'';[32]
but Peck did not believe the two could be so neatly separated.
Peck would have been in full agreement with Durkheim's
understanding of religion and society as it is expressed by
Edward Tiryakian. ''For Durkheim, not only is there an
acknowledgment that the values we cherish most highly
today have a religious origin, not only is there an acceptance
that 'Christianity was the chrysalis of Western culture itself,' but in more sweeping terms it may be stated that Durkheim finds in the phenomenon of religions consciousness and
activity the fundamental condition of social existence!''[33]

The settlements on the frontier to which Peck moved in
1822 were not models of social organization. The religion that
existed contributed little to alleviate the situation. The ministers were poorly paid and poorly educated.[34] Released from
the constraints of social pressure and control most frontiers-

men were indifferent to religion or vigorously irreligious.[35]
The temperance movement gained its impetus in this situation. In the early settlements the ministers often shared the
drinking customs of the lay people. This form of entertainment became so predominant that it is estimated that the
24,000 people (men, women, and children) in the Indiana
territory consumed 36,000 gallons of whiskey in 1810, not
counting the production of the domestic stills.[36]

In many sectors of the Illinois territory in the early
decades of the nineteenth century, crime and political corruption were highly organized. Relatively sophisticated in
their use of power, these deviant groups often exceeded the
ability of the settled communities to effect methods of social
control. The southern part of the territory was "overrun with
horse-thieves and counterfeiters, who were so numerous and
so well banded together as to set the laws at defiance. Many
of the sheriffs, justices of the peace, and constables were of
their number, and even some of the judges of the county
courts." To offset this condition, citizen's groups, called
"Regulators," were formed, "and the governor and judges
of the territory, seeing the impossibility of executing the laws
in the ordinary way . . . encouraged the proceedings of this
citizen organization."[37]

But however honest and worthy might have been the intention of
those who first formed this body of "Regulators," their proceedings,
as is the case with all anarchical confederations, soon became lawless, and defiant of all government. The system of torture carried
on by them, and inflicted on all suspected persons, had the effect of
causing the list of persons accused to become greater everyday. . . .
Some of the victims were dipped into the Ohio river, and held
under water until they divulged the names of their supposed
accomplices. Others had their thumbs pinched with bullet moulds.[38]
[Speaking more generally of social conditions on the frontier
Peck observed that] in moral and the essential principles of religion, this class of people are by no means so defective as many
imagine. The writer has repeatedly been in settlements and districts beyond the pale of civil and criminal law, where the people
are a "law unto themselves," where courts, lawyers, sheriffs, and
constables existed not, and yet has seen as much quiet and order,

and more honesty in paying just debts, than were legal restraints operated in all their force. . . . Industry, in laboring or hunting, bravery in war, candor, honesty, and hospitality were rewarded with the confidence and honor of the people. Regulating parties would exist, and thieves, rogues, and counterfeiters were sure to receive a striped Jacket "worked nineteen to the dozen," and by this mode of operation, induced to "clear out"; but truth, uprightness, honesty and sincerity are always respected. Many of the frontier class are *illiterate,* but they are by no means *ignorant.* They are a shrewd, observing, thinking people. . . . They have prejudices and fears about many of the organized benevolent societies [missionary organizations] of the present age, yet there are no people more readily disposed to attend religious meetings, and whose hearts are more readily affected with the gospel than the backwoods people.[39]

As in many informal and loosely organized communities the citizens depended upon quasi-charismatic leaders. Peck speaks of a Captain Joseph Ogle, an Indian fighter from Virginia who settled in Monroe County, Illinois. "Indeed he was just such a man as the people in all exposed and frontier settlements look to as their counsellor, guide, and commander. . . . Other pioneers, who had talents and influence, occupied the same position."[40]

But as in the classic instances of charismatic authority, it never prevailed in the face of established legal authority, permanent administration, and routinized decision-making. Without setting it in this theoretical framework, Peck illustrates this by citing the case of Daniel Boone, the archtypical charismatic leader of the American frontier.

As courts of justice were established, litigation in regard to land titles increased, until it was carried to a distressing extent. . . . A wide field of speculation was opened, and Colonel Boone, with hundreds of others, lost his lands from defective titles. His antipathy to the technical forms of law was great. He loved simple justice, was rigidly honest in all his engagements, and thought that all others, including the state, should act towards him on the same principles of natural equity. The law that prescribed the manner of entering lands was vague and defective, and its administration by the commissionors was still more so. . . . The old hunter employed

counsel, attended the courts from term to term, and listened to quibbles of the lawyers; but, on account of imperfect entries and legal flaws, he was ejected from the land he had defended so resolutely in the perilous times of savage invasion. After the vigor of life was spent, he found himself not the legal owner or possessor of a single acre of the vast and rich country he had so fully explored. . . . The shrewd speculators had the adroitness to secure legal titles by more accurate and better defined entries.[41]

The analytical contribution for which Peck is best known is his typology of social classes on the frontier. Frederick Jackson Turner in his best known lecture quoted Peck at length.

Generally, in all the western settlements, three classes, like the waves of the ocean, have rolled one after the other. First comes the Pioneer, who depends for the subsistence of his family chiefly upon the natural growth of vegetation, called the "range," and the proceeds of hunting. His implements of agriculture are rude, chiefly of his own make, and his efforts directed mainly to a crop of corn, and a "truck patch." The last is a rude garden for growing cabbage, beans, corn for roasting ears, cucumbers and potatoes. A log cabin, and occasionally a stable and corncrib, and a field of a dozen acres, the timber girdled or "deadened," and fenced, are enough for his occupancy. It is quite immaterial whether he ever becomes the owner of the soil. He is the occupant for the time being, pays no rent, and feels as independent as the "lord of the manor." With a horse, cow, and one or two breeders of swine, he strikes into the woods with his family, and becomes the founder of a new country, or perhaps state. He builds his cabin, gathers around him a few other families of similar taste and habits, and occupies till the range is somewhat subdued, and hunting a little precarious, or, which is more frequently the case, till neighbors crowd around, roads, bridges and fields annoy him, and he lacks elbow-room. The pre-emption law enables him to dispose of his cabin and corn-fields, to the next class of emigrants, and, to employ his own figures, he "breaks for the high timber"—"clears out for the New Purchase," or migrates to Arkansas or Texas, to work the same process over.

The next class of emigrants purchase the lands, add "field to field," clear out the roads, throw rough bridges over the streams, put up hewn log houses, with glass windows, and brick or stone chimneys, occasionally plant orchards, build mills, school houses, court houses, &c., and exhibit the picture and forms of plain, frugal, civilized life.

Another wave rolls on. The men of capital and enterprise come. The "settler" is ready to sell out, and take the advantage of the rise of property—push farther into the interiors, and become himself, a man of capital and enterprise in time. The small village rises to a spacious town or city,—substantial edifices of brick, extensive fields, orchards, gardens—colleges and churches are seen. Broadclothes, silks, leghorns, crapes, and all the refinements, luxuries, elegancies, frivolities and fashions, are in vogue. Thus wave after wave is rolling westward—the real *el dorado* is still farther on.

A portion of the first two classes remain stationary amidst the general movement, improve their habits and condition, and rise in the scale of society.

The writer has travelled much amongst the first class—the real pioneers. He has lived many years in connexion with the second grade, and now the third wave is sweeping over large districts of Indiana, Illinois and Missouri. Migration has become almost a habit in the west. Hundreds of men can be found, not fifty years of age, who have settled for the fourth, fifth, or sixth time on a new spot. To sell out and remove only a few hundred miles, makes up a portion of the variety of backwoods life and manners.[42]

Turner's thesis which stimulated so much scholarship and controversy[43] was directly derived from men such as Peck, western pioneers and scholars who viewed their section through innocent and hopeful eyes. The paragraph immediately preceding Peck's description of social classes could also have been cited by Turner. It expresses the nub of his theory.

The rough, sturdy habits of the backwoodsmen, living in that plenty which depends on God and nature, have laid the foundation of independent thought and feeling deep in the minds of western people.[44]

Peck's paragraphs bear remarkable similarity to Turner's thesis which is reiterated throughout his essay in various ways: "The existence of an area of free land, its continuous recession, and the advance of American settlement westward, explain American development." "American social development has been continually beginning over again on the frontier. . . . The frontier is the outer edge of the wave— the meeting point between savagery and civilization." "But the most important effect of the frontier has been in the promotion of democracy here and in Europe. As has been indicated, the frontier is productive of individualism."[45]

Peck's typology of social classes is incomplete. Even within his own writings, as the reader of the *Memoir* will discover, there are other classes delineated and described. "Squatters," for example, the lowest and economically most deprived people on the frontier, are described in considerable detail in his journals. These people followed the "trappers" and simply squatted on the land until they were forced off for various reasons. But in the section used by Turner, Peck was describing a vast and rapid population movement rather than attempting to develop a formal and systematic typology of class structure in a stable society. In the same book that Turner used Peck does describe ethnic groups and classes in the settled portions of the frontier. Selections will show that the typology is more extensive but even less rigorously defined than in the section cited by Turner.

Emigrants from Europe have brought the peculiarities of the nations and countries from whence they have originated, but are fast losing their national manners and feelings, and, to use a provincial term, will soon become "westernized." . . . [It is instructive to compare this with Turner's words: "In the crucible of the frontier the immigrants were Americanized, liberated, and fused into a mixed race, English in neither nationality nor characteristics."[46]]

The poorer class of French are rather peculiar and unique. Their ancestors were isolated from the rest of the world, had no object of excitement or ambition, cared little for wealth, or the accumulation of property, and were accustomed to hunt, make voyages in their canoes, smoke and traffic with the Indians. But few of them knew how to read and write. Accustomed from infancy to the life of huntsmen, trappers and boatmen, they make but indifferent farmers. They are contented to live in the same rude, but neatly whitewashed cabin, cultivate the same cornfields in the same mode, and drive the same rudely constructed horse cart their fathers did. In the neatness of their gardens, which are usually cultivated by the females, they excel the Americans. They are the *coureurs du bois* of the West.

The European Germans are now coming into the Valley by thousands, and, for a time, will retain their manners and language.

Cotton and Sugar Planters. These people, found chiefly in Mississippi, Louisiana, and the southern part of Arkansas, have a great degree of similarity. They are noted for their high-mindedness, generosity, liberality, hospitality, sociability, quick sense of honor, resentment of injuries, indolence, and, in too many cases, dissipation. . . . Having overseers on most of their plantations, the labor being performed by slaves, they have much leisure, and are averse to much personal attention to business. They dislike care, profound thinking and deep impressions. . . .

Farmers. The farmers of the west are independent in feeling, plain in dress, simple in manners, frank and hospitable in their dwellings, and soon acquire a competency by modern labor. . . .

Population of the Cities and Large Towns. The population of western towns does not differ essentially from the same class in the Atlantic State, excepting there is much less division into grades and ranks, less ignorance, low depravity and squalid poverty amongst the poor, and less aristocratic feeling amongst the rich. As there is never any lack of employment for laborers of every description, there is comparatively no suffering from that cause. And the hospitable habits of the people provide for the sick, infirm and helpless. Doubtless, our *circumstances* more than anything else, cause these shades of difference. The common mechanic is on a social equality with the merchant, the lawyer, the physician, and the minister.[47]

It is clear that there are a greater number of factors and variables included in Peck's use of the word "class" than is found in contemporary sociology. Peck had a tendency to class people by region, occupation, stability or transiency, education, habits, customs, mores, and morality. He describes in extensive and interesting detail the artifacts of the "frontier class," which he divided into the three groups cited by Turner. Their clothing is carefully described along with their dwellings, including the difference between a "cabin" and a "log house." Their furniture is depicted as well as their sleeping, eating, and living quarters, their cooking utensils and methods of preparing food and their hunting techniques.[48]

If it is a matter of interest at all it remains for the historians to judge the measure of Peck's influence on Turner. But however slight or great it may have been it appears evident that Turner did not study Peck carefully enough. In another essay, Turner says of the pioneer that "he had a passionate hatred for aristocracy, monopoly and special privilege; he believed in simplicity, economy and in the rule of the people. . . . Among the pioneers one man was as good as his neighbor. He had the same chance; conditions were simple and free. Economic equality fostered political equality. An optimistic and buoyant belief in the worth of the plain people, a devout faith in man prevailed in the West. Democracy became almost the religion of the pioneer."[49] This is undoubtedly true of what we would call the lower-class or revivalist preachers, and perhaps, therefore, of the greater number of evangelists; but Peck, and a significant number of educated and influential missionaries, did not share this unqualified faith in man and uncritical and innocent view of democracy, although they did possess the profound conviction that God's awesome power would prevail to make the West a "city on a hill," a "light to all the nations." Peck denounced what he believed to be the simple Arminianism of those preachers whom he considered to be corrupters of the gospel. It is only in recent years that scholars have taken more seriously the social and theological significance of frontier religion rather than concentrating on its eccentric forms. This will be further pursued in succeeding sections.

Religion and Social Control on the Frontier

Charles Foster says that "the virtues to be propagated in the newly arrived citizenry bore a one-to-one relationship with religion in respectable minds of the day."[50] Whether we speak of the preacher-missionaries or of the eastern businessmen who supported them, morality and harmonious community without religion were inconceivable in their minds. Before the twentieth-century anthropologists developed it into a formal theory, the conservative powers of the eastern states viewed religion primarily as an integrating and conserving social force. The primary purpose of missions was to sustain society and preserve traditional morality. Religion, to be sure, was the vehicle which transported its passengers to glory, but only after their lives had been productive, disciplined, honorable and just.

The political power which had been enjoyed by that minority of wise and good people headed by the clergy had been rapidly dissipated on the eastern seaboard after 1812. As Lyman Beecher said in his autobiography, when the clergy "got together, they would talk over who should be governor, and who lieutenant governor, and who in the Upper House, and their counsels would prevail."[51] But now in the age of Jackson and the split in the Federalist party those days had passed and it was necessary to seek new ways to control the rampant egalitarian impulses which stirred the masses. The situation was further confused by general social upheaval marked by "increasing drunkenness and violation of the Sabbath."[52] Religious benevolent societies (moral, missionary, Bible, and publication) appeared in great number in the eastern states. Crusades were organized to stamp out gambling, profanity, and intemperance. Sunday school societies were organized no less to enhance general culture—facility in reading and writing—than to stimulate morality and further the cause of evangelical religion. The Sunday school was the forerunner of the public system of education. Everyone, low or high, slave or free, was—at least in the early days—urged to attend. This provided the foundation of social equality and mutual respect which became the ideal of the secular schools.[53]

Peck moved to the Mississippi Valley on the crest of this fanatic fervor to establish religion and morality as the normative American way. Despite the strength of his religious

convictions and the overwhelming power of his personal sense
of destiny he was a moderate evangelist in a day when most
Protestant Christians agreed that "the very essence of every
system of manners, moral, and religion, [which is] not
evangelical, is corruption—gross, foul, deep, total corruption."[54] Peck's strong convictions were balanced by an unusual quality of toleration. He knew first hand the people
whom the eastern leaders feared, reviled, and sought to
control. During his extensive travels he had preached and
prayed with them, visited in their homes, eaten at their
tables, and slept in their beds. Perhaps this is the reason he
recognized that there were gradations of religious types
existing between the extremes of piety and atheism. While it
it clear that he viewed religion as an effective instrument of
social control as well as the path to salvation, he realized that
some men can be moral without the fear of hell or hope of
heaven. Therefore, implicit within his journal is a rudi-
mentary typology of religious and moral people. The reader
can extract the following types from the *Memoir* (pp. 85–90):
(1) actively anti-religious; (2) immoral rowdies; (3) moral
but not religious people, moral and respected by the community; (4) nominally religious; and (5) actively religious.
Peck is not to be given credit for developing formal sociological categories which he perceived only in the vaguest way,
but it is significant that such categories were implicit in his
work.

Historically, Christian missionary work has always been
motivated in great part by the impulse to establish respectable middle-class morality. This was true of foreign missions,
of American home missions in the past and present century,
as it is in the mission to the impoverished non-whites in the
East Harlem Protestant Parish.[55] But just as traditional
ecclesiastical structure and evangelical methods are un-
suitable in Harlem, they were inappropriate and ineffective
for capturing the allegiance of the frontier people. Thus the
influential Protestant establishments of the East, represented
by the Congregationalists, Episcopalians, and Presbyterians,

were for the most part content to leave the frontier to the
Methodists, Baptists, and Disciples whose ministry in any
case was believed to approximate the barbarity of the pioneer
mind. The frontier was penetrated by itinerant farmer-
preachers ''called of the Lord'' and, who, with no significant
training, moved into the new settlements as quickly as they
were organized. In the early days all the denominations
cooperated in the effort to ''christianize'' the West. At first,
pastors from the East were released for six month missions,
but as the frontier moved beyond the Alleghenies this proved
unfeasible; so individuals were sent out under the aegis of
the interdenominational American Home Mission Society.
About the same time denominational home mission agencies
(state and national) were established and the benevolent
work increased with the movement of the frontier.

The threat of complete social disorganization in the West
was not manufactured by pious pastors and conservative
businessmen. It was very real. An unprecedented cooperative
effort was put forth and the combination of financial, moral,
and religious resources that descended upon the frontier was
enormous. The ministry was so effective because it was itinerate and indigenous and identified with the people. The
preachers gained their livelihood from the land and persuaded the people themselves to contribute their pennies for
''maintenance of the gospel.'' Charles Foster rather cynically
but wryly observes that when Peck had once experienced a
discouraging period in his work he ''received a windfall, a
great stroke of good fortune: the Baptist Missionary Society
of Massachusetts hired him at the salary of five dollars per
week for time actually spent in the field. He could raise that
five dollars himself.''[56] But this was a significant event because unwittingly these people were utilizing the therapeutic
technique of contributing to the remedy of their own problems; it is significant also because Peck was among the
minority of missionaries who took the trouble to request
official endorsement to use the money he raised.

Because the threat of social disorganization was so real,

religion as an instrument of social control was necessary. A plea for western colleges was made by the religious people, and modern scholars have listed the reasons which were offered to solicit support.[57] It was recognized that every community required a stabilizing influence, that western society was plastic and could flow in any direction, that the unprecedented pluralism enhanced the divisive forces and strengthened the position of those who sought power, that demogogues and popular agitation increased the incohesiveness of society and the tendencies toward delusion and agitation, and that the general illiteracy and lack of rootedness and sense of history contributed to all of these. Finally, the intellectuals of the day feared the development of Roman Catholic colleges. Using different language, Peck indicates an awareness of all of these factors throughout his writings, especially in his journal entries of 1819, the year that he opened the college in Alton.

As a form of social control religious discipline was remarkably effective in the eighteenth and nineteenth centuries. Church leaders were not concerned primarily with the population growth of their congregations but first with the number of well-disciplined and pious souls.

Peck and Lawton, the missionary-historians in New York, discussed the social effects of discipline in the churches. The Baptists were notorious for their informal and relaxed procedures in the recruitment of ministers. This worked reasonably well in settled communities but on the frontier where strange pastors passed through and sought jobs without offering references this method of recruiting leadership broke down. A Baptist association in western New York established more rigorous methods of selection.

The adoption of these rules excited the wonder of friends and the malice of enemies. . . . The country being new, and the settlements small, many men who had lost their characters in the eastern and southern parts, supposing the wilderness to be favorable to their designs, were purposing to come into this country. . . . In consequence of the almost entire desecration of the Lord's day, it was necessary to enjoin upon the church at their formation, and make it an article in their covenant, that they should religiously observe the day; and also that all heads of families should maintain the worship of God in their houses, by reading the scriptures and vocal prayer.[58]

The West was subdued not only by the courage of the pioneer and the hard labor of the farmer and businessman, but by people who gathered in their churches and who exercised rigorous control over their members and profoundly influenced the total life of the community. Contrary to popular assumptions the interest of the church extended far beyond the well-known strictures against gambling, drinking, and hilarity on the Sabbath. Church records show that Baptists on the frontier were excluded from communion for an impressive list of major and minor offenses including adultery, stealing, swearing, "selling an unsound mare," calling another member a liar, "swapping horses," deceiving and defrauding, fighting, tale bearing, threatening a slave, quarreling, "misusing one's wife," and failure to attend church.[59]

A table can be developed from statistics included in the history of the New York Convention. It is instructive to notice how rapidly the Otsego Association grew in twelve years. While the number of actual "exclusions" was small, it is indicative of the change that has occurred in the churches to hazard the guess that one would have difficulty finding a single expulsion of a member in all of the major Protestant denominations in the entire state of New York over the past decade.

The influence of the church was pervasive and affected the entire social order. At a much later date when disciplinary strictures had undergone a general decline, Max Weber records an incident in which he visited a German Baptist Church in North Carolina. He asked a relative why he anticipated the decision of a certain man to be baptized.

"Because he wants to open a bank in M."
"Are there so many Baptists around that he can make a living?"

Otsego Association, N.Y., 1795–1807[60]

Year	Churches	Ministers	Members	Excluded
1795	13	5	424	—
1796	17	9	653	6
1797	25	12	1054	11
1798	27	14	1292	40
1799	34	14	1659	22
1800	37	15	1764	23
1801	40	19	2031	37
1802	42	19	—	34
1803	45	16	2116	43
1804	46	16	2334	37
1805	50	24	2622	47
1806	53	26	3903	61
1807	55	28	3265	50

"Not at all, but once being baptized he will get the patronage of the whole region and he will outcompete everybody."

Further questions of "why" and "by what means" led to the following conclusion: Admission to the local Baptist congregation follows only upon the most careful "probation" and after closest inquiries into conduct going back to early childhood (Disorderly conduct? Frequenting taverns? Dance? Card Playing? Untimely meeting of liability? Other Frivolities?) The congregation still adhered strictly to the religious tradition.[61]

Admission to the Methodist or Baptist sects was a guarantee of moral quality and fidelity in business matters.

As one pursues the literature about the early frontier, it becomes apparent that despite the obvious indifference to morality and religion, the social environment and the attitudes of the people were ripe and prepared for revival. The preachers had a difficult task but had they not received such clear assistance from a morally and religiously inclined populace their efforts would have been unimpressive. The pioneers who moved west were people who sought a new community and a new way of life, one which encouraged individual freedom and rewarded creativity and initiative, but they were eager to establish social forms and to develop the communal controls that were essential for the achievement of their ideals. The readiness of the people can be illustrated by an incident recorded by Peck, and indicates that even before the churches appeared the people wanted what they had to offer.

[A certain innkeeper who was indifferent to religion refused money from Father John Clark because] "your bill, Sir, is more than paid. It is not customary to charge preachers, though everyone of that class who travel this road don't keep the house in as good order as you did last night." [The landlord noticed that if it had not been for Clark's religious discourse the night before,] "we should have had drinking, swearing, and fighting through the night, to the annoyance of all quiet people."

[One may wonder why the landlord, however much he loved peace, was apparently willing to lose whiskey sales.] The bottle or jug of whiskey was always set on the table at such houses of entertainment, with a bowl of sugar, and a pitcher of water fresh from the spring, and "help yourselves strangers," was the courteous invitation. Whether the traveller drank more or less, or none at all, made not the least difference in his bill. Fifty cents for horse-keeping, supper, and lodging, was uniform for nearly half a century.[62]

Baptist Polity and Theology
in the Nineteenth Century

The purpose of the frontier according to Timothy Dwight was to drain off the dregs of the excess population of the seaboard states.[63] The fact is that this was one of the functions of the West just as it had been of the colonies in their relation to Europe. Peck obviously did not share the view that this was the purpose of the frontier, but there were times when he was deeply involved in turmoil and controversy with the "anti-mission Baptists" that he must have sympathized with it.

The Baptists, Methodists, and Disciples were the three great religious movements which depended on the revival technique and profited by the isolation and simplicity of the people. The arrival of an itinerant preacher was an occasion for the gathering of the folk from the surrounding farms and settlements. The social function of religion is evident in Peck's description of a tent meeting in Georgia.

In all frontier settlements in the south-western States, it makes very little difference in gathering a congregation, whether the preaching is on the week day or the Sabbath. All classes turned out in their ordinary working dress, for which they had a change of clean garments ready. They knew nothing and cared little for which Christian sect the strange preacher belonged; as all preached very much alike, and iterated the same common place truths of the Bible on such occasions. Men wholly worldly, and not very moral; who fingered bits of spotted pasteboard [gambling], drank whiskey, and attended horse-races and shooting matches, would turn out to hear a strange preacher, or go to a "big" meeting, as these large convocations were called; where several preachers of diverse gifts were expected.

The youngsters of the family were on their horses before the sun peered . . . and rode throughout the settlements, and halooed at every cabin to give the inmates notice that "mother's preacher" had come and would preach at 'Squire Redman's that day. . . . Though the people were scattered over the hills and along the vallies for many miles distant, the news spread, and by eleven o'clock men, women and children, two and three often on one horse, were approaching 'Squire Redman's plantation from every point of the compass. A full compliment of dogs to every family were . . . coursing along the margin of the woods near the pathway, smelling for game, and barking up hollow trees. The children, of course, large and small, had to be taken, or the mothers could not go, and the dogs, accustomed to follow their masters and the horses would go, whether wanted or not. And should the young children cry and the dogs bark, both preacher and hearers were used to such trifling annoyances.[64]

Peck's thoughtful analysis of the techniques of the revival preachers is recorded in the *Memoir* (pp. 200 f). He criticized the method on theological and psychological grounds and observed that the mass excitement and fervor was artificially stimulated, having nothing necessarily to do with religion as he understood it. Nonetheless, Peck shared the evangelical emphasis upon the necessity for a visible conversion experi-

ence as the starting point of the Christian life. He was only
critical of the mass revival method as a legitimate technique
for initiating the experience. He left us the record of a conversion, which, measured by the fashion of that period, was
a relatively quiet and secluded experience. It occurred in a
private home.

Very soon she despaired of making herself better, and felt her
dependence on the Lord to that degree, as to beg the preacher to
pray to God to have mercy on her; while with an audible voice she
cried out in agony, "Lord have mercy on me, a miserable sinner."
. . . Mrs. Wells, who lay prostrate across her chair, groaning, and
crying for mercy, as if wholly unconscious of what she said or did,
sprang to her feet, clapped her hands in a joyous ecstasy, and at
the top of her voice, in exultant tones exclaimed, "Glory to the Lord
Jesus! Glory to the Lord Jesus!—he's pardoned my sins;—he's
pardoned my sins!" and with continuous shoutings and exclama-
tions, until nature was exhausted, she sunk into the arms of Mrs.
Lowe, who placed her in the chair. Here she sat, still rubbing her
hands in ecstasy, and in a subdued voice, nearly powerless, still
cried, "glory, glory."

"Well, I don't believe in such conversion as that," says a sentimental lady;—a church member;—though she spent the half of
the preceding night over a specimen of the yellow-colored "light"
literature . . . and sighing and sentimentalizing over an unreal
and mawkish story of love and suicide.

"'Tis all fox-fire," declares a grave and reverend divine, whose
intellect is as clear and cool as an iceberg, and who has not enough
of impulse to raise the slightest emotions in his soul. . . .

It is a very queer kind of philosophy that admits persons to
faint, fall, and even die under the pressure of some sudden and
overwhelming calamity, or from ecstasy from hearing joyful news
of an earthy kind, and yet account such paroxysms as Mrs. Wells
had as "fox-fire," "enthusiasm," and the fruits of "ignorance." Mrs.
Wells was a woman of strong emotions, easily excited, and never
trained to disguise her feelings under a cold, conventional ex-
terior.[65]

The rapid growth of the Methodists and Baptists on the
frontier were due, of course, in great part to the success of
the revival method as it was employed by the itinerate
preachers. The Western Conference of the Methodist church

leaped from 2800 communicants in 1800 to 30,000 in 1811. The Baptists started more slowly. In 1830, a decade after Peck arrived in St. Louis, there were only 3600 Baptists west of the Alleghenies, but by 1850 there were 30,000 members, the nation as a whole having about 800,000 Baptists at that time.

In the first half of the century the Baptists were represented by a variety of sub-types. There were General, Particular, Regular, Separate, United, Primitive, Free Will, and Two-Seed-in-the-Spirit Predestinarian Baptists, each emphasizing a theological peculiarity or adhering to a particular liturgical form or polity. But there were several principles which were considered essential by all groups: adult baptism and conversion as a condition of church membership; immersion as the legitimate Scriptural form of baptism; congregational church government, assocations of churches possessing only advisory authority; direct responsibility of the individual to God without the mediating assistance of minister or sacrament; and separation of church and state.

The Particular Baptists were strict Calvinists holding to a doctrine of limited atonement and grace by predestination, while the General Baptists were Arminian, holding to a general atonement, free grace, and greater responsibility of the individual in his relation to God. The Regular and Separate groups had appeared during the Great Awakening in New England; the former group criticized the revival method while the Separatists departed from the fold in large numbers and supported the revival. In 1801 these groups joined forces and were called United Baptists. The Free Will, Two-Seed-in-the-Spirit, and Primitive or "Hardshell" Baptists gained their greatest strength in opposition to the mission activity on the frontier and can be included under the general rubric of "antimission Baptists," the groups that plagued Peck throughout his career.[66] The antimission controversy, as we shall note below, had significant theological overtones by which the contending parties justified their acts, but it is doubtful that the primary causal forces were theological. For the most part, frontier Baptist theology was a blend of Arminian and Calvinistic doctrines. Arminianism, which amphasized individual freedom and responsibility, was more amenable to the spirit of the frontier than strict predestinarian Calvinism. But the Arminian Baptists from New England tended to slide toward the middle-of-the-road in the direction of Calvinism, perhaps because the Methodists, who were their primary competitors, stressed free will and personal moral responsibility before God.[67]

But the crucial question for the Baptists and the one which distinguished them most clearly from the frontier Methodists was centered in the issue of ecclesiastical polity and the problem of authority. According to traditional Baptist polity, the saying attributed to Jesus, ''Where two or three are gathered together in my name, there will I be also,'' signifies the existence of a fully legitimated church in the local situation and without any formal connection with other churches. In fact, it was believed (and still is maintained by a powerful minority) that any formal connection involving authority and requiring subordination and superordination, constituted a corruption of the gospel. Thus according to traditional Baptist polity the local congregation is fully empowered to choose, license, and ordain a minister and to conduct all its spiritual and material affairs without reference to any other person or group. As Peck discovered, this arrangement contains a tremendous potential for anarchy. Associational discipline was (and is) virtually nonexistent. Without commonly accepted and rational ordination standards it is impossible to criticize effectively or discipline any preacher, no matter how bizarre his behavior or beliefs.

In actual practice, however, the modes of social and ecclesiastical control, although organized on an *ad hoc* and informal basis and in response to situations as they arise, are far more rigorous than the traditionally permissive system of the Baptists would lead the casual observer to suppose. It is obvious to the sociologist that no social institutions as large and effective as the Southern and American Baptist Conventions could survive if permissiveness where the rule rather than the exception.[68]

The Methodists were more effective than the Baptists even though the circuit preachers had to accede to the rigorous authority and control of the Methodist bishops. The Methodists and Baptists entered the frontier with virtually absolutely contrasting forms of church government, and yet both denominations were manifestly successful and caused the Episcopalians, Congregationalists, and Presbyterians to become permanent minority denominations in the nation.

Despite centralization of authority the Methodist church was elastic and fully capable of adapting to rapid social development and change. The best preachers were transferred from circuit to circuit year by year ''until vast numbers of people . . . had come under the influence of their preaching. . . . In effect, under the executive leadership of the bishops of the church . . . it was a self-perpetuating aristocracy of the traveling elders organized in their various conferences; while in its quarterly meetings, love feasts, class meetings, and the like, it gave opportunity for lesser officers, local preachers, and class leaders, and even the rank and file to bear their share in the local government under the guidance of the traveling eldership.''[69]

The most effective preachers were often men of astounding eloquence and charisma. The Methodists offered free grace for those who were sincerely repentant and promised transformation of the world by the simple arithmetic of adding together the power of individuals who were redeemed. Such preachers could sway their audience until it seemed ''to wave back and forth like fields of grain.'' On a good day, the sinners would ''fall slain by the hundreds'' and they would then be led to the mourners' bench where under the guidance of the elders divine ecstasy became rapture and peace or they were carried home in a paroxysm of emotional fatigue.

Baptist work was hampered by lack of organization, undefined channels of authority, and an unmanageable system for the recruitment of ministers. Scattered efforts to remedy the situation were attempted but were frustrated by the fundamental presupposition that associations and conventions could legitimately possess nothing more than advisory power. Every state convention or local association that was formed for reasons of mutual discipline and effective administration and policy formation possessed only an "advisory" authority.

A convention of delegates from every part of the State will afford an opportunity to such as are assailed with efforts peculiar to their section of the country, or involved in distressing and perplexing cases of discipline, and other difficulties, to consult their brethren who have gained wisdom by experience, and prudence by the things which they have suffered; and who are remote from those predilections which sometimes bias the judgment of the best of men.[70]

The Baptist theology of the church contained a fundamental contradiction which Peck apparently sensed. According to the tradition, both the redeemed individual and the congregation of believers were completely free and responsible agents. But the degree and constitution of these competing freedoms and the character and precise nature of the responsible parties has never been defined. The anomoly persists to this day because formal definitions require an official authority and the formal tradition is opposed to the creation of any such authority. Evidence that Peck detected this contradiction is found in the *Memoir*. He distrusted the "inalienable right of private judgment" and says that individuals must surrender their freedom and accept the discipline of the church and of the association of churches. He understood better than most of his contemporaries the sociological and psychological complexity of the relation between group authority and individual conscience.

There were a number of preachers in Lincoln [Kentucky] and the adjacent counties, all Baptists, who were somewhat divided on certain points of doctrine, and not altogether friendly in ministerial intercourse. Each possessed his share of the imperfections of human character; each was more or less selfish; petty rivalries prevailed, and small differences were magnified, as each party looked at the other through the medium of prejudice. In a word, the pioneer preachers of Kentucky were very much like the ministers of the Gospel in every age, nation, and country; no better, no worse; only a little more frank, and even blunt in their personal intercourse, and did not conceal their thoughts and emotions with the same ingenuity and tact as has been done in some places. Hence, if there were petty jealousies, rivalries, and surmisings, (all of which traits are wrong and unchristian everywhere,) they let their passions be seen and the want of union and mutual cooperation was the natural result.[71]

The Antimission Controversy

According to the *Memoir* the first overt antimissionary act involving Peck occurred in a little church in Missouri in 1818. The people voted to burn voluntary pledge notes which they had given Peck for the support of his work. A large portion of the Baptist constituency across the entire frontier was sympathetic to the breaking of the pledge. Antimission sentiment flared spontaneously in the southern and western states. By 1820 virtually every Baptist church and association in the Mississippi Valley was divided over the issue of missions. "Not a man ventured to open his mouth in favor of any benevolent enterprise or action. The [local] missionary societies were dissolved, and the associations rescinded all their resolutions by which they were in any way connected with these measures, and in this respect, the spirit of death rested upon the whole people!"[72]

Three men, John Taylor, Daniel Parker, and Alexander Campbell, stood out as antimission leaders. In 1819 Taylor published a pamphlet called "Thoughts on Missions," in which he said that the resident preachers were aroused by the assumption on the part of the new missionaries that the frontier was a religious desert and that the missionaries were the first to introduce true religion. He said the primary object of missionaries was to get money. Their efforts also were illegitimate because the missionary system was unscriptural.

He compared the missionaries with Judas and to horse leeches which suck blood "with a forked tongue." The missionary society, he said, was an aristocracy which was absolutely contrary to Baptist theology.

Parker, the founder of the Two-Seed-in-the-Spirit Predestinarian Baptists, agreed that missions would destroy Baptist democracy and church government. He observed that the national society usurped the work of God by calling men to preach, assigning them to fields, and requiring an educated ministry. The "denomination" he founded still exists, reporting 201 members in 16 churches in 1945.[73] Parker taught that two seeds, good and evil, entered the life stream of humanity in Eden, the evil seed being planted by Satan. Every child is born with one seed or the other and is, therefore, predestined. Since nothing can be done about this, missions are useless and a paid ministry is blasphemous since Christ came to save sinners and his work is completed. Parker was also an extensive pamphleteer.

Alexander Campbell and his father Thomas withdrew from association with the Presbyterians in 1809 to form the Christian Church (Disciples of Christ). The Disciples count this as their historic beginning but actually the denomination formed about twenty years later after several abortive attempts to unite all Protestants under one denominational banner. Alexander was a Baptist from 1813 to 1830. In 1829 he published the *Millennial Harbinger* in which he attacked every practice for which he could not find scriptural proof including creeds, mission societies, associations, synods, presbyteries, doctors of divinity, bishops, confessions, constitutions, titles such as "reverend," etc. He claimed to favor missions but not national agencies, those "great engines" which seek to dominate the nation. He opposed ministerial education and asked, "did God ever call a man to any work for which he was not fully qualified, and in the performance of which he was not successful?"[74]

The causes and reasons for the antimissionary controversy were more complex than their immediate participants realized. Peck, as the *Memoir* indicates, recognized that the dispute was neither purely theological nor exclusively religious in the widest sense. It was also a matter of class and educational competition. It was an important struggle for power within the denomination and reflected deep-seated tensions which existed, and still exist, between the East and the West.

Theologically the antimission groups were ultra-Calvinistic and Antinomian. Newman hypothesized that this was a reaction to the encroachment of the Methodists whose Arminian teachings stimulated the radical reaction, but he offered no support for this.[75] More likely, hyper-Calvinism offered an appropriate theological apology for opposition to all organized activity generated in the East. The antimission Baptists taught that God would bring his elect to repentance and redemption without any human aids. Such assistance was presumptuous and wicked. Of course, the antimission forces neglected to observe that they used human means to oppose the missionary work. Had they been theologically consistent they would have done nothing to oppose or assist the mission endeavor.

They argued that God's acts were absolutely free and always arbitrary and that it did no good to attempt to support the divine predestinations. The movement was radically individualistic and dependent upon ''intuition'' rather than ''reason'' to perceive God's will. Parker said that God did not send Jonah to Nineveh through a mission society, nor was he ''sent to a seminary of learning to prepare him to preach to these Gentiles; but was under the tuition of a special order of God, and was in no case under the direction of any body of men whatever, neither did he look back to a society formed to raise money for his support.''[76] On the grounds of their radical individualism and emphasis upon personal responsibility for one's acts—or on the grounds of the complete opposite that one could do nothing about his acts due to the arbitrary predeterminations of God—the antimission preachers were adamantly opposed to cooperative welfare programs of all kinds, religious or social. These were a proud people who wanted to control through their own leaders the social instruments by which they assisted each other.

They were fanatically anxious to preserve the autonomy of the local congregation. The formation of missionary societies with officers and field secretaries was a direct threat to the authority of the local church. The activities of the missionary agencies reminded John Taylor of the operations of Tetzel, the "hawker of indulgences when the Pope of Rome and the Mother of Harlots were at their zenith."

This represents the substance of the arguments based on theology and on the "intention of Scripture" for church government. The issues were serious but they were never seriously discussed or resolved on the theological level by the more sophisticated intellectual powers from the East. It was judged by them to be purely a non-theological issue arising out of jealousy and threatened loss of status on the part of the indigenous preachers. At both the theological and non-theological level the debate still goes on in all Christian groups regarding the "essential" and "unessential" in ecclesiastical polity, the nature and method of salvation, the legitimate locus of authority in the church, the nature of the ministry, the proper role of ecclesiastical benevolent and welfare agencies, and so on.

The theological issues, then as now, were complicated by secular factors. The anti-missionary preachers were threatened by a loss of prestige, money, and authority. The missionaries from the East were far better educated men than the farmer-preachers of the frontier. Opposition in one church minute was generated because "our land suffers a vast loss of money. . . . Money and theological learning seem to be the pride, we fear, of too many of the preachers of our day."[77] Peck observed that the antimission preachers were not paid but that they dearly loved the power and influence which they exercised over the population of the West. He reported that one preacher said, "you know the big trees in the woods overshadow the little ones; and these missionaries will be all great, learned men, and the people will all go to hear them preach, and we shall all be put down.''

As a causal factor the tension between East and West cannot be underestimated. The sections feared and distrusted each other with greater intensity than exists in the present political era. The cleavages in the churches reflected the divisions in the larger society. The anti-mission Baptists were concentrated in Georgia, North Carolina, Virginia, Tennessee, Kentucky, Ohio, Missouri, Indiana, and Illinois. The established power of the churches resided in the East and was supported by all the resources of the settled American communities. The westerners knew that the seaboard aristocrats looked down upon them and feared the tremendous population shift that was occurring in the nation. Like the Baptists in the seventeenth century, the frontiersmen developed theological support for their anti-aristocratic notions. The East was commercial and urban in relation to the agricultural and rural West. The West, in turn, was a debtor section while the East was the creditor. Philosophically, the East was conservative, tending to emphasize natural law, social harmony, and justice for all men through the alleviation of hardship through benevolent and philanthropic societies. The West was more inclined to favor natural rights, equality, and the immediate cooperation of kinship and communal groups for the help of the poor and the sick. The average westerner, moreover, did not view himself as an eternal backwoodsman but as an entrepreneur and capitalist on the make.[78] At least for the time being, higher education and the cultural refinement of the arts were superfluous and would never, in any case, operate as an effective substitute for common sense and practical judgment.

The Baptists were the only denomination which experienced the dissension of the antimissionary movement. The reasons are not easy to detect. It has often been suggested that Methodist doctrine which emphasized the Arminian principles of free grace and personal responsibility was in accord with the secular hopes and ideologies of the frontier people, but this does not explain the successful reaction of the antimission Baptists which was expressed in hyper-Calvinistic terms. More likely the reason is to be discovered in the differences between the Methodist and Baptist theologies of the church than in their theologies of salvation. The Baptists had a longer history of resentment toward absentee authority, and more to the point, the authority of the Methodist church was focused in the bishop who was resident in the area in the person of the very able frontier missionary, Bishop William McKendree, who lived in Illinois and was the chief ecclesiastical officer of the Western Conference. Thus, when the Methodist circuit preachers received orders or sought advice, they did not have to refer to New York, Boston, or Philadelphia. The Methodist hierarchy was directly represented in the West. Further, the hierarchical system of the Methodist church penetrated to the lowest levels of the denomination, and a greater number of people seemed to have a part in the policy and decision-making process as well as in the work of the church. The local Methodist churches had "lay-elders," who stood immediately below the preachers in the hierarchy, and who were ordained by the bishop. Peck commented on the efficacy of this post in conducting religious duties and in meeting the needs of the people.

> This office, now unknown in Baptist churches was regarded in Virginia and afterwards in Kentucky, as an appendage to the pastoral office. Lay-elders had no authority in government and discipline, as in a Presbyterian church, but aided the pastor in conducting religious meetings by exhortation and prayer, visiting the sick, instructing the ignorant, and confirming the wavering.[79]

Thus, the duties of absent or heavily burdened preachers could be met by the ablest lay officers while at the same time their status was officially limited and clerical authority strictly maintained. The Disciples was the only group which approximated the Baptists in doctrine and polity, and they appeared on the frontier in part as an antimissionary protest.

William Warren Sweet expressed a dominant opinion of later historians when he assessed the antimissionary controversy as "harmful to religion generally and to the progress of the Baptists in particular," and that it had a critical influence on the development of the West at a time when educational foundations were most sorely needed.[80] But such an opinion should not close the books. Thus far, specialized research on the influence of religious movements on the development of the ideologies of the western states has been sparse, and for the most part has been confined to the "purely religious" effects.

National Baptist Agencies and the Mission Controversy

The mission controversy can be analyzed in terms of the church-sect typology. The anti-mission preachers would be called sectarians and the missionaries would be representatives of the church, Christian realists who recognized that no religious and moral goals can be achieved and "no ideal can be incorporated without the loss of some of its ideal character."[81] Troeltsch observed that this paradox was resident in the form of an ambiguity in the Gospel ethic, the sayings of Jesus registering both a positive and negative evaluation of the world. The simplicity of the church-sect analysis, however, results in a tendency to overlook the morally ambiguous character of the sects as well as the churches. Troeltsch emphasized the "ethical rigor" of the sectarian type, but this generally persists for no more than a generation, and the motives of the first-generation rigorists are never purely moral. In an effort to correct the church-sect hypothesis several scholars observed that sects tend to evolve into churches or denominations, and more recently it has been noted that all churches possess "sectarian" inclinations in certain of their sub-groups.

It can be said that this inclination was present in the antimission controversy. An emerging Baptist sect conflicted with a "more advanced" sectarian group—also Baptist—which was well on its way to achieving denominational status. This kind of analytical confusion occurs in part because *both* groups needed to organize in order to achieve religious and moral goals which, in turn, would be compromised by the tendency of their organizations to frustrate the attainment of their goals, and by the further complication that a minority within the church-type will always seek to alter the organizational status-quo in order to remain true to the rigorous ethic of the Original Founder.

According to contemporary usage, Peck would be called a conservative, an organization man, one who believed that religion could not progress effectively apart from the traditions, institutions, and civilized philosophy of western culture. For example, he argued for the associational form of church government and in this sense he was opposed to one of the main tenets of Baptist tradition. He was disinclined to recognize any virtue in the argument of the farmer-preachers, who, however self-interested they may have been, recognized correctly that the civilizing influence tends to secularize religion, and from the perspective of the primitive Christian ethic it does corrupt the gospel. This is the valid emphasis of every "fundamentalist" group, and it is almost universally ignored and deplored by the members of the "churches" until their institutions have become so accommodated to society that they are rendered ineffective as critics of civilization. The organizational delemma is inescapable. Although the disadvantages of organization may be greater for religion than for other types of social institution, there is no effective alternative for the achievement of goals and communication of ideals to succeeding generations. Peck was sensitive to these issues. He was fully aware of the civilizing power of religion, and in turn, of the essential contribution that culture makes to religion. He thought and acted in the spirit of Tillich's observation that "religion is the substance of culture, and culture is the expression of religion.''

The development of the State Convention in western New York is illustrative of Baptist intentions and problems. Its proximity to the seaboard states contributed to a more rapid advancement of organizational structures. Nonetheless, it did not escape the destructive impact of the anti-mission controversy as the following report demonstrates.

The object of the convention is . . . to produce a greater sum of good: not by destroying, superseding, or opposing, those benevolent missionary societies already in operation; but by combining, improving, and maturing them.

The benefits which it is devoutly hoped will result from this institution, are, (1) a combination of energies, efforts, and funds. And let it be remembered that "combined exertion is powerful exertion." . . . In relation to doing good, the strengh of the churches of Christ . . . consists in a union of their wisdom, their talents, their graces, their charities, and their exertions, in mutual and friendly co-operations. . . . (2) A collection of important and extensive information. A convention of delegates from every part of this State and its vicinity will bring together numerous interesting and essential facts, concerning the want of the church, destitute portions of country, and the operations of the hand of God in different places. And through the medium of that correspondence, which the constitution provided, the moral as well as the local situation of that vast and gloomy region in the west will be laid open to the view of the Board, and by them to that benevolent public. . . . (3) A judicious distribution and destination of missionaries. Owing to an ignorance of each other's proceedings, different societies, in some instances, send more missionaries to some particular places than are needed, while others are left entirely destitute, and, for want of proper information, often direct them to fields of labor far less important and promising than many that remain unoccupied.[82]

It would be difficult to find a statement that more precisely reflects John Mason Peck's interests, interpretation of the Bible, and social philosophy than this report from the area in which he was converted and ordained to the Baptist ministry, and to which he often returned on his eastern visits. At the same meeting in which the above report was given, the President of the Convention, Elon Galusha, answered the objections of the antimissionary preachers, who said of the convention,

that it tends to aggrandizement, by promoting some of the brethren to more honor than others share; *that large ecclesiastical bodies are dangerous to the cause of Christ.* In answer to the first objection, we need only say that no honor is conferred on any brother by this body but that of a servant. And if any are desirous of the honor of devoting much time, much labor, and some cash, too, (without pecuniary reward) to the precious cause of truth, let them share it largely as their benevolent hearts may crave; for the heavier they are laden with it, the more will God be glorified, and suffering humanity relieved.

To the second objection, we would reply, that all ecclesiastical bodies are dangerous, in proportion, not to their numbers, but to the independent power they possess, the temptation they are under to abuse it, and the encouragement they give to unholy ambition. But this Convention, as may be seen by its constitution, is invested with no such power—can acquire none; consequently can abuse none.

Its members are chosen annually by the brethren. Its funds are all derived from free donations, and must be appropriated according to the direction of the donor. It affords no encouragements to unholy ambition, as it enjoys no emoluments, pays its officers no salary, no perquisites, and confers no honorary titles. . . .

System, so essential to the efficiency of our missionary operations, is less visible in the accumulation than in the distribution of our funds.[83]

This statement is of historical importance because it expresses ideas and principles which are still accepted in both the American and Southern Baptist Convention and which continue to operate as the fundamental rationale for these national organizations. In these sentences Galusha explained the procedures which were used by the New York Convention and which were adopted by the American Baptist Convention at its founding in 1907, and for the most part, still remain in force. For example, the officers of the national convention—president, vice-president, etc.—who are elected on a one year basis are still paid no salaries; the professional agents—executives, administrators, missionaries, etc.—are appointed by the boards of elected officials; they are salaried and oftentimes enjoy life tenure on the basis of successive appointments.

Although Peck fully recognized the necessity for the rationalization of religious work, he was not idealistic and naive about the nature of the organizations in which he participated. He recognized that controversy and jealous competition were not confined to the antimission groups. In several instances he regretfully alluded to the rivalries among the officials of the missionary societies. It is unfortunate for historical and sociological interests that he did not amplify these difficulties, or that Babcock did not include them in the *Memoir*, but we do know that most of the controversies centered around the competing interests of foreign and home missions. The *Memoir* alludes to a conflict between Luther Rice and William Staughton on the one hand and the advocates of foreign missions on the other. Torbet says, "in 1826 the Triennial Convention took steps to extricate itself from involvement in home mission work and Columbian College [of which Staughton was President]. . . . Many [were] accusing Rice of negligence and even of dishonesty (these charges were proved to be unfounded). . . . The result was a loss of financial support from some quarters."[84]

Peck's deep interest in the rationalization of denominational efforts did not signify for him a need to proliferate and extend organizations. He futilely sought, as have many of his Baptist heirs, to unite publication efforts whenever possible. Long before Parkinson was born Peck was aware of the ubiquitous tendency to amplify bureaucracy as an end in itself. Peck was the grandfather of the conservative western politician and religious man in the sense that he actively opposed the multiplication of executive and administrative posts in the East. Efficiency of operation meant for him the reduction of expenses and elimination of new offices whenever possible, limitation of power whenever feasible, and the creation of new offices only when no alternative existed. He was probably the only man in Baptist history who succeeded in reducing all executive salaries by 20 per cent—including his own—when he assumed office in the Publication Society. Nevertheless, as mentioned above, he was fully aware of the need for organization and efficiency. He called it "comprehension and distribution of duties," which are respectively similar to Weber's concept of "rationalization" and Durkheim's "division of labor." Finally, the *Memoir* indicates that Peck was ahead of his time in his sensitivity to the problem of depersonalization in bureaucracy. He insisted that the highest executive officials must maintain personal contact with their constituency. When he was executive secretary of the Publication Society, he found it within his power to maintain a correspondence and travel schedule that would overwhelm most men and may have contributed to his comparatively early death.

There can be no doubt that the antimission forces lacked a great deal in terms of the finesse that is the companion of cultural advantage and theological sophistication. It is also true that they often placed their personal concerns above the apparent needs of the developing frontier, and that in this they were shortsighted and self-interested. But there was truth in many of their charges, and they fully recognized that they were engaging a powerful and implacable antagonist. The Protestant establishment was concentrated in the East and consisted of an impressive interlocking directorate of which Peck was an influential itinerate representative. What Foster calls a "convention circuit" started to develop as early as 1820. Most of the major denominations and interdenominational organizations held their "Anniversary Meetings" in May in Philadelphia, New York, and Boston. Many of the same people traveled from one city to another as delegates to these various meetings. The *Memoir* indicates that Peck proceeded from convention to convention in his effort to attract support for the western enterprises. The American Bible Society was the crucial organization. "Since essentially the same people formed the nucleus of each successive 'national' Evangelical enterprise, the best time to

organize a new venture was when the Bible people got together.''[85] The formidable power of the eastern forces was
due in part to the fact that in the nineteenth century the
religious establishment consisted much more than today of
people who also were active in the highest political and
economic affairs of the nation.

But ignorance, in the form of inadequate information and
poverty of experience, was not monopolized by the farmer-
preachers. There is no evidence that any but a minority of
the most influential religious leaders of the East had ever
been west of Pittsburgh or St. Louis. Peck fought a battle
against ignorance on two impressive fronts, not one, as the
histories tend to emphasize. There was an influential anti-
mission faction in the East as well as the West, although
their argument was based on different premises. On theological grounds the eastern leaders favored the ''settled
pastors'' rather than the missionaries. Only a minister was
believed to be the legitimate instrument of God for a congregation; therefore, missions should be established only in
those places that are unchurched. It was partly on this basis
that foreign missions were favored over domestic enterprises. The Triennial Baptist Missionary Convention withdrew support from Peck and other home missionaries in 1820
on the grounds, which Peck called ''erroneous,'' that ministers were moving to the West in sufficient numbers to obviate the need for missionaries. The eastern people did not
share Peck's knowledge of the character and training of the
itinerate preachers. He was one of the few men of his time
who knew the East as well as the West and could deal intelligently and effectively with both parties.

Peck's Political Activity and Writings—
The Anti-Slavery Movement

Peck's awareness of the mutual relationship of social and religious forces has been mentioned several times. He was, for
example, sensitive to the ''social sources of denomination-

alism,'' and mentioned in his journals that he served both the Negro and white churches in St. Louis which had divided as early as 1825. Niebuhr considered it significant that the Methodist and Baptist denominations had split on the slavery issue fifteen years prior to the political division. Peck's sociological sensitivity, his social concern, and his awareness of the inevitable interdependence of religious and secular forces were the sources of an unusual interest in theoretical politics and an eagerness to be active in political affairs. In the *Memoir* he notes that the northern and southern religious leaders placed sectional loyalty before their commitment to the churches, to the detriment of both. ''The majority of southern men of intelligence,'' he wrote, ''did not in heart approve of it; but for the sake of union among themselves, as they said, consented to what was neither wise nor right. They and others are now reaping the bitter fruits of such concessions.''[86]

During the slavery controversy Peck, the indefatigable moderate, was criticized by people on both sides of the issue. His attitude toward slavery would not permit him to accept the southern view; his political and social realism precluded sympathy for the abolitionists. He spoke favorably of the Friends of Humanity, an antislavery group which was attempting in his view to deal with the issue in politically responsible terms. This group

differed widely from modern abolitionists of the Northern States and New England, at least in the following particulars.
1. They never adopted the dogma that slaveholding is a "sin *per se*,"—a sin in itself, irrespective of all circumstances. . . . Hence they could consistently buy slaves and prepare them for freedom; or contribute funds to enable slaves to purchase themselves. . . .
2. They never aided fugitive slaves to escape . . . in violation of the law of the land.
3. They never interfered in any objectional way with the legal and political rights of slaveholders. . . .
4. They aimed to do good both to master and servant in a quiet, lawful and peaceable mode.

5. They endeavored to consult the true interests of all parties concerned.

6. They upheld the constitution and laws of the country in a peaceable way.[87]

Peck was more in accord with the current methods of the Civil Rights leaders than this conservative statement would indicate. He demonstrated willingness to oppose powerful political and legal forces when he deemed it justified and necessary. This occurred in St. Louis when he educated Negroes in his school.

To prevent any difficulty slaves were required to bring certificates from their masters, though we did not wish to confine ourselves to this rule in every instance. By this prudent measure, the approbation of many cititzens of the first respectability was secured.

But not everyone was satisfied. He and James Welch received the following letter from a local resident who simply signed the letter, "Justice."

Gentleman: As you have but lately arrived in this country and perhaps may not be acquainted with our laws, I would beg leave to refer you to the 7th section of an act for the regulation of slaves, and leave it to yourselves to decide, whether or not you have incurred heavy penalties by your negro school.

It might also be made a question by the patriot and philanthropist, whether it is prudent and humane to give instruction to those who must be made by it either more miserable or rebellious. I warn you that the sanctity of the clerical character will not here screen the offenders against the law from punishment.[88]

The *Memoir* gives some indications of Peck's attitudes toward slavery, but his other writings offer a fuller view of his opinions. They bear remarkable similarity to recent "revelations" by the so-called Negro radicals who are now informing the white community that it is a myth that the slaves were a happy people whose contentment would be disturbed by efforts to improve them.

The barbarous and unwise regulations in some of the planting states, which prohibit the slaves from being taught to read, are a serious impediment to the moral and religious instruction of that numerous and unfortunate class. Such laws display on the part of the law makers, little knowledge of human nature and the real tendency of things. To keep slaves entirely ignorant of the rights of man, in this spirit-stirring age, is utterly impossible. Seek out the remotest and darkest corner of Louisiana, and plant every guard that is possible around the negro quarters, and the light of truth will penetrate. Slaves will find out, for they already know it, that they possess rights as men. . . .

Slavery, under any circumstances, is a bitter draught—equally bitter to him who tenders the cup, and to him who drinks it. . . .

This state of society seems unavoidable at present, though I have no idea or expectation that it will be perpetual. Opposite sentiments and feelings are spreading over the whole earth, and a person must have been a very inattentive observer of the tendencies and effects of the diffusion of liberal principles not to perceive that hereditary, domestic servitude must have an end.

Nonetheless, he favored ''state's rights'' in these matters.

This is a subject, however, that from our civil compact, belongs exclusively to the citizens of the states concerned; and if not un-reasonably annoyed, the farming slaveholding states, as Kentucky, Tennessee, and Missouri, will soon provide for its eventual termi-nation. Doubtless, in the cotton and sugar growing states it will retain its hold with more tenacity, but the influence of free prin-ciples will roll onward until the evil is annihilated.[89]

Following the War of 1812 the territories of Indiana and Illinois served as a refuge for slaveholders who wished to emancipate their people. Edward Coles, a native of Virginia, and one-time private secretary for President Madison, ''had been educated at William and Mary College, under the tui-tion of Bishop Madison, where he received the conviction of the wrong and impolicy of Negro slavery. . . . He effected the sale of his plantation, and removed his slaves to Illinois. . . . He was elected governor of the State in 1822, and, as it turned out, at a most important crisis.''[90]

Missouri had just been voted into the Union as a slave state. The wealth of the South was by-passing Illinois and as it moved westward a powerful pro-slavery faction arose in the state. A vigorous effort was put forth to force the legis-lature to vote favorably for a constitutional convention.

Clarence Alford wrote that "it may be said to the eternal honor of the clergy of Illinois of that day, that they were almost without exception, opposed to the Convention, and that they exercised great influence in securing the rejection of the Convention Resolution at the polls. The prevailing denominations in the State at that time were the Methodists and Baptists, and most of the preachers were from slave states."[91] And Pease said, "Illinois tradition affirms that John Mason Peck labored assiduously against a convention though no contemporary evidence of his activity appears."[92]

Babcock did not include the entries from the Journal of this period although his lengthy remarks on the subject in the *Memoir* indicate that he understood the importance and controversial nature of the event. It is apparent that Peck was accused by the pro-slavery faction of being instrumental in their defeat. But Babcock stuck firmly to his personal conviction that true piety negates the propriety of legitimate political activity no matter how virtuous the end.[93] He interprets Peck's entries to minimize Peck's role in this affair. Peck is said to have acted "in a quiet, unobtrusive manner" to bring about the favorable result, but "however deeply he may have felt as a citizen, there is no evidence that he made himself a partisan. Against ministers of the gospel doing this he always raised his voice and wielded his pen." Unfortunately, this sentence is ambiguous, for he does not tell us whether "always" includes this critical instance. That Peck played a role—perhaps significant—is clear even from Babcock's remarks. In the *Annals of the West* which he edited twenty-two years later, Peck characteristically includes no reference to himself, nor in fact, to the clergy in general.

Elections were biennial, and the question could not be decided until the first Monday in August, 1824; the contest was spirited. The people who were opposed to the introduction of slavery, became aroused; public meetings were held; and the societies organized for "the prevention of slavery in Illinois." The first move was made in the county of St. Clair, where the convention party was strong, and led by some of the strongest political men in the state.

A county society was organized, officers appointed, an address to the people of Illinois was published, and an invitation made to form societies were organized [sic] in as many counties, and a correspondence established in them through persons who could be trusted, in every county and election precinct. This system was in full operation before August, and a year remained to gather strength.

The opposite party relied on quiet and concealed operations. Many denied, and doubtless honestly, that the introduction of slavery was the object; and believed that there were objectionable features in the constitution, that should be removed. . . .

The members of the preceding legislature, who had protested against the convention question, contributed each fifty dollars from their wages, to meet expenses in printing and circulating papers. The governor was in the opposition, and at once resolved to expand his four years' salary in the contest, and nobly did he redeem the pledge. . . .

Governor Coles had purchased an interest in the press; David Blackwell, of Belleville, had been appointed Secretary of State, to fill a vacancy, and conducted the paper as editor. From that time until August, the contest was carried on vigorously by both parties and finally decided against a convention, by about eighteen hundred majority. The number of votes given in the State, was nearly twelve thousand. . . .

In six months, after the question was settled; a politician who was in favor of the introduction of slavery in the State, was a *rara avis*.[94]

A careful program of research would be valuable and necessary to determine Peck's precise conduct in this affair. But two points are clear: Peck was not as reticent in the declaration of his own views as Babcock would have us believe, and he criticized the secret and indirect machinations of the pro-slavery faction; secondly, he did not share Babcock's purified view of the role of the clergy in political affairs. Alford's account of the episode indicates that Coles was at the head of the anti-Convention forces,

but the man who accomplished most against the Convention by personal exertion and by untiring work was the Rev. John M. Peck, of St. Clair county. . . . He was a man of excellent education, of a strong and comprehensive mind and with an energy and perseverance rarely surpassed. The attempt to make the state of his adoption a slave state awakened in him the most intense feeling of opposition. Endowed with a strong constitution and great physical strength, he entered into a personal canvass against the Convention scheme and labored assiduously, in season and out of season, during the long campaign. . . . Establishing his headquarters in St. Clair county, he extended his organization to fourteen other counties. . . . It was with the religious element of the community and with the clergy that he most labored. Uniting the establishment of Sunday schools and temperance societies with the distribution of the Bible, he preached a crusade against slavery wherever he went.[95]

Peck wrote two speeches which are indicative of his sophistication in democratic political theory and the theological foundation of his views. First, his comment on the purpose and function of government.

Government is necessary to defend communities from intestine discord, injustice, and violence. Its necessity springs from the ignorance, depravity and selfishness of human nature. It is equally indispensable to protection from the injustice of violence of other nations, and from those individuals, who have thrown off the restraints of national government, and, as pirates and robbers, depredate upon the property of individuals and community.[96]

He indicated that one of the primary prerequisites of public officials, especially in a democratic government, was wisdom in every branch of human history that may have a bearing upon diplomatic activity.

Public men should possess considerable knowledge of the history of men, nations, and governments—knowledge of the whole circle of human affairs—particularly of the condition, resources, policy, and designs of the neighboring nations, that they may know how to direct the affairs of their own with advantage—and more particularly of the constitution, principles, history, laws, and peculiarities of their own government.

The peculiar organization of our national government, with the co-ordinate and subordinate relations of each state, the different circumstances in which some are placed in relation to others, and to the confederate republic, make it indispensable for a well qualified statesman to bring to this subject a mind habituated to severe and patient investigation, and well-stored with previous reading.[97]

He concluded this passage by indicating that men in high office should possess a knowledge not only of the law, but of human nature, and of the operation and nature of group interests and of individual passions.

In a discourse called "The Principles and Tendencies of Democracy" Peck wrote many things that will be considered routine by the modern scholar, but it is of value in an introduction to this man's thought and presents an illustration of the nineteenth-century political faith of America, of the faith in America itself, the land engaged in a unique political experiment which assumed the status of a religious crusade. The principles of the Declaration of Independence, Peck writes,

are as old as time, but here is the first instance when they have been proclaimed as a nation's faith; presented as the chief corner stone of a nation's existence.

Heretofore governments had been established by conquest and arbitrary power which the few obtained over the many. But this declaration was the first solemn proclamation ever sent forth by a nation of the only *legitimate* foundation of civil government. It was the corner stone of a new political temple. . . . It declared to the world in a practical form the transcendent truth of the unalienable sovereignty of *the people,* of the capability and right of man to govern himself. It proved that the social compact was no fiction of the imagination, but a sacred bond of union. . . .

In its general sense the term Democracy denotes the sovereignty of the people as the source of all political power and civil government. . . .

I have intimated that the great principles of democrac, were first proclaimed as a nation's political faith in the Declaration of Independence, yet they were not new discoveries. The very elements of democracy were matters of divine revelation to man. They are spread over the pages of the Bible. The government and discipline of a Christian Church as to ministerial and executive power, as exhibited in the New Testament, is purely democratical.

[This is obviously the Baptist (congregational) interpretation of the Bible, not the view of the "pure church" traditions represented by the Roman Catholic, Episcopalians, Methodists and others. A third interpretation is offered by the Presbyterians who have traditionally claimed that the Scripture prescribed republican ecclesiastical and political forms rather than hierarchical or democratic structures, and that they were the progenitors of the actual American republican system. In recent decades greater modesty and more careful biblical criticism have prevailed, and it is recognized that antecedents for all of these polities exist in the New Testament.]

The elementary principles of democracy will now be stated with great brevity.

1. *Self-government.* He who has not the control of himself, his passions, appetites and propensities, will make but a poor democrat. . . .

2. *Due regard to the rights and interests of others.* "Thou shalt love thy neighbor as thyself." . . . Where this principle [and the golden rule] does not prevail, selfishness will invade the rights, abridge the liberties, and destroy the happiness of other men.

3. A third element of democracy is manifested *in seeking the greatest good of the community to the least injury of individuals.* . . .

4. A fourth principle . . . is *that a majority should govern.* . . .
The sovereignty exists somewhere, and if not in the majority, then it must rest with the minority. But this would utterly subvert the democratic principle. . . . Abuses and evils can be corrected on democratic principles, only by the "sober, second thought of the people," expressed through the ballot box. . . .

5. I regard *mutual co-operation* as a fifth element of democracy.
. . . In a democracy there are no privileged classes. All are mutually dependent, and all mutually confer and receive benefits.

6. As a sixth elementary principle . . . all the members of the social compact, *who contribute to the expense, or the defence of the body politic, have the inalienable right to govern, and to say what laws shall be made.* . . . Every male citizen . . . who pays taxes, or performs militia duty, has the right of suffrage. The right of suffrage, then, is a democratic principle, and is not derived from constitutional regulations, or any conventional understanding of society. It lies behind all these, and constitutes an elementary principle in a democratical government.

7. I have but one more elementary principle. . . . It consists in submission to constitutional and legal authority. . . .

A revolution in a democratical government is political suicide.

Constitutions, laws, and forms may be changed . . . through the silent operation of the ballot box, but these principles remain unchanged.

Democrats, as men, may become apostates, but they can never revolutionize, and remain democrats. . . . They ought to perceive there are but two ways a democracy can be destroyed.

1. It may be destroyed by the conquest of a more powerful nation. This is the application of force. Such a method . . . is hardly probable. The world has never yet had a sample of such a triumph of despotism, where the people were truly democratic.

2. Its danger of destruction consists in apostacy from democratic principles. . . . A democratic nation may prove its own destroyer. . . . The people may turn traitors. They may rebel against the law, revolutionize, break up the government . . . but they must first surrender the principles of democracy. Hence all mobs and riots proceed not from the democratic principles, but are essentially despotic in their character, and subversive of true democracy.

If laws are unequal and oppressive in a democratic government, they must be amended or abolished in a constitutional way. Every other mode of redress does violence to the fundamental principles of democracy.[98]

The remainder of the address is devoted to "obvious tendencies" and "practical results" of democracy. The first tendency is for democratic people to form voluntary, non-political societies "for the promotion of religion, morals, literature, science, and the various branches of industry." But in the spirit of the Early Fathers, Peck is opposed to secret societies "for the purpose of managing and controlling political action." He quotes extensively from Washington's Farewell Address to the effect that all "combinations and associations" which attempt to "control or awe" the proceedings of government are destructive of democracy.

The second tendency is for true democrats to seek for universal education of its citizens, and the third is to maintain freedom of "intercommunication" between the government and the people. Fourth, the "diffusion of moral and religious principles are indispensable to the maintenance of a pure democracy, as vice and irreligion will inevitably subvert and destroy its radical principles." In describing the fifth tendency he does not view democracy in realistic or Calvinistic terms as a necessary instrument for the balance of powers because of man's inclination to injustice, rather he draws an analogy between ideal Christianity and ideal democracy. "True democracy is public spirited, kind, benevolent, humane, liberal, tolerant, seeks to do good to others, and wishes well to the whole species." Democracy did not succeed in "France, Spanish America, and Greece," because the people must first be "made democrats themselves." "Christianity—pure, enlightened Christianity is the precursor of democracy. These principles are spreading—fast spreading over the earth, and as they expand governments will be modified and changed until man everywhere shall be qualified for self-government, and despotism in every form be driven from the earth."[99]

Peck was given to prophecy and was generally good at it, but this prediction indicates his ultimate inability to avoid completely in sharing the innocence of his times. The peculiar tension which Troeltsch observed in the New Testament, and which he saw manifest in the "churches" and "sects," abided deeply within the mind of John Mason Peck. He embodied the opposing inclinations of idealistic hopefulness and critical rationalism which provided the principal currents of Baptist life in nineteenth-century America, and which, in a broader sense was reflected in the life and thought of all the Protestant churches.

John Mason Peck was the representative embodiment of the ideological conflict that divided the Baptists. The tension in that denomination reproduced the struggle of the nation in its search for a heroic reconciliation of two views of the nature of man and society. It needs to be emphasized that these views as they have been delineated by the scholars are at the very most, "ideal types," analytical constructs which have been abstracted from the social and intellectual milieu for the sake of clarity and explanation. They were never fully accepted or perfectly expressed by any class, group, or individual, despite the fact that historical and social analysts have often imparted the contrary impression. "All the lines of thinking of the eighteenth century," Sidney Mead writes, "converged on the idea of free, uncoerced, individual consent as the only proper basis for all man's organizations, civil and ecclesiastical."[100] These ideas were supported by the pietists who had a naive faith in man's moral inclinations, and by the rationalists who inordinately magnified man's intellectual capacities and disinterested desire for justice. Mead says, "it is important to emphasize in passing that for neither the rationalists nor the pietists was acceptance of the principle of free, uncoerced, individual consent an acceptance of guidance through individual whimsey. . . . For both the rationalists and pietists, the individual became free only as he consented to necessary authority, discipline, and responsibility."[101]

But this is precisely the disjunction which constituted the elements of ideological conflict which were expressed in every significant sphere of intellectual and practical life in America. Mead does not generally emphasize this merely in passing for he knows it was a fundamental root of the American controversy. The thought of men such as Peck cannot be grasped if they are simply placed on one side or the other of the issue. It was the pro and con of this momentous debate that Peck internalized and for which he sought a solution.

Expressed in ideal typical terms, the Protestant heritage, notably of the early Reformation, taught that man is sinful, corrupt, and incapable of consistently seeking justice or achieving his ideals. Ecclesiastical and secular government were more than helpful instruments for the administration of human affairs. They operated also as essential dykes against sin which should protect the civil or religious society from exploitation by self-righteous and powerful minorities. Both internal and external means must be maintained, however, to check the pretentious ambitions of the governing leaders. But there was another strand in the Protestant tradition which provided a view of man and community for the more hopeful and optimistic majority on the frontier. Man, while not spontaneously good, was capable of redemption. Collective man, represented by religious and civil governments, however, was neither good nor capable of being redeemed. Therefore, society could only be reformed by the quantitative multiplication of transformed individuals. The government must not interfere in any way with this process, nor should it assist in the process since it is incorrigibly corrupt; in fact, its pretended efforts to seek justice must be rebuffed by the power and voice of the people whose hearts are potentially pure and in whom God-given sovereignty truly resides. The autonomy of the local church or local community must be protected since they were the only legitimate instruments through which both God and the people express their will to the national powers. The role of the national organizations was defined in instrumental terms. They were merely a convenience, necessary agencies for the administration of policies which were determined by the people as they spoke and acted in their congregations and local governments.

Peck drew from both of these traditions and yet he was wedded to neither. He shared the hope that by God's grace man would be redeemed and would effect the transformation of political society, but he never could have agreed with the revivalist, Charles Finney, who said that to be religious is to do one's duty and one would not be required to be dutiful if he did not possess the inherent capacity to do it.[102] Man's inclination to sin, in Peck's view, more often than not overwhelmed his ability to love and his desire for justice. It is true, as we noted above, that he predicted that democracy will ride on the wings of Christianity and that it shall peacefully overcome the world. This was said in a public address and may have had a homiletical intent. His sermons indicate that he was very much impressed with the progress of the nineteenth century and that he shared the optimistic view that the foreign mission enterprise was rapidly "christianizing and democratizing the heathen throughout the world."

But beside this hope must be placed his realistic estimate of the moral and rational capacities of man. He fully recognized that the autonomy of the congregation and the local government could become an absolute dogma and foster the illusion that whatever the people willed reflected the will of God. He recognized both the danger and the necessity of effective national administration in both ecclesiastical and secular affairs. These things can be seen in another prophecy he made, in which, as early as 1839, he appears to have had a premonition of the Civil War and the need for a man like Lincoln.[103]

In all government there are broad, fundamental principles, which must be regarded and maintained, whatever may be the risk. On these principles the course of a statesman should never vacillate. The right of the people to instruct their representatives is unquestionable, for they in the aggragate, and not the privileged few, possess the governing power. But there may be occasional emergencies when a public man has to take the responsibility, and risk his popularity for the benefit of his country. . . .

It is only when constitutional principles are at stake, the national compact to be preserved, or great and paramount interests are in jeopardy, that the firmness and integrity of the patriot should be brought in collision with the will of his constituents. Yet he should never be obstinate or selfwilled, but proceed with due deliberation, and make up his mind to fall a sacrifice to popular resentment, rather than betray his country, or violate his conscience. There is a moral sublimity in the conduct of a man who will risk this much for the public good.[104]

The reader of the *Memoir* will detect that despite his Baptist heritage, and yet because of it—because of the incipient anarchy within the system—Peck was able to perceive that men in community, especially in times of crisis, can only be stimulated to creative and cooperative endeavor by a purpose and by a leadership that transcends their personal and parochial interests.

Paul M. Harrison

yours fraternally,

J. M. Peck

FORTY YEARS OF PIONEER LIFE.

MEMOIR

JOHN MASON PECK D.D

EDITED FROM HIS JOURNALS AND CORRESPONDENCE.

BY

RUFUS BABCOCK.

PHILADELPHIA:

AMERICAN BAPTIST PUBLICATION SOCIETY,

530 ARCH STREET.

PHILADELPHIA:
STEREOTYPED AND PRINTED BY
S. A. GEORGE.

TO THE CHURCHES

WHICH WERE GATHERED AND EDIFIED BY HIS MINISTRY;

TO THE SUNDAY-SCHOOLS WHICH HE PLANTED;

THE SEMINARIES WHICH HE FOUNDED OR FOSTERED,

AND TO

ALL THOSE BENEFITED BY THE EVANGELIZING, HUMANE, AND ENLIGHTENING

INSTRUMENTALITIES WHICH HE ASSIDUOUSLY PROMOTED,

THIS MEMOIR OF ONE CALLING HIMSELF

"AN OLD PIONEER,"

IS RESPECTFULLY INSCRIBED BY

THEIR FELLOW-LABORER AND FRIEND,

THE EDITOR.

We are likely in our efforts, in and for the present, to forget what is due to pioneers—to those who went forward in the cause of missions, amidst the scorn of the worldly and the doubt of the pious, relying with a sublime faith on the promise made to prophets and apostles.

PRESIDENT M. B. ANDERSON.

———

Some men are born to greatness, or have it thrust on them others worthily achieve it.

———

So have I strived to preach the gospel, not where Christ was named, lest I should build upon another man's foundation.

PAUL.

PREFACE

No compiler of a biography could desire to be favored with more abundant and reliable materials. They consist of a very extensive correspondence from the year 1808 to that of Dr. Peck's death, covering full fifty years of his eventful life. Then in addition to these well-arranged letters, which a thousand hands have contributed, with the substance of his more important replies, there are his journals for almost this entire period, filling fifty-three volumes, some few of them small and portable for his convenience in traveling, but most of them large, either folios or quartos of some hundreds of pages each, full of all facts and incidents which his inquisitive and almost ubiquitous spirit of research brought under his observation. The superabundance of these materials has indeed proved the principal embarrassment in this compilation. They are ample, and by Dr. Peck himself were designed for a more full and extended memoir of his life and times than it seemed advisable to the publishers now to send forth.

The embarrassment and perplexity of deciding what to reject entirely, and what to condense, and to what extent, has been the chief difficulty, and is the very point where most fault is likely to be found with this volume. Many readers of it will no doubt fail to find some of the things they had looked for with fondest expectation, and which, in their partial judgment, would have been more interesting than other things which are here preserved. Let all such charitably remember how many there are of different tastes, judgments, and personal predilections, and at least pardon, if they do not fully approve, the earnest endeavor here made wisely to compromise conflicting claims.

I have been mainly desirous to give with impartial fidelity the forty years of pioneer life—its preparation, its experiences, and its results—which was the grand specialty of Dr. Peck. It embraces the years of *preparation*, begun in privation, vexed with incessant struggles by a very narrow, imperfect education, which he was constantly striving to enlarge and improve; by indigent circumstances and various connections and concomitants not of an encouraging character. But through all this environment of hindrances, a brave heart and steady persistence enabled him to press his way successfully to the point where he was commissioned by the Board of the Triennial Baptist Convention a missionary to the great West, regarded by such men as Baldwin and Furman, Sharp and Mercer, John Williams, H. G. Jones and Staughton, as *one well fitted for this service.*

Then follow through the two-score years of widely-varying *expe riences* in this kind of life; his generally successful efforts in the different but nearly related fields of evangelical enterprise—preaching the gospel, establishing churches, Sunday-schools, Bible and tract societies, educational institutions to train preachers and teachers of common-schools, as well as calling into requisition and sustaining the religious periodical press for its manifold uses; and while all this network of evangelizing processes was vigorously pressed into requisition, he labored to surround, and supplement. and sustain it by all desirable civilizing and humane instrumentalities; encouraging a better class of settlers to follow his "Guide for Emigrants" and make permanent homes and thriving communities in the fertile Western valley, or, as he finally insisted it should be called, the Great Central Valley of North America, to make them temperate, Sabbath-keeping, and free. His indefatigable labors in this incidental sphere have been productive of vast and indeed the very best success. The venerable Dr. Lyman Beecher used to say, with emphasis, a quarter of a century ago, that J. M. Peck of Illinois had led more valuable settlers into the Northwest than any other ten men. Looking at what the mighty West now is, and ever must be, in its relations to the other portions of our country, this service can be scarcely over-estimated.

His personal privations and endurances in all these years do not stand forth in any marked degree of prominence. At the time of their severest experience he measurably overlooked them, so completely were his thoughts and heart absorbed in contemplation of the great benefits which were to result from them; and when they were passed he would make no effort to recall them, his motto ever being to forget the things behind and press forward for new and higher, worthier attainments. Yet the reader of these pages will catch many a glimpse of hardship and of actual peril and suffering —physical, intellectual, and spiritual—just enough, it is hoped, to win the full tide of generous sympathy, without such overshadowing excess as would tinge the review with discouragement and gloom. The hopeful ever largely predominated in the subject of this memoir, and if it shall awaken in those perusing it, either at the East or West, a spirit of cheerful self-sacrifice for the public good, akin to that which it records, it will not be read in vain. Self-denial in other and bloodier fields is now winning its meed of fair renown to an extent formerly unprecedented. Let it be known also that peace has its demands for large sacrifices and generous offerings as well as war; that their product on this field is to say the least equally beneficial with the other.

The *results* of this pioneer-life are but beginning to be seen. Yet how cheering to one who had adventured his all in this cause were the beginnings which his closing years witnessed. Little less than two thousand Baptist churches were in flourishing existence in his field ere he left it, where there were not a score on his entrance. More than twice that number of Sunday-schools, of which he and his yoke-fellow, Welch, planted the first; with colleges, universities, and professional seminaries of promising character and sufficiently numerous which were planted and flourishing in his day and greatly by his aid. And had he lived a little longer, he might have rejoiced that his own Illinois, which he had watched over from infancy, and aided in every stage of its transition and advancement, had given a wise and faithful President to the Republic, and a commander-in-chief of unsurpassed valor and skill to lead her armies, with one hundred and thirty thousand valiant soldiers, to crush out the most atrocious rebellion the world has ever seen. Yea, more, and better still, he would have hailed with devoutest gratitude the emancipation of all the enslaved of African race in Missouri, foretokening the same result speedily in all the States.

It only remains to explain the delay in the publication of this condensed memoir. Four years since it was written and submitted for examination to the Board of that Publication Society which Dr. Peck had so faithfully served as its chief executive officer for some of the most active years of his laborious and useful life. Their committee of examination, after the thorough perusal of the manuscript, were pleased to express high satisfaction with its preparation, declaring it in their judgment worthy of a wide circulation and adapted to important usefulness. But at just that period the great Northwest, where its circulation was expected to be greatest was in such financial embarrassment from repeated failure in her crops that all experienced publishers dissuaded from immediate publication. Then came this fearful war, engrossing all thoughts and efforts.

Now, however, that the mighty giant of the West has thrown off its incubus, and we have become so accustomed to the war as not to disregard entirely other claims, and specially while that foreign mission, of which the subject of this memoir was one of the earliest appointed heralds to the region beyond the Mississippi, is now stirring our hearts with notes of preparation for the first jubilee, it seems an auspicious hour to send forth this volume. While it cheers the humble beginner in his efforts for self-improvement, and gives to the scattered immigrants into the wilderness the assurance that they are not forgotten, and to all of us increasing sympathy with pioneer-missionaries who go in jeopardy of their lives to obey the great commission, may it promote the Redeemer's glory and the extension and triumph of His peaceful reign!

R. B.

Poughkeepsie, N.Y., 31st *March*, 1864.

CONTENTS.

9

CHAPTER XVIII.
1826.

CHAPTER XIX.
1827.

CHAPTER XX.
1828—1831.

CHAPTER XXI.
1832—1834.

CHAPTER XXII.
1835, 1836.

CHAPTER XXIII.
1836, 1837.

CHAPTER XXIV.
1838—1840.

CHAPTER XXV.
1840, 1841.

MEMOIR

OF

JOHN M. PECK.

—◄●►—

CHAPTER I.

Birth—Genealogy—Education—Conversion—Marriage.

How differently the same object affects us as we know or
are ignorant of its relations. If in your casual wanderings
you pass some copious fountain, and step across the little
rivulet issuing from it, with only the vague conviction that it
must find its way to the ocean, the impression is slight. But
if after a thorough acquaintance with the Nile, or the Mississippi, for instance—after tracing for thousands of miles their
magnificent course, witnessing the fertility they spread around
them, or the wealth which commerce wafts on their bosoms—
you then follow them to their sources, and stand by the bub-
bling fountain from which each takes its rise, what a train of
musing such a spectacle suggests. With somewhat similar
feelings those of us who have known for scores of years the
beneficent and wide-reaching results of the life-labors of JOHN
MASON PECK go back to the origin of his career.

The quiet home of Asa and Hannah Peck at their lowly
dwelling in the parish of Litchfield South Farms, Connecticut,
witnessed his birth on the 31st of October, 1789; and there
for eighteen years he was reared in the simplicity, frugality,
and industry becoming a child of the Puritans. The genealogical track of his family leads directly to Deacon Paul
Peck, who in 1634 emigrated from Essex county, England,

and soon after, with the pious Hooker, came to Hartford **and** founded the infant colony of Connecticut.*

Nothing of peculiar interest occurred to mark the character of Peck's childhood, or early youth. His father was in very

---

* The following genealogical account of the ancestry of Dr. Peck has been carefully prepared from numerous valuable papers furnished by the Hon. Tracy Peck, of Bristol, Ct., a kinsman of the Doctor.

PAUL PECK and Martha his wife came to America in 1634. He was one of the proprietors of the town of Hartford, and died there, December 23, 1695, aged eighty-seven years. He had five sons and four daughters. The fifth son, *Samuel*, was born in 1647, and died 1696, at West Hartford, leaving one child also named *Samuel*, born 1672, and died December 9, 1765, aged ninety-three years. In the year 1700 Samuel, the younger, married Abigail Collyer, and they had a large family. Their son *Elisha*, the grandfather of Dr. Peck, was born in 1720, and married his cousin Lydia Peck. He died May 29, 1762, leaving six children. The oldest, named *Asa*—the father of Dr. Peck—was born March 8, 1744, in Berlin, Ct.; but in 1783 he and his mother moved to the parish of South Farms in Litchfield, where, in 1786, he was married to Hannah Farnum, who was born there July 25, 1755. They had but one child, *John Mason Peck*, who was born at South Farms, October 31, 1789. He was married, May 8, 1809, to Sarah Paine, who was born in Greene county, N.Y., January 31, 1789. They had the following issue, viz.:

1. *Eli Prince*, born in Litchfield, July 28, 1810, and died in St. Louis county, Mo., October 5, 1820.
2. *Hannah Farnum*, born July 10, 1812, and married Ashford Smith, of Rockville, Iowa.
3. *Hervey Jenks*, born September 28, 1814, and died December 17, 1855, leaving a widow and six children.
4. *William Carey*, born February 11, 1818; died September 14, 1821.
5. *Mary Ann*, born September 18, 1820, and married Samuel G. Smith, and resided in Galena, Ill.
6. *William Staughton*, born November 13, 1823, and resided at Spruce Mills, Iowa.
7. *John Quincy Adams*, born August 27, 1825, and resides at Rock Spring, Ill.
8. *An infant*, born December 10, 1827, and died *sine nomine*.
9. *Henry Martin*, born May 7, 1829, and resides at Rock Spring.
10. *James Ashford*, born September 27, 1831.

humble circumstances, and moreover was afflicted with lameness, which early threw a large share of the care and the toils of tilling the little farm upon this his only son. From the time he was fourteen years old his summers were faithfully devoted to farm work, while in the winter months he continued to enjoy the benefits of the common school—that pride of New England, and especially, in that period of her history, of the State of Connecticut. True, the range of studies was not more than half as extensive as at present. The aim was to teach boys and girls, gathered in the same little apartment, to spell and read well, to write a fair, legible hand, and acquire such familiarity with the fundamental rules of arithmetic as would enable them to keep their simple accounts correctly, to cast the interest which they paid or received, and generally to familiarize themselves with the established forms requisite for the transaction of ordinary business. Some geographical and historical books were used for reading-lessons, and thus a smattering of knowledge in these branches was secured. A geography with an atlas of maps, or a historical book adapted to the capacity of children, had not then been introduced to the common schools; and grammar was chiefly or wholly learned by imitating good usage without much knowledge of its rules. Good elocution was sometimes attempted to be taught by rehearsing *memoriter* fine select specimens of prose and poetic compositions; but lest this should too much attract attention and pave the way for stage exhibitions, which were deemed too theatrical, judicious cautions were frequently administered both to teachers and scholars by the official visitors —the parson being one.

The common school which young Peck attended must have been rather inferior to the usual average of that period; or he was, as he frankly admits, more stupid and sluggish than ordinary lads, even with his scanty advantages; for when he was eighteen years old, and himself began to teach, his orthography and chirography too were sadly deficient—and to correct grammatical usages he seems to have made no pretensions Yet his mind and judgment were considerably exercised; and the common remark in the neighborhood was that John, though uncultivated, was no simpleton. He regularly heard the gospel preached on the Sabbath, and enjoyed the advantages of personal intercourse with those more intelligent than himself; and especially after beginning to keep school during the winter months, and board around among the families of his employees, he seems to have made rapid advances in acquiring general information.

At just about this period also his religious nature seems to have been quickened to new activity. I find among his papers a sketch of his early religious exercises, hastily written by him, as early as 1811, from which a small portion may here be properly extracted :

The early period of my life was spent like the generality of youth in willful opposition against God, and in pursuing those vanities and follies which children and youth generally follow. About the age of ten or eleven years I had fearful apprehensions of the danger of eternal punishment, and used to attempt to pray to God to deliver me therefrom; but I knew nothing of the way of salvation through the righteousness of a Redeemer.

These impressions wore off, and I remained for the most part stupid and senseless until I arrived at the age of eighteen. The Lord was then pleased to stop me in my rebellion, and turn me unto himself. The summer previous I had been peculiarly thoughtless; but on the evening of the 15th of December, 1807 (a time never to be forgotten), I was induced, rather from motives of curiosity, to attend a meeting about three miles from home, where the work of God's converting grace was progressing in a most remarkable manner. Here I was brought to see myself a guilty sinner before God, deserving his wrath. These exercises continued and increased for about one week. I viewed myself as lost without the interposition of God's mercy. My distress increased, and my burden became heavier, until the end of the week, when I was delivered, and found a peace of mind and a joy in God which I had never felt before. Insensibly, my heart was drawn out to love and praise the Lord. I looked around on the works of creation with a satisfaction and sweet delight before unknown; for they seemed manifestly declaring the glory of God. I then feared nothing so much as relapsing into carelessness and stupidity.

My hope was not at first as clear and bright as it afterwards became when a fuller discovery was made of the way of salvation through the merits of Christ. Little by little this faint hope increased. The character of God, his law, his providences, and the plan of grace as far as I understood it, appeared glorious and excellent. The total depravity of the human heart was a doctrine I was early acquainted with. I felt a pleasure, therefore, in ascribing the whole work of salvation to the Lord, being sensible of my own weakness and my absolute dependence on Divine grace.

It would be an interesting and profitable study for the mental philosopher to consider fully the development which this one impulse gave to the whole mind of the young man. He who before had vegetated rather than lived, now rises by rapid evolutions to a worthier elevation; he breathes a purer air, he sees through a clearer medium. He shakes himself from the dust in which he was so willingly buried before, and pants for the privilege of doing and being something worthy of his new, his immortal nature. Aside from the mere deliverance from the thraldom and degradation of his moral nature, he is now mentally a new creature—old things have passed away: behold, all things have become new.

With this quickening impulse there soon comes the yearning solicitude, and then the importunate cry of the converted Saul of Tarsus, " Lord, what wilt thou have me to do ?" In after years he tells us—though probably he told no one then —that to him also the Lord seemed to say by his Spirit: " Thou art a chosen vessel unto me to bear my name to the Gentiles, and I will show thee how great things thou must suffer for my sake." It would have seemed next to impossible, then, that this rude, uncouth, poor, and almost friendless boy should become a minister—and an able minister—of the gospel; that for scores of years he should fill some of the most prominent and responsible positions among the ambassadors of Christ. No education-societies then sounded out their welcome words of encouragement to those who are willing, but unable, to give themselves to the work of needful preparation for this high and holy mission. The prevalent opinion

then inculcated among his religious associates was that a full
and thorough course of classical and scientific training was
the indispensable prerequisite for preaching the gospel.   He
saw himself the chief reliance of poor, infirm, and loving
parents; and he said to the promptings of the Spirit: "No,
no; this can never be.   I must abide in the useful calling of
husbandry, and serve God in a private station."   This he
honestly, and for a period as considerable as two or three
years, attempted.   But ever and anon—as he followed the
plough, or swung the scythe, as he delved with the hoe or the
mattock, or felled the forest, or tended his farm stock in the
barn, or drove his flocks afield—the sweet voice of the good
Shepherd would be sounding in his ears and reaching the
depths of his soul: "If thou lovest me, feed my sheep, feed
my lambs: go and publish the glad tidings to every creature."
This he especially remarked, that when God gave him most
religious enjoyment, when his heart was warmed with love to
his Saviour, and his own hopes of heaven were clearest, brightest, and the peace of God was keeping and filling his soul,
then he could not at all repress these exercises in regard to
preaching.   But when he was dull and stupid in his religious
feelings, then this voice calling him to public duty died away.

Partly perhaps with the hope of driving such an idea from
him effectually and forever, he formed the next year after
his hopeful conversion a matrimonial connection.   He married, however, in the fear of the Lord; and, as John Bunyan
said in his own case, his mercy was to light on one eminently
fitted to be to him, religiously as well as in temporal things, a
true helpmate.

In so important a matter no doubt he sought and found the
Divine guidance; and that his memoir may contain his views
of the case, it will be proper here to give his own sketch, prepared many years later, and embracing much in regard to the
domestic and social habits of that age and vicinity.   So rapid
have been the changes in society in these respects, that the
simple practices in our fathers' days are even now a refreshing
novelty.

At the period we allude to—the early part of the present century—every farmer's daughter, and every girl raised in a farmer's
family of the best credit, was trained by theory and practice in the
routine of household affairs. This was not peculiar to New England. In New York among the Dutch settlements in the older
parts of that State, as well as in the families from New England
that planted themselves in middle and western New York, in New
Jersey and Pennsylvania, in Kentucky and Tennessee—even in
the "Old Dominion" and further South where servants performed
the more onerous labor—the mistress of the family was the over-
seer in her department. The daughters were trained to follow the
footsteps of the mother. The dairy, the poultry, and the garden,
showed proofs enough of their industry and skill.

In the Northern and Middle States no girl raised on a farm was
deemed fit to marry, until her bedding, clothing, window curtains
towels, table-cloths, and every article of domestic manufacture,
were made with her own hands in quantities sufficient for respectable housekeeping. And no young man who had enterprise, industry, and forethought, would marry a peevish, whimsical, senti
mental, lazy slattern. Young men, then, who made visits to families for a specific purpose were ingenious in finding out the domestic habits and qualities of the mother before they committed themselves to the daughter.

We have drawn this portraiture that our readers may under
stand to what class the writer was guided by Providence in the
selection of the woman who, for nearly forty-eight years, proved
his true helpmate.

She is thus described by his own hand.

SALLY PAINE—as was her customary designation in childhood
—was born in the county of Greene, N. Y., January 31, 1789. Her
mother died before she was twelve years old. Sally (who assumed
the legitimate name SARAH on entering womanhood) kept house for
her father, and had the charge of three younger children for two
years. The mother she had lost was an excellent housewife, but
one would think her daughter was too young to learn domestic
economy. Yet her father and others in the neighborhood ever
spoke of her as an extraordinary girl for tidiness, economy, and
domestic cultivation. She had but a few weeks opportunity of
school education, yet she taught herself and her brothers, and set
them an example which would have done credit to any female of

mature age. After her father's second marriage she went to reside
with her mother's parents—plain, old-fashioned farming people in
Litchfield, Ct. Then she had opportunity of attending the common
district school some part of each season. Slight as were these advantages, she obtained from them, as was the common result of the
training of those days, a hardy, robust constitution, high health, a
vigorous mind, and a reasonable supply of common-sense.

In 1807, during an extensive revival of religion, in the first
parish of Litchfield, Sarah Paine professed to be savingly converted
to God, and next year joined the Congregational Church then under
the pastoral care of Rev. Danl. Huntington. It was at that period
we became personally acquainted, which resulted in *esteem* for each
other.

We knew nothing of the sickly, sentimental, mixed emotion
called *love*, so faithfully and foolishly portrayed in the novelettes
and periodicals of this age. We were joined in marriage on the
8th of May, 1809. About one month later, the young husband
with his chosen bride might have been seen on a farm-wagon with
a load of household furniture. The chairs, table, bureau, kitchen
utensils, and a few other articles, were the gift of her grandparents;
but every article of bedding, table-linen, and personal clothing for
home wear, with many other et ceteras, were made by her own
hands. And yet she was but twenty years and four months old,
and her husband was nine months younger. We moved into the
house where the writer was born, and lived with his father and
mother about two years.

Some of the correspondence between these parties before
their marriage, and much afterward, has passed under review
in the preparation of this chapter, and if it does not imply
mutual *love*—the purest and the best—it certainly looks very
much like it. Yet it is singularly free from what would be
rightly called foolish sentimentalism. A confiding esteem
based on the sterling excellencies discovered in each other,
controlled by Christian principle, expresses briefly and justly
what was the nature of their affection. How noble were its
achievements, and how faithfully and perseveringly it enabled
them to illustrate with beautiful and winning simplicity their
sacred union for nearly half a century, these pages will confirm.

CHAPTER II.

Removes to York State—Joins the Baptists—Begins Preaching.

WHEN their eldest child was a month or two old, the expectation was that the infant would be taken to the meeting and "dedicated to God by baptism," as the phrase was. The mother, for some reason, had no confidence in the Scriptural authority of infant baptism when she joined the church; and the father, who had previously examined the subject, until he honestly supposed he had proofs enough of it by inference, at that period was in such perplexity as to stay proceedings. The winter following, these parents had a number of interviews with Rev. Lyman Beecher—since the venerable Dr. Beecher—who by a series of fair and candid efforts was unsuccessful in convincing either of them of the Scriptural authority of this Pedobaptist rite.

Next, and at no remote period, they were found revolving the question of a removal to Mrs. Peck's native region. The reasons for this procedure were probably such as often in that day and since have induced the enterprising and hardy families of New England to seek ampler room and more encouraging prospects beyond her narrow boundaries. But the sundering of ties which bind them to their early homes always costs a pang. Theirs, too, was a Christian home. In that humble dwelling the morning and evening sacrifice had been offered to God, their early vows had there been recorded, and the day when they bade those hallowed scenes farewell could not but have been tinged with a tender sadness. But they were young and hopeful; and they felt that while the wide world was all before them where to choose, Providence would be their guide. This transition and its results are thus presented by the pen of Dr. Peck at a comparatively recent period :

REMINISCENCES OF "YORK STATE."

It was in the spring of 1811, I moved my family, consisting of a wife and one child, from South Farms, my native parish, in Connecticut, into the town of Windham, Greene county, N.Y. The place of my residence for the summer was then known as *Big Hollow*, a deep, narrow valley or gorge, near the head of one of the *Kills* or mountain streams that united with East-Kill, West-Kill, and other streams, to form Schoharie-Kill. It meandered through a settlement further down, long since known as Prattsville, the site of an extensive tannery.

With the exception of fifteen or twenty small clearings, on the mountain sides and along the hollow for several miles, the country was a dense wilderness, consisting of massive hemlocks, intermixed with sugar maple, beech, birch, fir, and ironwood. Occasionally there were clumps of pine. The Big Hollow settlement consisted of seven families, mine making the eighth, within the distance of three miles from the center. This was distinguished by a small log building which was occasionally occupied as a school-house, and on Sabbath by a religious meeting, conducted by Deacon Hitchcock, the patriarch of this little settlement. The venerable deacon originated from Connecticut, belonging to the race of Congregational Puritans, and of course was a rigid Pedobaptist, as were most of the members of his family, who made half the population of the valley.

The writer and his wife were then, nominally, of the same denomination; but a year's careful investigation had brought them, theoretically, on to Baptist ground. On invitation of the deacon, I joined in the meeting. Having acquired the faculty of reading with fluency and correctness, and being in possession of a number of printed sermons, new to the hearers, I aided the deacon in reading, and making the concluding prayer. Occasionally, if the sermon was short, I spoke a little *extempore*. This habit, and that of praying in social meetings, had been acquired in the "Young People's Conference," held during an extensive revival in Litchfield, Ct.

It was during the period of the earlier settlement of this village, before my first visit, when twelve or fifteen families, and as many professors of religion, made up the community, that Deacon Hitchcock made an abortive attempt to get a Presbyterian church organized. It so happened, that at least one-half the professors had their doubts about the Scriptural claims of Pedobaptism. But what made the matter the more unpleasant to the good old deacon was the fact that a daughter-in-law and her husband began to show symptoms of believing in Scriptural baptism. As this question must be settled, and doubts removed, before a Pedobaptist church could be formed, the deacon made application to the Rev. Mr. Townsend, then pastor of the Presbyterian church in New Durham, to make them a visit, and remove the doubts Baptist principles had engendered. A day was fixed, and some of the people sent word to Deacon Rundell, who belonged to a Baptist church called Cairo, on the east side of the mountains. The parties met, and Mr. Townsend, by a very familiar illustration, showed how the infant children of believers were brought into covenant relation with their parents, and became entitled to baptism. "It is done by grafting," said the shrewd divine. "You all know when the scion is inserted in the stock by grafting, there are little buds on it that are grafted in also. These buds represent the infants, who are received to baptism by virtue of the faith of the parents." This was all plain, and no mistake; for the minister had proved it by reference to the eleventh chapter of Romans. Some of the company called on Deacon Rundell for his views. Now it so happened, the deacon had a large nursery, raised and sold grafted fruit-trees to the farmers throughout the country, and was a quick-witted, shrewd man withal. "Deacon Rundell, you understand all about grafting, and know the Scriptures too," replied one of the doubters. "Why, yes," said the deacon; "I have supplied all the people with fruit-trees of my own grafting on t'other side of the mountains, and guess I shall furnish several hundred for Windham this fall. But in grafting I always noticed one thing that the minister has overlooked. The little buds, when grafted in with the scion, always produced *good fruit*. If the children of believing parents always produce the fruits of righteousness, I think they ought to be baptized, because they are in spiritual union, not with their parents, but with the Lord Jesus Christ, the Head of the Church." The response from the minister was: "Mr. Rundell, we did not meet here to controvert disputed points; religious controversy is very unprofitable. We will close the meeting." This story was told the writer by some parties interested. It prevented the formation of a Presbyterian church at that time.

Learning that the Baptist church of New Durham held meetings monthly in a school-house on the Batavia turnpike, some five miles north of our residence, and over the mountain by a winding path, the writer might have been seen, with wife and babe about thirteen months old, wending his way up the side of a steep mountain, on a beautiful Sabbath morning, the 10th day of August. We arrived at the place of worship before any of the members who lived near

made their appearance. As they dropped in, one after another,
they greeted the strangers with a hearty welcome, inquiring, of
course, if we were Baptists. The facts being stated, the welcomes
became more cordial than before, and conversation on religious subjects occupied the time till the pastor arrived, which, according to
usage, was rather late. This was Elder Hermon Harvey, who was
a descendant of a Baptist generation of that name. His father was
Deacon Obed Harvey. The family, I think, was originally from
Rhode Island, but at a later period from "Nine Partners," in Dutchess county. Elder Harvey was a person of middle size and stature,
between thirty and thirty-five years of age. He was a plain, com-
mon-place preacher, studious in the Scriptures, mild in temper, and,
like other Baptist preachers at that period, worked a farm, received
casual contributions from the brethren, and was quite as self-denying, and devoted to the work of the ministry, as the men of modern
times. I suppose he is still living, though he must be quite advanced in live. I met him for the last time at the Rensselaerville
Association, in 1842.

The brethren introduced us to the pastor before he had time to
take his seat by the rough table that served for the pulpit, behind
which he stood to preach the gospel to an attentive congregation.
By that time we were made acquainted with every Baptist and some
other persons within the house. In this mode of reception there
was nothing new or strange with the plain, country Baptist congregations at that period in New York State. There was much of fraternal feeling and social hospitality. Those who came from a distance were provided with refreshments by those who lived near.
Their attire was plain homespun garments, put on clean and tidy
for the Sabbath, and worn by laboring men and women through the
week. Generally, the people were in straitened circumstances. If
any vehicles brought the family to meetings, they were plain, rough,
farming wagons. Men, women, and children, often walked three or
four miles. In one thing they had the advantage of the present
generation. Neither custom, fashion, pride, nor luxury, compelled
them to pay heavy taxes for the benefit of their neighbors' eyes.
In this manner was I first introduced to the Baptists of YORK STATE.

On the 13th of September, 1811, accompanied by my wife and
child, we were again climbing the mountain range, to the same place
of meeting mentioned above. It was on Saturday; for once in three
months the regular covenant meetings of New Durham church were
held on the mountain. This time we carried a small bundle of light
clothing. A great question of practical duty in obedience to Jesus

Christ had been settled for many months, and the opportunity had arrived when it could be carried out practically. Let not our readers express surprise at two persons, in early life, with a lusty infant, and a bundle of clothing, walking five or six miles over a high mountain to a church meeting. The young men and women of that day were hardy, robust, and thought no more of a walk, than some of the present effeminate race do of lolling in the easy-chair, or on the lounge.

> They breathed the pure, reviving air,
> That's born upon the mountains high ;
> They saw health's roseate offspring there,
> And hope beamed bright from every eye.

The members of the church assembled, and the customary greetings and hearty expressions of Christian affection passed around. The pastor made his appearance, and after giving out a hymn from Watts, and repeating the lines, all the brethren sung it who had the least pretensions to the gift of modulating the voice in harmony, and a prayer was offered, in which every member present joined with sincere devotion. The pastor then introduced the old custom of " renewing covenant" by all the members, male and female, giving an expression of their feelings, and their trials, their hopes, aspirations, and joys, during the past month. All spoke with frankness and apparent sincerity. The " door was opened" to hear " experiences of grace" from others ; and the writer and his companion gave a narrative of their conviction of sin and their gracious deliverance that had occurred nearly four years previous. His union with the Congregational Church, and being the subject of a ceremony that was regarded at the time as a substitute for Christian baptism by that sect, were, of course, narrated. This ceremony consisted not in pouring, nor in sprinkling water on the subject, but in the minister dipping the tips of his fingers in a basin of water and gently touching the forehead.

Questions then were propounded by the pastor, and opportunity was given for each member of the church to question the candidate on points of doctrine and experience. Far more pains were taken in the examination of candidates for baptism and membership in all our churches, than in this "fast age." Churches moved slow; and it was no unusual occurrence for candidates, after the hearing of their relation, to be advised to wait for one or more months. Apostasies were rare; church discipline was strict—far more so than at present; and excommunications less, in proportion to baptisms, in all the churches.

3

At the close of the public exercises at the school-house, every person in the congregation walked half a mile to a clear, beautiful, mountain stream, of sufficient depth, hid away in a romantic dell, where the two candidates put on the Lord Jesus Christ, and made the oath of allegiance to the King of Zion, in the Scriptural form of administration.

After the customary intermission, in which the hospitable brethren and neighbors vied with each other in providing refreshments for all who came from a distance, the members of the church, with a few spectators, repaired again to the school-house, where, after a brief address from the pastor, the Supper of the Lord was celebrated.

The day was remarkably pleasant, and a large concourse of people assembled to witness the baptisms. The countenances of all wore a solemn aspect, and the utmost regularity and good order was observed by every individual present.

Commencement of the Ministry—Suggestions on the Christian Ministry.

On Saturday, the 12th of October, 1811, the Durham church held its covenant-meeting in the Union School-house, on the east side of the mountains. This was in the Harvey Settlement.

On our first acquaintance with the members of this church, even before receiving baptism, nearly every male member had had conversation with us on what appeared to the writer a momentous question. "Don't you think you ought to preach the gospel?" was seriously asked in every instance of private conversation. The pastor, in particular, was too inquisitive to permit an evasive answer. How these brethren, who were entire strangers, till within the last two months, came to entertain such surmisings, I could not guess.

It was a fact known only to the writer, that, from the first hour that he indulged a hope of pardoning mercy, this subject lay with weight on his mind, which at times was fearfully oppressive. Every excuse had been put to his conscience, and yet he found no relief. The only periods of rest were those of backslidings in heart, and accompanied with doubts of his title to the divine promises. And as the period of his baptism drew nigh, the pressure of duty returned. During the past month, since his consecration to Christ by baptism, the question of his duty to preach the gospel had become quite agitating. Still, had the brethren, and especially the pastor, not mentioned it, probably the subject would have remained for a much longer time a private grief.

Before the church came to order, two or three of the brethren, with the pastor, urged a disclosure of my feelings to the brotherhood. When it came to my turn to speak, as was then customary, I gave a statement of my views and feelings on preaching the gospel, and of the trials I had experienced for nearly four years on that subject, and thus submitted the matter to the church, desiring them to judge prayerfully and impartially what they considered my duty, and left the hou e. In a few minutes a brother called me in, when I learned the church had voted to have me "improve my gift," as they expressed it, within their limits, until they gained evidence of my call to, and qualifications for, the work of the Christian ministry. They also voted that I conduct the meeting, and speak to the con gregation in the afternoon of the next day. All this, I learned afterwards, was in accordance with the old Baptist practice, especially in country churches. I was not wholly unprepared. At various times, in seasons of thoughtfulness and study, I had drawn out plans of discourses from texts of Scripture. One subject had primary place in my thoughts and affections : that of Christian missions, or preaching the gospel to every creature.

Next day, in presence of a crowded congregation, I made my first essay in speaking from a text. This was Mark xvi. 15 : "And he said unto them, Go ye into all the world, and preach the gospel to every creature." At the close, I thought that no temptation or despondency would ever cause me to doubt the Divine mission, but one week had not passed away without sore trials on this question.

I have given this sketch of personal history to call the attention of readers to the old practice in Baptist churches, of praying the Lord of the harvest to thrust forth laborers, and especially the anxiety and restlessness of the brethren in finding out who had the "call" and the "gift."

I have not a word to object against the efforts made to look out and educate *young* men who give evidence of the gifts and graces indispensable to the ministry, but the great and serious mistake consists in the following particulars :

1. In fixing the impression on the churches, that young men, *and none but young men*, are to be looked for in relation to that office. Nothing is said about men with families, and settled in business, becoming preachers. This *omission* has done the mischief, until what was once most common has become a rare exception.

2. That these young men must be *first* educated, all to the same extent, and in the same school, in classical literature, science, and theology. Many men, in some parts of our country, and in other

countries where the gospel is preached and Baptist churches exist, by self-tuition, under the guidance of ministers of experience, without a classical and scientific education, become qualified for the ministry. They make useful and successful pastors and evangelists, by the thorough training they get in the Word of God, by personal efforts and constant practice. They learn *to preach the gospel* with power and success, and to perform the duties of the Christian pastor, or the itinerating evangelist, though they may learn little else.

3. That no others but young men, thus educated, will answer for pastors in the churches.

All these exceptionable notions have been borrowed from the Calvinistic Puritans within the last thirty years, and no more fit Baptists for the work they have to do than Saul's armor suited the stripling David. Do the Baptists in "York State" look among their enterprising men of thirty or forty years, or even amongst obscure members of strong common-sense and ripe experience, for the materials of their ministry? Has the instance occurred at meetings on ministerial education, among the agents, lecturers, and other speakers, urging the churches to look for ministerial gifts from any other class than *young men?* Is there evidence of any such anxiety and persevering effort in the churches throughout the State, to learn the private feelings and convictions of duty, as the members of the little mountain church of Durham showed towards an individual, who two months previous came amongst them a stranger? This course was not singular or unusual in Baptist churches at that period in "York State."

Nor, with all their eagerness and anxiety to look out for ministerial gifts, were they hasty and inconsiderate in acknowledging them. The church first voted to invite the writer to exercise his "gift"— whatever it might be—within its own limits. In about three months they extended the limits to neighboring churches. In the spring of 1812, being about to make a journey to Connecticut, the last was recalled and a new one given, but still in the phraseology of the Northern churches the expression was: "Liberty to improve his gift wherever Divine Providence might open the door." This was no license to officiate, and to pass as a regular minister of the gospel, but only to exercise such gifts as the person possessed. Nor did the writer ever receive any other license until after his ordination. And why should men be licensed as ministers of the gospel until, by a suitable probation, they give evidence of the "call," the "gift," and the qualifications for that office? Why hold a brother up to the world as designed for a "sacred profession," until it is known that ne is fitted for that profession, and has evinced a settled determination to enter the ministry and abide in it, either as a pastor or an evangelist. If he has the gift and grace of a true minister of Christ, he will make that the paramount business of life. To use a Western figure, attributed to the eccentric Crockett, " He will stand up to the rack, fodder or no fodder." If he has the gift and enterprise that is characteristic of Christ's ministers, he will not wait till a church *call him*, but go into some destitute field, sustain himself and family by his own industry, *and proceed to call a church*, as many of our old pioneer preachers have done.

At the church meeting last mentioned, when the writer made his first essay in preaching the gospel, a messenger to the Rensselaerville Association had to be appointed to fill a vacancy, and the new member was chosen. I use the old term, MESSENGER, which is the correct word to be employed, to designate all persons sent on errands by the churches. Baptist churches cannot transfer to individual members, or through them convey to associations, conventions, councils, or any other body of man's contrivance, *delegated or representative power*. Hence the tendency to unscriptural notions and practices in calling things by wrong names. Messenger was the old Baptist term, when it was understood that Baptist churches could not be *represented*.

This body contained fifteen churches, when the session for 1811 closed, and thirteen ordained ministers. Total number of members eleven hundred and thirty-one. It had been a season of dearth for a long time. Only two churches indicated any thing like a revival the preceding year.

Elder John Winans was elected Moderator, and Deacon Nathaniel Jacobs, Sr., Clerk.

On the second day, Elder Wayland, Sr., preached from 2 Cor. iv. 15; and, after an intermission for refreshments, Elder Pettit gave a discourse from John x. 27, 28. No collections were taken for philanthropic purposes; nothing was said about missions, or even providing preaching for the destitute. South and west, within the reach of this Association, was quite a destitute region, and the people lived in small settlements, separated from each other, through the valleys and mountain gorges. For the churches entirely destitute of pastoral visitations, monthly visits were volunteered by the Elders. The church of Rensselaerville and **Coeymans**, of thirty members, and the church of Catskill, of thirty-two members, were thus supplied monthly.

CHAPTER III.

Preaching in Catskill—Ordination—Labors and Efforts for Self-im
provement—Illness—Necessity for Removal.

A SHORT time after the events above narrated, Mr. Peck,
having received a full letter of license to preach the gospel
from the church at New Durham, of which he was a member,
and having frequently exercised his gift where the providence
of God opened the way before him, was invited to visit the
little Baptist church in Catskill, the county-seat of Green
county. He found here a few brethren and sisters, neither
united nor enterprising, and continued occasionally to visit
them till the spring of 1812.

His family were then absent on a visit to his native Litchfield, Ct., and on his way to see them he passed a day or two
in Catskill, and was encouraged to make arrangements to
remove there, keep a school for his support, and preach for
the little Baptist church when they had no other supply. They
had no house of worship, but met in private dwellings, and
sometimes in the old court-house. They proffered no salary;
but whoever preached for them on the Sabbath received the
amount of the penny collection. This he was careful to note
in his journal; and the amount was less than an average of
one dollar a week, though he ordinarily preached three or four
times. But he loved the work rather than the wages, and
therefore made no objection to these arrangements. His diary
at this period breathes a pure and excellent spirit. Indeed one
cannot read it without being deeply impressed with the fer-
vency of his devotedness to God his Saviour, and a deep
abiding sense of his dependence on him. It would be easy to
fill many pages with extracts breathing most fervent desires
for entire conformity to Christ, and the pantings of intense
solicitude to be made useful to the souls of his fellow men

At the end of March, 1812, the following entry appears in his journal, which is interesting as indicating how early he became imbued with a desire for preserving accurate statistics. They are the beginnings of what proved in his life a mighty aggregate of such gathered, accurate facts.

I find by enumeration that in course of my past life I have had the privilege of hearing twenty-four Baptist preachers improve, many of them repeatedly. Fifteen of them I heard in Connecticut, the other nine since I removed to this State. [N.Y.] I have seen besides myself and wife three persons baptized, all of Litchfield, Ct. Seven times I have had the privilege of communing since I joined the Baptists. [Here follow the names of the preachers.] In Connecticut, Rufus Babcock, Sr., Isaac Bellows, Asa Tallmadge, Benjamin Baldwin, Jesse Hartwell, Asa Niles, Samuel Miller, Henry Green, Joshua Bradly, John Sherman, Asahel Morse, Isaac Fuller, Oliver Tuttie, Wilson and Joseph Graves. In New York, Joseph Arnold, Herman Hervey, Hezekiah Pettit, Orlando Mack, Francis Wayland, Sr., James Mackey, Levi Streeter, Wm. Stewart, and Josiah Baker.*

I have attended nine monthly church meetings, and five extra church meetings, in cases of discipline; have voted for the exclusion of two members; also have attended one Association and one General Conference; and have myself tried to preach twenty-seven times.

The following month he visited his family in Litchfield on foot, stopping after a weary walk each day where he could preach the gospel to those hungering for the bread of life. The journey and the visit occupied two or three weeks, in which he traveled chiefly afoot one hundred and eighty-two miles, and preached fifteen times. His old neighbors had not seen him since the change of his ecclesiastical relations, and, on the whole, rigid Pedobaptists as most of them were, they seem to have received him and treated him with as much

---

* Most of these men were personally known to me, as humble, unlearned, and self-sustained ministers of Christ. Some toiling on their little farms, others in their shops, that they might preach Christ, and administer his ordinances, where otherwise they could not have been enjoyed. Their record is on high.—EDITOR.

respect and affection as could have reasonably been expected. The Congregational church in Litchfield South Farms still claimed him as their member, since he had never sought a dissolution of his covenant-engagement to walk with them; and they now insisted on their right and duty to discipline him. They stated to him that what they had against him was' neither scandal, nor heresy, nor even his renouncing their sentiments and joining the Baptists; but for leaving them before giving them a hearing—thus virtually excluding them without giving them an opportunity to defend themselves—and, if they could, to reclaim him. The case came before their church, where he was regularly arraigned, and the parties impleaded one another. His defence was in brief this: he did not deny that it was his duty to make the effort for reclaiming them from what he regarded their error in reference to baptism. But according to the rules of the gospel he must first reform himself, by being baptized, and then endeavor to reform them, which he was now willing to attempt, both by precept and example; by Scripture argument and the alluring act itself—the best of all arguments. In brief he found, as he thought, himself and his brethren in a practical error, consisting in the neglect of the believer's first duty—baptism. Hence he deemed it his duty first to reform himself, and then endeavor to reclaim his erring brethren. To which his opponent, Esq. Morris, replied that it was a principle applicable to all associated bodies, that one who had entered into a voluntary covenant engagement should not abandon his associates without at least giving them fair notice, or asking leave; that it was unmanly to do so.

There was perhaps an element of truth in the positions of each; and to the praise of the candor and forbearance of the church it should be stated, that when they could not bring their delinquent brother to acknowledge that he had done wrong by leaving them *in the way he did*, they did not harshly and summarily excommunicate him, but laid the case over, from April to September, exhorting him meanwhile to consider their expostulations. How much better and more

Christian-like was this than severer measures and an unlovely spirit which churches not in ecclesiastical fellowship with each other often evince. Their personal relations and their Christian intercourse through it all remained unbroken; and finally, some dozen years later, they invited him to preach in their meeting-house, thus virtually canceling their slight censure. Whenever he visited his native town, all classes gathered around him with a loving and fraternal interest, and on the occasion of the centennial celebration of the organization of the county in the summer of 1851, he was invited by the committee—almost exclusively Pedobaptists—to take an important part in the interesting public services. But Harvard University had before this time honored him with one of its highest badges of distinction; and Litchfield might well be proud of a son, who had reflected more honor on his birthplace than she could now confer on him.

The summer of 1812 found him diligently plying his double duties in Catskill. His school flourished and yielded him and his little family the amount of support which their frugality and industry made suffice. His preaching was pretty regularly continued, and somewhat extended—wherever most urgently demanded—in the regions around. He frequently visited Hudson; and before the end of this year found in the excellent pastor of that church, Rev. Hervey Jenks, a neighbor of congenial and truly fraternal spirit. This excellent man—alas, so early cut down by death—was a recent graduate of Brown University; for a short time had been preceptor of its grammar-school in Providence; and having enjoyed ample opportunities of intellectual and religious culture, was able to impart to the young licentiate in close proximity just the assistance in his earnest endeavors for self-improvement for which he was now panting.

Very instructive and delightful it is to trace the benign influence which was thus exerted on the young licentiate's mind. His reading, study, and labor, henceforth assume a higher and worthier aim; and the results were speedily manifest. Their correspondence too was frequent, animated and, to Mr. Peck, very improving, though they were located but six miles apart, and saw each other very frequently. But their full hearts could not wait for the expected Saturday interview, and hence those exercises of the pen which still remain, a memorial as beautiful and fragrant as the record of the union of David and Jonathan.

From the Rev. Dr. Porter, also, pastor of the Presbyterian church in Catskill, a man of some peculiarities, but able, and generally of genial and catholic spirit, Mr. Peck experienced many courtesies adapted to promote his improvement. They attended funerals together, and listened to each other's exercises frequently. Mr. Peck, as the younger and less improved of the two, would be likely to receive the greater benefit in this intercourse. Occasional entries in his journal would seem to indicate that he thought the Doctor rather marred than improved, by his deep tinge of Hopkinsianism, and a pretty plain implication is furnished that the strong and undiluted Calvinism of Dr. Chester, of Hudson, was more to his taste. Honorable mention is also made of the family of Judge Day, of Catskill, to whose hospitalities he seems to have been cordially welcomed; and when they were in deep affliction, and their own pastor, Dr. Porter, was either absent or indisposed, Mr. Peck was invited to officiate, and in all respects was treated with a marked degree of deference and esteem. Such traces, honorable alike to the givers and receiver, are the more noticeable and deserving of commendation on the part of the Presbyterians, from the fact that the Baptists were making inroads upon them continually. In his circumstances, having recently come out from a Pedobaptist communion, the ordinance of baptism was very likely to occupy a prominent place in his thoughts, his conversation, and his public ministry. In his diary he thus notices the first administration of baptism the month after he commenced preaching in Catskill, and a year before his own ordination:

LORD'S DAY, 21st June, 1812.—In the forenoon Elder Hervey being with us preached from Isaiah xxxv. 8. Afterward we repaired to the river side, where prayer is wont to be made, and after a short but appropriate address by the administrator the two young candidates were baptized in water—a beautiful emblem of Christ's death, burial, and resurrection. Such an interesting scene I never before beheld. The situation of the place, the devout attention of a large audience, the tears discovered trickling down the cheeks of many, together with the solemnity of the ordinance itself, seemed deeply to impress my mind with a profound sense of the propriety of strict adherence to apostolic precedent in the administration of baptism. At the close of the afternoon service, when the baptized had been welcomed into the fellowship of the church, I presented my letter of dismission from Durham church; and after relating my experience, was admitted to this church, and we had a precious season around the Lord's table. Truly we might say it was a feast of fat things, and the Lord was sensibly present with us. At six o'clock I preached at Brother Hill's house. Had a comfortable time; and after meeting, an aged gentleman came forward and related what the Lord had done for him, desiring to join with us, and was fellowshipped. In the morning, the youth forsake the vanities of the world, and profess to be dead to sin and alive to God. In the evening, the aged wish to enter on the service of the Lord, and go into the vineyard at the eleventh hour.

Well might he subjoin: "I never experienced such a day before." Then follows an affecting expression of his sense of great responsibility in ministering to that little church, now happily—and by the aid of an advisory council called in part at his instance—reconciled and walking in love. He was now employed in feeding the lambs of the flock with the sincere milk of the word, that they might grow thereby; in guiding inquirers to the Lamb of God; and again in meeting the wants of others who were tried about baptism and wanted light to guide them. Similar exercises and successes continue to be noted till the end of the year. By a careful devotement of all his spare hours when out of school, to self-improvement and to preparation for preaching, he was rapidly advancing in grace and knowledge. Soon after the end of his first year in Catskill, the following summary appears of his entire course of ministrations, with all which he had received in pecuniary recompense. He had preached in all 174 times, viz.: in Durham and vicinity, 42 times; in Litchfield, Ct.

16 times; in Hudson, 9 times; in Madison (a little village contiguous to his residence in Catskill), 15 times; and in Catskill, 92 times.   He had also attended 23 monthly church meetings, and 7 on special business; attended 13 funerals, 2 associations, and 1 general conference.   Had received as a compensation for preaching, as follows : Litchfield, $1 16 cts.; in Hudson, $4 12½ cts.; in Catskill, $15 88 cts.; in Madison, $21 87 cts.   By subscription, presents, and otherwise, $18 92 cts., or $61 95 cts. in all.   He enters no complaint, and apparently feels no grievance that his work was not more adequately remunerated.

The church in Catskill, at the end of his first year's residence and service with them, invited him to be ordained ; and a council was called for that purpose, which met June 9, 1813.   The Presbyterian church was cordially proffered and accepted for the services, and Dr. Porter was invited to sit and dine with the council, which he did.   After the usual examination, which was deemed satisfactory, the ordination sermon and right-hand of fellowship were by his neighbor and beloved brother, Rev. Hervey Jenks.   Other principal parts were performed by Elders Stewart, Streeter, Mack, Hervey, and Pettit.   All the services were appropriate and solemn, and were listened to with lively interest by a large congregation.

The next Sabbath he baptized several candidates, and administered the Lord's Supper; and within a week officiated at his first marriage, of which he has given us the written form which he adopted, and the amount of fee (one dollar) which was tendered him.   Thus was he very fully inducted into all the functions of the ministerial office.

His internal trials in the discharge of his duties seem sometimes to have been severe and protracted.   But he learned gradually that for all these seasons of darkness and depression there was an adequate cause, physical or moral, and he became an adept in this species of pathology, and by carefully securing a correct diagnosis of his own soul, he was the better prepared to minister successfully to the spiritual maladies, or the morbid imaginations of others.   Those who have only known him in the last half of his public life—who have seen his spirits so buoyant and his disposition so equable, would scarcely expect to find in his early years such evidences as his journal discloses of a spirit so widely dissimilar. This morbid succession of heights and depths he learned to estimate more correctly as he advanced to maturity.   These pages might be filled with the record of them, but they are not in harmony with his maturer judgment, and will therefore be passed over.   So, too, of the somewhat profuse recording of his pious resolutions very formally adopted on frequent occasions of self-examination, for the first few years of his public life, he early became apparently ashamed, and his practice in this respect changed from about the time of his ordination. His determination to do his duty to God and to his fellow men, to the very best and utmost of his ability, became more and more strong and equable, and would—so he thought—be more impeded and distracted than benefited by a superabundance of abstract rules and resolutions previously adopted.

At one period he had minutely mapped out his whole time, giving a specific appropriation of duties to every hour.   But the necessary interruptions and variations to which a pastor's and teacher's life in such a population as here surrounded him, is necessarily exposed, made adherence to this plan practically impossible.   Pastors will in the end very generally come to adopt Dr. Payson's apothegm : " The man who wants me is the man I want." The duty now most urgently pressing must first be met, despite all abstract rules.

The first indication of the missionary spirit which so thoroughly pervaded his subsequent life is found in his diary a few weeks subsequent to his ordination ; and in consideration of its wide-reaching and healthful results, it deserves to be here copied and preserved.   This, be it remembered, was just before the news reached us of the conversion of Judson and Rice to Baptist views, and the incipient steps were taken for commencing our foreign mission operations :

FRIDAY EVENING, *June* 25, 1813.   Received the last number of the Baptist Missionary Magazine.   The missionary accounts from India

4

are very interesting. How many thousands of the poor benighted heathen there are who worship the idol of Juggernaut and adore the river Ganges, but are ignorant of the way of salvation through Jesus Christ! How can Christians in this land of high privileges sit easy and unconcerned, without contributing out of their abundance to spread the gospel in distant pagan lands! My soul is grieved for them in their ignorance. Oh, how I wish I was so circum-stanced in life as that I might be able to bear the gospel into some dis-tant pagan lands where it never yet has shined! A large part of the American continent is also involved in darkness. Yes, under the immediate Government of the United States, there is an abundant field for missionary labor. How I should rejoice if Providence would open a door for my usefulness and labors in this way! [This prayer was certainly answered, but not yet was the door opened.] But alas, how idle and vain are my thoughts! In this place I am too faithless, too prone to wander. Oh, that I might first learn to perform the duties which come within my reach, and not presume to think I should be more faithful in another part of the vineyard!

One means of improvement adopted by brethren Peck, Jenks, and Lamb—three Baptist ministers living near each other—was to meet every fortnight at each other's houses and discuss some question previously proposed. In this way they appear to have gone over a number of the important topics of systematic theology much to their mutual satisfaction and edification. But before the year closed these multiplied efforts in his day school, in an evening school which he conducted to eke out a scanty support, and in his numerous evangelical labors, proved too hard for him. His health failed, and he was brought apparently to the brink of the grave. His wife also, at another time this year, was very dangerously ill; but both experienced recovering mercy. In the meantime his improvement became more and more obvious to his ministering and other brethren. He was made clerk of the Association for two consecutive years, and wrote by appointment both the circular and corresponding letter—the first of his compositions submitted to the press. The circular was on Election. This Scripture doctrine he explained and substantiated, and showed both its use and abuse. During this year, also, he determined no longer to attempt preaching without carefully studying each sermon. He acknowledges the injurious effect on his own mind, as well as on his hearers, of going before his audience without due preparation and trusting to the impulse of the moment for the thoughts and illustrations which he should employ. It was but too common with one class of preachers in that day (not of course the intelligent) to profess that they did not premeditate, but it was given them in the same hour—so they said—what they should utter. Yet such is the inconsistency of poor human nature, these very men, if they heard from a studious brother minister an excellent and well elaborated sermon, would not scruple, when they thought the plagiarism would not be detected, to appropriate to their own use such a discourse, and deliver it, nearly as they could remember it, as though it had been given them by a direct communication from heaven.

His inadequate support—the result in part of breaking up his school during his sickness, and the fact that two summers he had suffered in health by his residence and excessive labors in Catskill—began to prepare his mind for leaving that affectionate little flock. About the end of the year 1813 he received an intimation of the desire of the Baptist church in Amenia, Dutchess county, that he would come and labor with them. After two visits among them, and the repetition of their invitation, accompanied with the proffer of such support as would enable him to give up a school, and devote himself more concentratedly to the work of the ministry and to his further improvement in education, he felt it his duty to accept their invitation. The church in Catskill, in conformity to his request, yet with much reluctance on their part, granted him release from his pastoral care over them ; and in a letter, bearing date February 19, 1814, expressed their gratitude for his fidelity in the discharge of his onerous and almost unrequited labors among them for almost two years ; and the assurances of their love, their gratitude, and their prayers for his success in the new sphere where Providence seemed to call him. This love was mutual, and he seems to have ever borne towards the flock, whom he first served, unabated affection ; and it is pleasant to notice their mutual regard in all the future years of his course

CHAPTER IV.

Pastorship in Amenia—Missionary Zeal and Labors.

On his first visit to Amenia, he records in his journal that he found a respectable church and congregation, who appeared in union, though there was much complaint of coldness among them. Deacon Richard Gurnsey, one of the best of men, was a leading instrument of his settlement with that people. When our brother came to know them more intimately, he found many things of a discouraging character impeding the success of his labors. Discipline had been sadly neglected, and a great part of the efforts for the two years he remained with them had to be devoted to weeding out the disorders which had been suffered to accumulate until they threatened the ruin of the cause. The flock was somewhat widely scattered in their residences on the mountain, and indeed over it, as well as for a long distance up and down the fertile and beautiful valley where their house of worship was located. Some families, too, resided across the state line in Connecticut, so that a widely diversified field of active labor was continually demanding his utmost energies, intellectual and physical. His preaching was prized; and there were calls for lectures, or prayer and conference meetings, in so many different neighborhoods, that he was kept in lively motion a great part of his time. But relief from the drudgery of the school operated favorably on his health, and his thirst for improvement tasked his powers to the utmost. That noble man, and scholar and teacher, Daniel H. Barnes, was at this time Principal of Dutchess Academy in Poughkeepsie, and an esteemed member and ere long a licentiate of the Baptist Church. Mr. Peck formed his acquaintance, and by his generous proffer was encouraged to commence under his instruction the reading of the Greek New Testament, as well as other kindred studies which he prosecuted. Week after week he would devote four days or more to earnest study under the guidance of this most excellent instructor—living in his family, and spurred on by the enthusiasm which this teacher felt and communicated. The Rev. Dr. Aaron Perkins was then his fellow-student, and bears honorable testimony concerning the fidelity, conscientiousness, and vigor of his associate in study.

Early in the second year of Mr. Peck's pastorship at Amenia, his hopes were highly raised of an extensive revival under his labors. How ardently he desired it, how indefatigably he labored for its promotion, and with what pious confidence in God, and what a deep sense of self-abasement and personal unworthiness he relied on Divine grace alone, his journal at this period abundantly testifies. The zeal which he put forth to multiply his religious services, and the carefulness he evinced to promptly instruct and encourage inquirers, were highly commendable. But he seems to have failed—as many others there and elsewhere have failed—to awaken the zeal, the self-denying and hopeful activities of the church members, so as to induce them to co-operate with him in his pious and praiseworthy endeavors. Probably these members, or many of them at least, thought his zeal was not according to knowledge—that he had taken counsel of his desires, rather than of any unmistakable tokens of the Divine favor. They saw not the little cloud rising out of the sea, foretokening the abundance of rain, nor heard they "the goings in the tops of the mulberry trees" (a favorite emblem among these spiritualizing ministers and people of the olden times), and hence they did not expect at that time great things from God, and of course were very slow in attempting great things for God. Some of his brethren indicated their unbelief of a revival as near at hand, by reviving difficulties and church labors of discipline on trifling matters, most vexatious in their influence, which for weeks and months attracted the chief attention and absorbed the zeal and spirit which the young pastor had hoped to turn into a worthier channel. Thus his hopes were blighted, the Holy Spirit was grieved away, and but few souls were converted. How sadly and deeply he mourned over this and similar hindrances to the progress of the cause with which his soul was identified, is sufficiently manifest by frequent and characteristic entries in his diary. But God was evidently preparing him, by these very reverses, for a more cordial welcoming of what was to be his grand life-labor.

In the month of June, 1815, at the session of the Warwick Association, which met that year with the church at Lattintown, of which his Brother Aaron Perkins was pastor, he met for the first time with Rev. Luther Rice, who with characteristic ardor was posting from one association to another fanning the flame of missionary zeal. In this case the spark fell on a train already laid, where little effort was needed to kindle a soul already panting with intense desire to be and to do something worthy of its nature, its alliance, its destination. In a word, Mr. Rice found in young Peck a congenial spirit ready to drink in the words of fervent, glowing, holy love, in which one who had just returned from heathen shores portrayed the degradation of pagan gloom, and the duty and privilege of hastening to rescue the souls of the perishing heathen from destruction. After listening to the public appeal, the pastor of Amenia managed to take Mr. Rice home with him; and in the hours they thus spent together a plan was consummated for employing the former by the latter to visit in the coming months two or three associations in central New York to promote a missionary spirit among them. A better and surer method could not have been taken to perpetuate in his own bosom the holy devotedness with which he was now beginning to be imbued.

Ere long, therefore, having already made a hurried visit, with success to the Franklin Association, by the consent of his church, as it may be presumed, he set forth for a more thorough labor with the others on this, to him, most important and decisive tour. The record of it, very nearly filling his Diary No. 5 (the first of those of a small, portable form), is peculiarly interesting from the nature of the services in which he was then for the first time engaging, and from the persons with whom he then first came in contact, and the incipient missionary movements which he was instrumental in setting in motion, as well as some of the scenes he visited—since so hallowed in their associations, and where so many of the devoted missionaries have been trained. For all these reasons, our readers will justly prize the reproduction of considerable portions of this journal in our pages.

HAMILTON, *September* 10*th*, 1815. Lord's Day. In the morning I heard Elder Hascall preach a funeral sermon from Luke xii. 37. He is a moderate speaker, but of sound judgment. In the afternoon I preached with a great degree of freedom from Luke xix. 10. The audience solemn, attentive, and many affected. May the word be blessed for their good! Spent the night at the house of Brother King. Had a very agreeable interview with him and his family. Conversed on the beauties of poetry to which Mr. King is much attached.

11*th*. Still I enjoy the presence of my Redeemer. I can truly say my cup runneth over with blessings. I find kind and endearing friends wherever I go, who strive to make me comfortable. My mind is no longer harassed with the cares of the world, and perplexed with the embarrassments of my temporal concerns at home. Now and then a thought of anxiety and grief steals across my mind in reference to my family. But this is hushed when considering that I have dedicated them to my God, and left them in his hands. With the greatest confidence in the rectitude of his government, I can anticipate the time of meeting my dear companion and my prattling babes as they gather around on my return. In the evening preached in the meeting-house in Hamilton from Psalm lxxxv. 10. Weather rainy, so that not many were present. Enjoyed considerable freedom in opening and explaining the doctrine of the atonement. My mind still continues engaged. I feel an ardent desire of doing good wherever I go.

12*th*. In company with Brother Hascall I went to Eaton—eight miles—where the association is to meet to-morrow. [Here was the residence and pastorship of that eminent man of God, Nathan'l Kendrick, D.D., so long Divinity professor in the Hamilton Institution, and who shared with Dr. Hascall the honor of founding it.] Put up at Brother Eels. In the afternoon the Hamilton Domestic Missionary Society met and arranged their affairs for the year en suing. This society is greatly assisted by female auxiliaries who manufacture cloth and other useful articles. It is in encouraging circumstances. In the evening I conversed with some of the brethren on forming a missionary society for the foreign mission. It is thought this is practicable. My mind still is peculiarly happy in Divine things. Oh, my blessed Saviour! all this I receive for thy name's sake.

13th. Spent the morning in further conversation on missions. At ten o'clock the Madison Association met, and Elder Lathrop, from Warwick, preached from Ezekiel x. Many interesting ideas were communicated, but his discourse in general was confused, and his manner disagreeable. Not in general liked by the brethren. In the afternoon the churches made their returns. Religion generally is flourishing. Some churches complain of coldness, but many are quite encouraged, and made returns of considerable additions. Five churches joined the association this session. It is already a large body, and embraces a number of flourishing and respectable churches. The ministers are mostly valuable men, sound in doctrine and much engaged to advance the cause of Christ. The churches in this western country are generally liberal to their ministers, affording them a comfortable support. This is usually done by an average according to ability. The justness and propriety of this method is very apparent. Before the day closed, I presented the letter from Mr. Rice, which I read. The association in a very spirited manner took up the subject and appointed a committee to confer with me on the question, and also requested me to preach a missionary sermon on the morrow. At evening the committee conversed on the subject, and agreed to form an auxiliary society. I drafted a report and prepared a constitution to be presented to the association. The spirit of missions greatly prevails in this quarter. It does not appear to be a hasty passion, but a settled conviction of judgment, and a principle of duty.

14th. How greatly I am favored! I share every comfort. What a checkered scene is human life! But a few weeks since I was repining at my lot. Then my mind was filled with constant embarrassment. Now I share and rejoice in the light of life.

Presented the report of the Committee on Foreign Missions to the association, which was readily approved. Some remarks were then made. An address was read by Elder Lawton. The spirit of missions seemed to kindle, and glow, and flame through the congregation. Public worship commenced at ten o'clock. I preached from Ezekiel xxxvii. 3—enjoyed peculiar freedom　Should I attempt to describe the effect on the congregation I could not do it justice. The solemn attention, the trickling tear, the sob and groan disclosed that the tenderest feelings of the heart were touched. It appears that we can hardly be enthusiastic on the subject of missions. Here is full scope for the most benevolent and feeling heart to exercise itself. It ill becomes me to say any thing respecting my own performance. This, however, I can freely say, if I am not grossly deceived, that to God—only wise—all the praise is due. A collection for the benefit of the mission was taken amounting to eighty five dollars, which was increased before the close of the session to one hundred and three dollars, paid into the treasury in one day When I reflect that but a few years since all this country was one vast wilderness—properly missionary ground—I must exclaim: What hath God wrought!

This is a specimen of nearly fifty pages of the characteristic journal of Brother Peck, which furnishes the true key to his future movements. The three weeks of his experience, as here developed, shows that his heart was fired with missionary zeal; and that perhaps unconsciously to himself he was beginning to loathe the kind of mixed employment—partly secular and partly sacred—in which his public life had hitherto been passed. Not unlikely, too, the hindrances he had unexpectedly experienced in the work of the Lord in the church at Amenia, their dilatoriness in furnishing him the stipulated support, and the pertinacity with which some of the members insisted on pushing their disciplinary action to wards a brother or two, who had fallen into disfavor, and whose wrong-doing the pastor thought some of the brethren inclined unduly to magnify, so as to turn off the regards of the community from what he reckoned as now more important—all conspired to move him to the result which appeared rapidly approaching. The letters which passed between himself and Mr. Rice, as well as his report to Dr. Staughton as Corresponding Secretary of the Board of Missions, all tended to the same result.

On his return from this tour, in which he rode four hundred and forty miles, preached nineteen times, and took five missionary collections, he entered with characteristic ardor on the performance of his duties both in Amenia and Hudson (to the church in the latter city he seems to have preached regularly for several months a portion of the time) ; but the cause did not prosper. Early in October he attended the Hartford Association, meeting that year in North Colebrook, Ct., and enjoyed the services very greatly, as a revival was then progressing there ; and his favorite missionary object continued to increase in the interest awakened in its behalf. Early the following month, he commenced teaching a school in Amenia, led to it as he says by the necessitous circumstances of his little family, and in hope of being of some benefit to the youth placed under his charge. The same week he sent in a letter to the Amenia church, giving notice of the discontinuance of his pastorship at the termination of the year.

Various ecclesiastical duties and engagements led him away from his school for a day or two at a time, for successive weeks, to Poughkeepsie, to Hudson, and elsewhere. And the double duties he was now attempting were unfavorable to his health and his religious enjoyment. Of this his journal takes frequent and sad notice. Notwithstanding, he appears to have borne up under these discouragements in a manful and·vigorous manner. Twice a month he lectured before his school, and probably a few others, on topics sacred and historical—endeavoring to arouse them to a livelier interest in mental as well as religious exercises.

December 8th he mentions that within one week he had married three couples and received for it sixteen dollars, of which he was in pressing want, and could therefore regard this in no other light than as a special providence, for which he would render a tribute of praise to his ever bountiful Provider.

Before the close of this year, he aided in the ordination of Rev. J. G. Ogilvie in Hudson, to whom he gave the charge, the first time he had ever attempted this service. It seems to have been much blessed to his own soul, awakening a very solemn sense of his responsibility in watching for souls. Returning from this ordination, he perused by the way the memoir of Thomas Spencer, and found his soul more and more kindled to holy emulation of his brief but distinguished career. While riding along the road he frequently lifted his heart in prayer to God, and felt assured of a gracious answer—comparing his own feelings on this occasion to those of President Edwards, which the latter describes as an inward sweetness, or ravishing desire of soul, taking the greatest satisfaction in the adorable presence of God. "I thought"—says Mr. Peck —"I could be happy in any situation of life, even the most trying. I felt not only willing, but ardently desirous to be wholly devoted to the cause of Christ."

Friday evening, December 15th, occurs the first mention made of the name of a dear brother, with whom he was to be most interestingly associated for more than forty years in kindred labors and trials for the promotion of Christ's kingdom. The minute in his journal is in the following words: "I wrote a letter on missionary business to a minister by the name of James E. Welch, he having written to me first. It is pleasing to hold correspondence with any of the friends of Jesus, especially with such as devote themselves for life to the missionary cause."

Towards the close of the year, he remarks that "Teaching a large school, and then preaching in the evening, is quite fatiguing to this frail tenement of clay;" and his religious enjoyments and depressions seem to have alternated frequently in this period of his history. How could it be otherwise? The bow constantly bent must lose its elastic, recuperative force. The chief marvel is that either mind or heart could retain a healthful vigor when so constantly taxed beyond their power of endurance. At the end of the year 1815, he notices that he had preached the past year one hundred and thirty-five times.

CHAPTER V.

Removal and Student Life.

THE opening year, 1816, witnessed several events of most important influence upon his future history which may be appropriately noticed here. January 5th he mentions having written to Dr. Staughton with a view of obtaining some assistance from the Elucation Society. In that letter he says:

For more than two years past I have had my mind frequently exercised about the situation of the perishing heathen, and have ardently longed to be the humble instrument of imparting to some of them the word of life. My situation in life, and the want of requisite qualifications have precluded the hope of ever entering that field until a few months past. The difficulties in the way do not seem quite insurmountable, since I have had opportunity of becoming more attached to the missionary interest and learning the wants of the poor heathen. By communications from Brother Rice I learn that it is in contemplation to establish a mission in the Missouri Territory. On this subject I found in my own mind such a correspondence of feeling and sentiment that I could not forbear opening my mind to him. Ever since I have thought upon the subject of missions, I have had my eye upon the people west of the Mississippi, particularly the Indian nations, and have often wondered why no attempts were made to send the gospel to them. I have often thought that if it was my lot to labor among the heathen, the Louisiana-purchase, of all parts of the world, would be my choice. Since receiving the last communication from Brother Rice, I have had serious thoughts of making a tender of myself to the Board of Foreign Missions. As I am in great want of sufficient literary acquirements, I have thought of spending a few months the ensuing summer in Philadelphia could I obtain some assistance in board and tuition from the Education Society. This would be, however, for the exclusive purpose of qualifying myself to engage in the cause of missions in some part of the heathen world. . . . As I earnestly wish your friendly advice in what I have proposed, it may be proper to inform you of my circumstances a little more particularly. I am twenty-six years of age, and have a family consisting of a wife and three children. I began to preach in 1811, and was ordained in June, 1813. The opportunity I have had for an education has been quite small. I have made some advance in the several branches of an English education, and have paid some little attention to the Greek and Latin languages, but without the help of an instructor, except a few weeks which I spent with Mr. Barnes, late of Poughkeepsie. I am not able to translate much of the Greek Testament without the help of a lexicon.

This last letter from Brother Rice alluded to in the above communication, and which Mr. Peck mentions in his diary, as fixing his future destiny, is too important and characteristic to be omitted or curtailed. The allusion to other things than those immediately relevant to Mr. Peck's case are too interesting, for other reasons connected with the history of that period, to be omitted. The letter is given entire.

South Fork of Lick Creek, Knox Co.,
Indiana Territory,
November 30th, 1815.

To the Rev. John M. Peck.

Very Dear Brother :—Your very kind and highly interesting letter, of October 12th, came duly to hand, and I intended to answer it shortly, but have not found time till now. Brother James E. Welch was with me when I received it, and at my request he wrote to you immediately. He thinks of undertaking a mission to the West, should it be thought advisable. Possibly you may be fellow-laborers in this great field. Your success at the several associations you visited—viz. : the Franklin in June, the Otsego and Madison in September, and the Hartford in October—gives me very great satisfaction indeed. In your next, I will thank you to furnish me with the address of some principal minister, or private member, belonging to the Madison Association, to whom a parcel of the next Annual Report may be forwarded. Also furnish me with the address of the President and of the Corresponding Secretary of the "Madison Society Auxiliary," etc., and the *date* of the formation of said mission society ; and send me, if you can, a copy of their constitution. In answer to your inquiries :

1st. Is it contemplated to form a permanent mission-station in the West ? Yes ; certainly.

5

2d. Would it be best to have schools connected with the mission? Yes.

3d. Any particular place in view for the seat of the mission? St. Louis, probably.

4th. What literary attainments would be indispensable? A good English education, to say the least, so as to be able to conduct a school to advantage. In addition it would be *very desirable* to possess an acquaintance with the Latin and Greek, if not the Hebrew; and indeed it would be desirable that the missionary should be a graduate of some college, though this should not be considered indispensable. A thorough acquaintance with grammar, rhetoric, geography, and history, are of very great importance.

5th. Would it be thought necessary for some person to accompany you in this Western tour? Should some suitable person find his heart moved to offer himself to the service of the Board, as a missionary to the West *for life*, it might be very proper for him to travel with me some time in the country for the purpose of ascertaining the best position for the seat and commencement of his missionary labors. I thank you for the freedom with which you have described your views and impressions relative to personally engaging in the missionary service. It gives me great satisfaction, too, that your views are so much inclined to the West. Not only do I conceive it to be *proper* that a mission should be established in the West on account of the importance of this region in itself, but indispensably *necessary* to satisfy the wishes and expectations of pious people in all parts of the United States. So that by no means could I think *it best for you to abstain from these reflections;* much less that *you ought to give them up as vain and hopeless.*

From these observations you will receive the idea that I think it not improper to encourage you in the consideration of undertaking a Western mission. This is done by me on the ground that you possess an education amply sufficient to enable you to conduct an English school to advantage, as well as from the very pleasing impression, relative to your talents, piety, industry, and zeal, left on my mind by my short acquaintance with you last spring. You have at least *shown yourself faithful over a few things*, and I cannot but cherish the hope that the Head of the Church designs in his providence and grace to *make you ruler over many things.*

You mention a brother, Zalmon Tobey in Williams College, who thinks of directing his attention to the Western Indians. I hope this is of the Lord. No information could have imparted to me more sincere pleasure. Who knows but you and he may labor together? Consult him upon the subject, and let me hear about the matter. I beg you will request him to write to me, and to direct his letter to Nashville, Tenn., provided it be written in season to arrive there by the 1st of February; if not, direct to Augusta, Ga. Direct your own in the same manner. Since my letter to Brother Cushman, to which you allude, I have been present at the formation of four new auxiliary mission societies in Kentucky. In that State I have received more than eleven hundred dollars. In Lexington, the contribution after a missionary sermon was two hundred and forty dollars—the largest I have received on any one occasion. I expect to spend all the winter and part of the spring in ranging the Western and Southern States; shall probably not reach Philadelphia earlier than April—perhaps not till the 1st of May; fear I shall not be able to visit New England again in all next year, as there is much, very much to do yet in the Middle, Southern, and Western States, besides my contemplated tour into the Missouri country.

I beg you will write me as soon as convenient, and let me know if you would like to engage in the contemplated Western mission for life, and whether you would like the business of teaching a school; and whether you would be willing to offer to the Board next spring, and would be ready to set out next season distinctly to engage in the mission itself. It would afford me great satisfaction to see you in Philadelphia next spring; and I believe you might be highly useful in this Western country, whether as a missionary or otherwise.

Best regards to your dear lady, and believe me most sincerely and affectionately yours,

LUTHER RICE.

While Mr. Peck was waiting for a full decision of the momentous questions now before him, his school was continued, and he preached in Amenia, in Sharon, in Ellsworth parish, where was an interesting boarding-school, in which a precious revival was then progressing; and by request of pious Pedobaptist conductors he visited and preached repeatedly to students and others with happy effect. He also visited Hudson and Catskill near the close of January, and enjoyed much freedom in preaching and visiting among his old friends. On leaving Catskill to return to Amenia, he commenced reading the life of David Brainard, which he had just purchased. His

mission labors and success among the Indians seem to have
fired his soul with fresh ardor.   These impassioned utterances
occur in this connection :

Oh, what would I not willingly do or suffer if I could live as devoted as this eminent servant of God ! His singular piety and
devotedness to the cause of Christ affected me so much that frequently I shut up the book and indulged myself in meditation and
prayer.   I felt an inward longing or panting of soul after more devotion.   I had very clear views of my exceeding sinfulness and
depravity.   But notwithstanding, I felt that with the presence of a
holy God I could be happy anywhere.   I felt not merely to submit
to the hardships of a missionary life, but I ardently longed to enter
the field.   Frequently did I lift up my soul in prayer to God ; and
toward the latter part of my ride my soul was much drawn out for
the youth in my society, particularly those in my school.   I felt as
though I could wrestle with God in their behalf.   Oh, that these
desires and impressions might be lasting !

Some weeks later, when going again to Hudson to preach,
he thus writes in his diary :

I am so much taken up in my school through the week that I can
hardly find time for religious meditation.   Oh, how dreadful is the
thought of separation from God ! Stopped at an inn to feed my
horse, where there was a lewd, drunken, wicked set.   It pained my
soul to be in such company.   I felt a degree of joy that I was not
always to dwell in the tents of wickedness.

March 1st, he notices having just received letters from Brother
Welch and Dr. Staughton.   From the first he learnt some
particulars of interest about the Missouri Territory ; and from
the last a favorable prospect of entering the theological school
in Philadelphia next summer.   The Doctor recommended him
to apply to an education society in New York city where he
would no doubt obtain the needed assistance.   In the letter,
the first of a long and interesting series, official and otherwise
which the writer addressed to his subsequent pupil, Dr
Staughton says :

I am happy to find your mind impelled to devote your days to the honorable and laborious service of a missionary of Jesus. I trust the Lord in his providence will open before you a sphere of useful action, and assist you to fill it to the honor of his blessed name. I do not conceive that any difficulty will attend your introduction into the Education Society for a few months, or a longer time should it be found desirable.

He then points out the method for him to proceed in securing the assistance desired ; gives the last information received from Brother Rice, indicating the vigor and success with which he was prosecuting his laborious agency ; then mentions the sailing of the missionaries Hough and wife, with Mrs. White, and closes in a most fraternal manner.

Mr. Peck's visit to the several associations in the summer and fall brought him into correspondence with several distinguished brethren in those bodies. Room can only be found here for extracts from the letters of two of them—Rev. Elon Galusha and Rev. John Peck. The former, under date of Whitesborough, 17th January, 1816, says :

I was highly gratified to learn your great success in the missionary cause, and the information with which you favored me from Brother Rice was very grateful. Wonderful indeed are the mercies of God. How transporting to contemplate the latter-day glory, to which the pleasure of the Lord, now prospering with our missionary brethren, is doubtless a prelude. Oh, that men would praise the Lord for his goodness, and for his wonderful works to the children of men ! Nothing special has occurred in the place of my late residence, since I saw you, except the establishment of the "Shaftsbury-and-vicinity Missionary Society," of which my father is President, and Elder Mattison Corresponding Secretary. In subscription by members of said society I obtained more than one hundred dollars. The missionary cause also flourishes here. The Female Mite Society, established by your request, now consists of seventy members, twenty-three of whom pay annually one dollar each, the others half this sum. Five or six dollars have also been added as donations, amounting in all to between fifty and sixty dollars already, and the year not half expired.

Oh, dear brother, pray for me that I may be more engaged in the glorious cause of our precious Redeemer. May the pleasure of the Lord prosper with you, and his special blessing rest upon you.

Your cordial friend and unworthy brother in gospel bonds,

ELON GALUSHA.

Father Peck, as he has long been called, wrote as follows:

CAZENOVIA, *May 24th*, 1816.

Dear Brother:—It is with pleasure that I learn your resolution to devote yourself to the service of God in the missionary cause. You inform me that you are on your way to Philadelphia to spend some time in the theological seminary preparatory to your engaging in the blessed cause of preaching the gospel in the regions of superstition and idolatry. I rejoice that you find the means of accomplishing your desires. And I pray God that he may continue his blessing to you, and grant success to all your endeavors for his glory. I will take the liberty to inform you that the Lord has graciously been pleased to visit us with an outpouring of his Spirit: sixty-five have been added to this church since July last. In the town of Eaton, where the Madison Association was held which you attended, free grace is now gloriously triumphing. Within a month past, on two Sabbaths, thirty-eight were immersed in the name of the Holy Trinity. In Homer, where Elder Bennett is pastor, Zion's glorious King is exhibiting his matchless power. Last Sabbath, twenty-four were added to that church. In Pompey the Lord reigns: twenty-four have been added to the church in that town. In Sherburn and Sangersfield God is doing wonders. According to your request I send a copy of our last minutes, also a copy of the sixth and seventh numbers of "The Vehicle." I request you to take an interest in the promotion of this work. And if you could continue your correspondence with me, I should esteem it a great pleasure; and I desire you to send me any intelligence or other communication suitable for the magazine. I consider your situation favorable for this purpose, and all communications will be thankfully received. I know of no person in the Cayuga Association more suitable to be intrusted with missionary reports and other communications than Deacon Squire Munro, of Camillus, who is now President of the Auxiliary Foreign Missionary Society. I feel to congratulate you on the glorious triumph of our adorable Sovereign. Almost every breeze wafts to our ears some pleasing intelligence of the increase of Christ's kingdom. Go on, victorious King, nor stay thy hand until all thy enemies are subdued, and the whole earth is filled with thy glory. This is the sincere prayer of, dear brother, your sincere friend,

JOHN PECK.

Brother Lawton presents his respects, and desires to be remembered by you.

Peck and Lawton, Bennett and Kendrick, Hascall and Galusha, are names not likely ever to fade from Baptist recollection in Central New York; and to all of them the subject of this memoir had linked himself for a life-long affection by his brief visit to them the preceding autumn.

At the end of March he closed his school, to which he had become much attached, and it was hard parting. So he found it in taking leave of the churches in Catskill, in Hudson and Amenia, in all of which he left many loving, friends. This and the business cares of settling up his accounts, and providing for nis family's comfort through the summer, and especially taking leave of them for so long a period—all tended to depress and almost sadden him. Near the end of April he left them, and stopped in Poughkeepsie; he afterward spent five days in New York, where he preached in the principal Baptist churches, and received the marked attention of ministers, deacons, and influential brethren and their families. On some kind and generous notices of his preaching which came to his knowledge, he expresses in his journal the fear that he was in danger of becoming popular. For Elders Parkinson in Gold street, Williams in Fayette (now Oliver) street, and Maclay in Mulberry street, he preached more than once each, thus filling up his time and wearying him almost beyond his power of endurance. Then on the 1st of May he set forth at seven o'clock in the morning—and *in a steamer too!*—for Philadelphia, reaching as far as Trenton before midnight. Here he stayed over, and reached Philadelphia by another steamer, down the Delaware (which much delighted him by its earlier vernal beauty than he had left behind him), before noon the second day. He found Dr. Staughton's residence, and was introduced to him and his lady and his three fellow-students,

Farnsworth, Wilson, and Meredith. Somers having just left for a settlement in Troy, and Welch not having arrived.

His residence in the city of brotherly love—boarding in the family of Dr. Staughton with his fellow-students, and mingling freely with all the Baptist and other ministers who were then accustomed to be the frequent guests of his renowned preceptor, and who often preached in his pulpit as well as ate at his table—gave to this young man opportunities of improvement to which he had never been accustomed, and not unlikely were of quite as much benefit to him, by their direct and indirect influence, as the opportunities of study which he enjoyed. He entered soon on the vigorous study of Latin, and obtained a little knowledge of the Hebrew tongue, besides reviving and enlarging his acquaintance with the Greek of the New Testament. He also listened to the instructive lectures of Dr. Staughton on botany and other branches of natural science. He wrote essays and other compositions and sermons, and submitted them for criticism to his fellow-students and their teacher. Occasionally, too, he preached even in the great Sansom-street church edifice, which was then his especial admiration for its magnitude and unique construction. Gladly would we transfer to these pages his first admiring impressions of the house, the audience (which by a popular exaggeration, then as now by no means uncommon, he greatly over-estimated) rated at four thousand hearers *seated*, besides multitudes standing in the aisles and about the lobbies and doors of the edifice. It was then a time of revival in this church. The first Sabbath he spent there, he saw eleven baptized in the spacious font in the centre of that great theatre, which for that purpose especially he greatly admired. The next month fourteen were received by the same church.

No feature of the novelties now rushing on his attention seems to have more interested him than the Sabbath-schools, then very recently introduced. That in the Sansom-street church, where he soon became a teacher, embraced some four hundred pupils; held two sessions each Sabbath, which were begun with reading the Scriptures, accompanied often with brief familiar expositions, with exhortation and prayer, at the end of which all the children repeated in concert the Lord's prayer, Then they divided off into classes of fifteen or twenty each, having two teachers to every class, and pursued for an hour the method thought best for imbuing the young minds with religious knowledge. They were closed with some general remarks, or exercises of review, and with one or more appropriate hymns, in which all these young voices, as far as possible, were taught to unite. The deep interest which he soon came to take in these schools, his visits among the poor, the sick, the ignorant, to whom his connection with the children of his class introduced him, were all happily conducive to that eminent fitness which he early attained for performing an immense amount of successful and blessed labor of this kind in the West.

As he had been for years an ordained minister, and as his services were needed and welcomed in a somewhat wide circle in and around Philadelphia, he found not a little interruption to the regular course of his studies by such calls and diversions. At times he regretted this; but so much stronger was his love for evangelizing labors of all kinds than for mere book-learning, and so facile had the habits already required rendered the performance of these semi-pastoral or missionary labors that he very readily yielded himself to nearly every solicitation of this character; and almost every Sabbath, and not unfrequently considerable part of the week besides, he was exercising himself actively as a minister of Christ. Nor was this by any means a total loss. For by the various intercourse thus secured with all classes, he became a successful and rapid learner in the great field of the knowledge of mankind.

'Considering his own want of early scholastic advantages, it is interesting to notice the method he employed for supplying these deficiencies and overcoming the bad habits into which he had almost necessarily fallen. A letter of advice which he about this time wrote to a dear young friend whose early years had been passed somewhat as his own, but who had the pros-

pect now opening of becoming a public character, and needed
therefore to be improved in many respects in intellectual furniture and acquirements, develops, I doubt not, somewhat minutely some of the methods which he had found it necessary
to pursue in order to correct bad habits and elevate himself
to a worthier level of intellectual attainments. A few sentences of that letter will indicate its general character :

I am pleased with your improvement in writing, and hope you will
not be discouraged by any difficulties that may present. If you
intend to be a missionary, you must acquire the habit of pressing
through many difficulties to obtain important qualifications. I most
earnestly intreat you to spend at least half your time in reading
and writing. To facilitate your writing, it may be best for you to
make a little book and keep a diary of what is passing. But while
you are attending to writing, it is also indispensably necessary that
you should attend to *spelling*. I do not say it to criticise, nor must
you let it hurt your feelings, but your spelling is very bad. In
order to correct this, whenever you write, it is best you should have
a small dictionary lie before you, and look out every word whose
spelling you are not sure you know. You can easily find any word
in the dictionary by its alphabetical arrangement. You had better
also study the spelling-book, and regularly teach some child a lesson
in it every day, thus helping to fix what you learn more firmly in
your memory.

Then follow some directions for learning grammar without
much aid from teacher or books, of which a specimen in
orthography may suffice :

In writing, you must begin every sentence after a period with a
capital letter. Also the name of any person or place. So when
you have the letter *i* or *o* by itself, you must use capital letters.

Then follow a number of corrections of this friend's bad
spelling, or faulty use or neglect of capital letters. Thus
anxious did he show himself that others should be early imbued with the spirit of intellectual improvement, and should
be shown some of the first steps of the ladder, for which he
had been obliged to feel his way in the dark.

The presence of Mr. Rice in Philadelphia some part of the time while he was engaged in study, helped to keep his heart still warmly alive to missionary duties. At his instance, Mr. Peck was often sent forth to visit churches, associations, and missionary societies at their anniversaries, to fan the flame of holy zeal for the evangelization of the heathen. One of the earliest of these tours took him into Delaware to attend the Delaware Baptist Association. He describes its exercises, preachers, subjects, etc., and indicates pretty clearly the blighting influence of some of those hyper-calvinistic views among them, which eventually dwarfed to nothingness most of those churches. In these and like visits, and in the extensive facilities he had for associating with the ministers of that day, he came to know somewhat intimately a large portion of those who figured most conspicuously in that early period of our annals. To some of these he only briefly alludes, scarcely more than mentioning their names; others he very briefly characterizes, with a free and generous frankness, ever more ready to record their excellencies than to dwell on their defects. Others again he portrays more fully and minutely. Dr. Staughton and S. H. Cone—then a young man, and a still younger preacher, having left the stage and political life to preach the unsearchable riches of Christ—were his favorites as pulpit orators. He draws a life-like picture of their manners in the pulpit, and the effects which attended their most powerful and successful public appeals. A sermon of the latter, when on a visit to Philadelphia seeking some aid for the little church in Alexandria, to which he had just begun to minister, brought forth a collection of nearly two hundred dollars—a large sum for that day. "The greatest pulpit orator *of his age* I have ever heard, but appears humble and discovers no disposition to gain the applause of the people. His address most pleasing," etc.

Revs. John Williams of New York, Luther Rice, Daniel Sharp, of Boston, and H. G. Jones, of Roxborough, were his chosen counselors. The varied biblical learning of Dr. Staughton and Irah Chase, recently from Andover Seminary, he highly esteemed ; while with all his fellow-students above-named, as well as Welch, Murphy, H. Malcom, Ashton and Walker who joined them subsequently, he maintained a most fraternal union.

Near the close of July their studies were intermitted for a vacation of five or six weeks, most of which he spent in aiding his dear Brother Rice in getting out and distributing the annual missionary report of the Board ; and then in a kind of volunteer missionary tour in lower New Jersey, where he enjoyed very much the hospitality of Rev. Mr. Sheppard, of Salem, and some others. He preached abundantly in the counties of Salem, Cumberland, and Cape May, not only in the Baptist churches, but in destitute neighborhoods, and wherever the providence of God opened a door before him. He seems to have enjoyed this tour very much, and also to have been eminently welcome and useful. Wherever practicable he was, both privately and publicly, promoting the foreign mission spirit and effort.

Just about this time also, both his journals and letters indicate that he was much exercised in mind in regard to the path of his personal duty. The Foreign Mission Board, at their annual meeting in New York, had discussed but not decided the question of establishing a mission in the Missouri Territory. While all admitted the great desirableness of this step, the more considerate and cautious brethren deemed it the prerogative of the Convention (which would meet the next year), and not of the Board, to decide a question of so much magnitude. This conclusion necessarily deferred any definite action on the case of Messrs. Peck and Welch, who were quite willing at that time to have offered themselves to the Board for this Western mission. What should he do therefore ? Dr. Staughton and Mr. Rice advised that he should pursue his studies in Philadelphia until the next spring or summer. Dr. Sharp, with whom he then for the first time appears to have taken counsel, suggested his temporary employment by the Massachusetts Missionary Society, to travel and preach under their auspices in central and western **New**

York, and perhaps extend his labors to Ohio. Another plan
was for him to teach school again for the winter in Amenia,
which would have brought him into close proximity to his
dear family, from whom this long separation was most unwelcome. All agreed, it seems, that for the ultimate benefit
of his proposed devotement to the mission in the great West
the first of these plans was the most desirable, provided he
could secure the comfortable support meanwhile of his little
family. Generous friends, chiefly in Philadelphia and New
York city, made up a purse for this object; and thus his
way was cleared of impediments, and his heart leaped with
joy at thought of spending the winter in the very place of all
others most adapted to secure his personal improvement.
Somewhat more extensive plans of study were therefore
marked out for him and his destined associate, Welch, on
which he prepared to enter with vigor. Preliminary to this,
he spent a few weeks in a visit to his family. The joy of
returning to their embrace after an absence of five months or
more was great indeed. What added very much to his sacred
delight was the revival now progressing in Amenia, in which
many of his old friends and a remarkable proportion of the
dear pupils of his late school had personally shared. With
what holy joy he now returned to see the valley of dry bones,
which he had left so lifeless, quickened to blessed vitality;
with what religious fervor he preached, and prayed, and visited from house to house, is recorded in his journals and
letters of this period, and is still cherished in the grateful
recollections of some who then witnessed his joy and shared
his labors. In this visit he found it practicable to attend the
anniversaries of the Hartford and the Rensselaerville Associations, with both of which as a pastor he had been pleasantly
connected. In both of these bodies he watched with interest,
and in the latter especially he helped to promote and deepen
the missionary zeal of his late associates. With his family he
also visited Hudson, Catskill, and Durham, where troops of
old friends gathered around them with glowing affection.
Rev. Dr. Porter, of Catskill, opened his church to him, and he

6

there preached in behalf of his favorite theme—missions—
with decided success.   So he did also in Amenia, where he
not only took up a collection twice as large as usual, but also
formed a juvenile missionary society of nearly forty members,
a majority of them his former pupils.   To his father's house
in Litchfield, Ct., he also made a brief visit, and records his
thankfulness that his old Congregational brethren no longer
exhibited coldness to him on account of his change of ecclesiastical relations, but loved him as of yore.

Passing through New York city, both going and returning,
on this visit to his family, he spent several days, and as usual
preached to several of the churches with increased acceptance.
On reaching Philadelphia again (November 8), he found that
he had traveled by land and water eight hundred and twelve
miles, had preached twenty-seven times, seven of which were
for missionary collections.   Just about this time also, he
received from the indefatigable Rice a characteristic letter.
It should be remembered that he had left Philadelphia in
July, putting into the hands of Mr. Peck the work of sending
off the last half of the annual reports for that year.   The
Napoleon-like movements of Mr. Rice—over the mountains,
crossing and recrossing State lines, through Virginia, North
Carolina, Kentucky, and Tennessee, with a celerity which
nothing but the boldest zeal, and the most indomitable perseverance could have planned or executed—were well adapted
to kindle a similar spirit in those with whom he came in
closest contact; and they did not fail of this result on him to
whom these hurried lines were addressed.   To this letter
Mr. Peck promptly replied, giving to his honored friend all
the recent missionary intelligence.   Thus imparting and receiving impulse in the chosen work to which his life was
devoted, he was the better prepared to enter again upon his
course of studies.   The following plan he sketched for his
daily guidance through the winter; and he adhered to it when
unavoidable interruptions did not turn him aside.

Rise in the morning at six o'clock.   Engage in private prayer,
which I can well do, as my fellow-students will not have risen at

that hour. Then spend one hour in studying the sacred Scriptures, with the assistance of Henry, Gill, Scott, or some other judicious expositor. Commence and continue regular study till breakfast, reviewing the Greek grammar first. After breakfast pursue regular studies of the day, except the hours given to medical lectures. After dinner come the recitations, after which miscellaneous reading and writing till tea-time. The evenings—except two each week given to lectures on osteology — to be devoted to studying the classics, to writing, copying, etc., except some times an hour or two given to attending public worship. Then give the closing hour, till half-past ten, to such study of the Scriptures, as occupies the first hour of the morning. Regular daily studies were : Monday and Wednesday, Hebrew and Latin ; Tuesday and Thursday, Greek ; Friday, natural philosophy, use of the globes, astronomy, etc. ; Saturday, composition of sermons, lectures on theology, and systematic reading.

He also resolved to be economical of time, frugal in expense, temperate in diet, not over indulgent in sleep, nor to allow himself in idle, unprofitable talk, and sacredly to keep up secret communion with God.

Dr. Staughton, conceiving that his pupils, Welch and Peck, would be greatly benefited in their vocation as missionaries, by such improvement as a course of medical lectures would furnish, procured them tickets from the principal professors in the medical college ; and they gladly availed themselves of this additional means of generous culture. It may readily be understood that with such an amount of demand on them, taking full notes as they did of the lectures they listened to, their time would be literally crowded with engagements. Yet Mr. Peck preached on an average about three times a week the whole winter, visited the prisons, conversed with and preached to the prisoners, and made himself very useful among the poor and ignorant of that city. It is no marvel that under this system of overtasking, both body and mind began soon to falter ; and many are the mournful intimations spread on the pages of his private journal of the nature and amount of his sufferings—physical, mental, and religious. Not yet had he so fully learned, as he did subsequently, how certainly the

overdone frame and the mind strained beyond its healthful
tension are sure to spread over the whole soul the tinge of
depression, or the fitfulness of unwholesome exhilaration,
which, as it cannot be sustained, will alternate with stupidity
and gloom.   Affecting are the jottings down on successive
Sabbath mornings of his "stupidity, deadness, want of engagedness in the cause of Christ," when he should have had
time for repose, but was obliged, as he and others thought, to
preach repeatedly.   Can we wonder that he complains of a
heart so little attuned to the services on which he was required to enter ?   They who give to mind or body no rest,
when both by the great Sabbath law are allowed it, must
expect to receive in their own abused nature the due punishment of the violation of these wholesome ordinances.

To add to his embarrassments the health of one of his
children failed, his family needed comforts which he was
unable to supply them, the aid which had been proffered him
for their support partially failed, and the remainder came but
tardily, so that his mind for February and March was continually harassed with almost agonizing apprehensions in
regard to the welfare of those most dear to him.   His letters
to his family, and especially his diary from day to day, bore
conclusive and sad evidence of what he in this respect suffered.
At length, with the advice and consent of his kind preceptor,
Dr. Staughton, he made a little tour among the churches in
the vicinity of Philadelphia, where his gratuitous labors had
been so largely given, aided by his fellow-students, Welch and
Meredith.   At the home of the latter he addressed a cheerful
epistle to his wife ; and making known to the pastors and some
of the principal brethren, delicately as possible, his straitened
circumstances, they made up in small sums nearly sixty dollars, which proved to be a timely relief in this trying exigency.
He was busily engaged in this business when the time arrived
for the assembling of the triennial convention for missionary
purposes in May, 1817, to whose decisions he had looked
forward with such mingled fear and hope, as certain to have
a decisive bearing on all his future course.   He was, therefore

a deeply-interested spectator of what transpired on that momentous occasion; and as more than one generation has since passed away, it may be interesting to reproduce on these pages the more important portion of his condensed records of those transactions. The principal actors have all been removed, and their sayings and doings may without indelicacy be reviewed by us, with interest certainly, and perhaps with profit.

WEDNESDAY, *May* 7, 1817. The missionary convention assembled at Sansom street. Credentials were received from the delegates, and they took their seats. Rev. Dr. Furman was chosen President, and Rev. Daniel Sharp, Secretary—when further business was adjourned till to-morrow morning.

At evening, Rev. Dr. Baldwin preached the convention-sermon, from John iv. 35, 36. He contemplated, 1st, the fields of missionary labor; 2d, the qualifications of missionaries; 3d, the encouragements assured. His discourse was interesting, but wanting in animation.

Thursday, 8*th.* The convention heard the report of Brother Rice, their general agent. It was very interesting. Oh, how much does the zeal and activity of this devoted servant of the Redeemer reprove the slothfulness of others in this holy cause! Communications were ther read from our brethren in India, both from the Serampore missionaries and our own missionaries in Rangoon. A church has been formed at the latter place, and all things prosper. Were it not for some particular circumstances, I should think it my duty to devote my life to that region. The Board made a report in part, in which they express their desire that a Western mission be entered upon.

Friday, 9*th.* Heard the further communications from Burmah— a joint letter from Brethren Judson and Hough: their plan of missionary operations. They utter the Macedonian cry: "Come over and help us." They declare their intention never to give up the missionary cause. Committees were then appointed to investigate the minutes of the Board, and to prepare the business of the convention. The Board recommended some necessary alterations in the constitution so as to embrace home missions; also to provide for the education of missionaries.

Evening. A general prayer-meeting was held in Sansom street for the blessing of God on the convention and for the success of our efforts to spread the gospel.

Saturday, 10*th*—Heard the report of the committee to whom that part of the report of the Board concerning alterations in the constitution had been committed. Considered the recommendations in committee of the whole, and reached this result:

1. Incorporated with the foreign field certain portions of our own country under the denomination of a Domestic Mission. This secures the great object of a Western mission.

2. Directed the Board to raise a fund for the establishment of one or more classical and theological seminaries to educate missionaries and others.

This, also, I view as a most important object, nearly concerning the welfare of the mission. To qualify young men as missionaries is a preliminary to sending them out. All this business was conducted with the utmost love and harmony. Never did I see so eventful a period in the cause of religion as the present. Events of the utmost importance are depending on the developments of every hour. From first to last the hand of God is clearly seen. It is to be hoped that the present exertions will arouse every supine professor, and excite every latent principle of piety amongst the Baptists in our land.

Evening. Rev. Mr. Baptist, from Virginia, preached in Sansom street from 2 Timothy vi. 12. He is a popular young man, and in many respects an orator.

Monday, 12th. Convention still engaged in the consideration of the important business before them. Besides favorably confirming the recommendations of the committee of the whole, from Saturday's sitting, the subject of a more permanent agency in this country was considered. It is with no common emotions of delight that I have to mention the harmony and union which prevail in our councils.

Tuesday, 13th. After several important resolutions considered and adopted, the convention unanimously approved the doings of the Board for the three years past, censuring those individuals who have opposed and attempted to injure the mission. Next they took into consideration the subject of a mission to Africa; then heard the communication of two young men from Massachusetts (Coleman and Wheelock), who offer themselves to the Board. Their letters were very animating.

Received also a communication from New Orleans, setting forth the state of things in that region and the great, the pressing need of missionary labors. A Board for conducting the missions the next three years was then chosen.

Wednesday, 14th.—Convention continued its sessions both forenoon and afternoon. All things progressed with the utmost harmony. Much business of importance was transacted, which I trust will be of lasting benefit to the churches. It was an affecting time at the close. Dr. Baldwin made a short address, which awakened tender and tearful emotions in nearly all present. The one hundred and thirty-third Psalm was then sung, and the convention adjourned till the last Wednesday in April, 1820. It is probable that I shall never see these fathers and brethren any more in this world, but I hope to meet them in the next. Rev. Mr. Leonard preached in the evening from Luke xxiii. 42, 43.

Next day (the 15th) the Board commenced its important business. Evening, Rev. Mr. Bates preached from Malachi i. 11. Doctrine: The worship of the true God will prevail in all the earth. An interesting discourse.

Friday, 16th. The Board still in session. Messrs. Coleman and Wheelock were accepted, and appointed missionaries to Rangoon. The subject of a domestic mission in the Southwest was brought forward. A letter from Rev. Mr. Ronaldson, of New Orleans, was read, and an appointment given him with the provision of five hundred dollars per annum for his support.

The business relating to myself was then brought forward. [He had presented a written document, fully explaining his views and feelings, offering himself as a candidate for appointment in the Western mission.]

The business was not taken up in a manner quite satisfactory to me; and the views of the Board seemed rather discordant on the question, *What should the Domestic Mission embrace?* Some seemed to entertain the idea that it must only embrace an itinerant mission among destitute churches and such places as are already Christianized. The business was finally deferred till to-morrow.

This view of the case brought a heavy trial on my mind. Indeed I see no way to obtain my object in the mission, but either to engage as a mere itinerant for a limited time, or to go *exclusively* among the Indians. The first I do not think my duty under existing circumstances; the last does not seem expedient. What will be the result I know not. But I feel to trust in a gracious God who will do all things well.

Evening. Heard Rev. John Peck preach from Psalm xxx. 5. Retired to rest, but slept little, on account of the agitation of my mind and the painful suspense under which I labored with regard to the mission.

Saturday, 17th. This day, I suppose, will decide my future pros-

pects.   How solemn the thought that a few hours must decide not
only with respect to what I have been pursuing for two years past,
but what relates to my whole life in the future !   I feel a degree of
resignation to the hand of God in whatever he may please to appoint.
To *Him* will I commit the whole concern, believing that he will order
what is best for his kingdom and glory.   At ten o'clock met the
Board of Missions.   After some business of minor importance,
Brother Welch made his communication to the Board.   I made
some further explanations, and then we withdrew.   The decision is
now pending.   What will be the issue I know not.

Six o'clock.   The long agony is over.   The Board have accepted
Mr. Welch and myself as missionaries to the Missouri Territory
during our and their pleasure ; and have appropriated the sum of
one thousand dollars to defray our expenses in getting to St. Louis
and for the support of the mission.   In this I think I see the hand
of God most visibly.   From this moment I consider myself most
sacredly devoted to the mission.   O Lord, may I live and die in the
cause !

Lord's-day, 18*th*.   Attended worship in the morning at Sansom
street.   Rev. Daniel Sharp preached from Psalm cxix. 97 an excellent, eloquent, and appropriate discourse.   After sermon Brother
John Walker (a fellow-student) received ordination.   Dr. Staughton
asked the usual questions, and presented him the Bible.   Dr. Furman made the ordaining prayer, while all the ministers present imposed hands.   Dr. Baldwin gave an excellent and very affecting
fellowship with the right-hand, and Rev. John Williams gave the
charge to the candidate.   The exercises were solemn and impressive.

This day is one never to be forgotten.   My fellow-laborer Welch
and myself are to be solemnly set apart for the work of the mission.
The exercises are to commence at five o'clock.   It is a solemn
consideration.   I have now put my hand to the plow.   O Lord,
may I never turn back—never regret this step.   It is my desire
to live, to labor, to die as *a kind of pioneer* in advancing the gospel.
I feel the most heavenly joy when my heart is engaged in this work.

At the appointed hour in Sansom street Rev. Dr. Furman preached
an appropriate discourse from Acts xiii. 2 : "Separate me Saul and
Barnabas for the work whereunto I have called them."   Dr. Staughton called on Brother Welch and myself briefly to explain why we
desired to engage in this mission.   Dr. Baldwin offered the prayer.
Dr. Staughton gave the right-hand of fellowship with a most affecting address, in which he adverted to our residence in his family
Rev. Jesse Mercer gave the charge.   One expression in the charg'

deserves to be indelibly impressed on my heart. Speaking of the success which, under the blessing of God, he hoped would crown our labors, and enforcing the necessity of prudence in every respect, he added: *"A little imprudence may spoil the whole work."* The solemn exercises were closed by singing Rev. Saml. Pearce's favorite missionary hymn: "O'er the gloomy hills of darkness," etc., etc. After Dr. Staughton gave the right-hand of fellowship, all the min istering brethren gave us their hands and bade us God-speed. When I came to take the hand of my ever-valued and much-endeared friend, *Rice*, my heart well nigh failed. The thought rushed on my mind with peculiar force: "Soon we separate, perhaps never to meet in this world; but I hope we shall meet in heaven."

After the services closed, many of the dear flock of Sansom street came and took me by the hand, bidding me an affectionate farewell.

Two pages of his journal are here filled with a very appro-priate review of the months he had so pleasantly and profit-ably spent in Philadelphia, the kind friends who had there gathered around him, the obligations under which he was now laid to devote himself unreservedly to the great cause of evan-gelizing the destitute. A humble sense of his own conscious weakness, and his dependence on Divine grace mingles with his fervent gratitude to God and to his brethren for the privi-lege of being allowed thus to devote himself on the altar of duty. Then girding himself anew to the work before him, he seems doubly resolved that no efforts or sacrifices on his part shall be wanting to promote the cause to which his life is now consecrated.

CHAPTER VI.

Preparation and Journey to the West.

MR. PECK immediately hastened to his family that he might prepare them for the long and toilsome journey to the place of their destined residence and labors. He spent one night in New York city, hearing Dr. Baldwin preach in Fayette (now Oliver) street church, and another in New Haven, where he formed the acquaintance of Rev. Mr. Lines, pastor of the Baptist church, and of a young brother, Lindsley, a student in Yale College, a candidate for the Baptist ministry; and with unutterable emotions reached his father's house, and embraced his dear family after his long absence and their many trials. This was on the 22d of May. The next two months, besides the requisite arrangements for their journey, and the leave-taking of his and his wife's families and their many friends in the places where he had resided and the churches he had served, he performed a large amount of pioneer missionary work, of an agency kind, throughout a somewhat extensive region of Connecticut, Massachusetts, and eastern New York. He attended the anniversaries of the Shaftesbury and the Saratoga Associations, before both which bodies he was permitted to plead the cause of missions. He traveled during these few weeks by private conveyance or on foot seven or eight hundred miles; and in preaching, visiting, writing letters, and arranging for, and actually forming, auxiliary societies, he performed an almost incredible amount of labor, and apparently with gratifying success. He notices in his journal the kind courtesy of several Pedobaptist churches in New Haven, in Catskill and elsewhere, that opened their houses of worship for him cordially, and allowed him to plead the cause dearest to his heart before their people, and receive their willing offerings. In Troy, Albany, and Hudson also,

his labors were welcomed and blessed. In West Stock-
bridge he examined and baptized five candidates, among them
Nathaniel Colver, then a young man.

Indeed, were the names of all the loved and honored servants of God whom then he met with, and to whom no small
share of the fire of his own zeal was communicated, here
enumerated, the catalogue would be found to embrace a large
number who have worthily carried forward the work on which
he was then entering. Merely preparatory to his great life-
labor—as he regarded these services—it may reasonably be
doubted whether they were not directly and indirectly as
useful as any which he ever rendered. The holy zeal thus
enkindled in so many breasts, of both pastors and influential
members of churches, was indeed a quickening leaven, giving
greater vitality to their own affections and to all with whom
they came in contact; and by linking them in thought and
sympathy to the masses of the unevangelized at home and
in pagan lands, they experienced the benign influence of the
moral dignity of the missionary enterprise. On an average
he preached nearly one sermon a day (on some days not less
than four), and wrote and received twice as many important
letters on this great subject during this whole period. No
wonder he groaned out under this self-imposed burden, and
instead of recruiting for the great labor before him, as he
needed to, he was absolutely exhausting both his physical and
mental forces. The tender, heart-moving adieus which day
after day he was taking of dear and valued friends, with the
feeling in most instances that it was a final parting, was also
exhausting and depressing. To counterbalance these things,
he had only the invigorating influence of faith, but this was
all powerful.

Friday afternoon, 25th of July, see a little one-horse wagon
leaving the door of Asa Peck, in Litchfield, with its precious
freight—his only son and wife with their three little ones. They
had together read the closing part of the twentieth of Acts,
had knelt down and prayed together, and with such sad fare-
wells as were almost overwhelming, our brother with his

little family here set forth on their journey of more than twelve hundred miles, not expecting ever again to meet on earth. This was the external aspect of the scene. He who would look beneath the calm aspect of the surface might there discover a violent internal struggle.

This son, now leaving the parental mansion, is not a heedless young man, unacquainted with the depth and tenderness of emotions which swell a father's heart. He has for years been a father himself—has known the pain of parting with his own offspring. He can, therefore, and he does, more deeply and thoroughly than he thinks it wise at present to manifest, sympathize with the agonizing sensations which his feeble and decrepid father now evinces. That aged and infirm man has not the faith of his son, nor the heroic fortitude of his own wife. She, the tender-hearted mother, with a Christian heroism which her sex are so often enabled to exercise, rises above the weakness of woman and the fondness of a doting parent. Her lip quivers, but her heart is firm. There are tears in her eyes, but there is also a triumphant, exulting joy on her countenance as she says: "If the Lord hath need of him—only son as he is, and we are growing old—let His holy will be done! *He* gave, and though very precious to us was this his gift, yet, if there is a needs be for the sacrifice, God forbid that I should hinder his devotement to his Saviour and mine."

The father yielded to his own overmastering sensibilities; he groaned and wept aloud; and as the little wagon drove from the door, his loud outcries of grief were the last sounds which fell on the ears of the departing ones. Again and again had this grandsire plead that one of the children at least might be left to gladden his loneliness. It could not—must not be; and as all this now comes over the minds of these wayfarers, doubt not that they too are glad of the shelter of their covered vehicle; for they can give vent to the long pent-up emotions which perforce they have endeavored to restrain.

The religion of the great Cross-bearer is essentially a system of sacrifices; but it has also its compensations. The very next Lord's-day this aged pair wiped away their tears, and went up to the house of God to worship. They asked (as was then and is now common in parts of New England) an interest in the public prayers for themselves and the dear ones on their long journey who had just parted with them. And no doubt they felt even then, when all eyes and all kindly hearts were turned to the pew which Asa Peck and wife occupied, that they were privileged and honored in giving up such children to the service of the Lord. Nor were these children without their rich recompense. In many ways and forms, the bread which they cast upon the waters was found by them after many days multiplied an hundred-fold.

In no one aspect, scarcely, have the last forty years of our country's history shown a greater advancement than in the facilities for rapid and easy journeying from one remote point to another. Now it is very easy in three or four days to remove a family with all their substance from the Connecticut to the western banks of the Mississippi. Then it required as many months of time, with not a little of toil, exposure, and even peril. Will not the readers of this memoir very naturally desire a pretty full view of what were the actual experiences of this family in this their great transition, very little more than forty years since? And as very many of them are able to draw the favorable contrast, by their own recent experience of a journey over the same extent, will not their gratitude be awakened by the facilities, the comforts, the expedition now realized? Mr. Peck thus states the distances from one point to another, in the route then most frequented, in a letter to his wife, some months before their actual setting out: From Litchfield, Ct., to Philadelphia, two hundred miles; thence to Pittsburg, three hundred; to Wheeling, sixty; to Zanesville, fifty-five; to Chillicothe, seventy-two; to the crossing of the Ohio river, sixty-three; to Lexington, Ky., sixty-eight; to Louisville, seventy-three; to Vincennes, Ind., one hundred and twenty-two; through wilderness to Kaskaskia, one hundred and forty-five; to St. Louis, fifty-seven. Total, twelve hundred and fifteen.

7

For brevity's sake, pass over the journey to Philadelphia, which had now become familiar to him, and which occupied ten days, and the week which he spent in that city getting his final instructions from the Board, and introducing his wife and children to many of the families who, by previous acquaintance with him, had become most interested in their welfare. The subsequent itinerary, with such abridgment from the original journal as can be made without essentially marring its interest, had been faithfully prepared for insertion in this place ; but the publishers cannot allow its introduction here : it must find a less conspicuous place, in the appendix, or be left out entirely.

Nearly one month was occupied in passing from Philadelphia through the State of Pennsylvania over the Alleghany mountains, till on the 10th of September he passed into Ohio. Three weeks he journeyed in that State, and on the 23d of October recrossed the Ohio river into the State of Kentucky, where he met with his associate, Welch, and wife, and soon left in company with them, and on the 6th of November again crossed the Ohio river, into the then territory of Illinois, at Shawneetown. Here again some extracts are given from his journal.

THURSDAY, *October 6th.* Our arrival was late, and little could be learnt in regard to this wretchedly-appearing village. Here the glad tidings of salvation are but seldom heard. We are now properly on missionary ground, which from its location and destitute state must belong to our field.

This was, indeed, their first entrance into Illinois—then a territory—in which Mr. Peck and family were destined to spend the greater part of their long and useful lives. How full of morally sublime interest, now that we can look back upon the whole history, was this entrance on his field ! Not Cæsar and his legions crossing the Rubicon involved interests so vast and blessed, as the humble transit of that little covered wagon with its precious contents over the swollen flood of the beautiful Ohio on the evening of that dark November day. To the eye of sense how insignificant! But faith invests the scene and its results with new and hallowed attractions.

FRIDAY, *November 7th.* Weather cloudy, with some rain. We are now at the public house kept by Dr. H. Oldham, where we are lying an expense, waiting for a turn of weather in our favor. Gentlemen, lately from St. Louis and Kaskaskia, represent the roads for fifty miles as extremely bad; but, as every kind of carriage is passing, we apprehend no insuperable difficulty. O Lord, preserve us from harm!

Met with Mr. Paine, my brother-in-law, who has been waiting here for us nearly three weeks. He is designing to accompany us to St. Louis.

The waters in the Ohio are still rising rapidly. Should the banks become full, this village must be overflowed. Immense quantities of driftwood are floating down the river, rendering the crossing very difficult.

In the evening I preached, at the house where we lodge, to a goodly number of people, from Acts xiii. 26, last clause. A decent and solemn attention was given. Oh, that the word of salvation may be sent with power to the people of this village!

Saturday, *8th.* Through the whole night the rain has fallen in torrents, and continues to pour down. The river has risen the past night between two and three feet, with the certain prospect of overflowing the town, should it long continue to rise. What is to be done, I know not. In addition to the deep mud, hitherto our chief obstacle, we are now to encounter the swollen creeks and rivers, rendered, for some days at least, impassible. Still I am not disheartened. Divine Providence will open some way for our relief. Should a convenient boat come down the river, bound for St. Louis, I am inclined to think it will be best to send on my family by water.

Evening. The rain has continued unabated, and the river rises rapidly, threatening to deluge the town. Several times it has been overflowed and destroyed by water, but always in the spring. Never was it known to rise so high at this season of the year before. Back of the town, only one-half mile distant, the water has become so deep as to be impassible with our wagon. Just at sunset there was a breaking away of the clouds in the west, indicating fair weather to-morrow. But passing is impossible until the waters on our road are fallen. Here we are obliged to remain till the providence of God shall relieve us from our present perplexed condition.

I stepped into a grocery where were assembled a number of wild fellows, swearing and blaspheming at a most horrid rate. I have seen enough of Shawneetown to justify what is reported of it as a most abandoned place. There are some decent, clever families; but I have conversed with none who seem decidedly religious. To-morrow will show how the Sabbath is regarded. I never saw a place more destitute of religious instruction; and yet unless very prudent measures are pursued, little good can be expected to result.

Lord's-day, *9th.* At an early hour a boat came along, bound to St. Louis; and, leaving Brother Welch to conduct the religious services which had been announced, my family and I stepped on board it, compelled thereto by our necessity, as I thought, and took our leave of Shawneetown. The arrangement was that Brother Welch and wife should wait for the subsiding of the waters, and come on by land; and my Brother Paine should take on my horse and wagon, while my wife and little ones would be more comfortable in the little six-by-ten feet cabin of the keel-boat, which my family shared with the captain, having accommodations for cooking and eating in what they call the "midships" section of the boat. The captain, J. Nixon, appears very friendly, and is to carry me and my family to St. Louis for twenty-five dollars. The hands are young men, going into the Western country, and as yet conduct themselves with decent civility. Though a little crowded, we feel ourselves comfortable and happy. Down the Ohio we are pleasantly floating with the gentle current, while nothing opposes our course but a slight breeze from the west, which only renders our passage more agreeable. The banks present little diversity for a considerable distance except a few moderate hills on the Illinois side. The flat country back from the river is now overflowed. The day is given to devout meditation.

Evening. The sun has just set behind the woods of Illinois, exhibiting a most beautiful sight after so much bad weather. In a figure, I seem to see in it Jesus, the Sun of Righteousness, shining upon the last hours of the dying saint, whose hope is in the Redeemer, and whose glory then begins. With much pain I reflect on the necessity which seemed to demand of us such a use of the Lord's day. I can truly say: "How amiable are thy tabernacles, O Lord of hosts! My soul longeth, yea, even fainteth for the courts of the Lord. While traveling by land, it was not always practicable to have regular morning and evening worship. Now, in our little, retired cabin, we hope to regularly engage in this important and delightful service. Read Isaiah i. and united in prayer with my dear companion.

Monday, 10th. Weather delightfully pleasant. Some of the time the wind is in our favor. We ran with the current all the last night, and a little after sunrise found ourselves opposite the mouth of the Cumberland river. About noon we passed the mouth of the Tennessee. Soon after we stopped at Fort Massac, on the Illinois shore, seeking for boat-stores, but could obtain nothing but potatoes. Most of the way the banks are low on each side, and the country overflowed at the present high water. In some few places, however, the banks are bold, and the country back swells into gentle-rising grounds. Most of it is still in the state of nature, through which the wolf and bear roam and the timid deer frisks its light gambols.

We are happy in our situation, though destitute of many ordinary comforts. Confined in a small keel-boat, with few utensils for cooking, our fare coarse and, in the article of bread, scanty, yet we are far from complaining Ours is destined to be a life of privation, trial, and hardship. All this I anticipated before engaging in the missionary work. I now begin again to feel the same devotion to the cause, and the same willingness to be a sufferer, if that will advance the cause of the Son of God, which used to animate me.

Towards night the clouds gathered, and a storm seemed coming on. Our boat is heavily loaded, and the prospect induced our captain to put in shore, and lie for the night, under a hill on the Illinois side.

Tuesday, 11th. Last night proved rainy, with some wind, and much thunder and lightning. This morning the wind and rain keep us in harbor. My fears are not a little awakened for the comfort and safety of Brother and Sister Welch. They have to make their way overland; but if stormy weather continues, their journey must be extremely uncomfortable, even if the roads should be passable. Through the day the rain continued to fall copiously, and the wind blew so hard that we did not venture to proceed, Captain Nixon, who commands the boat, in the morning took his gun and went out for game. At dark he had not returned, which excited considerable uneasiness, lest some accident had befallen him. A short distance from where we are lying are the ruins of an old fort or encampment [Fort Wilkinson], where are the ruins of several houses which have been burned. Near by is a burying-ground, where are multitudes of graves. We were informed by a young man that it was a fortification, occupied in 1801, but evacuated on account of the sickly condition of the troops stationed there. Near sunset the rain ceased, and prospects of fine weather cheered

8.

Wednesday, 12*th*. Last night was the most dismal we have yet experienced. The wind began to rise in the evening, and continued to increase until it blew a gale. It was from the southwest, and from that quarter alone we were unsheltered. It was found necessary to moor both head and stern of our boat, which was done by fixing strong ropes to small trees and saplings, the yielding of which to the strain gave us some play. We were under fearful apprehension of breaking from these moorings, in which case our wreck on the shore or against some huge tree would be inevitable. Our skiff drifted from the boat, and we expected we would be stove or lost. These gloomy prospects, in the absence of the captain, whose skill was now so necessary, seemed fearfully depressing. Every countenance was covered with gloom. Yet even in the midst of all this I found comfort in the reflection that the winds and waves are under the Divine guidance; that even the smallest events occupy a special place under the economy of God's providence. Immediately after breakfast we agreed that assistance should be obtained from the only two families living within twelve miles, and that such of the hands as could be spared from the boat should go in search of the captain. I volunteered to go with one scouting-party, and spent most of the day searching the woods, but without success. Nor were the others more fortunate. One party, however, had the good luck to kill a deer, whose meat was a seasonable supply.

About four o'clock, afternoon, the captain arrived, quite worn-out with fatigue and hunger. Having lost his way yesterday while eagerly following a deer which he had shot, he wandered about among dismal swamps and ponds till night, when he was obliged to stop. In the morning he directed his course by the sun. After swimming one wide sheet of water, and wading through several others, he at length reached a path which enabled him to find his way out. Late in the afternoon the wind died away, promising us a still night. Thus after all our threatening discouragements we again have pleasant prospects, and are enabled to rear our Ebenezer. "*Hitherto hath the Lord helped us.*"

Thursday, 13*th*. The weather proves delightful—a little frosty and cold. Soon after sunrise the boat was on her way again, moving with all the velocity which the swollen current could give. The banks on each side are low, except some bluffs on the right or Illinois shore. Many places were overflowed by the high water. Now and then a solitary cottage gave variety to the scene. At eleven and a half o'clock the majestic Mississippi presented itself before us. The land on every side appeared too low to admit of much settlement. Opposite the mouth of the Ohio, on the Missouri shore, were a few houses and an encampment of soldiers. Got up our sail, after considerable delay, and were wafted about five miles up the river, and came to under the east shore.

Friday, 14*th*. Weather rainy. About sunrise the boat was under weigh again, proceeding up the Mississippi. Various methods are employed in propelling a boat against the current in these large rivers. When the wind is favorable the sail is used; but often we are obliged to creep along shore, and by the help of oars, or long poles, and sometimes by catching hold of bushes, the men are enabled to drag the boat along. In some cases, where the banks are sufficiently high, a rope of a hundred fathoms length is attached to the top of the mast, and men walking on the shore drag the boat after them. A little past noon the wind and rain obliged us to lie to, under the Missouri shore, where we spent the night.

Saturday, 15*th*. The day fair, the air cool, and all things favorable, for an early departure. We are now proceeding around the great bend which the Mississippi makes in this part of its course, and which is very accurately delineated on Mellish's new map of the United States. The flood-water of the Ohio sets far up the Mississippi, and neutralizes the current so as not much to impede our progress.

Lord's-day, 16*th*. Cloudy, cold, with wind from northeast, bringing some flakes of snow, or rather hail. None but those deprived of the privileges of the sanctuary can duly appreciate the blessed enjoyment of meeting with the people of God. David seems clearly to intimate this in the eighty-fourth psalm, where he envies even the swallow who, through the desertion of the altar-worship, nestled in the sacred place. This day, as the last Sabbath, must be spent on board the boat; but, oh, let a proper remembrance of it be impressed upon my heart! Enjoyed some freedom while engaged in secret devotion. Towards noon, the boat being near the Missouri shore, I went on shore at a small settlement. Here I found two families of Baptists, and from them obtained considerable information respecting religion on the west side of the river. There is a Baptist church about fifteen miles above, where a Mr. Edwards preaches to-day. Oh, that I were there to aid him in declaring the name of Jesus!

Monday, 17*th*. Called at a house on shore to inquire for provisions, and learned from the people that there is a great opening in this region for schools. My thoughts are much exercised on some systematic plan to be formed for planting and sustaining schools in all this country. How much wisdom is requisite to originate a judicious system promotive of the cause in which I am engaged!

Our progress up the river is slow and often retarded. We get forward not more than eight or ten miles a day. About two o'clock the boatman ran on a cleft of rocks, which threatened serious injury, but, through a merciful Providence, we at last got off safe. The land on each side of the river here assumes an aspect unlike that below. Moderate hills give a pleasing variety to the scenery, while the rugged rocks projecting from the banks remind the traveler of dear New England. We are now just below Ross point, where several Baptists reside.

Tuesday, 18th. Cloudy and cold. The ground is frozen in many places. Last evening we lay a little above Ross's Ferry. Called on Mr. Ross, a Baptist, and Mr. Edwards, a Baptist minister, in this region. Was agreeably surprised to learn that there were seven churches associated in this part of the territory of Missouri. Here is a vast field for labor, and the work is already commenced.

Wednesday, 19th. To-day we passed Cape Girardeau. At night, when the boat was moored, I went ashore to walk back to the Cape, which was thought to be only a mile and a half distant. It proved to be three miles. Walking there and back the same evening, the exertion was too much for my feeble frame. This overdoing, with a severe cold which I have recently taken, has thrown me into a fever, which now confines me, and threatens some severe sickness.

CHAPTER VII.

St. Louis—its condition forty years since.

DECEMBER 23D. A long blank here occurs in my journal. We arrived here December 1st. Near Cape Girardeau sickness seized me, and I have been unable to write. I am even now in a critical situation. My disorder threatens to be of a pulmonary character. Our trials are great, but we try to bear with patience. I have consulted a skilful medical man, and he advised me to put myself immediately under the care of some regular physician in the place for a thorough course of medicine.

The above entry bears marks of having been made when the writer was scarcely able to hold a pen, and wrote from a kind of forced necessity. It is followed by another blank in the journal almost as long. But we have now reached a point where it is possible to substitute the later "reminiscences" of Dr. Peck, recorded by his own hand, and prepared by him for the public eye, instead of the abstract of the journal which the editor had prepared. These recollections of St. Louis, which will occupy the present chapter, are prefaced by some account of his manner in reaching it, and they shall be presented entire.

On two occasions, and for the first time in the history of the Great River, steamboats had passed up to St. Louis and returned the preceding summer. The first steamboat that ascended the Mississippi above the mouth of the Ohio was the General Pike, commanded by Captain Jacob Reed, which reached St. Louis, August 2d, 1817. The second was the Constitution, commanded by Captain R. P. Guyard, which arrived October 2d, the same season. Captain G. was an Englishman, a professor of religion and member of a Baptist church before he left his native country. He was a man of great enterprise; had followed the seas, as commander, with success; and came up the Mississippi from New Orleans with a cargo for the then remote French village of St. Louis.

The keel-boat containing my family reached Cape Girardeau on the 19th of November, and passed on above a point of land where the "old town" was situated. Having letters to persons in the village, and supposing it not to be over two miles, I went down in the evening, following a trail that wound around the bluffs the distance, as I found on experiment, of nearly four miles. At the Cape, as the village was called, I was introduced to Hon. Richard Thomas, afterwards a judge of the circuit court in that district, and several other gentlemen, and learned many facts about that part of Missouri.

Being under the necessity of lodging on the boat, as we started at the first appearance of daylight, I walked rapidly, became fatigued, took a severe cold, and next day found myself too ill to leave the cabin. We were ill-provided with medicine, no physicians of course to be had, and suffering under a severe fever, while the boat by the hard labor of the hands made about ten miles daily against the strong current. I heard from the captain about the "grand tower," the "devil's bake-oven," the "boatman's tea-table," and other singular formations, as we passed, but could not see them. It was somewhere above these places that a large sycamore had fallen from the Missouri shore into the current, and stretched its long arms into the river and down the stream. Around this the boat had to pass against the foaming, rushing current. All the hands were on shore tugging with all their force at the cordelle. I could hear the water rush up the side of the boat where I lay, and knew there must be danger, for the captain at the highest pitch of voice was calling to the men, and, sailor-like, swore profanely, which he never did in my hearing before or since. In a few moments the noise of the rushing waters and the cry of the captain ceased. He entered the little cabin, pale, ghastly, and in a tremor though he had the character of a brave and fearless man. Soon as he could gain the power of utterance, he replied to our inquiry, "What's the matter?"—"You have had a perilous escape. Had the cordelle broke, or the men not exerted themselves to the utmost, the boat would have been in the bottom of the river, and no power on earth could save you." Aided by the captain, I crawled out of the cabin to survey the perils of the Mississippi. The boat lay safely moored to the shore in an eddy, above the body of the tree. Around its top and among its huge limbs the water was rushing furiously, and it really seemed marvelous that we escaped. I resolve all such deliverances by a firm belief in that particular Providence whose ceaseless energy is constantly employed in the sustenation and preservation of all his creatures. How heathenish and unphilosophical is it for men of scientific attainments to talk, write, and lecture about the "Laws of Nature," as though the infinite and all-creating God had made a universe, containing some of his own essential attributes—a sort of machine that, when once put in motion, can move itself by its own imaginary "laws."

I recollect only one more incident on our voyage, for I was too sick to make entries in my journal. At the mouth of the Platin creek, a few miles below Herculaneum, is a flat rock extending some distance under the river. Here so strong a current rushed along shore that the hands could not pull the boat with the cordelle, and it fell back below two or three times. At last the cordelle parted, and the boat fell below the current, being kept in shore by the captain at the steering-oar. The aid of some men being obtained, the hands succeeded in getting the boat to a safe landing.

As the keel boat, with the "last of the boatmen," has passed away, with other conveniences and appendages of pioneer life, in this "age of steam," many of our readers will not understand the nature and mode of working this craft without further description.

A keel-boat in shape very nearly resembled a canal boat, but with a gunwale on each side twelve or fifteen inches in width. Besides hoisting a sail in a favorable wind, especially when going down stream, there were three modes of propelling a keel-boat in passing up stream. These were the use of the cordelle, the setting-pole, and occasionally bushwhacking.

Except in crossing a river, when oars were used, the boat had to creep along shore. The *cordelle* (French for little rope) was a long rope fastened to the bow of the boat, and drawn over the shoulders of the men, who walked in a stooping position along the shore. The setting-pole was ten or twelve feet long, the lower end shod with iron, and the upper end terminating in a knob, which was pressed against the shoulder. In using this where the water was of sufficient depth, the men placed themselves on the narrow gunwale, with their faces toward the stern, their heads bent low, and as the boat moved ahead they walked toward the stern. The one in front would turn about, pass the others, and take his station in the rear. When the hands on the gunwale dropped their setting-poles, and caught the limbs and brush along shore, and thus dragged the boat ahead, it was called "bushwhacking." A long, heavy oar, with a wide blade, was attached to the stern, and moved on a pivot, which the captain or pilot managed while standing on the roof, or, in boatman slang, the deck.

It was early in the morning of the first of December we found ourselves lying about at the foot of Elm street. Rev. Mr. Welch, and wife, my colleague, my brother-in-law, with our horses, had reached this place a week previous, and had made some acquaintances in the village. I was still sick, with a low intermittent. He had procured for my family a shelter—a single room at the corner of Myrtle and Main streets. It was the only tenement that could be found in the village, and had just been vacated by the now venerable Matthew Kerr and his partner Mr. Bell, as a counting-room. There I lay confined with illness two months. For three weeks I had no physician, knowing that such a remote village would be the point to which incompetent persons might resort, and attempt to act the doctor. The late Dr. Young, who came from Kentucky, and planted himself in the present county of Warren, and located Marthasville, came to St. Louis. Mr. Welch, who knew him personally in Kentucky, as a regularly educated physician, brought him to my house. He recommended immediate application to Farrar and Walker, then practicing physicians of skill and fidelity; and Dr. Walker attended daily, and Dr. Farrar occasionally, until I was restored.

At the commencement of 1818, St. Louis was crowded with inhabitants, including families temporarily residing there for the winter. Every house and room that could shelter persons was occupied. There was no regular hotel, nor were there even boarding-houses, that afforded nightly accommodation. Alexandre Bellissame kept a French tavern at the corner of Second and Myrtle streets, where farmers from the country found food and shelter for themselves and horses. The storekeepers, most of whom were without families, in many instances, kept "bachelor's hall" in their counting-rooms, and cooked their own meals. "Shin-plaster" currency abounded. The bills were the droppings of the first generation of banks instituted in the far West without any adequate specie basis. Their leaves were scattered over the frontiers like the leaves of the trees by an autumnal frost, and the price of every article of necessity (for articles of luxury were not thought of) was high in proportion.

This bore heavily on us as missionaries, under sacred obligations to use an economy bordering on parsimony, in all our expenses. It was "California times" for families to live in St. Louis in those days. The houses, shops, and stores were all small. Many only one story, and limited to two or three small rooms, were thought to be quite commodious. For the single room my family occupied for nine months, we paid twelve dollars per month. Mr. Welch engaged a room in the rear of a store, for school purposes, about fourteen by sixteen feet, for fourteen dollars per month. Eatables were not easily obtained, and only at extravagant prices. Butter was from thirty-seven to fifty cents per pound, sugar from thirty to forty cents, coffee from sixty-two to seventy-five. Flour of an inferior quality cost about twelve dollars per barrel. Corn in the ear, for horse-feed, from one dollar to one dollar and twenty-five cents per bushel. Pork, raised on the range, was regarded a cheap article at six to eight dollars per hundred pounds. Chickens sold readily for thirty-seven cents each, and eggs from thirty-seven to fifty cents the dozen.

Oppressive as were the prices of every article of living in St. Louis at the commencement of 1818, and inconvenient as were our accommodations, the morals and religion of the place were the most likely to awaken our attention and call forth our sympathies.

It is here expedient to draw an accurate picture of St. Louis as it appeared to the writer, during a few months of his early acquaintance, in the beginning of 1818. There was a class of gentlemen of the bar, the medical profession, merchants, and officers in civil and military authority, Indian traders, etc., whose character and behavior, for men of the world, and destitute of any strong religious principles, were not gross, but respectable. They played cards for amusement, and of course bet liberally. They had social "sprees" occasionally, and indulged in habits of conviviality. Yet they exhibited some noble qualities, were generous and liberal, and governed by principles of honor. Some of these men in 1831, and at subsequent periods, made a profession of true religion, joined a Christian church, and lived and died as Christian men should do. Some, with hoary heads and feeling the infirmities of age still live, and are honored, respected, and beloved by all who know them.

We would delight in giving the impressions, as among our most vivid reminiscences, made on our mind from the casual social intercourse, without any attempt at intimacy, with many whose names and peculiar traits of character come within memory's vision. But the field is too large, and propriety and delicacy forbid saying any thing. Of the law profession there was the late Judge Carr (Wm. C.), Edward Bates—still among us in the vigor of his profession—David Barton, his brother Joshua, who was killed in a duel by one of the rectors in 1823. This victim was an intelligent man, of a sprightly mind, and possessed many amiable qualities, but fell a sacrifice to the barbarous and unchristian practice of dueling. There had been several duels within a year; and I gave out an appointment to preach on the subject at my next monthly visit to St. Louis, with

8

the resolution that I would not spare. In the interval of time, two more duels had taken place. One had proved mortal to one of the party, from a shot through the abdomen; while his antagonist, who escaped without a wound, took a severe attack of fever, caused, probably, by the preternatural excitement, and died within a week. My text was from Isaiah i. 15, last clause : "*Your hands are full of blood.*" The old Baptist church-house, which stood on the corner of Third and Market streets, was the place; and it was crowded by all classes, amongst whom I discovered the Hon. David Barton, then a Senator in Congress, whose lamented brother was one of the victims, and the late Rev. Samuel Mitchell, whose eldest son was another. I had taken the precaution to write out every word of my discourse. I did my utmost to hold up the practice of dueling to the abhorrence of all right-minded men, as a crime of no small magnitude against God, against man, against society.

The discourse made a little "town-talk" in the village, and I received the thanks and approbation of many citizens. I made no personal reflections, but portrayed to the best of my ability the disastrous effects of dueling on the social relations, and the folly of obtaining satisfaction for injuries in such a mode.

But I have wandered ahead, and perhaps anticipated events that belong to a future period of these reminiscences, and must now take the "back-track." And what shall I say of Robert Wash, afterwards on the Supreme Bench of the State; of Judge Tucker, who lived in a log cabin, and had his law office in a hollow sycamore, a few miles east of Florissant; of a Mr. Cozzens (his first name forgotten), who was assassinated in 1826; of James H. Peck, afterwards district judge of the United States court; and of many others, whose names for the moment have escaped my memory.

The Hon. Henry S. Geyer, now (1856) in the United States Senate, I thought was the keenest for wit and sarcasm, and the most biting satire, of any lawyer I had ever heard before a jury. The distinguished ex-Senator of "thirty years" T. H. Benton, who, whatever his political friends or enemies may think, has certainly made broad and deep lines in the political history of this nation, was at the bar in St. Louis at the period alluded to; but it so happened, I never heard him make a regular address to either court or jury.

Of the physicians, I have already mentioned Doctors Farrar and Walker, both kind-hearted, respectable, and highly-respected physicians. Dr. Walker died early with the bilious fever—that common and fatal disease that carried off so many vigorous young men every summer for several years. Dr. Farrar lived to an advanced period, highly respected, and died some half dozen years since. Dr. Simpson and Quarles kept a druggist shop and also practiced. Dr. S. is known to many as a kind-hearted and good-natured old man, past threescore and ten, and may be found regularly by his old acquaintances in the counting-room of the Republican office about nine o'clock, A.M. Then there was Dr. Garuiort, who had a respectable line of practice, and the venerable Dr. Saugrain, who lived on Second street, low down, and kept a neat garden. He had the confidence of the French families, as a physician, and I think was something of a naturalist and botanist in his pursuits.

There was another class in St. Louis at the period of these reminiscences that merit only that sort of notice which will place in wide and vivid contrast the advances in morals and social order by the American and French population. One-half, at least, of the Anglo-American population were infidels of a low and indecent grade, and utterly worthless for any useful purposes of society. Of the class I allude to, I cannot recollect an individual who was reclaimed, or became a respectable citizen. The reader will keep in mind that at that period there were no foreign emigrants from their native country among us.

This class despised and villified religion in every form, were vulgarly profane, even to the worst forms of blasphemy, and poured out scoffings and contempt on the few Christians in the village. Their nightly orgies were scenes of drunkenness and profane revelry. Among the frantic rites observed were the mock celebration of the Lord's Supper, and burning the Bible. The last ceremony consisted in raking a place in the hot coals of a wood fire, and burying therein the book of God with shoutings, prayers, and songs.

The boast was often made that the Sabbath never had crossed, and never should cross the Mississippi. The portion of the Anglo-American population who had been trained to religious habits in early life, and manifested some respect for the forms of worship, were kept away from the place of worship by an influence of which perhaps they were not fully conscious. Though the profane ribaldry of the class already noticed did not convince their judgments of the fallacy of all religion, it affected their feelings and pride of character. But there was another class whose influence was far more effective, because it carried with it a degree of courtesy, respectability, and intelligence. I refer to the better-informed French population. These constituted at least one-third of the families. They were nominally Roman Catholics, and their wives, sisters, and daughters adhered to the Catholic faith, attended mass, and went to con-

fession regularly. The men attended church on festival occasions.
But every Frenchman, with whom I formed an acquaintance, of
any intelligence and influence, was of the school of French liberal-
ists—an infidel to all Bible Christianity. But they would treat
Christian people, and even Protestant ministers of the gospel, with
courtesy and respect. Romanism was the religion of their fathers,
but the casual correspondence held with France, where infidelity was
demolishing the thrones of political and religious despotism, and
tearing up the foundations of superstition, led them to regard all
religion as priestcraft, necessary perhaps for the ignorant, super-
stitious, and vicious, but wholly unnecessary for a gentleman—a
philosopher.

The good-natured jokes and *badinage* of their French acquaintances, and the bitter taunts of the profane and drunken scoffers,
made it unpopular and unfashionable to be seen on the way to
church on Sunday, except on special occasions.

The Sabbath was a day of hilarity, as in all Catholic countries.
Mass was attended in the morning by females and illiterate French-
men ; and in the afternoon, both French and Americans assembled
at each other's houses in parties for social amusement. Dances,
billiards, cards, and other sports, made the pastime. Four billiard-
rooms were open throughout the week, but on the Sabbath each
was crowded with visitors and gamblers. With few exceptions, the
stores and groceries were open on that day, and in some of them
more trading was done then than on any other day in the week.
The carts and wagons from the country came to market, and sold
their provisions at retail through the village.

Another source of irreligion may be traced to officers in the
United States Army, who, with few exceptions, were irreligious them-
selves, having vague notions of a future state, with some crude
Universalian notions as the basis of their own prospects.

There was one family connection in St. Louis, the head of which
was a prominent officer of Government, and who had an influence
over many young men in his official relation. The influence of this
family in demoralization was by no means small. And when we
say family, let no one associate the idea of mother, wife, or sister ;
for females were not their associates, except an abandoned class.
It is a singular, but Providential retribution, that not one of the
name is now to be found on the city register. All the old ones
have gone to their graves and been forgotten ; and if any of the
younger branches are left, they must be sought for in other States.

It is here proper to allude to the great changes since wrought—

partly by the immigration of Christian professors from older States, and partly, to the power and grace of God, by individual conversion. Leaving out the Germans and Irish of foreign birth, there are now as great a proportion of pious Christian church-members and of church-going people, in the ratio of the whole population, as in Philadelphia, New York, or any other large commercial city in our country.

The Rev. Salmon Giddings was the pioneer missionary in St. Louis, and the first minister of the gospel who preached there in view of a permanent location. Baptists and Methodists, though scattered throughout the country, had never preached the gospel in this town. Messrs. Mills and Smith, as evangelical explorers, visited and preached in St. Louis in November, 1814. The late Rev. Dr. Blackburn, of Tennessee, made a visit to this remote village the preceding summer, and preached to an audience respectable for numbers. *This was the first gospel sermon ever preached in the town*, for I never call the addresses of Romanists gospel preaching.

The labors of Mr. Giddings for eighteen months were wholly itinerant, in which he visited most of the villages and settlements on both sides of the Mississippi. One object of these labors kept in view was to search out persons who had been members of Presbyterian churches, and, as wandering sheep, to gather them into the fold. The first church he gathered was in Bellevue settlement, Washington county, about ten miles south of Potosi. There a colony of Presbyterians had settled. This was on the 2d of August, 1816. It was the first Presbyterian congregation ever gathered west of the Great River, and consisted of thirty communicants The next was the church in Bonhomme, thirty miles west of St. Louis, and included sixteen communicants. The third was the First Presbyterian church in St. Louis, of ten members, formed in November, 1817, to which he ministered as stated supply and pastor till his death. He did not confine his labors wholly to the town, but continued to itinerate, occasionally visiting the villages and settlements. For four years he supplied the church in St. Louis onehalf the Sabbaths, and during ten years he gathered five churches in Missouri and six in Illinois. He was one of the most quiet, patient, plodding, self-denying and faithful missionaries.the Presbyterians, or Congregationalists, ever sent into this country.

In addition to the obstacles to the propagation of a pure Christianity found in the laxity of morals, want of reverence for the Sabbath, and disinclination to regular attendance on a preached gospel, there is another class which should be noticed. I refer to the colored people, both free and bond. The number of free blacks and mulattoes was small in comparison to the whole population. Of these, two persons, the late J. B. Meachum and his first wife, were Baptists, and truly religious. Of the rest, some were more moral than others; but all alike were without religious instruction. The Sabbath to them was a relief from toil. There was an open space, of a square or more, between Main and Second streets, and not far probably from Green street. Here the negroes were accustomed to assemble in the pleasant afternoons of the Sabbath, dance, drink, and fight, quite to the annoyance of all seriously-disposed persons.

On the 11th of April, 1818, we had an introduction to the late William Clark, Governor of the Territory, who had been absent at Washington city during the winter. We had letters of introduction from distinguished citizens of Kentucky. The moral condition of the negroes was one topic of conversation, and the best mode of instruction. The governor, alluding to the scenes of dancing, riot, drunkenness, and fighting on the Sabbath, already referred to, stated that the preceding summer he had to call out a military company three times to suppress riots amongst this class. The character of negroes in general is a tolerably correct index to that of the white population among whom they reside. They are characteristic for imitation, and are quick in catching the living manners, and quite successful in cultivating the low vices of their superiors. Such was the condition of the negroes, which prompted us as missionaries to make an effort to reclaim them through religious instruction.

The persons who gave evidence of true piety in St. Louis at that period can be easily enumerated. Of Presbyterians of the General Assembly, we have already mentioned ten as united in covenant-relation in the First Presbyterian church. The most prominent and influential of these were the Hempstead family. The venerable patriarch and his wife lived five miles north of the town on the farm where the beautiful cemetery called Bellefontaine is now situated.

He was eminently a religious man, while by untiring industry, a commendable economy, and strict integrity in business, he acquired property. His eldest son, Edward, was educated for the bar, and possessed talents of a high order. He came to Missouri soon after the treaty of cession, probably as early as 1806 or 1807. Three other brothers came soon after. In 1811, the father with his family arrived.

Mr. Hempstead was active in correspondence with clergymen and others in the Eastern States to obtain a Protestant minister. He obtained a box of Bibles from the Connecticut Bible Society, rode over the country, visited the families and supplied them with copies ot the Word of God. Previous to that effort, in 1814, no Bibles could be obtained on this remote frontier. The only chance for a family to obtain a copy was to send by some friend or neighbor, who was about to journey to the old States, to purchase them a Bible and bring it in the saddle-bags. During the period of his residence in the country, he was active in "works of faith and labors of love;" sought out and administered to the sick, the poor, and the friendless, and prayed with the bereaved and distressed. He was ordained the first ruling elder in the Presbyterian church, and became a prominent pillar therein.

The most prominent Baptist in St. Louis was *John Jacoby*, who carried on the business of a saddler and harness-maker. Mr. Jacoby was a native of Virginia, born in 1781, but his parents migrated to Kentucky when he was a small child, where at an early age he left his father, and was bound to a trade. After serving out his apprenticeship, with honor to himself and fidelity to his master, he commenced business, and, in 1806, married Miss Jane Starks. He was exemplary in morals, but remained a stranger to the power and consolation of the gospel till 1810, when the death of his two eldest children became such an admonition of Providence as led him and his wife to the Saviour of sinners, and to hope in his mercy. This was in October, 1811. The next April he and his wife were baptized, and joined the Little Huston church in Bourbon county. He emigrated to St. Louis in the autumn of 1816, and commenced business under flattering prospects. His character for industry, sobriety, and unwavering integrity in business, soon gained him the confidence and esteem of the citizens. He became one of the constituents of the Baptist church; was soon after elected deacon, and took a deep and active interest in all its affairs.

In the autumn of 1820, he gave possession of his position to Mr. Thornton Grimsley, whom he raised, and removed his family to St. Charles. He died of a malignant bilious fever on the 15th of September, 1822, aged forty-one years.

By his death the church in St. Louis lost one of its main pillars, society one of its brightest ornaments, the cause of truth and justice one of its firm supporters, the poor and afflicted a sympathizing friend, his surviving widow a tender and affectionate husband, and his children a worthy parent.

At the period of our arrival, there were two young men from Ireland who were Methodists. They are still living, and well-known to the citizens as the Messrs. W. and J. Finney. In the spring, two others came and remained for a time. In June, 1818, the late Bishop

McKendree made a transient visit and preached once in a building used as a court-room. The circuit preachers made several efforts to organize a class and bring St. Louis within the circuit, but without success. Without a room in which to hold meetings, and weekly ministrations, nothing effective could be done.

There was a Cumberland Presbyterian preacher and family who resided in the place and kept a small store. His name was Green P. Rice. He preached in our congregation and that of Rev. Mr. Giddings whenever he could get an opening. He appeared to be a good man, with promising talents, especially as an exhorter, and was very desirous of establishing a church of his own sect on what he considered very liberal principles of union. His doctrines would compare well with what I have occasionally heard from Baptists whose heads were muddy by a mixture of metaphysics with Bible truths. He spent some time in each sermon to show and prove that God had done all he could to save *sinners*, and, *ergo*, if they were not saved, the Lord was not to be blamed. The fair implication of such notions is that if God had not done all he could to save sinners, he would have been the guilty one, and they, poor innocent creatures, would have suffered wrongfully. To such presumptuous nonsense and blasphemy are men driven by their vain efforts to *reason* about matters of faith.

Mr. Rice left St. Louis for Edwardsville the next autumn. At a subsequent period we heard of him as a lawyer and a politician in Alabama.

Rock Spring, Ill., *February 28th*, 1856.

CHAPTER VIII.

Early Evangelizing Efforts in the West—Recollections of towns in
Illinois and Missouri in 1818.

SOON as Mr. Peck had sufficiently recovered from the illness
which affected him on his arrival at St. Louis, he and his colleague, with their accustomed vigor and enterprise, set themselves
selves to work in various ways to accomplish the important
objects of their mission.   They rented a school-room, and
commenced teaching; while for want of better accommodations, they occupied the same room on the Sabbath and on
Wednesday evening for preaching.   In February, they constituted a small church.   In April, they baptized several candidates, for the first time, as they thought, using the Great
River for the solemn burial of believers with Christ, in the
ordinance sanctified by his example as well as his command.
Very soon they opened a subscription for building a church-
edifice, and were greatly cheered by obtaining on it nearly
three thousand dollars.   In June, they had purchased an eligible site and broken ground for the building.   Public exercises
appropriate to laying the corner-stone were duly attended.
Their day-school flourished; and not to be outdone by their
Catholic neighbors, they determined, in the lower department
of the school at least, to admit all who would come, whether
they could pay for tuition or not.   To enhance the interest and
value of their seminary, Mr. Peck commenced courses of popular lectures on topics of chief interest in elementary instruction, which were well attended, and were continued from week
to week for some time.   In the meantime, they opened a
Sunday-school for the instruction of colored children and
adults, and were soon cheered with finding nearly one hundred
names enrolled as pupils.   The Holy Spirit's blessed influence
was manifest in this school very graciously, and several were

hopefully converted. Most of these colored people were
slaves; and though the missionaries were careful to admit
none without the permission of their masters, yet when the
religious influence began to manifest itself among them, the
sons of Belial began to sound out the notes of remonstrance
and alarm, and some were withdrawn from the school. Their
success in other respects also awakened some denominational
and other hostility, which for a time considerably retarded
their progress.

They sedulously endeavored to unite all Protestant Christians in common endeavors for the advancement of the cause of
Christ. For this purpose the monthly missionary concert was
regularly attended as a union meeting, held alternately in
Rev. Mr. Giddings' school-room (which was also his preaching-
place) and their own. The Cumberland Presbyterians and
Methodists, when visiting St. Louis, were often accommodated
(as they had then no preaching-place) by the Baptist brethren
with the use of their own place of worship, even when they
would have preferred to occupy it themselves, so anxious were
they to present as unbroken a front as possible to the predominant Romanists.

Nor did they, by any means, confine their efforts to the place
of their residence. Nearly every Sabbath, and often on the
week-day, they would ride forth among the destitute settlements, and fulfill appointments for preaching which had
been made for them, sometimes quite at a distance from
St. Louis. Here is introduced the account of several tours
for evangelizing purposes, as given by Mr. Peck, from his own
journals.

As these reminiscences are not confined to Missouri, it is time
to pay a little attention to Illinois. Our first visit from St. Louis
to this territory was to the Badgley settlement, in St. Clair county,
on the 20th and 21st of June, to attend the meeting of Ogle's Creek
church. This was one of several little churches that had originated
from a general rupture among the churches on the western side of
this territory in 1810. At the period of our visit, there were three
parties of Baptists in Illinois that had about the same fraternal in

tercourse with each other as the Jews and Samaritans of the old time. Ostensibly the question of correspondence with slaveholding churches in Kentucky was the bone of contention; but the fact is there were a few impracticable men who aspired to be leaders, who had been quarrelsome from the beginning. We have the old records ·of half a dozen of these churches, which have been extinct for a long time, and these tell a monthly story of bickerings, "hurts," and complaints—imperfect as these records were kept. Among the singular and mischievous "rules" introduced, one was requiring a unanimous vote on all matters "touching fellowship." This was called "working by oneness." One selfish or headstrong man or woman could keep a little church in a state of turmoil for a twelve-month : an admirable method of keeping "the unity of the Spirit in the bond of peace." Allied to this was a rule of decorum which, whether written or unwritten, was always put in force by a class of preachers. Upon the opening of church-meeting, the first question was to inquire " if all were in peace." This, when practically trans-lated, always meant : "Now, brethren, think over your grievances and 'hurts,' and see if you can furnish any cause of complaint against a brother or sister." It is astonishing to notice what trifling things made these "hurts:" for this was the slang term to express their grievances. The most frivolous and insignificant charges would get into the church through this back-door. It is really Providential that not one of these litigious communities have had a permanent existence; but the effects of the spirit indulged and the habits formed remained a long time, to the grievance and an noyance of pure Christianity. We preached twice on this visit, and was kindly received.

Our next visit to Illinois was on business, but it was at the old town of Kaskaskia, and during the session of the convention, then organizing a State Government. I rode on horseback along the American Bottom, through the ancient village of Cahokia (or as called by the Jesuit missionaries, "*Notre Dame des Kahokias.*") Adjacent to it, on the south side of the creek that came in from the bluffs and gave its name, was the little hamlet of *Prairie du Pont.* The " Caoquias" and " Tamaroas" Indians occupied these villages when Charlevoix visited them in 1721. Here were located two ecclesiastics from the Seminary of Quebec, who had been stu-dents under Charlevoix. I followed the trace leading over the hills of Monroe county to the old " Whiteside station," where I called on the venerable widow and received her hospitality.

The Whiteside connection originated from Amherst county, Va., from whence they emigrated to Kentucky, and from thence to Illinois and Missouri. Colonel William Whiteside, who had died a year or two previous to my visit to his widow, though not a public speaker, was a leader among the early Baptists in Illinois. His name occurs as clerk in the church, and other meetings, for many years; and the neat plain hand he wrote, and the structure of his sentences, shows him to have been an able and useful clerk. He was also selected as a leader in the parties of defense, during the Indian assaults from 1786 to 1796. His house, with others attached, was a stockade-fort, and a protection to his neighbors for many years; and to this day, "Whiteside's Station" is a well-known locality in the north part of Monroe county.

An hour before sunset found me at the hospitable residence of James Leman, Sr. It was a sort of half-way house between St. Louis and Kaskaskia—a common stopping-place or house of "private entertainment" to all travelers. I had previously formed an interesting acquaintance with Rev. James Lemen, Jr., as he then wrote his name, and who was then in Kaskaskia, in the convention, engaged in framing a code of fundamental laws for the State. The old people who had emigrated from Western Virginia to the Illinois country in 1786, and were among the first converts ever baptized in this remote wilderness, did not seem to be burdened by age. They were hale and vigorous persons, perhaps a little over fifty years, and exhibited the marks of health and constitutional vigor. Two or three stalwart men, with large bone and muscle, six feet high, stood around. I learned they were two of the youngest sons, and one a son-in-law. The appearance of these persons, with that of others seen on this route, has any thing else than evidence of a sickly country. The men and women who were born here, and had grown to manhood on these prairies, had large, robust frames, healthy constitutions, and gave proof direct of health. What was it for them, if an occasional shake of the ague, or a touch of the autumn intermittent annoyed them for a few days? Since that period I have gathered statistics of those and hundreds of other families among the early American settlers that prove, past contradiction, that Illinois and Missouri, off the rivers and out of the low bottoms, are the healthiest regions within the United States.

Our conversation was chiefly religious. Elder Lemen was frank, open, very decided in his way; but kind, benevolent, and conscientious. He preached nearly every Sabbath, and often rode thirty or forty miles to visit destitute settlements. He and family, and many others who lived in this settlement, had their membership in Can tine (now Bethel) church, in the north part of St. Clair county. The distance was thirty-six miles, which they rode on horseback. The meetings were held on alternate months in Cantine, and New Design settlements, the first Saturday and Sabbath in each month; and for more than ten years, neither sickness, bad weather, much less indolence, prevented the regular attendance at the church-meetings, which never included less than two days at each meeting.

Old Mr. Lemen was a man of remarkable punctuality. Family-prayer was attended regularly, evening and morning. During his absence on his preaching excursions, or at any other time, his wife performed this duty. The two youngest sons, the able-bodied men already mentioned, were not then professors of religion. Another ——, but he had become wild and wayward, and was in an excluded state. As the customary hour drew near for family-worship, both parents requested the writer to pray for these sons, while tears and sobs expressed their strong, pious, parental feelings.

Next morning found me pursuing a lonely, but pleasant route, for sixteen miles, without a house, to the French village of Prairie du Rocher. This village was located about 1745, along the American bottom and a small, sluggish creek adjacent to an immense range on Cliff Rock, from whence its name. In 1766, it had fourteen families. It is a low, unhealthy situation, and about three miles to the southeast of the ruins of old Fort Chartres. One incident in this village deserves notice. The Jesuit missionaries were ordered home by their superior-general, from the Illinois country, about the time of its coming under the British Government in 1765. Father Meurain was the last, and he was ordered away, but at the urgent request of the Kaskaskia Indians he returned and became their father-confessor. He died at a very advanced age in Prairie du Rocher in the year 1778. He was a learned man, and left a valuable library and a manuscript dictionary of the Indian and French languages in twenty-four volumes.

Our business at Kaskaskia had no connection with government affairs, and we spent only one night. We called at the only hotel kept in the place, by Mr. Bennett, who subsequently became a pioneer in Galena. We had a slight acquaintance with him at St. Louis, but he regretted to inform me that he did not think it possible to accommodate me. Every room was occupied, and every bed had two or more lodgers. I laughed at his scruples, and told him I was a real missionary, and could camp on the floor with my saddle-bags for a pillow. At last it occurred to him that one of his beds had but one occupant that night, the fellow-lodger being absent. It

9

was a small room, and the bed, none too wide for two, was occupied by Adolphus Frederick Hubbard, Esq., one of the delegates from Gallatin county. Mr. H. had seen me in Shawneetown, and no sooner was my name announced to him by the landlord than he insisted I should share the hospitality of his bed. Being thus made comfortable, I learned from my room-mate something of the progress made in the construction of the new Government. There are a few incidents, gathered at a subsequent period, that may be admitted in these reminiscences.

In the formation of new States, from territorial possessions under the Government of the United States, but one uniform rule was observed in the pristine period of our national history. Congress, under the authority of the Constitution, exercised the entire powers of government. The first step after marking out the boundaries of a new territory was to endow the Governor and Judges with the authority to make a code of laws for the people. Soon as the governor saw the population and orderly habits of the people justified the measure, he made proclamation, and authorized the election of the House of Representatives. This body came together and nominated certain citizens—twice the number to which they were entitled—for a "council," or Senate. These names were sent to the President, who made a selection, and brought them before the House for confirmation. The House and the Council constituted the territorial Legislature. In this mode the territories of the Northwest, Indiana, Illinois, Mississippi, Orleans (now Louisiana), Upper Louisiana (afterward Missouri), and Arkansas, came into existence. Each of these territories became a State by virtue of a special charter from Congress; conventions were elected by qualified voters; a constitution adopted, and each was received as one of the States in union. Arkansas was an exception in forming a *State* government. The people, without law, formed a constitution in 1836. It was a period of the prevalence of a spurious democracy or rather anarchy, which sets at defiance all law, and claims what no person has any right, or can possess under a government of laws—that of *popular sovereignty*. No such fallacy exists, or can exist, wherever the boundaries and laws of a State, an organized territory, or the Constitution and laws of the United States exist.

But to return to Illinois. The territory had been divided into fifteen counties, which, according to population, sent thirty-two delegates. St. Clair county being the oldest and most populous sent three; Madison and Gallatin, being next in population, sent also three each.

Madison, Bond, and Crawford were the three northern counties across the State. All north was a wilderness, and one-half of the territory then was supposed to be uninhabitable. By a grant in the charter of 1787, of the Northwestern Territory, five States, within prescribed limits, could form constitutions and be admitted into the Union upon evidence of sixty thousand inhabitants; but on a special act of Congress the same district could form a State government on evidence of forty thousand population. Illinois, by its territorial legislature, the preceding winter petitioned Congress, and the charter was granted for forty thousand. Marshals were appointed in all the counties to take the census. As the period of their labors drew nigh, it became doubtful whether the requisite number could be obtained. The public roads leading across the territory were watched; families were found that were said to have been missed; and after every effort to make up the number, it was officially proclaimed that the requisite number, with some two or three hundred surplus, had been found. The emigration that season was large; and no doubt, before the constitution was submitted to Congress in December, some three or four thousand additions were made to the population.

Elias Kent Kane, Esq., of Kaskaskia, a man of superior talents, made the draft of the Constitution. Hon. Jesse B. Thomas, of Cahokia, St. Clair county, was the presiding officer. William C. Greenup, Esq., was Secretary to the body. In addition to Mr. Thomas, John Massinger, Esq., and James Leman, Jr., were the delegates from St. Clair county. The convention assembled at Kaskaskia in July, and closed their labors by signing the constitution they had framed, on the 26th day of August.

In the month of September, I made two excursions into the settlements south and southwest of St. Louis. The first originated in a misunderstanding of both the time and place of the meeting of the Bethel Association.

My first tour led me into the region about St. Michael, in what is now Madison county. I passed down the country, seeing only occasionally a log cabin, to Herculaneum, then a river town, landing, and a place of some importance. It then contained three or four stores and about thirty dwelling-houses. It was situated on the narrow, alluvial flat of the Joachim (called by the old settlers, *Swashen.*) The flat on which the village was laid off was narrow, and bounded at each end by perpendicular cliffs, rising two hundred feet high, and which formed cheap and natural towers for the manufacturing of shot. The Plattin was another stream that entered

the Mississippi a short distance below the Joachim. On these
streams were several water-mills and distilleries at that early period.
Herculaneum at that day, and for several years after, was the depot
for the lead trade of the interior.

A few miles north, and which we passed as we came down the
country, are sulphur springs, which at that period bid fair to become a watering-place when the country became settled.

My route lay in a southwesterly direction, towards the heads of
the Plattin, to McCormick's settlement. One object, never lost
sight of in my travels, was to examine into the condition of schools;
and I found at least three-fourths of all the masters and schools
were public nuisances, and ought to have been indicted by the
Grand Jury. Mr. McCormick, an old settler in this range, and regarded by all his neighbors as a sort of captain, to whom they
looked for guidance, though a backwoodsman, with very little school
education, had sound common-sense, and was determined to have
a good school for his large family and the children of his neighbors. He enlisted some of his friends in Herculaneum to send him
a "rale teacher," "none of those whisky-drinking Irishmen, such as
got into our settlement last year, or, sure as I'm a Methodist, we'll
lynch him!" So Mr. B., who knew "how the land lay" in that settlement, sent out a Mr. Bellknapp, just from Connecticut. Mr. B.
was an experienced teacher, and being a man of observation and
strong common-sense, he soon found out how to manage some
thirty or forty stalwart young men and women.

Introducing myself and my object to Master B., I was invited
into one of the most primitive school-houses then to be found in
the Territory of Missouri. I was pleased with the regulations, and
the pupils were evidently in favor of the teacher, and they were
making good progress under his instructions.

Leaving the school-house I called on Mr. McCormick, had my
horse fed, and took dinner. The only preaching in the scattered
settlements among the hills was by the Methodists. The country
for many miles was very hilly, and the road I traveled a mere bridle-
path—that is, a trail for a single horse. I could learn nothing of
any Baptist association. Night found me at a Mr. Hale's, who kept
a house of private entertainment on the wagon-road from Mine-au-
Burton to Ste. Genevieve. Mr. H. was a Methodist, and could tell
me of all the Methodist preachers and meetings in that part of the
territory, but knew nothing of Baptists. Finally he proposed to
give me directions in the morning to a Baptist family who lived a
few miles off the main road, which I could reach by traveling

through a "hurricane" of two or three miles in extent. Now let the reader know that a "hurricane" is a tract of timber over which a tornado has passed, crushing all the trees, and throwing them in every direction.

Next morning, ere the sun appeared, I was on my horse following a devious horse-trail over logs and through brushwood. About two years previous, large hickory, oaks, and other timber, two or three feet in diameter, had been twisted from the stump, often splintered for fifteen or twenty feet in height, and then thrown in every direction. The width in a direct line did not exceed one mile; but the pathway was so devious, and it was so difficult for the horse to jump over the fallen timber, that two hours time passed away before I gained the distance.

About nine o'clock I found the family to which I was directed. As this family was a specimen of the squatter race found on the extreme frontiers in early times, some specific description may amuse the reader, for I do not think a duplicate can now be found within the boundaries of Missouri. The single log-cabin, of the most primitive structure, was situated at some distance within the cornfield. In and around it were the patriarchal head and his wife, two married daughters and their husbands, with three or four little children, and a son and daughter grown up to manhood and womanhood. The old man said he could read but "mighty poorly." The old woman wanted a *hyme* book, but could not read one. The rest of this romantic household had no use for books or "any such trash." I had introduced myself as a Baptist preacher, traveling through the country preaching the gospel to the people. The old man and his wife were Baptists, at least had been members of some Baptist church when they lived "in the settlements." The "settlements" with this class in those days meant the back parts of Virginia and the Carolinas, and in some instances the older sections of Kentucky and Tennessee, where they had lived in their earlier days. But it was "a mighty poor chance" for Baptist preaching where they lived. The old man could tell me of a Baptist meeting he had been at on the St. Francois, and could direct me to Elder Farrar's residence near St. Michael. The old woman and the young folks had not seen a Baptist preacher since they had lived in the territory some eight or ten years. Occasionally they had been to a Methodist meeting. This was the condition of a numerous class of people then scattered over the frontier settlements of Missouri. The "traveling missionary" was received with all the hospitality the old people had the ability or knew how to exercise. The younger

class were shy and kept out of the cabin, and could not be persuaded to come in to hear the missionary read the Scriptures and
offer a prayer.   There was evidence of backwardness, or some other
propensity, attending all the domestic arrangements.   It was nine
o'clock when I reached the squatter's cabin, and yet no preparations had been made for breakfast.   The beds, such as they were,
remained in the same condition as when the lodgers first crawled
from their nests in the morning.   The young women appeared listless.   Their heads, faces, hands, clothing, all indicated slothfulness
and habitual neglect.   Soon the old woman made some preparations
for breakfast, and as the culinary operations were performed out
of doors, very probably the younger women assisted, but no other
female entered the cabin but the old lady.   In an hour's time her
arrangements within commenced.

Not a table, chair, or any article of furniture could be seen.
These deficiencies were common on the frontiers; for emigrations
from the "settlements" were often made on pack-horses, and no
domestic conveniences could be transported, except the most indispensable cooking-utensils, bedding, and a change or two of clothing.
But the head of the family must be shiftless indeed, and void of all
backwoods' skill and enterprise, who could not make a table for
family use.   There were two fashions of this necessary article in
the time to which I refer.   One was a slab, or "puncheon," as then
called, split from a large log, four feet long, and from fifteen to
eighteen inches wide, and hewn down to the thickness of a plank.
In this were inserted four legs, after the fashion of a stool or bench,
at the proper height.   The other was a rough frame, in which posts
were inserted for legs, and covered with split clapboards shaved
smooth, and fastened with small wooden pins.   We found one of
these descriptions of tables in hundreds of log cabins where neatness, tidiness, and industry prevailed.

Our landlady having nothing in the shape of a table, substituted
a box.   On this she spread a cloth that might have answered any
other purpose than a table-cloth.   The table furniture was various.
For knives, two or three hunting-knives answered.   The plates were
broken or melted pewter ones, except a single earthen one with a
notch broken out, which, with a broken fork, was placed for the
"stranger" to use.   We could readily have excused the kind old
lady for this extra trouble; for, being dim-sighted, in washing, or
more strictly in wiping it, she had left the print of her fingers on
the upper surface.

The viands now only need description to complete this accurate picture of real squatter life. The rancid bacon when boiled could have been detected by a fœtid atmosphere across the yard, had there been one. The snap-beans, as an accompaniment, were not half-boiled. The sour buttermilk taken from the churn, where the milk was kept throughout the whole season, as it came from the cow, was "no go." The article on which the traveler made a hearty breakfast, past ten o'clock in the morning, was the corn, boiled in fair water.

According to universal custom among the squatter race, the men eat first, the women followed, and, if the company were numerous, the youngsters and children followed in regular succession.

We give this portraiture as a fair specimen of hundreds of families we found scattered over the extreme frontier settlement in 1818–19.

Pursuing our route, we left appointments to preach on our return in Cook's settlement in the day-time, and in Murphy's settlement Sabbath night. And in passing from Cook's to Murphy's settlement, Sabbath afternoon, who should we meet but the identical family of squatters where we had taken breakfast, with an old wagon, a pair of steers, two old horses which the women and children rode, with their "plunder," moving to the southwest, on the waters of Big Black. The day I left, some newly-arrived immigrant came upon them, bought out their "crap" and claim for the old wagon and yoke of steers, and they were on their way to Big Black, where a few squatters and bear-hunters had commenced a new settlement.

On the 25th September, 1818, I set out on horseback the second time to find the Bethel Association. The route was the same one I last traveled until I got below Herculaneum, and then gradually bearing to the left and down the direction of the Mississippi, through an extensive tract of barrens very thinly settled. It was in passing through these barrens that Joseph Piggott, a Methodist circuit preacher, in the year 1820 came near freezing to death, in an extremely cold night, and without food for himself or his horse. He gave the writer a narrative of his sufferings that night, four years a'ter, at his residence on the Macoupin, Ill., and yet we were so hard-hearted as not to express a word of sympathy. A few stunted and gnarled trees, and a sprinkling of brushwood, with now and then a decayed log, appeared above the snow. He was nearly chilled, after wandering about a long time in search of a path; and with great difficulty, with his tinder-box, flint and steel, could he get a fire. He then scraped away what snow he could, and with his blanket lay down, *broadside to the fire;* but before he secured much warmth the other side was nearly frozen. Then he would turn over, but finding no relief, would get up, stamp his feet, while the wind seemed to pass through him. When daylight appeared, he was too cold to mount his horse, but led him while he attempted to find his way on to some lonely cabin which proved to be not many miles distant. There he spent the day and enjoyed the hospitality of the squatter family. We listened to the distressing tale with amazement! This man was born and raised in Illinois, and accustomed all his life to the frontiers, and yet had never learned one of the indispensable lessons of a backwoodsman—how to camp out, make a fire, and keep warm. Eating was not so very important; for any man in the vigor of life, in those days in this frontier country, who could not go without food for twenty-four hours, and more especially a preacher of the gospel, ought to be sent back, where he came from, to the kind care of his friends.

The writer had not been in the country one year before he had learned half a dozen lessons in frontier knowledge of great value in practical life. One branch was how Indians, hunters, surveyors, and all others who had to travel over uninhabited deserts, made their camping-place, and kept themselves comfortable. The first thing is to select the right place, in some hollow or ravine protected from the wind, and if possible behind some old forest giant which the storms of winter have prostrated. And then, reader, don't build your fire against the tree, for that is the place for your head and shoulders to lie, and around which the smoke and heated air may curl. Then don't be so childish as to lie on the wet, or cold frozen earth, without a bed. Gather a quantity of grass, leaves, and small brush, and after you have cleared away the snow, and provided for protection from the wet or cold earth, you may sleep comfortably. If you have a piece of jerked venison, and a bit of pone with a cup of water, you may make out a splendid supper, provided you *think* so; "for as a man thinketh, so is he." And if you have a traveling companion, you may have a social time of it. So now offer your prayers like a Christian, ask the Lord to protect you, wrap around you your blankets with your saddles for pillows, and lie down to sleep under the care of a watchful Providence. If it rains, a very little labor, with barks or even brush, with the tops sloping downward, will be no mean shelter. *Keep your feet straight to the fire,* but not near enough to burn your moccasins or boots, and your legs and whole body will be warm. The aphorism of the Italian physician, which he left in a sealed letter as a guide to all his former patients, when he was dead, contains excellent advice to all frontier people : *"Keep your feet warm, your back straight, and your head cool, and bid defiance to the doctors."*

I got about half-way through the tract of barrens between Her culaneum and Ste. Genevieve, and stopped at a small cabin, where I got such refreshment for "man and beast," and such lodging as its inmates could furnish. Before noon the next day I was passing through Ste. Genevieve.

As this was the first visit I made to this ancient town, I may as well give a brief sketch of its early history.

Ste. Genevieve is the oldest French village in Missouri. When Lalede and the Chouteans came from New Orleans to establish a trading-post at St. Louis, in 1763, they stopped at Ste. Genevieve, which contained about twelve or fifteen families, in as many small cabins, but finding no warehouse or other building in which they could store their goods, they went on to Fort Chartres and wintered. We date the commencement of Ste. Genevieve as a village from the period of the erection of Fort Chartres, the second, about 1756. Very probably there were previous to this, as there were in the lead-mining districts, what are. called in patois-French, *cabanes*, a term expressing the idea of "shanties," a cluster of shelters for temporary purposes. Such cabanes were in the lead-mining district when Philip Francis Renault had his exploring parties out at various points in the upper valley of the Mississippi. And, by the way, I find no evidence that lead-mining was followed in the mining-country after Renault, disappointed, and a "broken merchant," quit the business about 1740, until the possession of Illinois by the British about twenty-five years thereafter. Many of the French inhabitants who held slaves left the Illinois country ; some went to the newly-established town of St. Louis ; others to Lower Louisiana. Many families also went to the lead mines in Missouri, while others stopped at Ste. Genevieve and New Bourbon with their servants. This gave an impulse to the former town, which before 1770 became the depot and shipping-port for the lead business. The French at St. Louis, as a *nom-de-nique*, called Ste. Genevieve *Misere*, as they did Carondelet *Vide Poche :* and in their turn received the nick-name of *Pain Court*, to indicate they were short of bread.

The old town of which I am writing was near the Mississippi, and about one mile below the ferry and landing. From this point, where the rock forms a landing, for seven miles down the river, was an extensive tract of alluvial bottom about three miles in width. On this rich alluvion the French of Ste. Genevieve and New Bourbon made one of the largest "common fields" to be found along the

Upper Mississippi. It contained within the common inclosure from three thousand to four thousand acres. The repeated inundations of high water, and especially the great flood of 1784, drove the inhabitants to the high ground in the rear, where they built the old residences of the new town, or the existing Ste. Genevieve. Each successive flood tore away the rich bottom along the river, until that of 1844 about "used up" the great common field of the village. No passenger in passing up or down the great expansive bend of the river would hardly realize that the largest steamers now float in a channel that is more than two miles from the Mississippi river, as it ran in 1780.

Protestant Christianity has had but feeble influence in this ancient French village.

Having no time to tarry, we found our way by the Saline works (where General Henry S. Dodge was manufacturing salt in the barrens of Perry county, then known far and near as the name of this tract of country) to the house of Mr. Duvol, where we arrived Saturday evening after sunset. One day of the Association was over, and though an entire stranger, and excessively fatigued from our long ride, no excuse would be taken : we must preach : and preach we did, a missionary discourse, off-hand, from Isaiah xlix. 20. Here were two preachers from the Boone's Lick country, William Thorp, and Edward Turner, who were messengers of correspondence from the Mount Pleasant Association, then recently formed. They were among the earliest settlers in that far-out-of-the-way region. Thorp (we think) came there from Kentucky in 1810, and Turner soon after. Of course, they knew not a single fact about missions, nor any thing correctly of the progress of the kingdom of Christ on earth, or of its destiny. A set of crude and erroneous notions had been stereotyped in their minds, in Kentucky, about gospel doctrine and moral obligation, and they were fixedly resolved to learn nothing else. Having come from a new association to solicit correspondence, and perceiving the writer was received with great promptitude as a visitor, and invited to preach on the spot before the association, which held a night-session, they were not openly hostile. They only whispered about among a few of the brethren, and shook their heads doubtingly. For several successive years we met those brethren at associations, when they took a bolder and more decided stand against all organized efforts to publish the glad tidings to a sin-ruined world. They maintained that missions, Sunday-schools, Bible societies, and such-like facilities, were all men's contrivances, to take God's work out of his own hands. Their views of the plan of salvation through Christ were exceeding limited and imperfect, and their success was quite as limited as their Biblical knowledge was deficient.

The Bethel Association this year consisted of five churches and eight ordained ministers. The churches were Bethel, Tywappity, Providence, Barren, St. Francois, Dry creek and Salem. The last had been constituted on Fourche-a-Thomas, in Arkansas, and was the first church ever gathered in that region. It had two ministers (Benjamin Clark and Jesse James) and twelve members. Mr. James disappeared from the minutes in after years, as we suppose by death, but Mr. Clark lived and labored in that desolate region for many years with great self-denial, zeal, and success. In the early period of the Home Missionary Society, we obtained for him, as we did for many other laborious frontier preachers, an annual perquisite of one hundred dollars, and mission funds were never better laid out. The last we heard of this excellent brother was a vague rumor that he had gone to Texas.

The Bethel Association had held a correspondence with the Little River Association in Kentucky. That year the messenger was Josiah Horne, who preached an excellent sermon on the Sabbath. On the preceding session the association had taken up the subject of Foreign Missions, having received an annual report of the Board. They now had a regularly-appointed missionary under the Board, as their visitor, and seemed disposed to use him freely. We copy from the minutes:

"The business relating to missions, postponed last year, was taken under consideration, and Brother Peck called on for information on the subject. Several interesting communications were read, a circular from the Baptist Board of Foreign Missions presented, and the great efforts of the Christian world to promote the cause of Christ stated, together with the views, proceedings, object, and success of the Baptist denomination generally in this great and good work;

"*Therefore, resolved*, That Elder Thomas P. Green (near Jacks:n Cape Girardeau county) be our Corresponding Secretary, to open a correspondence with the Baptist Board of Foreign Missions, transmit to their secretary a copy of our minutes, and receive communications from them."

The missionaries at St. Louis, after conferring with their friends, had concocted the plan of a society, embracing such of the denomination in Illinois and Missouri as chose to unite in it, the outline of a constitution was read, and the project explained. Upon this the following entry was made in the minutes :

" Heard a plan, drawn up by Brother Peck, to promote the gospel and common-schools, both amongst the settlers and the Indians in this country, which plan, we think, would be highly useful, and which we earnestly desire to see carried into effect;

" *Therefore, resolved,* That we view with pleasure the exertions of our brethren J. M. Peck and J. E. Welch, united in the Western Mission, to spread the gospel and promote common-schools both amongst the whites and Indians, and that we recommend the above plan for the consideration of the churches and a liberal public. As Brother Peck engages to communicate an outline of the plan, it is hoped each church will consider it, and instruct their delegates against the next association."

The plan and constitution of this society was brought before the Illinois Association, and approved by that body on the 10th of October and by the Missouri Association on the 24th of the same month, where its organization was completed.

As this was the first society ever organized west of the Mississippi for philanthropic and missionary purposes, some more details of the plan and proposed method of operations are deemed expedient.

NAME.—" The United Society for the spread of the gospel."

OBJECT.—To aid the " Western Mission" in spreading the gospel, and promoting common-schools in the western parts of America, both amongst the whites and Indians.

TERMS OF MEMBERSHIP.—Persons of good moral character by paying five dollars annually. Each [Baptist] association, contributing annually, could send two messengers. Each branch or mite society, church, or other religious society, contributing ten dollars annually, to send one delegate.

MEASURES TO BE ADOPTED.—The society, at its annual meeting, to consult on the best measures to promote the gospel and common-schools ; devise measures to assist ministers in obtaining an education, and to qualify school-teachers ; consider the moral and religious welfare of the Indians, and devise means for their reform ; and use every means in their power to send forth missionaries on the frontiers and destitute settlements.

QUALIFICATIONS OF MISSIONARIES AND SCHOOL-TEACHERS.—The first must be in full standing in the Baptist churches, and give satisfactory evidence of genuine piety, good talents, and fervent zeal in the Redeemer's cause. No person of immoral habits, or who, in the judgment of the Board, was not qualified, could be employed as a school-teacher.

It was not expected the society would pay teachers among the white settlers, but to aid in introducing good ones, and thus encourage the people in an entire reformation in the schools throughout the country. Thus the society, or rather its secretary, who also made extensive excursions as a general agent, by an extensive correspondence, found out where teachers were wanted and where they could be had. It is not extravagant to say that in three years, by so simple and cheap an agency, more than fifty good schools were established in Missouri and Illinois, where common nuisances, with drunken, illiterate Irish Catholics at the head, had before existed.

FUNDS.—The funds of the society were included in three departments: the Education fund, the Indian fund, and the Mission fund.

Having failed in establishing an Indian school amongst a band of natives then located near the Pilot Knob, in Madison county, Mo., no further effort was made for that object. The education-object made no demand for funds. Several missionaries in Missouri and Illinois were employed as itinerants, at the rate of expense of hired men, that is from sixteen to twenty dollars per month, according to locality. The labors of most were successful and performed with fidelity. Some received their compensation from voluntary contributions. The writer being under patronage of the Baptist Board of Foreign Missions made frequent collections without charge to the society; for which, a few years after, when a class of Baptists turned against their brethren, declared non-intercourse with all in favor of missions, Sunday-schools, etc., the slang of "money-begging missionary," "the gospel going on silver wheels," and "Judas having the bag," was reiterated from that class. One well-meaning, but short-sighted old preacher received seventeen dollars and twenty-five cents, for a month's itinerant service and traveling expenses. Hearing that he used this stereotyped slang, where he ought to have preached repentance towards God and faith in our Lord Jesus Christ, we sent him word by a common friend, acknowledging our position analogous to that of Judas, who had been appointed treasurer of the company by the Divine Master. But who got the thirty pieces of silver? Elder —— got seventeen dollars and twenty-five cents, for which we hold his receipt. It troubled the old man to no small extent when we turned the "silver wheels" upon him.

There was an honest, but mistaken basis on which the objections against missions were founded. These preachers were quite de-

10

ficient in correct and Scriptural views of church government. Its extreme simplicity, and the large liberty it gave to its members in their selection of objects, and divers modes of benefactions they did not comprehend. Associations were called "advisory councils," but the *advice* had the effect of *law*. Hence, by a confused series of far-drawn inferences, they arrived at the conclusion that all other societies except churches and associations, not being specially thorized in the Scriptures, must be forbidden.

Then in many minds crude antinomian notions were intermingled with scattered and detached fragments of gospel truth. They had no clear and correct notions of the connection of Divine purposes and means to accomplish them. Because God worked in us to will and to do his own pleasure, they had no conception of human duty and responsibility. There was a mulish obstinacy about some of these men, as there is about the same class now. They would not examine the subject candidly and prayerfully; they shut their own eyes against the light, and as far as in their power kept the members of their churches in darkness. They made the singular blunder in denying the use of all means and instrumentalities in the conversion of sinners and sending the gospel to the destitute, while they were active and zealous in using means and trying to be instrumental in opposing gospel measures. A third cause of this anti-mission spirit and practice among a class of preachers, originated in sheer selfishness.

They knew their own deficiencies when contrasted with others, but instead of rejoicing that the Lord had provided better gifts to promote his cause, they felt the irritability of wounded pride, common to narrow and weak minds. They got no compensation for their preaching; but the smallest degree of power and influence over others is more precious than gold to such men. As an illustration of the nature and extent of this course of opposition to missions, I will narrate an incident that occurred in Sangamon county, Ill., some five or six years after the date at the head of this article.

A little association had been formed; and after a hard struggle, and by a bare majority, an article was adopted of this purport:

"It shall be the duty of the association to debar from a seat any Baptist who is a member of a missionary society."

By a previous act they had made their articles of faith, and provided that they could not be altered except by a unanimous vote, and then appended this little anti-mission and unscriptural rule by a majority of one to their articles of faith. At that time, and for ever after, there was a large majority of members in the churches opposed to the rule, but they could not rid the association of it, as long as one selfish. crotchety member remained. The church where the association was held were to a man opposed to this rule; and fearing it might prevent Baptist ministers from visiting them, a resolution was introduced to the purport that they would invite any orderly Baptist minister to preach for them, although he might be a missionary. To give full opportunity to investigate the subject, the question was postponed one month. Fearing such an investigation might expose the designs of the anti-mission party, four preachers rode from thirty to fifty miles to attend the church-meeting. It was in the month of February; the creeks were high; and two of these zealous visitors swam Sugar creek on their horses, at the risk of their lives. One of these men was quite a simple-hearted, weak brother, whose small mind was led by the others. But he loved to hear himself talk, while in a confused manner he uttered words that lacked ideas. He was interrupted by a motion, which was put by the moderator and decided in the affirmative, of this purport:

"That Brother J——n be requested to state explicitly his ob· jections against missionaries."

His reply was honestly made, as follows:

"We don't care any thing about them missionaries that's gone amongst them heathens 'way off yonder. But what do they come among us for? We don't want them here in Illinois."

The moderator replied: "We live in a free country, and Baptist churches love liberty. We need not give them money unless we choose, and we are not obliged to hear them preach if we do not like them. Come, Brother J——n, let the church know your real objections."

"Well, if you must know, Brother Moderator, you know the big trees in the woods overshadow the little ones; and these mission· aries will be all great, learned men, and the people will all go to hear them preach, and we shall all be put down. That's the objection."

Indian Councils.

On my return from the Bethel Association, I found the Rev. John Ficklin, from Kentucky, in town. He was on an agency from the Kentucky Mission Society to certain bands of Indians in Missouri, to obtain some of their children to commence an Indian school in that State. This was the embryo of the Indian school, subse· quently sustained by the national government, on the farm and

under the supervision of the late Hon. R. M. Johnson, at the **Blue**
Springs, Scott county. Mr. Ficklin was a self-sacrificing, zealous
Baptist preacher, and for a long series of years was a member of
Great Crossings church, and connected with the Elkhorn Association. He (with Mr. Short, his traveling companion) had made an
excursion to several places in the territory, where bands of Indians
resided, one of which was on the Fourche-a-Courtois in Washington
county, another was at Indiantown between the Bourbeuse and Merrimac rivers. Here was a band of Shawanese and Delawares, called
Rogers' band, from their chief or head man. Mr. Rogers was originally a white man, taken prisoner in boyhood, and so trained in Indian
habits and tactics, that in mind, temper, disposition, and inclinations, he was completely an Indian. He took for a wife a squaw,
who was the daughter of a chief, and through his influence and his
own superior talents he held the office of commander in that band.
During the series of wars between the Indians and white people,
in their early migrations to Kentucky, Rogers commanded a ma-
rauding party on the Ohio river, who displayed their prowess in
plundering boats, and murdering the owners when they met with
resistance. The victory of General Wayne, in 1794, and the treaty
of Greenville that followed, put an end to these depredations. Previously to this period, however, Captain Rogers had accumulated
wealth enough to satisfy the wants of himself and band, and ap-
prehensive they might be trailed out by some of the war-parties
of the whites, prudently migrated across the " Great River," and
located themselves at Village-a-Robert, afterward called Owen's
Station, and now Bridgton, in St. Louis county.

Rogers had not lost all predilections for the lower grade of civili
zation. He had two sons, James and Lewis, who grew up to manhood, and two or three daughters. One daughter married Cohun,
a Delaware brave, and a fine, noble specimen of humanity. He
was a man of strong sense, industrious, generous, and a firm friend
to his white neighbors.

When, and under what circumstances, Captain Rogers died, I never
learned. His successor in office was Captain Fish, who also was one
of our race, but taken a prisoner when a small boy, and acquired
the Indian character so perfectly, that a stranger would not have
suspected his white blood. He married a daughter of Captain
Rogers, and perhaps this connection tended to place him in office,
which was for life.

This band of Indians cultivated little farms. Captain Rogers
took an active part in getting up a school in the village, in which

the American settlers united, and the white and Indian boys were at their books in school hours, and engaged with the bow and arrow and other Indian pastimes, during intermission. Amongst these scholars was the late Rev. Lewis Williams, who obtained his education in boyhood in this half-Indian seminary.

About the time, or a little before the cession of Louisiana to the United States, Rogers and his band removed to the Big Spring at the head of the main Merrimac. Here the water suddenly bursts from the earth into a large basin from which flows a river more than fifty yards in width, and from two to three feet deep. It proved very sickly to the new-comers, and several died. I think probably Captain Rogers was of the number. Supposing they had intruded upon the dominion of a *Matchee Monito*, or Evil Spirit, they broke up their lodges, came down the country, and built their cabins on the borders of Indian prairie in Franklin county. This spot is a few miles south of Union.

Captain Fish, the Rogers, and others, met Mr. Ficklin in St. Louis, where, on the first day of October, we held a talk about sending their children to Kentucky. Lewis Rogers, who could read and write as well as most of the frontier settlers, offered to go, provided he could be permitted to take his wife and all his family with him. To this proposal Mr. Ficklin consented. These Indians were thrifty farmers, and brought the best cattle to St. Louis market the butchers had received. Next year, in company with Elder Lewis Williams and Isaiah Todd, I visited these Indians at their hunting-camps, some eight or ten miles above their town. We were treated with great hospitality. They heard favorable accounts from Lewis Rogers at the school in Kentucky, and consented to send on more of their sons.

About the same time two large parties of Indians came to settle difficulties and make peace. These were on the one side Cherokees, with a few Delawares and Shawanoes; and on the other side, Osages, or, more correctly, *Wossoshes*, as they pronounce their name. These two bodies had been at war for more than two years, and by the advice of their Great Father, the President of the United States, had met in presence of their good father (Governor Clark), who superintended the affairs of the Indians over a vast district of country. The ostensible cause of this war may serve to show that mistakes are made by commissioners, that eventually produce ruptures between Indian tribes. Indian boundaries and Indian titles to particular tracts of country, among themselves, unless established by the government that acts as their

common guardian, are vague things. Floods of sympathy have
been poured out by those who know nothing truthfully about Indian
titles, boundary lines, and Indian rights ; or their character, history,
and habits. "Attachment to the graves of their fathers" is all
poetry. From the earliest period that we can obtain any knowledge
of this race, they have been migratory.

In 1808, through the late Pierre Choteau as United States Com-
missioner, at Fort Clark, on the Missouri, a treaty with the Osages
was negotiated, in which a line due south to the Arkansas was to
become the eastern boundary, and down the Arkansas to the Mississippi. These Osages some years after set up a claim to hunt on
the lands south of the Arkansas. In 1808-9, the President entered
into an arrangement with the Cherokees, for a portion of the nation
who desired to remove westward, to exchange their lands east
of the Mississippi for lands on the Arkansas river. They claimed
the right of hunting indefinitely westward. The Osages, not liking
these intruders, as they regarded them, broke up their hunting-
lodges, and plundered them of their peltry. One depredation pro-
voked another, until they came in collision ; murders were committed ; and finally the Cherokees made a formal declaration of
war. They took up the line of march in the spring of 1817, with
two field-pieces, mounted and drawn by horses, and the men armed
with rifles. The Cherokees were half-civilized, and understood and
kept up military discipline ; and adopted into their nation were not
a few "white skins," and the Shawanoes and Delawares. They
made a rapid march into the Osage country, surprised them in
their villages, made them run, killed a dozen or so, and took as
many prisoners, chiefly women and children, whom at the time we
are writing about they held as hostages.

The Great Chief of the Cherokees, on the Arkansas, was a most
venerable man named Tolrentuskee. He was one hundred years
of age, and entirely blind. It was not his business at that advanced
period of life, with his locks white as the mountain snow, to go out
to war. This duty, his braves, commanded by an experienced war-
rior, had performed under his authority. But his presence was
indispensable to the ratification of peace. He had traveled on
horseback from the Indian country on the Arkansas on a mission
of peace, accompanied by a beloved daughter, who appeared about
forty years of age. She was a pattern of filial affection ; for she
led her venerable sire to and from the council-room, and waited on
him with the greatest tenderness.

The council between the tribes was held in the Indian office, in the presence and under the presiding influence of the late Governor Clark. Few men in the nation had so extensive an influence over the Indians, and so much tact in conciliating as this Superintendent of Indian affairs. The parties were seated on opposite sides of the room; the Governor, his aids, secretaries, and interpreters, around a table in the center; and the spectators, who were invited guests, on elevated seats back. The Cherokees were first called on to exhibit their complaints against the Osages, and the latter to respond. The Osages had several *talking*-braves, or those who claimed the gift of Indian oratory. The whole speaking on the part of the Cherokees, according to their usage, devolved on old Tolrentuskee; and a more dignified, grave, sententious speaker we never heard. The intonations of his voice, and his occasional gesticulations, were peculiarly impressive. He told of an interview between the chiefs of the Cherokee nation with his Great Father Washington in Philadelphia, in 1794. Though he was not then a great chief, he opened his ears to the lessons of the Great Father, who told the Cherokees war was not good; it made people unhappy, and the Great Spirit became angry with his children. The Great Father told them they must leave off war and plunder, cultivate the soil, raise corn and cotton, make good houses, and learn to talk from the book. His ears were opened wide, and every word of the Great Father sank into his heart. The same lessons had been taught them by the successive Great Fathers, and the Cherokees were fast learning the ways of the White-skins. They built houses like their white neighbors; they touched their mother earth, and she gave them corn, and cotton, and other good things. These clothes I wear, my daughter who sits there and leads me in the dark, made for me. She grew the cotton in the field, and made the cloth. We do not desire to go on the war-path: it is not good. When we came across the Big river, our Great Father told us to live in peace with the Osages, and Kanzaus, and Quppaws, and all the other Red-skins. We tried to do so, but the Osages came over the Arkansas to our hunting grounds. They destroyed our lodges, stole our meat and skins, and killed and scalped some of our men. We sent them word to keep on their own side of the Arkansas, and not molest us; but they grew worse. Bad birds flew through the air and told them lies; and they stole our horses and other property, and killed more of our people.

The venerable chief spoke an hour in rehearsing the depredations of the Osages, and proving the war on the part of the Cherokees was a necessity. His intellect was remarkably clear, and the tones of his voice melodious. The responses from the Osages were various, and a little contradictory. They claimed the country south of the Arkansas as their ancient hunting-ground, without producing any proofs from history or tradition. They regarded the Cherokees as intruders, because they came across the Big river. Tolrentuskee had alluded to the inferiority of the Osages in the war, and used an expression that stung to the quick one of the Osage braves, who proved himself to be not only a braggart, but a dastardly coward. He was a large, robust man, six feet in height, painted in true Indian style, with his head shaved close, only the scalp-lock being left, and this done up with long red feathers. Springing to his feet, and throwing off his blanket from his shoulders, with only his shroud around his waist, his eyes flashing resentment, addressing Governor Clark, as all the speakers had to do, he exclaimed:

"My father, I'm a MAN—an Osage brave; my heart is big; I never quail before Red-skins; I fear no Red-skin; I only bow in the presence of White-skins, my father"—at the same time making a somewhat awkward, but low obeisance.

Captain Cohun was sitting in front of the writer; and I saw by the curl of the lip, he was observing this Osage, and inquired: "Do you know him?" "Yes; that's the very fellow who pushed his wife off his horse when we drove them from the village, that he might run away. We have got his squaw among our prisoners."

The Governor adjourned the council till the next day, without any settlement, advising each party to yield something. Next morning the Osages argued resolutely their right to the hunting-grounds *north* of the Arkansas, thus tacitly relinquishing all claims to the disputed country. Peace was made, and the treaty signed by each party, and witnessed by the spectators—the Cherokees promising to give up the prisoners, whom they held as hostages.

CHAPTER IX.

A Missionary Tour in Southern Missouri.

On the 3d day of November I started from St. Louis, on horse back, on a tour through a portion of the churches of Bethel Association. Near the Merrimac I tarried with a Mr. Moore, who treated me hospitably, and furnished me with a buffalo skin, on which I lodged for the night very comfortably. The puncheon-floor, with a buffalo skin for a bed, and a saddle-tree for a pillow, furnished no mean lodging in those frontier times.

Next morning, before the sun appeared, I was wending my way down the country, in company with two men from Strawberry, in the Arkansas country. We passed the sulphur springs, and Van Zant's Mill, and rode on to Horine's, who kept a house of entertainment, for breakfast. For this and horse-feed, each traveler paid thirty-seven and a half cents—the customary fare, supper, horse-feed, and lodging for the night, was uniformly fifty cents. But if it was known the traveler was a preacher of the gospel, and engaged in that business, he was seldom charged, though the family might keep a house of entertainment as a means of support.

I parted with my companions at Herculaneum, and followed a "bridle-trail" near the bluffs of the Mississippi, and through an immense tract of barrens. In one place, amid the scattering and scrubby timber the fire was raging through the tall, dry grass, and even to the tops of dry trees. Beyond the fire, flocks of wild turkeys would start up and light on the trees, and the startled deer would bound away over the hills.

I reached Ste. Genevieve at eight o'clock, and put up at Donohue's tavern. The landlord, with a company of *gentlemen*, was busily employed at the card-table. Seeing that my horse was made comfortable, and getting quite an ordinary supper, I was successful in obtaining a private-room, a table and candle, and was occupied in writing until a late hour. One prominent object of my journeying was to carry into effect the missionary society already mentioned, and which was organized at the time of the Missouri Association on the 24th of October.

I had provided printed circulars, containing the constitution and other particulars, and these, with written letters, were sent off with appointments to preach on my return. At sunrise, the 5th, I was on my way down the country, and, after about fifteen miles ride, was at the cabins of General Henry S. Dodge, who was then a salt manufacturer at the Mississippi Saline. The Dodge family were from Connecticut, and anciently a family of Baptists. Doctor Israel Dodge, father to the gentleman whose hospitality I was sharing, came to Kentucky, and from thence to Vincennes, before the close of the last century. General H. S. Dodge, now the venerable senator from Wisconsin, was born in that French village. A brother of Doctor Dodge, Elder Josiah Dodge, from the same State, settled in Kentucky, and was an efficient Baptist preacher. His brother, the Doctor, had migrated to Ste. Genevieve before 1794; for in February of that year Elder Josiah Dodge made him a visit, came over to the Illinois country, and baptized four persons in Fountain creek.

The wife of General H. S. Dodge was a firm and zealous Baptist. She was a McDaniel, of St. Louis county, and joined the church in early life. After breakfast, and a season of devotion, I rode through the barrens to the place where I had attended the Bethel Association, as already narrated, to John Du Vol's, a Baptist, where I passed the night. In the vicinity the Roman Catholics were establishing a college and a seminary for the education of priests. Next day I reached the town of Jackson about sunset, and from thence to Deacon Thos. Bull's house, where I was cordially received and hospitably entertained. Deacon Bull was one of the constituents and stated-clerk of Bethel church. He was an elderly man, plain and old-fashioned in habits, and a warm-hearted Christian.

On the 7th (Saturday), I met the church in Bethel meeting-house. This was a log-building, rough in style, but quite as fashionable as any house of worship in the territory. Elder Wm. Street, who had come from a settlement down the St. Francois, had preached before my arrival. The church sat in order and transacted business. I then preached from Isaiah liii. 1, and Elder Jas. P. Edwards followed me from John xiv. 6. The people tarried during all these exercises with apparent satisfaction. Custom and common-sense are the best guides in such matters. Dinner was never thought of on meeting-days. The Cape Girardeau Society, auxiliary to the "United Society," had already been formed in this vicinity, and there were more real friends and liberal contributors to missions in this church than in any other in the territory. Yet in a few years, by the formation of Jackson and two other churches from this, the death of some valuable members and the removal of others, with the introduction of some members of a different spirit, Bethel church, the oldest in Missouri, had Ichabod written on her doors. It became a selfish, lifeless, anti-mission body.

On Lord's-day, November 8th, I preached a missionary discourse to a large congregation, from Exodus xxxiii. 15: "If thy presence go not with me, carry me not up hence." A collection was taken, amounting to thirty-one dollars and thirty-seven cents. This was the second missionary collection ever made in Missouri; the first was taken at the Missouri Association, on the 25th of October, of twelve dollars and twenty-five cents.

At evening I rode to Jackson, and preached at the house of Hon. Richard Thomas, where I was kindly and hospitably entertained. Mrs. Thomas and her daughters were members of Bethel church.

I continued visiting the settlements and preaching to the people for several days. I visited Cape Girardeau and Ross Point, and formed a Mite society at each place. On the 11th I preached again in Jackson, and aided in the organization of a Female Mite Society of seventeen members. Jackson at that time was the county-seat of Cape Girardeau county. It had been laid off in 1815; and at the time of my first visit, according to the notes made on the spot, contained between sixty and seventy dwelling-houses, five stores, two shoemaker-shops, one tannery, and two good schools, one for males and the other for females. The population in and around Jackson were more moral, intelligent, and truly religious than the people at any village or settlement in the territory.

I was now about to leave Cape Girardeau county, in a northwesterly direction, for St. Michael. The first prominent settlement was Bollinger's, the name of the leading patriarch. Mr. Bollinger and a number of other German families made their pitch here, under the Spanish Government, about the commencement of the present century. They were nominal Lutherans, but being destitute of a pastor, and without schools, they degenerated in religion, but were industrious farmers. Mr. Bollinger was a member of the first Legislature under the State government, and subsequently either he or his son has been repeatedly a member. A few years since a new county was laid off from Cape Girardeau and adjacent counties, and named after him.

The first night after leaving Jackson, I stopped with a Methodist family—an elderly widow lady, her son, his wife and three children. At first I did not make known my profession, but commenced a religious conversation. I soon found that though members of the society, neither could explain *how God could be just, sustain his law, and pardon sinners.* At first they supposed he would do it for our *prayers;* then for our *reformation;* and finally for our *sincerity.* This gave me a favorable opportunity to preach Jesus and him crucified, as the only way of pardon. They listened with peculiar interest; begged me to stay, give out an appointment, and preach the same doctrine to their neighbors. But I had appointments ahead, and left them at sunrise, after family-worship. My kind host would take nothing, though he kept a house for private entertainment, as one means of supporting his family.

After riding seventeen miles, under the affliction of a severe sick-headache, and calling on two families to rest, I reached Brother James James' cabin, near St. Michael, where I tarried. Here I found a venerable minister by the name of George Guthrie, formerly from Ohio, but now residing on the Mississippi, near the mouth of Saline creek. At night we both preached in St. Michael at the house of a Frenchman whose name was Labbe. Though raised a Catholic, he had renounced that fallacious system. His wife was a Baptist. Next day, the Providence church held their regular meeting in an old log-building called the block-house. Elder Guthrie and I both preached, and left time enough for the church to attend to its business. Next day, being Sabbath, we had the same arrangement. After preaching, Elder Farrar baptized two females. At night I preached again in the village of St. Michael. That village then was a very wicked place.

The following week I visited and preached twice in Cook's settlement, and obtained thirty dollars, subscribed by seventeen persons, to have Elder Farrar visit them, and preach monthly. I had conversed with the Elder, with Deacon James, and several other brethren, and found, if he could have one hundred and fifty dollars during the year, he could devote his whole time to the ministry. There was great destitution for fifty miles in each direction. Elder Farrar was a moderate preacher, but a godly, praying man, poor in this world's goods, but his heart was in the work. He had truly a missionary spirit, of which he gave evidence till his death, which took place in 1829. Before I left this field, I had in subscriptions over sixty dollars, and a fair prospect that the whole would be made up. But there was ignorance of the most inexcusable kind, apathy, covetousness, and bigotry in the church. There was a minority of brethren of excellent spirit and desirous of seeing the plan carried into effect. Some weeks after my visit, the subject was taken up in the church, which in fact had no business with it. The subscriptions were voluntary. No one was pressed to give any thing. The church, or at least the majority of the men who acted, were certainly under the influence of the Evil One. Like the persecutors of Christ, they were blinded and knew not what they did. The majority actually voted that the subscription-papers be brought forward and burnt! The deed was done! and I record this as the first overt act by the antinomian and anti-mission faction in Missouri. Nor have I ever heard in that State of as flagrant a violation of Baptist rights and privileges as this. The elder and the dissenting brethren bore all this treatment with Christian meekness and patience, but the church has never prospered.

On the 20th of November, in company with Elder Farrar, I started southward down the St. Francois river, to visit the church that was then the farthest south of any one in the Missouri Territory. We rode over a rough, unbroken tract of country about twenty-five miles, and reached the cabin of Elder William Street after dark. This church bore the name of St. Francois. Its location could not have been far from the site of Greenville, the county-seat of Wayne, which was established long after my visit. This church was constituted July 11th, 1816, by the aid of Elders John Farrar and James P. Edwards. There were ten males and thirteen female members in the constitution. Elder William Street, who had been accustomed to address his neighbors, and keep up religious worship, was ordained by choice of the church the same day. One of the constituents was Jonathan Hubbell, who, as I learned from Elder Street, came into the country and lived several years under the Spanish Government, near the present site of Jackson. Though never ordained, he preached to the people in a private way. He had been a Baptist for many years, and was one of the first who came into that part of the territory.

Both the Providence and Belleview churches were at first " arms' " of Bethel church. Providence church was constituted in August, 1814, by aid of Elders Wilson Thompson, John Farrar, and *James E. Welch*, from Kentucky, then a licentiate. The latter, by request, wrote their articles of faith and covenant. A year or more before this, Elder Farrar was ordained by Bethel church, aided by Elders Colden Williams (then a preacher in the church), and Fielding Wolfe from Kentucky. Elder Williams, shortly after this, was dismissed from Bethel church, and migrated to the Boon's Lick country, where I may notice him at a future time.

On Saturday, November 21, the St. Francois church held the
11

monthly meeting in a rough log-cabin in the woods. The plan of the "United Society for the spread of the gospel," was laid before the church. Elder Street had the intelligence, kindness of heart, and Christian spirit, to comprehend the plan, and engage heartily in the work. Not another male member of this body of Christian professors understood or cared about the object. They were stupid, listless, and apparently indifferent to every thing. The people throughout these extreme frontier settlements were quite ignorant; few could read, and fewer families had Bibles. They knew not the name of a single missionary on earth, and could not comprehend the reasons why money should be raised for the expenses, or why ministers should leave their own neighborhood to preach the gospel to the destitute. They manifested the same apathy in their worldly business. A small cornfield and a truck-patch was the height of their ambition. Venison, bear-meat, and hog-meat dressed and cooked in the most slovenly and filthy manner, with corn-bread baked in form of a pone, and when cold as hard as a brickbat, constituted their provisions. Coffee and tea were prohibited articles amongst this class; for had they possessed the articles, not one woman in ten knew how to cook them. Not a school had existed. A kind of half-savage life appeared to be their choice. Elder Street and family appeared to be an exception; and he was doing his best to raise his neighbors in the scale of civilization; but he had a hard field to cultivate. Doubtless, in a few years, when the land came into market, this class of "squatters" cleared out for the frontier range in Arkansas. Elder Street remained; others of more industry came in; and some ten or twelve years later, we heard he had organized a Bible-class and Sabbath-school, and taught it with success. He was a moderate preacher, a spiritually-minded man, desiring to do all the good he could. The last time we find his name on any document is as the preacher of St. Francois church, in the minutes of the Black River Association, of which he was Moderator in 1836. He died in 1843 or '44, at a very advanced age, probably near ninety.

I returned home with Elder Farrar, Sabbath night. My route that week was through Doe Run and Belleview settlements, where I preached and introduced the plan of missions; preached in several other settlements; was detained two days by a violent storm of rain, and preached at St. Louis on the 30th of November.

One specific object, during my excursions through the territory, was to examine into the condition of the schools that existed, and aid the people in procuring a better class of teachers than could generally be found.

After having gained correct knowledge by personal inspection in most of the settlements, or by the testimony of reliable persons living in such remote settlements as I could not visit, the conclusion was that at least one-third of the schools were really a public nuisance, and did the people more harm than good; another third about balanced the account, by doing about as much harm as good, and perhaps one-third were advantageous to the community in various degrees. Not a few drunken, profane, worthless Irishmen were perambulating the country, and getting up schools; and yet they could neither speak, read, pronounce, spell, or write the English language. These agents were encouraged by the priests to go among the people.

A custom prevailed extensively, which had existed in the Southern States from their early settlement, of turning out from the school-house the master at Christmas, and frequently at Easter. This custom can be traced back to the Feudal age in the mother country. It belonged to the rude sports and semi-riots encouraged by the Romish priests and feudal lords, to keep the common people from thinking about their down-trodden condition. These mock-festivals, when the masses elected their "abbots of unreason," "bishops of misrule," so graphically depicted by Walter Scott, are illustrations of the anarchy permitted and even encouraged by the authorities in Church and State. The half-reformed English hierarchy under Elizabeth, James, and the Charleses, gave countenance to similar disorders to gratify the whims, caprice, and the low sensualities of the people, just as the priests, with their " file leader" in St. Louis, now encourage and countenance the low vices and Sunday revelings of their degraded subjects.

The schoolmaster riot was a common occurrence in Missouri at the period of our date, and in not a few instances. The Irish masters to whom we have alluded, loved their *poteen* dearly; and frequently negotiated with the youngsters, who were ringleaders in misrule, for a " treat." " Cherry-bounce," sweetened with honey, was the favorite beverage. The year before our tour South, mentioned above, Mr. O'Flaherty, not a hundred miles from Ste. Genevieve, did more than his pupils exacted, the preceding Christmas. He procured a supply of cherry-bounce, whisky and honey; and while he took his full share, distributed it so generously that one-half his pupils were made " orful sick," as their parents expressed it. Some had to be carried home, and the doctor called in; while the master required a wide path, and made zig-zag tracks in reaching his lodging-place. He was turned out in fact by the indignant parents.

Our efforts were directed through the "United Society" already mentioned, to find out well-qualified teachers, and recommend them to such settlements as would sustain them. This measure, fraught with no small benefits to the people, cost us nothing but a little trouble in corresponding and in our explorations.

On the 6th of December, at night, agreeably to previous arrangements, I preached a missionary sermon in the Legislative Hall in St. Louis, from Mark xvi. 19, 20, and received a collection of twenty-six dollars and twenty-five cents for the "United Society," to sustain itinerant missionaries within the territory. This was the first collection for missions and the first sermon for that purpose in St. Louis.

A system of itinerant missions, or "circuit-preaching," as our Methodist friends call it, is the most economical and successful mode of supplying the destitute, and strengthening and building up feeble churches, that has been tried. It is truly the apostolic mode; and if the finger of Divine providence ever pointed out a method adapted to the circumstances of new and sparsely-settled districts, it is itinerating or circuit missions.

The new-fangled notion that has gotten into Baptist heads, and Baptist management of missions, that pastors of churches, and none but pastors, are the instrumentalities God has appointed to extend the borders of his kingdom, needs to be examined and brought to the test of the Scriptures and common-sense.

We know that bishops, or pastors, were provided among the ascension-gifts, and elders, or pastors (not one merely), were appointed in the apostolic churches. Their qualifications are specified in the epistles of Paul to Timothy and Titus. *But we find no report of the labors of this class of men.* I should like some one to give a sketch of the doings and success of these bishops, and references made to the Scriptures where the history of these men's labors is recorded. The Acts of the Apostles contains a sketch of the labors of the apostles and evangelists; but these were itinerants, and traveled from church to church, from country to country, as pioneers in the gospel field. They planted and watered new churches, and taught them to look out among their members men who were able to preside over them.

CHAPTER X.

Tour to the Boone's Lick Country.

PREVIOUS to this tour, and after consultation with Rev. Mr. Giddings and other friends, Mr. Welch and the writer first held a meeting with Mr. G. and drew up a plan for the Missouri Bible Society. An abortive effort had been made, at the visit of Messrs. Mills and Smith, to form such a society in 1814, but it proved a failure.* A public meeting was held in Mr. Gidding's school-room, on the 9th of December, and after a sermon by the writer from Psalm cxix. 97: " O, how I love thy law : it is my meditation all the day," the society was formed. It was of course made auxiliary to the American Bible Society, from which we received a supply of Bibles and Testaments in the spring. I mention this as a point from which a system of efforts proceeded in supplying the destitute population throughout Missouri and Illinois.

Having made provision for my family to reside in St. Louis during the winter, on the 12th of December I started on a tour on the north side of the Missouri river for two months. I left my family sick, but appointments had been sent forward; and I knew of no other way for an itinerant missionary, but to go forward, meet his engagements, and trust his family and all things else to the disposal of that Providence who watches over the birds of heaven, numbers the hairs of each one's head, and has given assurance of being with his ministers always, even to the end of the world. Nor have I ever been disappointed in this exercise of confidence in the Divine government.

From St. Charles, where I crossed the river amidst running-ice, mv route lay through the scattering settlements near the river,

---

* Rev. Samuel J. Mills and Rev. Daniel Smith, both natives of Connecticut, were sent forth as explorers by the missionary societies of Massachusetts and Connecticut, who traveled extensively in the Mississippi valley, distributing the Scriptures and finding out the spiritual wants of the new settlements. The latter, Mr. Smith, settled in Natchez, Miss., and the former Mr. Mills, became the pioneer of the Colonization Society in founding Liberia in Africa.

where I had appointments day and night. The "old Boone's Lick trace" through the prairies was no route then for a missionary. After passing the tavern-stand of Nicholas Kuntz, a rough, wicked, and yet hospitable old German, the next pitch was "Camp-branch," fifty miles above St. Charles, and the next Van-Bibber's at Loutre Lick. I followed a bridle-path through the hills and bluffs near the river. At old Brother Darst's house in Femme-Osage settlement, I preached and formed a Mite society to aid the "United Society for the spread of the gospel." Here I was met by Flanders Callaway, a leading member of the Baptist church near the mouth of Charette, called Friendship. His wife, an excellent woman, was Rebecca, the eldest daughter of Colonel Daniel Boone. After dinner we rode together a few miles to the cabin of Squire Boone, a nephew of Daniel. There has been a *Squire* and a *Daniel* in all the old Boone families I have been able to trace out. Daniel had a brother by the name of Squire. He had an uncle in Pennsylvania, who raised a large family of children, and amongst them were Daniel, Squire, and George. This coincidence of names in the Boone connection has made sad work in the "biographies" and "histories" of the veritable Daniel Boone. The Squire Boone and his wife where we lodged were Baptists from Kentucky. They were true-hearted people, and possessed and retained the true missionary spirit. A few years later I found them above the Loutre, and to the left of the Boone's Lick trace.

The morning of December 16th was clear, cold, and frosty. We started at the rising of the sun, and rode to Brother Callaway's cluster of cabins on the bank of the Missouri—the distance being twenty miles—where, in expectation, an excellent breakfast was in rapid preparation. Here, for the first time, I saw and conversed with the veritable Daniel Boone, the pioneer and hunter of Kentucky. Instead of writing a new article of the impressions made on my mind, as recorded in the life of Boone, found in Dr. Spark's edition of the "Library of American biography," written in 1846, vol. xxiii., two paragraphs are here inserted from that volume:

"On his introduction to Colonel Boone, the impressions were those of surprise, admiration, and delight. In boyhood, the writer had read of Daniel Boone, the pioneer of Kentucky, the celebrated Indian fighter; and imagination had portrayed a rough, fierce-looking, uncouth specimen of humanity, and of course at this period of life a fretful and unattractive old man. But in every respect the reverse appeared. His high, bold forehead was slightly bald, and his silvered locks were combed smooth; his countenance was ruddy and fair, and exhibited the simplicity of a child. A smile frequently played over his countenance in conversation. His voice was soft and melodious. At repeated interviews, an irritable expression was never heard. His clothing was the coarse, plain manufacture of the family; but every thing denoted that kind of comfort that was congenial to his habits and feelings, and evinced a happy old age. His room was part of a range of log-cabins kept in order by his affectionate daughter and grand-daughters.

" Every member of the household appeared to take delight in administering to his comforts. He was sociable, communicative in replying to questions, but not in introducing incidents of his own history. He was intelligent; for he had treasured up the experience and observations of more than fourscore years. In this and other interviews, every incident of his eventful life might have been drawn from his lips; but veneration being the predominant feeling which his presence excited, no more than a few brief notes were taken. He spoke feelingly, and with solemnity, of being a creature of Providence, ordained by heaven as a pioneer in the wilderness, to advance the civilization and extension of his country."

He was not moody and unsocial, as if desirous of shunning society and civilization.

A thousand-and-one tales told of Colonel Daniel Boone are as purely fictitious as the Arabian Nights' Entertainment.

I preached in the day and evening at the house of Mr. Callaway, with Colonel Boone for a hearer.

On Thursday morning, the 17th of December, I rode along a blind trail, or bridle-path, and over hills and through ravines, fifteen miles to the cabin of Mr. James Stevenson. My route lay along the bluffs that bordered on the Missouri river, the country thinly settled, and wagon-tracks seldom seen. I had sent on an appointment at Mr. McDermid's, but it had failed in being circulated.

Mr. S., of whose hospitality I was a welcome sharer, was an experienced hunter, then about sixty years of age. Two young panthers graced the one room that answered for kitchen, dining-hall, and lodging-room. My curiosity was gratified to hear and learn something of the exploits of the chase. In our boyhood the story of "Putnam and the wolf," so graphically described by Colonel Humphry, his biographer, had been often read with thrilling interest. But here was a man that threw old Putnam into the shade.

A few years previously to my visit, bear-hunting furnished both sport and profit on both sides of the Missouri. On one year especially (we think it was 1807-8), the common black bear was so plenty on this range as to satiate and tire out the hunters. Mr. S. narrated a most terrific account of a contest he had with a wounded bear, and finished the story by exposing one of his arms and side, where the teeth and claws of the enraged animal had left scars that were truly frightful. The old hunter obtained the victory. He had broken the barrel of his rifle over the head of the enraged animal, and while one arm and his side were at the mercy of the bear, he was successful in wresting his hunting-knife from its sheath, and plunging it into the heart of his assailant.

My next appointment, at twelve o'clock, was twenty miles, and no house on the route. Obtaining directions about the blind trail I had to follow I returned thanks to my kind host, and was on my horse before the sun peered his bright face over the bluffs, thinking I could reach the preaching-station and get breakfast before the people assembled. The day was pleasant, the air mild, and I found it expedient to mail one overcoat with my traveling-valise behind me. The morning wore away, and I must have traveled a dozen or fifteen miles, when I found the path I had followed came to an end. I had passed divers paths that diverged to the right and left, but the one I followed was the plainest, and the tracks of horses deceived me, until I found myself in a large rush bottom.

"Taking the back-track" is the only remedy in such cases. As I came to a fork I would follow that till it proved to be equally fallacious. After several trials, I found myself in sight of the turbid Missouri, and soon discovered that the path I had missed was a dim trail that wound around a point of the bluff. I now pushed on in hopes of making up for lost time, but I had not gone a mile before I discovered that my overcoat and valise were gone from behind me.

The only alternative was to "take the back-track" again, and ride till I found my missing property. This going and returning caused me a ride of a dozen miles. The overcoat and other articles lay unmolested in the path where they had dropped in the early part of the day. Just as the sun set I came in sight of a clearing, and, to my surprise, found more than twenty men and women, who had patiently waited from the hour of twelve to hear the "strange preacher." As some of the company had to return home, eight or ten miles, that night, I arranged to preach at once to the company present. Several stayed through the night, amongst whom were Brethren Smith and Coats, who came to meet and pilot me through to the monthly meeting of Salem church, on Coats' Prairie, the next day. The family where we stayed were Methodists, and once in three months a circuit-preacher visited them.

After the people had dispersed, our kind hostess set about pre-paring supper for the family and company who tarried. After commencing the evening meal, Mrs. C. remarked, rather apologetically: "I reckon that you have had no dinner to-day. I hope you will find something that will answer." "I purpose, madam, to eat my breakfast first, and then I will talk about dinner and supper." "Law me, have you eat no breakfast to-day?" "Not a morsel has entered my mouth this day till I sat down to your table." I then gave the company a brief sketch of my adventures during the day. "But why did you not tell us when you first arrived? I would have had a bite set before you at once." "Because I saw here a number of people hungry for the gospel, and I knew they would go home. I much preferred to do my preaching. Now I can eat leisurely, and get a comfortable night's rest, and be off with these brethren early in the morning." "And I shan't let you go before breakfast, so you may make yourself easy." And sure enough, our bustling, industrious, tidy hostess, had her table spread; corn cakes, venison, and fresh pork, with fine-flavored coffee, graced the board. and a hearty welcome crowned all. Having had a season of family-worship, we parted from this hospitable and pious family just as the rising sun threw his beams on the tops of the forest trees.

The weather was quite moderate, and a pleasant ride of fifteen miles brought us to the cabin of Brother William Coats, on the border of a little prairie that bore his name, as the first settler in all that region. Here my colleague gathered a small church the preceding June, and mine was the first visit of a Baptist preacher more than six months after. Prayer-meetings had been kept up by Brethren Coats and Smith. The church was called Salem.

Brother Coats had been a member of a Baptist church more than twenty years. During this period, whenever he enjoyed the presence of God, his mind was deeply exercised about preaching the gospel to his fellow-men; but when in a worldly, backsliding state, these impressions left him. He came from Tennessee in 1817, and made the first settlement on the prairie that bore his name. We held a long conversation with him about his duty, and in less than two years he was numbered among the preachers.

Lord's-day, *December* 20*th*. The people collected from the scat-tering settlements ten or fifteen miles around to hear the gospel. I preached from Ephes. ii. 8: "For by grace are ye saved through faith; and that not of yourselves; it is the gift of God."

There was a vein of crude antinomianism that ran through the minds of that class of Baptists who claimed descent from the party called "Regulars" in Kentucky and Tennessee. They could not comprehend that God in all the sovereign displays of his grace worked by means, and made use of instrumentalities in the conversion of sinners. Hence preachers, with crude and imperfect notions about God working in us to do his own will and pleasure, knew not how to preach the gospel to unconverted sinners. These mistaken notions lay at the bottom of opposition to missions and to all instrumentalities for the conversion of men. The mind of Brother Coats, before referred to, had been stereotyped with the fallacies he had heard, mixed up with gospel truth, from early life. He was a plain, strong-minded man, who read the Bible and thought out its meaning for himself; but he had been trained under that mode of preaching which hampered his feelings. He lost twenty years of usefulness for want of Scriptural instruction when he first joined the church. For, amongst other errors, this class of preachers taught that no one must intermeddle with those whom God called to the ministry; He would bring them out "in his own good time."

At the close of preaching, the "Coats' Prairie Mite Society, auxiliary," etc., was formed and several dollars raised. After meeting closed, I rode ten miles in company with Brother Thomas Smith, with whom I had formed an interesting acquaintance at the Missouri Association in October. He was an active, intelligent man, with a clear, strong mind, and one of the very few lay-brethren I found who understood the duty of a Christian professor. His wife was a daughter of David Darst, one of the old pioneers who came into the country and settled on the Femme-Osage, under the Spanish Government.

Brother Smith had none of the troubles of Brother Coats in reconciling the purposes of God with the means and instrumentalities He has directed us to employ. He was clear-headed in Scripture doctrine, and warm-hearted in Christian practice. But the mysterious providence of God saw fit to cut him down in a few years and take him to the kingdom on high!

Monday, the 21st, was spent with this hospitable family in writing and arranging my affairs for the further prosecution of the mission.

Tuesday, 22d. Accompanied by Brother Smith, I set off at an early hour. A ride of fifteen miles brought me to the French village of *Cote Sans Dessein* (literally, "a hill without purpose.") This village derives its name from an isolated hill or bluff that stands, as if by accident, near the left bank of the river, a short distance above the town site.

A colony of French families, at the head of which was Baptiste Louis Roi, settled here in 1808. The Indians began to be troublesome in 1812, and M. Roi, with a few others, erected a block-house and an inclosure with palisades to protect the families. But as danger approached, Roi was deserted by his comrades, who went down the river in canoes, and left him with his men and a dozen women and children to defend the fort. In the spring of 1814, they were assailed by a large company of hostile savages. One of the men took fright, hid himself, muttered over the prayers he learned from the priest, and crossed himself, till he was driven from his hiding-place by Roi, who threatened to shoot him if he did not quit his foolery and fight for his life.

The heroic women cast bullets, cut patches, and loaded the rifles while Roi and his unflinching comrade poured on the assailants a murderous fire in defence of the fort till fourteen braves were slain, and many more wounded. After several bold attempts to storm the fort, they were driven back with reduced numbers. They then fastened combustible materials to their arrows and attempted to burn the building. The supply of water in the fort was scanty, but the women used it with parsimonious economy. The blazing torches of the savages were sent on the roof with frightful accuracy from a ravine that sheltered the assailants, and each new blaze called out the demoniac yells of the Indians. At this crisis the water was drained from the last bucket, and the blazing fire oroke out afresh! Even Baptiste Roi himself looked aghast on .he helpless group around him; the house on fire, and no means to extinguish it! Must they be burned alive, or fall victims to the tomahawk and scalping-knife! Just at that crisis, Madame Roi appeared with the night-vessel from her lodging-room, the contents of which just served to extinguish the fire and save the lives of the party. The Indians with the howl of despair departed with their wounded, leaving the dead bodies of fourteen braves to be interred by the heroic defenders.

It was not till after the war that this extraordinary defense became generally known. The young men of St. Louis honored him with the present of a costly rifle for his gallant behavior.

Passing along the river bank, I reached the house of a Mr. Fergusson, where my reception was friendly and hospitable. Here I found a copy of Goldsmith's writings, and several other choice books—a rare thing in that early period of log-cabins.

On Wednesday morning, the 23d, I found my horse was sick and lame. It was the same horse that brought my family from the

State of Connecticut to Shawneetown, and which performed hard and valuable service through the summer and autumn. After some detention, I rode a short distance to the cabin of a Mr. Scott, where I preached to a small company.

Next morning, my horse being some better, I rode twelve miles to Round Prairie in company with a young man by the name of Henderson. Here I stopped a while to converse and pray with Mrs. Henderson, the mother of my traveling companion. She be-longed to the Presbyterian Church when she left the old States, and expressed great satisfaction to see a minister of Christ. It was no unusual occurrence to find intelligent and pious Christians in the scattered log-cabins on these frontiers. And no service is more important in the labors of an itinerant than family visits, and in-structing and consoling the people of God, who, like sheep scattered through the wilderness, are beyond the reach of the pastor. After a season of Christian conversation and prayer, and partaking of refreshments, I proceeded forward to the Two-Mile Prairie, and received the hospitality of a Mr. Brant.

December 25th. The people with whom I tarried last night are young, with one little child, appear to be in fine health and spirits, and have come to this new country to obtain land at government-prices when it comes into market. They are industrious, active, and keep private entertainment for travelers. They are not religious, but civil and quiet, as were four travelers who tarried at the same place. Learning by inquiry that I was a missionary, I was invited to pray with the company before we retired. This morning they refused pay for my entertainment, and invited me to call and preach when-ever I passed that way.

To-day my route was first across the Two Mile Prairie. It de rives its name from its average width, commences between two points of timber towards the Missouri, and extends a long distance northward until lost in the Grand Prairie. Here are about a dozen families in log-cabins scattered along its borders. Crossing this prairie in a horse trail, and after riding several miles through tim-ber and brushwood, I came to a Mr. H——'s, where report said break-fast could be obtained, and which offered quite a contrast with the family of last night. The cabin was a single room of most primi-tive fashion, spice-bush tea was a substitute for coffee, and the flesh of hog, bear, deer, and elk was plenty, of which the landlord showed me enough to supply a regiment. The corn-dodgers were cold and quite unpalatable; for the good woman had never learned the art of cleanliness and cookery. The man was a successful hunter, but probably understood very little of agriculture. I paid fifty cents for these accommodations ; for my horse was lame, and refused to eat.

As I proceeded westward, cabins and smokes from clearings became more frequent. The Methodist circuit-preachers, Messrs. McAllister and Jones, pass through and preach in these scattering settlements about once in six weeks, and Dr. David Doyle, a Baptist minister from North Carolina, settled the last spring to the left of my trail and near the Two Mile Prairie. He will soon gather the scattered Baptists in this region into the field.

I could only travel my broken-down horse in a slow walk, and night found me under the hospitable roof of Mr. Crump, where I was kindly entertained. He was not a professor of religion, but had the character of an orderly, excellent man. His wife was a neat, tidy person, and the mother of three children.

December 26th. As I was about to start on my way towards Franklin, a Baptist by name of Anderson Woods came along, and was hailed by Mr. Crump. He was on his way to the monthly meeting of Bethel church, at the house of Lazarus Wilcox, and finding my horse was no better, I struck into the trail, and in half an hour we were at the place of meeting, and soon surrounded by the members of the church and others. Brother Woods was not then in the ministry, but could lead a meeting in prayer and exhortation. By request, I preached to the little congregation before church-meeting, and again at night to six persons, one of whom was a deaf mute from his birth. He was singularly intelligent for one of that unfortunate class. He knew what we were about in worshiping God. His brother, Deacon Wilcox, related an incident that was proof of his knowledge and correct views of the infinitely Holy God. He had occasion to correct his little son for telling a lie.

The deaf mute was much attached to the child, and when the father had corrected and given him a serious talk, the mute got an old book in the house, with divers religious emblems for a frontispiece. One of these was the figure of a large human eye in one of the upper corners. The deaf mute placed the boy between his knees, and while the tears of sympathy and sorrow rolled down his cheeks, he pointed to the emblem of the All-seeing Eye, raised it upward and then to the boy as though he would pierce him. This was the most impressive way he could say : "The eye of God is on you, looks into your heart, and will punish you for lying." This was done several times. This man, as I learned at a sub-

12

sequent period, told his experience to the church by signs; his brother, being interpreter, was baptized and lived a Christian life.

Bethel church was situated on the waters of the Moniteau, twenty miles east of Old Franklin. It was organized June 27th, 1817, by the ministry of Elders David McLain and Wm. Thorp.

On Lord's-day, the 27th, the weather was pleasant, the sun shone bright, and all nature appeared gay and cheerful. The people report the season as unusually mild and pleasant.

I preached from 1 Pet. iii. 18. The house contained two rooms, and was crowded with people, who gave respectful attention. The settlers in this region, in general, appear to be a respectable class of citizens, tolerably well-informed, and enjoy gospel privileges to a greater extent than in most parts of the territory.

On Monday, I rode through the country to Franklin, found a Baptist family by name of Wiseman, where I had been directed to call. A hasty appointment was circulated, and I preached to a roomful of people.

Franklin is a village of seventy families. It is situated on the left bank of the Missouri, and on the border of an extensive tract of rich, alluvial bottom land, covered with a heavy forest, except where the axe and fires had destroyed the undergrowth, "dead ened" the timber and prepared the fields for the largest crops of corn.

If any one wishes to find the site of this flourishing town, as it then appeared to promise, he must examine the bed of the river directly opposite Booneville. Repeated floods, many years since, drove the inhabitants to the bluff, with such of their houses as could be removed, where New Franklin, not a very thriving place, now stands. At the period of our visit, no town west of St. Louis gave better promise for rapid growth than Franklin. There was no church formed in the village, but I found fourteen Baptists there.

The country on the north side of the Missouri above the Cedar, a small stream on the western border of the present county of Callaway, was known as Boone's Lick from an early period. Also under the same cognomen was the country designated on the south side and west of the Osage river. The particular salt-lick to which this appellation was first given was ten or twelve miles above old Franklin and about two miles back from the river. Tradition told that this spot, in a secluded place among the bluffs, was occupied by the old pioneer, the veritable Daniel Boone, for his hunting-camp. But the name came from the late Major Nathan Boone, who in company with the Messrs. Morrisons of St. Charles, manufactured salt at the spring in 1806–7. About the same time a settlement was made on the Loutre and on Loutre Island. This settlement, except Cote Sans Dessein, was the veritable "Far West" until 1810.

During the spring of 1810 several families from Loutre settlement, and a large number, then recently from Kentucky, moved westward and planted themselves in the Boone's Lick country, then reported as the *el dorado* of all new countries. Off from the river bottoms the land was undulating, the prairies small, the soil rich, and the timber in variety and of a fine quality. Deer, bears, elk, and other game were in abundance, and furnished provisions, and, in many instances, clothing, until the people could raise crops.

There were in all about one hundred and fifty families that came into the Boone's Lick country in 1810–11, when the Indian war stopped further immigration till 1815 or 1816. Twelve families settled on the south side of the river, not far from the present site of Booneville, and several more formed a settlement south of the Missouri, some ten or fifteen miles above Old Franklin.

Amongst the emigrants, both from Loutre and Kentucky, were not a few Baptist families and two or three preachers. A church had been organized in the Loutre settlement, a majority of which, with their church records, were among the emigrants, and became reorganized, and I think took the name of Mount Zion.

Soon the hostile Indians broke into these remote frontier settlements. It was in July, 1810, that a hostile band of Pottawatomies came stealthily into the settlement on the Loutre, nearly opposite the mouth of the Gasconade river, and stole a number of horses. A volunteer company was raised, consisting of Stephen Cole, William T. Cole, Messrs. Brown, Gooch, Patton, and one other person, to follow them. They followed the trail across Grand Prairie to Bone Lick, a branch of Salt river, where they discovered eight Indians who threw off their packs of plunder, and scattered in the woods. Night coming on, the party disregarded the advice of their leader, Stephen Cole, an experienced man with Indians. He advised setting a guard, but the majority exclaimed against it, and cried "cowardice." About midnight the Indian yell and the death-dealing bullet aroused them from sleep. Stephen Cole had taken his station at the foot of a tree, and if he slept, it was with one eye open. He killed four Indians, and wounded the fifth, though severely wounded himself. William T. Cole, his brother, was killed at the commencement of the fight, with two other persons. Next morning the survivors reached the settlement and told the dreadful tidings, and a party returned to the spot, buried the dead, but found the Indians gone.

This was the first of a series of depredations, murders, and robberies in these remote settlements that continued five years. The district of St. Charles had the Cedar for its western boundary. The Boone's Lick country was not recognized as within the organized territory of Missouri. The people were "a law unto themselves," and had to do their own fighting. Every male inhabitant of the settlement, who was capable of bearing arms, enrolled and equipped himself for defense. Each one pledged himself to fight, to labor on the forts, to go on scouting-expeditions, or to raise corn for the community, as danger or necessity required. By the common consent of all these volunteer parties, Colonel Benjamin Cooper, a Baptist from Madison county, Ky., was chosen commander-in-chief.

Colonel Cooper was one of Kentucky's noblest pioneers. He had also been a prominent man in the wars with Indians in that district, possessed real courage, cool and deliberate, with great skill and sagacity in judgment. He had also been an efficient man in the affairs of civil and political life, and a man of firmness and correctness as a member of the church.

Among the principal officers who occupied subaltern positions as the commanders of forts and partisan leaders for detached field-service were Captain Sarshall Cooper (a brother of the Colonel), William Head and Stephen Cole.

To guard against surprise, the people, under the direction of their leader, erected five stockade forts:

1. *Cooper's fort* was at the residence of the Colonel, on a bottom-prairie.

2. *McLain's fort* (called Fort Hempstead afterward) was on the bluff, about one mile from New Franklin.

3. *Kincaid's fort* was near the river, and about one and a half miles above the site of Old Franklin.

4. *Head's fort* was on the Moniteau, near the old Boone's Lick trace from St. Charles.

5. *Cole's fort* was on the south side of the Missouri, about a mile below Booneville. Here the widow of W. T. Cole, who was slain by the Indians on Boone's Lick, with her children, settled soon after the murder of her husband.

These forts were a refuge to the families when dangers threatened, but the defenders of the country did not reside in them only as threatened danger required. Scouting-parties were almost constantly engaged scouring the woods in the rear of the settlements

watching for Indian signs, and protecting their stock from depre
dations.

With all their vigilance during the war, about three hundred
horses were stolen; many cattle and nearly all their hogs were
killed. Bear-meat and raccoon-bacon became a substitute, and
even were engaged in contracts for trade. They cultivated the
fields nearest to the stockade-forts, which could be cultivated in
corn with comparative security, but not enough to supply the
amount necessary for consumption.

Parties were detailed to cultivate fields more distant. These
were divided into plowmen and sentinels. The one party followed
the plows, and the other, with rifles loaded and ready, scouted
around the field on every side, stealthily watching lest the wily foe
should form an ambuscade. Often the plowman walked over the
field, guiding his horses and pulverizing the earth, with his loaded
rifle slung at his back.

With all these precautions, few men but would tread stealthily
along the furrows. As he approached the end of the corn-rows, where
the adjacent woodland might conceal an enemy, his anxiety was at
its height. When these detachments were in the cornfield, if the
enemy threatened the fort, the sound of the horn gave the alarm,
and all rushed to the rescue.

It was in the autumnal season of corn-gathering, that a party of
these farming soldiers were hard pressed by a party of savages. A
negro servant drove the team with a load of corn. He knew nothing
of chariot races among the ancients, but he put the lash on the
horses, and drove through the large double-gateway without touching either post, as had been too often his unlucky habit. The
Indians were on the opposite side of the clearing, saw their prey
had escaped, raised their accustomed yell, and disappeared in the
woods. "Oh, Sam," said the Captain, whose servant he was,
"you've saved your scalp this time by accurate and energetic
driving!"

"Yes, Massa, I tink so," at the same time scratching his wool as
if he would make doubly sure that the useful appendage was not
missing. "De way I done miss dose gate-posts was no red man's
business. I never drove trew afore without I hit one side, and
sometimes bose of dem."

These pioneer Boone's Lick settlers deserve to be known and
had in remembrance by the present generation in that populous
and rich district of the State. I regret exceedingly, now it is too late,
that I did not gather many more facts, and record the names of the

principal families. They suffered as many privations as any frontier settlement in western history. The men were all heroes and the women heroines, and successfully and skilfully defended their families and the country about three years without the least aid from the national or territorial government. Throughout the war but ten persons were killed by Indians in all the settlements about Boone's Lick. Several other persons besides those already mentioned were killed in the Loutre settlements and below.

Those killed in the Boone's Lick country were Sarshall Cooper, Jonathan Todd, William Campbell, Thomas Smith, Samuel McMahan, William Gregg, John Smith, James Busby, Joseph W. Still, and a negro man. Captain Sarshall Cooper came to his tragic end at Cooper's fort, where his family resided. It was a dark night; the wind howled through the forest, and the rain fell in fitful gusts, and the watchful sentinel could not discern an object six feet from the stockade. Captain Cooper's residence formed one of the angles of the fort. He had previously run up a long account with the red-skins. They dreaded both his strategy and his prowess in Indian warfare. A single brave crept stealthily in the darkness and storm to the logs of the cabin, and made an opening in the clay between the logs barely sufficient to admit the muzzle of his gun, which he discharged with fatal effect. The assassin escaped and left the family and every settler in mourning. Among a large circle of relatives and friends, the impressions of their loss were vivid at the period of our first visit.

After nearly three years of hard fighting and severe suffering, Congress made provision for raising several companies of 'rangers' — men who furnished their own horses, equipments, forage and provisions, and received one dollar per day for guarding the frontier settlements—when a detachment was sent to the relief of the people of Boone's Lick, under command of General Henry S. Dodge, then major of the battalion. The mounted rangers included the companies of Captain John Thompson of St. Louis, Captain Daugherty of Cape Girardeau, and Captain Cooper of the Boone's Lick. An expedition under command of Captain Edward Hempstead was sent in boats up the Missouri. In the companies were fifty Delawares and Shawnees, and two hundred and fifty Americans. On the south bank of the Missouri, at a place now known as Miami, was an Indian town of four hundred, including women and children, who had migrated from the Wabash country a few years previous. They were friendly and peaceable; but bad

Indians would report bad tales of them, and Major Dodge, under instructions, guarded them back to the Wabash country.

One more disastrous event, though it occurred in the Loutre, deserves a brief record. Early in the season of 1814, the Sauks and Pottawatomies stole horses in the neighborhood of Loutre island. Fifteen or twenty rangers, commanded by Captain James Callaway, being out on a tour of observation, accidentally fell on their trail, and followed it. They came on the Indians in their camp near the head of Loutre creek, found the horses, but the Indians seemingly had fled. They retook the horses, and proceeded toward the settlement until they reached Prairie Fork. Here the captain, desirous of relieving the men who had charge of the horses in the rear, gave the command to Lieutenant Riggs, who went on with the main party. In a short time Captain Callaway and the men who had charge of the horses were fired on by a large party of Indians who lay in ambuscade, and he was severely wounded. He broke the line of the Indians, while men and horses fled; rode towards the main Loutre, where he was again intercepted by the savage enemy, and, being mortally wounded, fell from his horse as he attempted to swim the stream and expired. Four rangers of his party, McDermot, Hutchinson, McMillan and Gillmore, were killed.

Captain Callaway was the son of Flanders Callaway, and grandson of Daniel Boone. He was respected and lamented by all who knew him. The county of Callaway bears his name to posterity.

On my first visit to the Boone's Lick settlements, January, 1819, there were five preachers and five churches on the Baptist platform. Concord, I am inclined to think, had its origin in the party from Loutre, already noticed; and if so, it ranks first in the order of time. This church was in what is now Cooper county in the settlement south of Booneville. It gave name to the Concord Association, the history of which will be noticed in due time.

From this church, about the time or soon after my first visit to this part of Missouri, a preacher was raised up, and for a few years was remarkably successful in the conversion of sinners and establishing churches. His name was Luke Williams. It appears on the minutes of Mount Pleasant Association as a licentiate in 1820. He settled on a quarter section of public land, which he could hold by pre-emption for a limited period; for he had no money to buy land, and no means of getting any unless he should quit the min istry and engage in secular business, as some of his brethren did He was one of the most self-sacrificing itinerants in these days] ever knew. His zeal and Christian enterprise prompted him to ride and preach through all the settlements to the extreme western frontiers. No missionary society aided him; no churches—even those raised up under his ministry, and who claimed a share of his time and talents—gave him a dollar. He had put up a cabin, made a "truck-patch," and a cornfield, before he engaged in the ministry. He stayed at home only long enough to cultivate, with the aid of his industrious wife and little children, a crop of corn. The calls on him to preach to the destitute churches were numerous and pressing, but the members, not excepting the deacons, were too intent on saving every dollar they could get to buy land when it came into the market. Then a large majority of the Baptists that came into the early settlements of Boone's Lick had strong prejudices, as unreasonable as they were unscriptural, against giving any compensation to ministers. They made the egregious blunder that because the gospel was "without money and without price," therefore they might take the *time and the talents* of a minister of Christ for their own use, and rob him of the means of support due to his family. Luke Williams gave away many hundred dollars in his time and talents for the personal benefit of those who were too ignorant, too full of prejudice, or too avaricious to do justice to one of Christ's laborious and self-sacrificing servants. Yet God was with him, and scores of sinners were converted under his ministry. He died after a short but severe illness, early in September, 1824; leaving his land without a title, and his wife and little ones without a shelter they could call their own. An attempt was made after his decease, at the Fishing River Association, to raise a fund to enable the widow to enter the land for the children; but I am under the impression that for want of promptitude, and taking "pledges" and "promises" instead of dollars, the effort proved abortive.

Elder J. Hubbard, who was an old man and had been long in the ministry, was a resident and a preacher in Howard county on my first visit. He possessed a strong mind, and had received a better education in early life than his brethren in the ministry. He was clear-headed, Calvinistic in doctrine, and yet free from the blunders of those who could not reconcile the duty of sinners to repent and believe in the Lord Jesus Christ with the sovereignty of God in the dispensation of his grace. I found no preacher in Missouri, and few anywhere else, who had such full and correct knowledge of the Holy Scriptures as Elder Hubbard possessed. Yet he was modest and unassuming, without the least dogmatism in giving his views when solicited. He was quite deaf and could enjoy conversation only when his brethren spoke in a distinct tone of voice.

Elder Edward Turner was from Kentucky, and came to Howard county soon after the close of the war. He was a man of moderate abilities, and of correct deportment as a minister of the gospel. His name appears on the minutes of Mount Pleasant Association of 1820.

Elder Colden Williams was another of the early Baptist ministers in the Boone's Lick settlements. He came there from Cape Girardeau county, where he had been pastor of Bethel church. He possessed a strong discriminating mind, loved the work of the ministry, and was faithful in his calling. His membership was in Mount Zion church, where he furnished the monthly supply. I trace his name on the minutes of the association as a messenger from that church till 1830, when it disappears. He was much respected as a minister, and probably was called home about that time.

The only one that remains to be noticed is *Elder David McLain.* He was the first Baptist minister that came from central Kentucky to the Boone's Lick country with the first colony in 1810. Early in March, 1813, he started on horseback to Kentucky in company with a man by name of Young. They traveled without molestation till they reached Hill's ferry on the Kaskaskia river, old trace from St. Louis to Vincennes, Carlyle, the seat of justice of Clinton county, Ill. Three families that resided here, being alarmed by Indian signs, had left the ferry for one of the settlements in St. Clair county. The ferry-boat being fastened to the west bank, the two travelers crossed with their horses, and had not proceeded more than half a mile before they were fired on by Indians. Mr. Young was shot, and fell from his horse. Mr. McLain's horse was shot through the body, and fell; but the rider extricated himself, threw his saddle-bags into the bush, and ran for his life with several Indians in chase. Soon after, all the Indians fell back but one stout, athletic fellow, that seemed determined not to lose his prey. Elder McLain was encumbered with a thick overcoat, with wrappers on his legs, and boots and spurs on his feet. The Indian fired and missed him, which gave him the chance to throw off his overcoat, in hopes the prize would attract the attention of his pursuer. The other Indians having fallen back, Mr. McLain made signs of surrender as this one approached him, having loaded his gun. In this way he deceived his foe till he got within a few feet, when he assumed an attitude of defiance, watched his motions, and, at the instant he fired, dodged the ball, and then, with all the energy he could command, ran for his life. The contest continued more than one hour, during which his foe fired at him seven times. In one instance as he threw his breast forward, unfortunately he threw his elbow back and received the ball in his arm. During the chase he contrived to throw of his boots and spurs. They had run three or four miles in the timbered bottom down the river, and at a bend came near the bank. Elder McLain found himself nearly exhausted, and it seemed to him his last chance of escape was to swim the river. He plunged in, making the utmost effort of his remaining strength, and yet he had to keep an eye constantly fixed on his wily foe, who had loaded his gun for the eighth time, and from the bank brought it to a poise, and fired a second of time after McLain dove in deep water. By swimming diagonally down the stream he had gained on his pursuer, who, with the savage yell peculiar on such occasions, gave up the chase and returned to his band. Doubt less his report to the braves was that he had followed a "great-medicine," who was so charmed that his musket balls could not hurt him.

On reaching the shore, Mr. McLain was so exhausted that it was with the utmost difficulty he could crawl up the bank; for he was in a profuse perspiration when he plunged into the cold water. He was wet, chilled through, badly wounded, and could not stand until he had rolled himself on the ground, and rubbed his limbs to bring the blood into circulation. It was thirty-five miles to the Badgley settlement, where Elder Daniel Badgley and several Baptist families lived, which Mr. McLain, after incredible effort and sufferings, reached the next morning. There, with his wounded arm, and a burning fever, he lay several weeks, till some of his friends came from the Boone's Lick settlements, and took him to his family. A party of volunteers went over the Kaskaskia river, buried Mr. Young, found McLain's saddle-bags, with the contents safe, but saw no Indians.

I will now resume my journal, commencing January 1st, 1819, on which I left Franklin, and rode twenty-five miles a northwestern course to Chariton, where I called on and received a cordial welcome from General Duff Green and his family. It may now amuse the inhabitants on my route to read my remarks and speculations about the new country in which I traveled for a month:

"The country over which I rode is naturally rich and fertile and rapidly settling. This part of the territory will soon become the garden of Missouri. The surface of the land over which for a few miles I traveled before I reached this new town is rough and broken, but will probably become valuable.

"Chariton, containing about thirty families, has been laid off on a stream of the same name. In the winter of 1816–17, it was the wintering-ground of a tribe of Indians. The following summer, three or four log-cabins were erected. Within a year the increase has been rapid, and, in view of trade and business, it is thought to be superior to any situation on the Missouri river. The Chariton consists of three principal streams or branches that take their rise in the great prairies far in the north, each of which when not unusually low is navigable for keel-boats. These branches unite their waters in one noble channel as they approach the town, forming a stream navigable for steamboats, and a safe harbor at all seasons.

"This stream forms a beautiful semi-circle, in the bend of which lies the town site, the lower end of the circle touching on the Missouri. On the east side of the town-plat lies a range of hills or bluffs, giving a romantic and variegated appearance. Some, like pyramids, rise abruptly into the air, and from their summits show one of the most delightful prospects in nature. Ascending one of these bluffs, which rose majestically from the town site, I had an extensive view of the surrounding country. To the west and north-west the prospect is almost boundless."

On the Sabbath (January 3d), though in constant pain from swollen and inflamed face, I preached at twelve o'clock and again at night.

There are several very respectable and intelligent families in this town, and several unquestionably pious. At night I called the attention of the ladies to the formation of a "Female Mite Society," to aid the "United Society for the spread of the gospel," in sustaining some of our preachers in traveling and preaching in destitute settlements. This "Mite Society" was organized the following week, of twenty-two members, who subscribed thirty-six dollars. The officiating persons chosen were Mrs. Lucretia M. Green, President; Mrs. Henrietta C. D. Finlay, Secretary; Mrs. Polly Allen, Treasurer; and Mrs. Mary Ann Campbell and Miss Ann Green, Assistant Directors. In the following spring, the first Sabbath-school west of St. Louis was commenced in Chariton. It became auxiliary to the "Philadelphia Sunday and Adult School Union," which was the progenitor of the American Sunday School Union. About this period the Baptist missionaries held some correspondence and had some thoughts of making Chariton a station for the "Western Mission."

On the 7th of January, I rode to Franklin and preached at night to a few persons. Next night I preached in Booneville, where the people gave good attention. On returning across the river next day, I found the *Rev. Nicholas Patterson* in town. Mr. P. was an itinerant missionary from Philadelphia, and sent to the Far West by the Board of the General Assembly of the Presbyterian Church. I had seen and formed an acquaintance with him the preceding summer at St. Louis. He was a graduate of Princeton college, N. J., where he also studied theology; of medium talents as a preacher, but possessed an amiable disposition, great simplicity of character, and was habitually devotional. We traveled in company through the frontier settlements, visiting every log-cabin we could find, read ing the Scriptures, conversing, exhorting, and praying with every family. When opportunity offered, we would send an appointment ahead, and gather in a congregation. Our principal range was south of the Missouri and westward to the farthest settlements. Many of the settlers then scattered through that region were real frontier squatters, who lived in single log-cabins of the most infe-- rior quality, and made a cornfield of half-a-dozen acres, and a " truck-patch," on which they raised cabbages, turnips, cucumbers, and melons. We visited families who had not heard a preacher of the gospel for twenty years.

I give a description of one family we visited, not a dozen miles above Booneville, as a specimen of many others. It is no disparage- ment to the pioneer settlers that, in two years after our visitation, they poured into the country from Kentucky, Tennessee and other States; bought out the "rights" of these primitive squatters; made farms and introduced the habits of industry and civilization. The " squatters" we saw " cleared out" for the frontiers of Arkansas, or some other unsettled region, where they would not be annoyed with "improvements."

The only appearance of roads we found were bridle-paths, that pursued a zigzag course from one cabin to another. Seeing a smoke at a little distance from the trail we were pursuing, we found a cabin, about twelve feet square, made of such rough black jackpoles, as any stout man could lift, with a sort of wooden and dirt chimney. Very little " chinking and daubing" interfered with the passage of the wintry winds between the logs. We had to " stoop low," as Cotton Mather advised Franklin when he bumped his head against the cross-beam, to get in at the doorway The floor was the earth, and filthy in the extreme ; and the lodging-places of the inmates were a species of scaffolds around the walls, and elevated on forks

In and around the dirty shelter we found eight human beings, male and female, and the youngest nearly full size. Soon as we entered, the youngsters rushed out with an expression that probably was a mixture of wonder and fear. The old man and woman remained. *He* was either offended by having his domicile invaded by decent-looking persons, or he was too stupid to converse much. *She* was more tractable, and answered our questions as though she felt some interest in the conversation. *His* shock-headed appearance was as though he had slept alternately on a heap of cockleburs and ashes. The young men and women would show their dingy faces through the crevices between the logs, and in the doorway. It was not from destitution of water that the whole family remained unwashed, for a fine spring burst out within twenty yards of the cabin. Their dress was an object that attracted my attention, while my colleague made the effort to instruct them in some of the primitive truths of religion. Not a particle of *cloth* of any kind did I discover about their bodies. Men and women were dressed in skins that once the wild deer claimed, but covered and saturated with grease, blood, and dirt. We gathered the following history, chiefly from the old woman. They were "raised in the States," which, on further inquiry, meant North Carolina; there they were married, and one or two children were born. There she and the "old man" joined a Baptist church, and heard preaching once in a month. Neither had been to school in early life. They soon moved "beyond the settlements," and had continued to move as the "settlements" came near them. They had been in Missouri some three or four years, and supposed they would have to move again soon; for they heard the "settlements" were getting into the Boone's Lick country, and the land was to be sold.

On conversing with the old woman about an experience of grace and the way of salvation for sinners, through Jesus Christ, she wept and said: "That's jest what I hearn the preachers say afore we left Carolina." She could read a little, but had neither Bible, Testament, or hymn-book. She "wanted a *hyme*-book mightily," and we gave her a small one, and also a Testament.

We read a chapter, gave some familiar explanations, and prayed with them; but all we could say, aided by the persuasions of the mother, we could not get one of the young folks into the cabin. She said "they had never heard a *human* pray in all their born-days."

One of the most striking contrasts in the character and habits of those we visited was in family government. Many of the fami-

13

lies we called on, like the one described, were not only wretchedly
ignorant and filthy, but wholly destitute of skill in family government. Children were left to act out their vicious propensities,
without the least effort on the part of the parents to assuage and
restrain their ungovernable passions. Some parents do not train
their children, from early boyhood to the period of manhood, to
habits of self-government. What helpless wretches, and how unfit
for social life, are those young men who have no government over
themselves; and in nine instances out of ten the blame, guilt and
crime may be justly charged to father or mother, or both.

Captain Stephen Cole survived the war, after making every effort
for the defence of the settlements, and being wounded several times.
After living through and enduring all the hardships and privations
in settling and holding the country ; just as the period of prosperity
came, and lands and other property increased in value, and invited
repose and contentment; in 1822 his love of adventure induced
him to become a pioneer in the trade to Santa Fe, from which he
never returned. He was killed by the red-skins on the plains !

Colonel Benjamin Cooper attained to a green old age. He was
a member of the territorial council, and much respected and beloved
by all classes.

Mount Zion church, situated in the interior of Howard county,
was one of the oldest, and my impression is that it was formed by
emigrants before the war. No real progress was made in church
affairs during the period of the war from 1810 to 1815. Church-
meetings and preaching were very irregular. The loss of about
three hundred horses that were stolen by the Indians, and a large
portion of the cattle and swine killed, and no opportunity to provide a surplus of corn ; the old settlers fared hard and had to be
very industrious. Then the "new-comers," like a mountain torrent,
poured into the country faster than it was possible to provide corn
for breadstuff. Some families came in the spring of 1815 ; but in
the winter, spring, summer, and autumn of 1816, they came like
an avalanche. It seemed as though Kentucky and Tennessee were
breaking up and moving to the "Far West." Caravan after caravan
passed over the prairies of Illinois, crossing the "great river" at
St. Louis, all bound to the Boone's Lick. The stream of immigration had not lessened in 1817. Many families came from Virginia,
the Carolinas, and Georgia, and not a few from the Middle States,
while a sprinkling found their way to the extreme west from
Yankeedom and Yorkdom. Amongst these was the writer and his
family in 1817.

Following in the wake of this exodus to the middle section of Missouri was a terrific excitement about getting land. It had attained the climax on my first visit. A delegate in Congress from the Territory of Missouri, by one of those political frauds common to political manœuvering, obtained the passage of an act for the relief of the New Madrid sufferers from the earthquakes of 1811–12. It turned out in the result, if there was any truth in hard-swearing before the courts, that there were fivefold more New Madrid claims than there were heads of families and single men in that district. There were honest claims, but the courts of justice in Missouri are not yet through with the fraudulent ones.

The late William H. Crawford, Secretary of the United States Treasury, decided that no pre-emption rights would be granted west of Cedar creek. He overlooked an amendment to a law that provided expressly for the Boone's Lick settlements. The mails at that period were at least a month in going and returning from Washington, and some three months passed away before the error was rectified.

It was in the summer of 1818, that, by proclamation of the President, the land-offices of St. Louis and Old Franklin were opened, pre-emptions confirmed and paid for, and public sales commenced. But pre-emptions in the Boone's Lick county were held in abeyance. In the meanwhile hordes of speculators in New Madrid claims were scouring the country and laying a claim on every farm that could be found.

Enterprising pioneers, who, like Colonel Benjamin Cooper, had defended the country in most perilous times, were in imminent danger of losing their lands and improvements. The Register and Receiver of the land-office, supposing Congress would make some provision in the case, held back these farms from sale, and made proclamation for those settlers, who ought to have pre-emption-rights, to come to the office, prove their rights, and have them placed on record. My first visit was at this crisis; and I could not call at a cabin in the country without being accosted: " Got a New Madrid claim?" "Are you one of these land-speculators, stranger?"

From the close of the war, the old settlers had been struggling and putting forth all the industry and enterprise possible to obtain money to pay for the pre-emptions at the minimum price of Congress land. I will leave the reader to imagine the just indignation of those pioneers, while in doubt about purchasing the land their own honest industry had improved. After some delay the law was found to be in their favor, and all excitement was allayed when they got their certificates of purchase.

During the war, when the people had to live in forts, and till 1818, no correctly-thinking person could expect Christian churches to be organized, revivals to follow, and the baptism of converts to be reported. With five Baptist preachers, and as many more Cumberland Presbyterians and Methodists, only five Baptist churches, with members not much exceeding one hundred in all, were gathered before 1818. That year the five churches united in organizing the Mount Pleasant Baptist Association. The churches were Concord, Mount Zion, Mount Pleasant, Salem, and Bethel. In 1820, these five churches report to the association, seven ministers and two hundred and thirteen members. Mount Pisgah, in Cooper county, fifteen or twenty miles south of Booneville, was formed by immigrants to that region in 1819–20, reported three ministers—Elders John B. Logan, Jacob Chism, and Lewis Shelton—and thirty-four members. Providence church, north of the Missouri, was formed about the same time of ten members. In 1820, the association was held with Concord church on the 9th, 10th, and 11th days of September, when seven new churches, including four ministers were received. The churches were Petite Osage Bottom (called Teetsaw), Mount Nebo, Double Springs, and Big Bottom, south of the Missouri; and Mount Arrarat, Little Bonne Femme, and Chariton, north. The elders on the south or right side of the river, all new-comers, were Peyton Nowlin, William Jennings, and Peter Woods. In the Chariton church, then located in the old town of Chariton, for the first time, is the name of the late Ebenezer Rodgers. From the same church, a licensed preacher by the name of John Bowles appears on the minutes.

CHAPTER XI.

Recollections of Missouri in 1819—A Seminary contemplated.

On the 15th of January we pursued our journey, visiting such families as we could find scattered along the points of timber, conversing and praying with them. After a ride of ten miles we arrived at the house of Mr. Ish, just in season to hear a Methodist circuit-preacher by the name of Jones. Here we spent the day and following night. Mr. Ish was a Presbyterian, and appeared to be a pious, intelligent, and liberal man. His wife was an amiable woman, and they lived in their double log-cabin, in a plain, but neat and comfortable style. In their family-circle there was peace and harmony, and their children were under the best government and instruction I had seen for many months. Mr. Ish lamented the low state of religion and the social habits that prevailed around him, but lived in expectation of a change in morals and habits soon as the land was brought into market, when the "squatter" class would sell their pre-emptions to industrious immigrants, and "clear out." This settlement was extensive, and called the "Big Bottom." It extended ten or twelve miles along the river, opposite the town of Chariton. There was no school, and a majority of the squatters wanted none. A Baptist church of a dozen members had been gathered a few weeks previous to our visit, in the upper part of the settlement, and may be found on the minutes of the Mount Pleasant Association of 1820 with the name, Big Bottom.

On the 15th, at night, we saw a comet plainly visible, which not a few regarded as the forerunner of another Indian war.

On the Big Bottom was a cornfield, under a common fence, of nearly one thousand acres, and occupied by more than twenty families, each of which cultivated their separate plat of ground. A majority of the families lived in the most primitive order of log-cabins around this field. Several we passed by were not "chinked nor daubed," and the chimneys were halves of logs, laid up as high as the mantlepiece, and served as a slight barrier to keep out the cows and hogs. Children and youth in almost countless numbers would show their tangled and matted locks, dingy faces, and squalid dress and appearance as we passed by. We had met with so little encouragement in visiting, conversing, and praying with this class that we concluded to pass them by, and go on to Mr. Job's house (a Baptist family) where I had sent an appointment to preach at night. This was on Saturday, the 16th of January. Though the appointment had not been circulated more than one hour before our arrival, the house was full and the people solemn and quite attentive. We conversed with several persons who appeared to be seriously inquiring the way of salvation. For mixed up with the ignorant, filthy, wretched squatters described, were many decent, respectable, and religious families, who were patiently waiting for the land to be brought into market, when the squatters would give place to an improved class.

On Sabbath, my colleague having gone over to Chariton to preach there, I preached two sermons during the day.

The Sabbath, as a day of worship and rest, as a memorial of the resurrection of Christ, being so much neglected and profaned, even by professors of religion, and knowing the people on this frontier seldom or never got any instruction from any source on this subject, I prepared myself, and preached to a crowded assembly from Isa. lviii. 13, 14, associating with it, Heb. iv. 9, 10. The people were attentive and solemn, and some seemed seriously impressed. After a short intermission I preached again from Romans x. 1. I dismissed the congregation as customary, but none seemed inclined to move. After a short time a few went out, while the rest stayed and sung hymns. I again exhorted, prayed, conversed, and by request I gave out an appointment to preach on Tuesday. Some were in tears. This was the only place in which I saw any indications of a revival in the Boone's Lick settlements during my first visit.

After dinner I rode to the house of Mr. Ish, and preached again after night. Though it was dark and rainy I had a house full to hear me. On Tuesday, accompanied by Mr. Patterson, I rode to Mr. Job's, where both preached to an attentive congregation.

Next day we bid farewell to our friends in Big Bottom, crossed the river to Chariton, and the next Sabbath both preached in that village.

On Monday, January 25th, I gave the parting hand to my traveling companion, whom I left to perform missionary labor in the Boone's Lick country, and rode to Franklin. My horse being lame, I had left him in Booneville, and hired one for the late tour. Finding his disease was the swinney, and that it would require many months to recover, I was compelled to leave him and buy another to take me to St. Louis. On my way down I had appointments for frequent preaching.

During the period of my visit to the Boone's Lick country, the winter was unusually mild and open; no snow of consequence, light showers of rain, and for one-third of the nights no frost. I reached St. Louis on the 5th of February.

February, 1819. It now became expedient to make such arrangements in the Western Missouri enterprise, as would save expense and promote its objects more effectually. It had been in our plan at first, even before we left Philadelphia for this region, to establish a seminary for the common and higher branches of education; and especially for the training of school-teachers and aiding the preachers now in office, or who may hereafter be brought forth in the churches. The education of the ministry is of primary importance in all new countries. A classical and scientific education, such as academies and colleges furnish, has never been regarded by Baptists as an indispensable requisite to entrance on the gospel ministry, or to perform the duties of a Christian pastor. But there are certain branches of education that are indispensable to ministerial usefulness.

The mind must be trained to habits of thinking; to logical reasoning, to readiness of speech; to systematical arrangement of gospel truth, and to a practical application of Christian duties. Mere declamation is not preaching the gospel. A man may stand up, rattle off words, tear his voice to tatters, and foam at the mouth, and yet not communicate one Scriptural idea, nor excite one spiritual emotion in his hearers. We have a very poor opinion of a man who has to write all his discourses, and read them off on the Sabbaths. If he has not, and cannot acquire the gift of "*aptness to teach*," he had better let this work alone. And yet the writer has written out in full, and read from the platform not a few discourses in early times through the old settlements of Illinois and Missouri. This was done, in part, on special subjects, that seemed to require a cluster of facts, and sometimes dates, to produce the desired impression; and partly to counteract the violent prejudices that prevailed against preparatory study and written outlines in pulpit discourses. The Puritans (Presbyterians and Congregationalists) since their origin, about three hundred years ago, have gone to the extreme in their reading lessons. Baptists and Methodists, until late years, may have erred on the other hand; and for lack of concentrated thought, and writing out their thoughts in logical and consecutive order, became mere declaimers; or, rather, like the blind horse in a mill, go round and round on the few Scriptural ideas they profess.

Our aim was not to establish a regular theological institution, or lay the foundation and build up a college. The writer never had the gift of anticipating and attempting great things. It has been his rule through life to do what he could for the present, and trust to Providence for the future.

As my family was the largest, and better adapted to a country life, and the burden of a boarding-school, while the circumstances of my colleague and his family made it expedient they should abide in town, we soon settled that question. The next was the location. Several points were thought of on both sides of the "Great River," but it was no easy matter then to find a village, or a country settlement, where a respectable seminary could be sustained and boarders accommodated. The Catholics had several institutions, they called seminaries and colleges; but for literary, scientific, or theological purposes, they could never do much good among the American and Protestant population. It was deemed expedient for the writer to visit several places within fifty miles of St. Louis. St. Charles was one point to which our attention was directed; and the preceding autumn we had aided in gathering a school, and by our influence with the citizens of that growing village to patronize a man whose initials were J. C. Mr. C. was a Baptist preacher, and we honestly supposed he would cordially co-operate in all our Christian enterprises. But to our sorrow, within less than a twelvemonth, we found out by documents received that he was of doubtful standing among Baptists in Kentucky and Ohio, and regarded a disorderly person. He had been raised a Quaker, without the honesty or truthfulness of that sect. He had been baptized, licensed, and ordained in Ohio, but never did have the confidence of clear-headed and sound-hearted Baptists.

His personal appearance and address gained attention, and made temporary claims to the respect of his patrons. He was a good penman, but deficient in orthography, grammar, and other branches of a good English education. He had made some progress in plain mathematics, and had studied and practiced surveying, though superficial in that branch. Yet he had shrewdness and tact to find out he could not succeed and gather a profitable school without an assistant or partner. He was anxious—all in kindness to the missionaries—to get one of us to join him. This made repeated visits to St. Charles necessary during the latter part of February and early in March

The late Hon. Rufus Easton of St. Louis, who had become interested in the landed property, projected as the site of Alton city,
exacted the promise that we should not decide on our location
until we had visited and explored that site, or rather the village
now known as Upper Alton, two and a half miles in the rear, and
on elevated and healthy ground. And we hope it will amuse and
not offend our readers in that vicinage if they have a truthful description of the two Altons as they then appeared.

We (singly—not our colleague) left St. Charles on February 23d,
1819, and rode down to the "Point" towards Smeltzer's ferry, then
located about three miles above the site for a city. Here we crossed
the river a little after sunset, and had five miles to ride to the inhabited village. For three miles the pathway lay along the brink
of the low water of the river under the cliffs. Not far from the
present site of the Alton House, there was a building, but whether
a rough frame or a log-house it was too dark to perceive. (There
were four cabins on the town site.) Here we obtained directions
how to find and follow the dubious pathway through the brush and
forest, up a long hill to the village. It was cloudy and dark, but
on emerging from the forest, we found on every side the appearance of camp-fires. Log heaps, piles of brush, old stumps and
other combustible materials were glowing with heat, and spreading
an illumination over the plateau. Inquiry was made for a tavern
or boarding-house, and we were directed to a long, low, ill-looking
log-house. It was about forty feet in length, and probably sixteen
feet wide, the doorway for entrance at the west end, and the dining-
room, as it seemed to be used for eating purposes, was the first
room entered. Our readers are aware we had been in some dirty
places. The table was supported by forks driven in the ground,
on which rough, newly sawed boards extended perhaps twenty
feet. An old cloth, filthy like the rest of the establishment, covered
a portion of the table. A supply of dirty dishes indicated that
several boarders might have had a late supper. The part from
which the dishes and cloth had been removed was occupied by
three parties with cards, or something resembling spotted pieces
of pasteboard; all in harmony with the rest, for the cards and men
were the dirtiest objects I had seen since our pilgrimage in the
Boone's Lick country. On inquiring for the landlord, a shock-
head, begrimed features, and soiled garment that appeared to
belong to a "human" came in. The first thing was to find a stable
and feed for a wearied horse.

On exploring the premises, I found him in a log pen with some

boards over one half the roof, and the mud mid-leg deep.   Seeing
no chance for better quarters, I left him munching corn, of which
ne had a supply.

It did not take many minutes to frame and carry into effect a
resolution to find better quarters for his rider.   While living in
St. Louis the preceding year, I had formed a slight acquaintance
with the family of Doctor Erastus Brown, who in autumn had
removed to Upper Alton.   Offering a dirty, ragged boy a dime to
pilot me to Dr. Brown's, slinging my saddle-bags on the arm, and
climbing over stumps and logs, brought us to the snug, neat,
newly-built log-house—no, we will call it a "cottage"—where we
found the doctor, his lady, and two or three little ones, in as
comfortable quarters as any decent folks deserved to have in those
frontier times.

" Doctor, I have called to impose myself upon your hospitality,"
and gave him a brief sketch of my recent adventure, amongst
wretchedness, filth, drunken ribaldry, and low profanity of the
boarding-house.

Both declared a hearty welcome, and regretted I did not call on
them on my first arrival.   I told the good lady not to get supper,
for I had eaten a late dinner, and it was drawing towards bed-time,
but in the quickest time she had the tea made and the table spread.
I told her I was used to sleeping on the floor with my saddle for a
pillow, and saddle-blanket for covering, but I was ushered into a
neat little room, with a bed and covering fit for a prince.   In all
my wanderings, I never experienced as great and sudden a transition
from wretchedness and filth to comfort and happiness.

In the morning, after an early breakfast, in company with my
friend, Dr. B., I made an exploration through the town, was introduced to several citizens, and learned all that was necessary of
Upper Alton *at that time*, as the site for a seminary of learning.

There were on the spot between forty and fifty families, living
in log-cabins, shanties, covered wagons, and camps.   Probably not
less than twenty families were destitute of houses ; but were getting
out materials and getting up shelters with industry and enterprise.
I had become acquainted with the extremes of the social state, and
had no opportunity to enlarge my experience.   Doubtless there
were other families living as comfortably as the one whose hospitality I had shared.

I found a school of some twenty-five or thirty boys and girls was
taught by some backwoods fellow, but the chance for a boarding-
school was small indeed.   There was the old settlement about the

forks of Wood river and Rattan's prairie that might furnish a few scholars. The Macoupin settlement—real frontier rowdies—was thirty miles north, of a dozen families; then three families had ventured over Apple creek. The emigrants to the Sangamon country went there the preceding winter. Peoria, on the Illinois river, was an old French village of twenty-five cabins. Morgan, Cass, Scott, and all those counties along the Illinois river were the hunting-grounds of the Indians. The late Major Wadsworth and half a dozen families had made their pitch in Calhoun county. All the country to the east and north was one vast wilderness. Where then could scholars be found to fill a seminary at Upper Alton? After deciding all such questions, I gave a fellow a quarter to clean the mud from my horse, paid for his fare, received a hearty invitation from Dr. and Mrs. Brown to call on them the next time I visited Alton, and made my way by another path back to Smeltzer's ferry. It was three or four years before I again visited Upper Alton, during which period quite a town had sprung up, but I never could find the locality of the dirty tavern house; never again saw the family or its inmates, and was so fortunate as not to learn their names. It is thought not one of that breed can now be found in Madison county.

Having crossed the river and rode a few miles, I preached to about twenty people, at the house of Mrs. Griffith, a widow lady, a dozen miles from St. Charles, which became one of my preaching-stations through the season. I rode home with Mr. Ayres, where I spent the night. Mr. A. and his wife were Presbyterians, and originated from Stamford, Ct. They were intelligent and respectable people and lived in comfortable style.

Myself and colleague were engaged in a *mission compact* in the F-a-r W-e-s-t, until it was dissolved by the joint action of the Board of the old Triennial Convention, and the missionaries.

I have previously given an account of the organization of the " *United Society for the spread of the Gospel,*" in Illinois and Missouri. This was the first missionary society that was formed in this part of the world. One object was to aid the preachers then in the country, to itinerate and preach the gospel to the destitute.

I had volunteered to officiate as collecting agent, without charge, to provide the funds to sustain the itinerants. It was in this business I was engaged while traveling, from October, 1818, to April, 1819. That is, while performing all sorts of work as an itinerant missionary, under supervision of the Board in Philadelphia, and in concert with my colleague in St. Louis, I did what I could to provide means for the local society, that had been organized by the advice and approbation of three associations. One mode to secure contributions, was to organize "*Mite Societies*" in the churches. I had formed three such societies during my excursion in the Boone's Lick country.

During the first week in March (1819) it was decided that a new mission station should be established at St. Charles, a seminary planted there, and that I should take charge of that station, and that my colleague should maintain the post at St. Louis. During much of this month the weather was stormy; rain, snow, and sleet frequent, the roads muddy, and vegetation late in putting forth.

On the 19th I crossed the "Great River,"* and rode to Elder D. Badgley's residence. The road was intolerably muddy, and before I reached there the cold air was piercing. My object was to spend a few days, in providing funds for the "United Society for the spread of the gospel."

The church I first visited in the Badgley settlement was called "Ogle's Creek," and the members were scattered over the field now occupied by Unity and the southern portion of Bethel churches. Here I formed the "Ogle's Creek Mite Society, auxiliary," etc. This was the first social organization for missionary purposes ever formed in Illinois.

On Monday, the 22d, in company with Elder Badgley, I started on a week's tour. We rode across the spot of ground where I have since resided for more than thirty-five years, crossed Silver creek by deep fording, and spent the day and night with brother William Padon, the father of our venerable Elder John Padon.

---

* This compound word as I give it includes every particle of meaning contained in the modern name MISSISSIPPI. Some fancy-monger, with more imagination than learning, since my first residence on its banks, gave the modern name, "*Father of Waters.*" It has just as much truth and real philology in it as another phrase, "*Dark and bloody ground,*" when applied to Kentucky. The word *Mississippi* is a compound word in the Algonquin language;—the most extensive language of the Indians of North America, though corrupted into different dialects by the Ottawas, Sauks, Foxes, Miamis, and the tribes towards the Atlantic. Mr. Schoolcraft says, (1820) "It is now spoken nearly in its primeval purity by the different bands of Chippeways. It is a compound of the word *Missi,* signifying *great,* and *Sepe,* a river." Let no crack-brained genius hereafter say or write "*Father of Waters.*"

Elder Badgley—like many of our frontier preachers, who never knew any rules for the interpretation of Scripture, but their own fancy, or as some of them mistakingly thought, the Spirit of God taught them the meaning—had some queer speculations, which he occasionally preached to the world.

We had a long but friendly talk about the fall of man, and the *kind of death* Adam died, according to the threatening denounced, on the partaking of the forbidden fruit,—"*ye shall not eat of it, neither shall ye touch it lest ye die.*" (Gen. iii. 3.) I have heard the whimsical dogma preached, not merely on these frontiers, but in "York State," in early times, that man did not die a *spiritual death* but a *moral death ;* so we held a profitless discussion about spiritual and moral death, and all the collateral circumstances and contingencies.

These crude notions had their origin in ignorance of the meaning of words, and the distinction between the literal and figurative meaning of words and phrases. A good English dictionary and a careful examination of the meaning of words, with a smattering of the elements of rhetoric, about "tropes and figures," and a slight touch of logic and mental philosophy would have been of great service to this class of preachers. But some of them were as much afraid of a dictionary as they were of a missionary.

It would be a capital thing if we could preserve the golden mean in the education of ministers, and especially young ones. But there is such a tendency to extremes in every thing, that it is next to impossible to keep the middle track, and educate our young ministry in the Scriptures. They are taught—or rather in our modern institutions, they are carried over superficially, a wide field in science and literature, and learn very little of THAT BOOK, doctrinally, practically and spiritually, which God has given, and out of which he has commanded them to teach the people. Some of these illiterate old men have studied the Bible carefully, and with prayer, and guided by plain common-sense, and deep reverence for the things of God, overflow with true Biblical knowledge, and spiritual emotions ; though they sometimes make blunders in speech and miss the meaning of figurative language. And yet young preachers who have dabbled a little in Latin and Greek, are apt to turn up their noses at these old fathers. Such is poor human nature in young and old.

Tuesday morning, March 23d, we rode a northern course between Silver creek and Looking Glass prairie to Elder Robert Brazil's house, where the heavy rains and our preaching appoint-

14

ments detained us till Friday. On this trip we rode over the town plat of Lebanon, then containing five log-cabins. We preached daily, visited some families, and formed the "Looking Glass Prairie Mite Society."

Elder Badgley (who was one of the managers) was soon after appointed an itinerant missionary for Illinois, and performed two months missionary service at sixteen dollars per month; and the Mite Societies I formed, as agreed upon, paid their funds over to the missionary, and he reported to the treasurer in St. Louis.

Returning to Mr. Padon's on the 26th, I preached in the vicinity at night. My congregation were three-fourths Methodist; for Payfield's settlement was a regular old "stamping ground" for Methodism.

Silver creek, from the heavy rains since we crossed it, was swimming deep, and the bottom land was covered with water, up to the mid-sides of a horse, and the prospect of reaching our next appointment was quite dubious. However, Brother Padon, who was inured to frontier life, had the *will* to help us onward, and "where there is a will there's a way."

Saturday morning the sun shone out, and after an early breakfast, our host yoked up his oxen, and hauled a big trough to Silver creek, and crossed over the missionaries with their saddles and luggage, and swam the horses along side the feeding-trough, converted into a canoe. It required three trips to do this.

Amongst the contrivances of Infinite Wisdom for man's accommodation is his providential operations in forming the banks of all our creeks and rivers in this valley, so as to leave a skirt of land along the border, some four or five feet above the overflow of the bottoms. This furnished a dry and convenient plateau for saddling and mounting our horses. We rode half a mile through deep water, and after crossing Ogle's and other creeks, and by following a "blind trail," we reached old Mr. Seybold's residence in season to meet the little Baptist church then called Cantine Creek.

The situation of Mr. Seybold's residence (one of our old pioneers, long since deceased) was about three miles north of west from Troy. Here we preached on Saturday night and Sabbath, and formed the "Cantine Creek Mite Society."

The state of religion throughout the whole country was very low; not a revival could be heard of in Illinois and Missouri. The ministers and many of the members of any degree of intelligence in the old Illinois Association, at that time, were friendly to these missionary announcements. At the preceding session (October

10th, 1818), the following record was placed on the minutes without opposition, and apparently with honesty of purpose. It was the twentieth item:

"Brother Peck presented the plan of a society to employ missionaries, and promote common schools amongst the whites and Indians, which we desire to see carried into effect, and which we recommend to the churches."

I also give the record for Lord's-day, October 11th, Elder William Jones being clerk:

"A respectable concourse of people having met, Brother Peck preached a missionary sermon from Exodus xxxiii. 15: 'If thy presence go not with me, carry us not up thence.' A collection for the Indian fund of the Western Baptist Mission Society, of eleven dollars and twenty-five cents, was received by Brother Peck."

[This money was applied to the expenses of the Indian mission in the Wabash country under Elder Isaac McCoy.]

The record further says:

"Brother Jones preached from Heb. iv. 3, and Brother Musick from Isaiah liii. 1. Brother Peck closed by giving some interesting accounts of religious revivals in the Northern States and elsewhere."

The "plan of a society" to employ missionaries took the form of the "United Society for the spread of the gospel." Five months after this act of the only association then in Illinois, the venerable David Badgley, the first Baptist minister who settled his family in the Illinois country, and the missionary of another Board, were forming "Mite Societies," auxiliary to the first missionary organization in the Far West.

On Monday, the 29th, after a violent shower, with some thunder and hail, I preached in the log-cabin of Messrs. Collins, three brothers, who came to St. Louis in December, 1817, at the same time the writer and his family arrived. They came over the river early in 1818, purchased a farm and the cabin they then occupied, and where I preached the first sermon ever heard on the site of Collinsville. The Brethren Lemen and others had preached in the adjacent settlements a dozen years previous.

On the 8th of April my family was removed to the town of St. Charles. Here we commenced a literary institution with the name of St. Charles Academy, having formed a partnership with J. C., heretofore mentioned.

The number of scholars was about thirty, but soon increased to forty. At the same time, Rev. Charles S. Robinson, a Presbyterian missionary from the Eastern States, established a meeting in the same village.   He received occasional aid from another missionary (Rev. Mr. T.)

I heard Mr. T. preach several times.   His sermons were good, sometimes eloquent; but — as the laborer said to the prophet (2 Kings vi. 5): "Alas, master!—it was borrowed."   One from Luke xiv. 18 was from Burder's Village Sermons.   At the monthly concert for prayer in St. Louis, he gave us a lecture from Daniel ix. 1–3.   This discourse was chiefly made up from one then recently preached before the East Tennessee Bible Society.   A portion I recognized as having been first preached and published in the Eastern States.

Ministers of the gospel ought to collect all the ideas and thoughts they can from every source, work them over in their own mental laboratory, and clothe them in their own language.   But, if they copy other men's sermons, and retail them off as their own, those present who recognize them, ought to exclaim: "Alas, master! for it was borrowed."

To lessen, as much as possible, the expense of the mission, I made every effort to sustain my family by the fruits of my own labor.   Attendance in school, domestic affairs, and cultivating a garden, kept me busily employed, and in a state of mind that was a poor qualification for a preacher of Christ   There is such a tendency in human nature to become worldly-minded, that it requires constant watchfulness, and the abiding impression that the ministry of the gospel is the paramount business of life, and every other pursuit to be kept in subordination to this one great calling. And I have no question that every man who has felt himself to be called of God, and been set apart by the Church to the work of the ministry, has no right to forsake it for any earthly advantage. And every one who does forsake this calling, because of its sacrifices and inconveniences, and enter on the business of the world that he may get rich, or that his family may be placed in respectable and fashionable circumstances, should be "unfrocked," as our Episcopal friends express it.   Such men have either made a sad mistake in getting into the ministry, without those elements of mind and character required in the gospel, or they will suffer the chastisement of a merciful Saviour, and fail in their pursuit of worldly prosperity and happiness.   There is an immeasurable difference between such men and those ministers who provide a support for their families by their own industry and the economy and household-management of their wives; while they feel and act as though preaching the gospel was the paramount business of life, and the class who give up that calling because it does not afford them the income necessary to gratify their earthly desires. Ministers who sustain themselves, and labor in the ministry for the salvation of sinners and sustaining feeble churches, deserve all praise. And while the ministers of Christ are entitled to a support from the churches they serve (wherever ability exists), they should be encouraged and commended whenever they devote such time and talents as they have to the cause of Christ.

During the summer of 1819, amidst the secular employments alluded to (for teaching school is no more a gospel service than plowing corn), I generally had appointments to preach in destitute neighborhoods, in the town of St. Charles, and occasionally in St. Louis. On the 18th of April we opened a Sunday-school, which was the first known in that town. Another department of labor was preaching to the colored people, chiefly slaves, on Sabbath evenings. Several became seriously disposed, professed to be savingly converted to God, and some were baptized.

During this season I suffered afflictions from impurity of the blood. A series of severe boils annoyed me for three months, and on two Sabbaths when I had appointments in the country, I was prevented, from inability to ride on horseback. Thus the summer passed away without any thing of particular notice. During vacation the latter part of June, I made a missionary tour to the Salt river settlements, and found a call for Bibles and Testaments in every neighborhood. The state of religion, even where small churches existed, was very low. There were two or three preachers without any regular standing in the churches of any evangelical denomination, whose conduct was suspicious, and who did more harm than good. Church-members were eagerly engaged in worldly pursuits. They attended church-meetings monthly, when they had nothing else to do, and preaching occasionally when some itinerants passed through the settlement; but I seldom found one who worshipped God at home, or trained up his children in the way they should go. If the mother was a real Christian, the children were not wholly neglected. There were instances that came under my observation, though few, in which the mother made it a matter of principle to talk with her children and pray with them; and the blessed effects are visible in some families to this day.

CHAPTER XII.

Review of the Western Mission—Position and prospects of Messrs.
Peck and Welch—Experiences—Dissolution of their connection
as Missionaries of the Board.

THE very full reminiscences of Mr. Peck, contained in the
preceding chapters, here close.   Before taking up the thread
of the narrative of the future years, to be gathered from his
journals and correspondence, it seems appropriate " to make
up the reckoning," in sailor phrase, in regard to the progress
hitherto secured.   Between two and three years had now
elapsed since Messrs. Peck and Welch had reached St. Louis
and commenced their mission and explorations.   They had
found in the territory and its neighborhood remote from Illinois, more Baptist churches and ministers (*so-called*) than
they had expected.   The larger part were feeble, unintelligent,
and peculiarly susceptible of prejudices against better-informed, more zealous, and ampler-sustained ministers, coming
among them, and, as they could readily perceive, supplanting
them in influence and favor with the people.   Neither of these
missionaries had then had as ample experience as afterward
in dealing with the prejudices, and guarding against the jealousy of this class of preachers and churches.   On a candid
and thorough review of all their proceedings during these
trying and eventful years, they might doubtless see how it
would have been possible to have so modified some of their
acts, and so have guarded some of their deportment, as to
have escaped, or at least diminished, a portion of the untoward influences which were raised up to oppose them.   The
anti-mission party among American Baptists was just then
taking form, and assuming its attitude of hostility to those of
their brethren who heartily engaged in evangelizing operations, both at home and abroad   It naturally allied itself to

the antinomianism and selfishness too prevalent in all partially sanctified hearts. It found, too, one of its securest intrenchments in ignorance, prejudice, and jealousy in the ministry. There would occur frequent opportunity for misrepresentation; and of this a portion of those ministers availed themselves with unscrupulous avidity. The best of men are imperfect; and there will be furnished abundant occasion among those seeking occasion to find fault with the spirit or the management of those who were struggling with all their might to introduce a more orderly, intelligent, and efficient system of operations among these sparsely-scattered churches, and their illiterate and, therefore, very naturally jealous and prejudiced ministers.

Some infelicities, too, were just beginning to manifest their influence in the associate in Mr. Peck's school operations in St. Charles. Indeed it was quite impossible to effect very much in teaching, while so many calls for preaching were responded to, at such a distance from the residence of the missionaries, either in St. Louis or St. Charles. A double object was regarded in attempting these schools. First, to furnish better specimens of teaching than hitherto existed in that vicinity, and to prepare more competent instructors for the many schools needed; and next, to secure in a great degree their support from the tuition they should receive. The former of these objects was measurably attained. But the latter signally failed. After deducting the expenses for rents, assistants, etc., and the various losses from those unable or unwilling to pay, the net income of the St. Louis school was never large, and that at St. Charles still less.

To some of us at this distance of time, and but little acquainted with the concomitant circumstances, it no doubt seems strange that these brethren had not, in the outset, concentrated their labors more on one or two important points, and by thus more fully demonstrating their full success and manifest advantages, have carried ampler and earlier conviction to the minds of all. The fact was that no small portion of the censure they incurred was for going and settling them-

selves in the chief towns to the neglect of the scattered pioneer-
dwellers in the wilderness. How baseless such an allegation
was, their abundant travels and exposures in the cabins of the
poor and destitute abundantly confirm; while the motive for
their efforts, and for their too frequent and long absences
from home, is made manifest. They tried very resolutely
to take away occasion of offense from those too ready to seek
such occasion.

As the natural result of this course, though themselves
very fully convinced of the importance of giving more time
and attention to St. Louis especially, they had been so much
diverted from and hindered in this work, that the church-
edifice, which two years earlier had been commenced, was
scarcely completed; their congregations had very much dwin-
dled; and their taunting opponents seemed likely to realize
their hope of the discomfiture of the missionaries in their endeavor to plant firmly in that important post the banner of
the Cross.

Very sad, though not altogether desponding, are some of
their letters and the entries in the journals of the mission at
this period. To add to the disquietude of Mr. Peck, he seems
to have suffered greatly at this period, in view of his own
want of more fervent zeal and pious devotedness to the spiritual duties of his high calling. His diary for some weeks is
filled with lamentations over his want of greater conformity
to his Saviour; and the fervent prayers here recorded show
how far he was in reality from the deadness of soul which he
lamented.

The autumn of 1820 brought also other experiences of a
most afflictive and trying character to our brother and his
family. That season proved very sickly, and disease and
death spread their pallid influences all around them. First,
his eldest son, a fine, promising lad between ten and eleven
years old, who had begun to prove a comfort and joy to his
parents, by rendering himself useful in his father's long and
repeated absences from home, was prostrated by the prevalent
fever, and for a few days hung trembling between life and

death. With agonizing importunity the cry was uttered: *Spare him!* SPARE HIM ! But such was not the will of Heaven. He died, and two days afterward the brother-in-law of Mr. Peck, a member of his family, Mr. S. Paine, also died. Thus God sorely tried the faith and the submission of his servant. But even in the furnace he found the sustaining presence and favor of his Saviour. Looking up to him with adoring reverence and love, he was enabled from the heart to say : "Though he slay me, I will trust in him."

He was himself called to pass through a severe attack of illness ; and when physicians and friends all gave him up for lost, it pleased the Lord almost miraculously to raise him up again. The sanctified influence of all this varied but severe discipline upon his own soul was eminently salutary. Fervently had he been praying that the Lord would quicken him again, and give to him the true appreciation of the blessedness of his chosen ones ; and specially that he would warm his heart to engage in his missionary and evangelical labors with the holy zeal which he had anticipated as he contemplated them at a distance. The prayer was now answered. And with a heart tremulous with deep emotion, and smarting from recent chastisement, he was enabled to cleave to the hand which had smitten him, not in anger but in tenderest love. His journal and his letters breathe now the spirit of deadness to the world, and an absorbed engagedness in his Master's work ; of concern for the welfare of souls around him, and the forgiveness of injury, which indicate the unmistakable presence and power of the in-dwelling Spirit of God. How readily he now found opportunities to plead with all the unrenewed around him to be reconciled to God. How easy it was, in every family where he gained admission, to converse personally with the inmates, and press home the urgencies of the great salvation. In preaching and prayer, too, he seemed like another man ; so much so, that it was very noticeable among his friends, some of whom thought it an almost sure indication that his work on earth was nearly done, and that the Lord was rapidly ripening him for the blessedness on high.

In the mean time very considerable changes were awaiting him in his external relations. In a private letter to his esteemed former teacher, Dr. Staughton, the Secretary of the Mission Board, he had intimated the difficulties experienced in his and his colleague's attempts to do any thing effective for the poor Indians from the point of their present location ; and Rev. Isaac McCoy was urging his coming to the aid of that mission under his care at Fort Wayne. It was thrown out rather as an inquiry by Mr. Peck to elicit further light as to whatever opinion the Secretary, from his intercourse with the Board, might be disposed to form, and *privately* communicate it to him. But not very unreasonably it was otherwise interpreted, and made the ground of rather a summary proceeding The convention of 1820 was much engrossed at just this period both with the Burman Mission and the founding of the Columbian college for the training of their missionaries and others, and, having listened with concern to some anti-mission complaints from the West, proceeded to direct the Board to discontinue the mission at St. Louis. The following is the minute entered on the records of the Western mission :

July 9th, 1820. The missionaries received official intelligence from the Secretary of the Board that this mission was closed for the following reasons :

1. The want of ample funds for its vigorous prosecution.

2. A supposition on the part of the Board that this region would be soon supplied by the immigration into it of preachers from the Middle and Eastern States.

3. The opposition in the West was also urged as a reason for its being abolished. The triennial convention had accordingly recommended this course, which the Board, as in duty bound, thus carried out :

Brother Welch is requested to continue his labors in St. Louis as a private minister and not as a missionary, no aid being promised him. Brother Peck is directed as speedily as practicable, on the termination of the present year, to remove to Fort Wayne, and join Rev. Mr. McCoy in his labors among the Indians. Thus terminates the Western Mission. *Attest :* J. M. PECK, *Secretary.*

The missionaries experienced no little mortification and surprise by this abrupt and unexpected termination of their arrangements and connection. Little more than three years had elapsed since their appointment, as they understood, for life. And though they had expected to have made their efforts in the school more remunerative, to lighten the expense of the mission to the Board; and though they had anticipated a more generous contribution from those to whom they ministered, and had in a too sanguine confidence relied on the hope of larger and earlier success in their missions, yet they were not prepared for so summary a winding up of their joint labors. It is noteworthy, however, that neither of them became in the slightest degree alienated from the mission cause, or even from the Board. On the contrary, both of them remained for scores of years the faithful and devoted friends of this cause. Mr. Welch, by domestic duties of an imperative character, was soon called away from that field for a long season. But he had too largely adventured his labors, enterprise, and even his little pecuniary patrimony, in the effort to rear the house of the Lord, and carry forward to mature strength the feeble Baptist Church in St. Louis, to prove recreant to its interests. For years afterward his best energies were often put forth to liquidate its debts and promote its welfare, though not permitted by Providence to become a resident preacher there.

The feelings and views of the other missionary may be learned from the following communication to the Board:

St. Louis County, November 17th, 1820.

To the Corresponding Secretary of the Baptist Board of Foreign Missions:

Rev. and Dear Sir:—After a silence of some months I resume my pen once more to address the Board. The hand of God has lain heavily upon me and the waves of trouble have rolled in frightful torrents over my head. First, I was attacked with bilious fever in its most malignant form, which soon brought me past all expectations of recovery; but when the hopes of friends and physicians failed, a good and gracious Providence was pleased to raise me, and the same mercy has now restored me to my usual health. Two of my younger children were sick at the same time.

The first week of October was a peculiarly trying time in my family. My oldest son—a promising, sprightly youth—was smitten by the destroying angel; and my brother-in-law, Mr. Paine, followed two days after. My oldest daughter then lay low, but has since recovered. Under these accumulated trials we have enjoyed a spirit of submission. Why should a worm complain at what infinite wisdom and goodness have done!

A letter from the Secretary, together with the annual report of the Board, announced to me the important change in this mission; but the intelligence was received while I lay on the verge of the grave. All things considered, perhaps the Board have pursued the best course by dropping the mission; but they widely mistake when they deduce their reason "from the numerous emigrations of ministers to our Western settlements, that the period has arrived when it is no longer necessary to support any brethren as missionaries at these places." But one Baptist preacher has emigrated to Missouri, within one hundred miles of St. Louis, since our arrival, and we heartily wish him back again; and not more than two or three in Illinois, within the same radius, from this centre. Nor is there a better prospect in future for this species of emigration in the same extent of country. To reiterate what has been repeated often, this region is DEPLORABLY DESTITUTE—the reports of professors of religion in Kentucky and elsewhere to the contrary notwithstanding.

The direction of the Board that I should repair, to Fort Wayne has deeply engaged my thoughts. What the Board have done I am not disposed to find fault with, but regret that they have expressed in so decisive terms "that Mr. Peck at the close of the present year immediately become a laborer with Mr. McCoy." On this point I have serious, conscientious difficulties. The field around me appears too important to be thus early vacated. The sphere of useful effort is certainly widening. With all the time I can spare I am unable to visit even occasionally one-half of the destitute churches and settlements that plead for the gospel. I hope I have no objection to living and laboring amongst the Indians and devoting the remnant of my days to their welfare; but by whom shall Jacob arise here, for he is very small? The distance from this to Fort Wayne is not less than five hundred miles, near the northwest corner of Ohio. The expense of removing must be considerable, and when there, continued expense must be incurred. Here I can minister largely to my own necessities. I have no wish to incur further expense to the mission. That has already been greater than I ever anticipated. I have felt intensely desirous for the time to come when missionary efforts here would no longer burden a liberal public abroad. That time, I think, has already come. Though my usefulness must be abridged greatly by it, I am willing to labor with my hands, or to use any lawful effort to support my family, for the furtherance of the gospel. It really seems to me as if the voice of Providence was saying to me: "Stay where you are," especially since the late distressing change in my family. May I offer one consideration more ? The health of Mrs. Peck is somewhat precarious. The vigor of her constitution has been impaired by her removal to this country. In case of the proposed removal to Fort Wayne, she must (with a babe but a few weeks old) have female help on the road, and that is next to impossible to get in this country. All these considerations induce me to request the Board to reconsider their resolution concerning the field of my future labor. I do not wish to relinquish the principles of a missionary, and it would be my desire still to be under the wing of the Board, though not as to support, in case they will recall my appointment to Fort Wayne. Should circumstances prevent Brother Welch's return to settle in St. Louis or vicinity, I do not see how I could leave this region ; for St. Louis must not be relinquished by the Baptists.

With sentiments of continued respect, I am yours, etc.,

                                        J. M. PECK.
To REV. WM. STAUGHTON, *Cor. Sec.*

Six months later, viz., in May, 1821, Dr. Staughton wrote to Mr. Peck : " The Board would have preferred your settling down with Brother McCoy, but the reasons you assign for continuing in the vicinity of St. Louis are so entirely satisfactory, that the propriety of complying with your wishes struck the mind of every member." Sufficiently equivocal this, certainly, for the most astute Secretary. But it seems to have been understood on both sides as closing the missionaries' relations of dependence on the support of the Board. To obviate all possibility of misconception hereafter, it has been deemed necessary to give these statements in full, from the records of the Western mission, which have been carefully preserved.

15

CHAPTER XIII.

New Position of Mr. Peck—Timely Aid from Massachusetts—Removal to Rock Spring.

It may easily be supposed that Mr. Peck would feel some solicitude in regard to his future course, after the dissolution of his connection with the missionary Board which sent him out, and hitherto had sustained him. For although their remittances had been neither large nor regular, and more than once the missionaries were for many months without answers to their letters, or supplies for their wants, so that they were left in great perplexity, yet eventually the Board made them remittances which relieved them from suffering, and they were thus enabled more vigorously to prosecute the important object of their designation. Now, however, all expectation of further aid from this quarter had been dissipated. At the same time they had done absolutely nothing to educate the churches which they had formed, or others which they in part supplied, in the duty of contributing of their carnal things, while the preachers were laboriously striving to promote their spiritual welfare. This, at first view, seems unaccountable and wrong. But there were peculiar circumstances warranting, or at least apologizing for it. These churches were very small and poor, their members struggling with the infelicities of a new settlement, and having every thing to do for themselves. The St. Louis church were deeply involved in debt for the church-edifice ; and it was thought better for the time being to encourage them to concentrate their efforts on paying the interest on this debt, rather than say any thing to them about salary for the preachers. Moreover they were aware of the prejudice existing in many minds against them as missionaries ; and for the same reason that Paul, in peculiar circumstances, would not be chargeable to young churches which he planted and preached to, lest odium should thereby be attached to the gospel, so these missionaries wished as far as possible to remove the reproach of having any worldly interest of their own in planting and watering these germs of a future and more perfect evangelization in that new field.

They had formed missionary societies wherever they had deemed it prudent and practicable, and devoted the proceeds faithfully to sustaining traveling preachers—the best which could be obtained in that region—to preach among the destitute. Moreover, they hoped by this means to conciliate the favor of these humble men to the idea of the wisdom and beneficence of the missionary cause. But probably the contributions were too small, irregular, and unreliable, to have much favorable effect of this kind. Certain it is that some of these recipients of the bounty of the churches, raised with utmost difficulty by the solicitations of Messrs. Peck and Welch, and paid over in full to those thus employed, turned against the very men who had tried to feed them. Some actually went over to the anti-mission party, and others evinced a jealous and unlovely spirit toward their benefactors which it was hard for the latter patiently to bear. In this way, one after another of the associations and churches, which they had influenced successfully at first to favor the missionary cause, now turned against it, and seemed inclined to repudiate them altogether.

It became, therefore, a matter of extreme difficulty and delicacy for Mr. Peck now to introduce this matter of needed support for his family, where he had been accustomed to give his labors freely. More than ever did he therefore feel inclined to obtain as early as practicable a little farm, by the cultivation and products of which he might in a considerable degree sustain himself. But even to make this experiment required a considerable outlay, and he was now penniless, the sickness of himself and family having entirely exhausted every means.

Early in the year 1822, a correspondence was opened between himself and brethren in Boston, which ere long led to his appointment as the missionary of the Massachusetts Baptist Missionary Society. His first commission in their service, signed by the honored names of Thomas Baldwin, President, and Daniel Sharp, Secretary, is dated Boston, March 12th, 1822. The correspondence which led to his appointment is interesting and equally honorable to both parties; but as it is chiefly a recapitulation of the facts above stated, it need not here be reproduced. The letter of the Secretary, accompanying the commission, stated that the society's appropriation would be five dollars a week for the time actually spent in their service, and that he would be expected to raise as much as practicable of this amount on the field of his labors, and make regular returns of his labors and receipts. Here, then, was a small but reliable foundation laid for some aid in his family's support. Relieved so far from anxieties which had preyed upon his spirit, he seems to have entered with unwonted ardor upon his chosen work. His family remained for some time in the vicinity of St. Charles, but we find him very often in St. Louis cheering on the feeble Baptist churches there; and the remainder of his time was pretty equally divided between the destitute portions of Missouri and Illinois.

After balancing all the considerations for and against this step, he came to the conclusion that it would best promote the interests of the mission and the cause of Christ for him to settle his family in Illinois. Accordingly, in the end of the month of April, 1822, he removed to Rock Spring, which henceforth became his family residence. Here he obtained a half-section of unimproved land, and with some little assistance from kind neighbors he was enabled to erect such buildings as made them measurably comfortable, and began the cultivation of a little portion of the land to aid in supporting his household. The time, and care, and toil, which he devoted to this seems to have been at times oppressive to him; but though he complains of its deadening his religious susceptibilities, he did not intermit or shrink from these endeavors till his family was made comfortable. His residence on the Illinois side of the great river, though still in proximity to St. Louis and the scenes of his former principal labors, brought him into closer connection with many brethren, ministers, and others, whom he ardently loved and esteemed till the end of his earthly course. The Lemens were among the former; and their living, increasing friendship and esteem were based on the solid excellencies mutually recognized and appreciated in each other. Very many others, both ministers and private Christians, and some who as philanthropists, patriots, and promoters of the welfare of these incipient settlements in the wilderness, became intimately connected with him in counsels and labors, will be often mentioned in the course of this narrative.

A little band of brethren, chiefly from Georgia, had settled around the new home he had chosen, and they desired to be formed into a church. Accordingly, on the 26th of May, 1822, the organization and public recognition of the church was consummated. The day being very stormy, many were detained from attending; but sermons were preached by Brethren Peck and Kinney, the church was constituted in due form, and the Lord's Supper administered. It was a solemn and interesting occasion.

The following Sabbath found him ministering to the St. Louis church, and on the 3d of June he set forth on a laborious tour of some weeks to the eastward, visiting the Wabash Association and several places of importance, both in Illinois and Indiana. The following extracts from his journal will indicate the state of feeling at that time in the association, and the efforts he made to promote the cause of truth :

SATURDAY, *8th June.* Reached the association, New Princeton, Ind., and was affectionately received by Brother William Polke and some other brethren, but soon discovered strong prejudices and jealousies on account of my missionary character. No seat was allowed me. However, the association appointed me to preach on the morrow. Preached at night at a brother's where I tarried.

Lord's-day, *9th.* A Brother Anderson and Brother Parker preached In my interview with Brother Parker I alluded to his address about missions, and told him I could cheerfully give him my hand, as a conscientious and well-meaning, though greatly-mistaken brother. He is a most determined opposer of the whole mission system. In the evening I preached in the court-house at Princeton on the subject of missions, and spent the night with Brother Devin. My mind quite engaged.

Monday, 10*th*. I preached before the association on missions The Wabash Association, though, while Brother McCoy was amongst them, warm friends of the mission—at least a majority were—have in too many instances become opposed. Prejudices have risen up, and some are, I doubt not, influenced by selfish motives. It appears very evident that Parker is determined not to yield, or give up the ground he has assumed. To effect his pur. pose he has been engaged for some time among a portion of the churches.

After some amendments to the constitution of the association had been discussed, the subject of missions came up. This was occasioned by one church having charged another with having supported missions as constituting a grievance. This gave full scope for a discussion on the propriety of missions. Mr. Parker opposed them with all the ingenuity in his power, and Mr. Wm. Polke as ably defended them. I then obtained leave to speak, and entered on a detail of facts connected with this subject. The whole discussion lasted about five hours, and excited peculiar interest in the public mind. A large assembly seemed unwilling to stir from the place till the decision was reached. I have never before met with so determined an opposer to missions in every aspect. But the decision gave a decided victory to the cause of missions, fully sustaining the church which had contributed to their support.

In the evening preached again on missions, and received a generous collection in aid of the cause at Princeton court-house. Passed the night with Judge Prince. The citizens in and about Princeton have treated me with the utmost affection and respect. I was invited to almost every house. A disposition to hear me preach was manifested beyond any thing before witnessed in the West. Let me never be so ungrateful as to forget the kindness they have shown. The Lord reward them.

Then he proceeded as far as Vincennes, and preached in various places, riding here and there, in sunshine and storm, striving to instruct and comfort the churches, and win the unbelieving to the Saviour. On returning home he thus reviews the journey :

"I have been absent from home twenty days; have rode four hundred and fifty-six miles, preached twenty-five times, visited many families and settlements, and gained much information in regard to the destitution of this part of our country, the great need of missionaries, and the promising fields which are ripening."

After a few days spent with his family, our brother left for a mission tour in Missouri. Passing a Sabbath in St. Louis, he officiated at the funeral of a poor Baptist brother, just arrived from Ohio, with a wife and six children. They were all sick and in the most distressing circumstances. He speaks with some admiration of the humane and generous attention manifested by the citizens generally in their great affliction—consoling them in the bereavement, and contributing to supply their needs.

Pursuing his route onward through Feefee and Bonhomme, in each of which churches he had endeavored to make an appointment for preaching, but found no hearers, or next to none, he laments pathetically the low state of piety prevalent among them. At the latter place, however, he met with an old disciple, Father Stephen Hancock, eighty years of age, mourning over the low state of Zion. Very sound in doctrine, a great admirer of salvation by grace. He was one of the enterprising emigrants who accompanied the celebrated Colonel Daniel Boone to Kentucky in its first settlement, and had long maintained a pious deportment. They rode together, in pious conversation, to Point Labadie, where the little church seemed to prosper. Our brother visited the sick, instructed and prayed with inquirers, and preached to them the gospel. Thus he went on from place to place, ministering the word and ordinances of the gospel to those rarely enjoying these privileges. At the end of two or three weeks he returned home, finding sickness and death in his way. A small assembly in St. Louis was addressed, containing in all but fifteen females, of whom it proved that thirteen were widows. His wife and two children were soon prostrated by bilious fever, and for some days their lives seemed to hang by a very brittle thread. Deeply was his mind exercised in regard to this discipline, and very humbly did he lie before the Lord, crying for his mercy; and at length it dawned upon them. His family's health having measurably recovered, the 24th of August we find him attending the Illinois Association at Wood river. General coldness in religion, with not a little of personal pique and jealousy toward our brother, was here also evinced. He preached, however, at the stand, while the business of the body was being transacted in the meeting-house. In this latter, his journal records, was brought to light much of the real nature of the opposition to missions in this country. It evidently arises from some of the most selfish and contracted feelings of the human heart. Even some real Christians, in a low state of religion, some-times evince much bitter prejudice, and such a disposition as is entirely repugnant to the gospel. He preached here, but without the good effects, apparently, which had lately attended his efforts in Indiana under somewhat similar circumstances.

First of September he again preached, baptized four, and administered the Lord's Supper in St. Louis. The sickness then prevailing much thinned the meeting. He found diffi-culties presenting themselves in the church, which he records his conviction that nothing but the special influence of the Lord's Spirit can reconcile. From this point he again pro-ceeded into the interior of Missouri, and preached in many of the places where he had before labored with various indications of success. Gratefully he speaks of a Brother Louis Williams, a preacher whom he met on this tour, and whose great im-provement within two years and the indications of whose use-fulness filled him with delight. In various parts of this wide field appearances of a genuine revival gladdened his heart. So much so, that again and again he swept over this wide circuit, visiting the feeble and young churches, and in some instances baptizing into their fellowship recently-converted souls. Abounding in labors of this cheering character, his mind and heart evidently became more buoyant and cheerful. Abounding in the works of the Lord was evidently his delight.

The church at St. Louis, whose pecuniary and other embar-rassments had occasioned him so much solicitude, he was at length enabled to snatch from pecuniary disaster. Early in November I find the following record in his journals:

This night (November 4th) we entered into an arrangement with the Presbyterian Society about holding and occupying the meeting-house in joint concern—they advancing fifteen hundred dollars to pay the debts and finish off the house, and the Baptist Society to have ten years in which to refund the money and resume the exclusive possession. This plan ultimately failed of execution.

On Lord's-day evening, the 12th of the same month, he preached a funeral sermon for the beloved Jacoby, in the legislative hall at St. Charles, where this good man had died a few weeks previously. He had been a main pillar in the Baptist church at St. Louis ; and for a long time afterward it seemed as though his removal threatened to terminate its existence. An appropriate memoir of him was also forwarded by Mr. Peck and inserted in the Massachusetts Baptist Magazine. (See vol. for 1823.)

His first quarterly report was forwarded about this time to the missionary society in Boston by whom he was in part sustained. It breathes a cheerful and confiding spirit, and earnestly pleads for more laborers to be sent into this wide field.

Near the end of December, we find him visiting Vandalia, the seat of government of Illinois. He preached in the legislative hall by the desire of the legislature then in session. Here, too, he met with the same Daniel Parker, his antagonist at the Wabash Association, and who was here as a senator of Illinois, as hostile as ever. A second time Mr. Peck preached to a densely-crowded assembly in the hall of the legislature in advocacy of Bible societies, to which form of evangelical benevolence, as he saw, it was more difficult for the anti-mission party to offer objections, than to some others where human infirmity is more mingled. To this topic, for some time after this, our brother successfully devoted much of his attention.

This same Parker also very considerably changed his track from a little after this time. Wearying or discouraged in his direct efforts in the anti-mission cause, he broached a new form of heresy and schism. His two-seed doctrine has been very fully described by Brother Peck at a later period of their history.

CHAPTER XIV.

Report of labors—Loss of Diary and other valuables, etc.

IN the month of September, Mr. Peck made a tour through Madison, Greene, and Morgan counties, Ill., for preaching the gospel; which excursion he speaks of as having been very satisfactory to himself, and he hoped of advantage to the interests of Zion. He preached one night in Edwardsville, and the next in Carrolton, where the sermon from Heb. xi. 25 was blessed to the fuller awakening and conversion of one individual, *Thomas Carlin*, subsequently Governor of the State of Illinois The two following months also found him frequently revisiting these scenes, where there were distinct evidences of the Spirit's presence and power. We give from his journal a single day's experience in each of these months, indicating the prevalent spirit which now possessed his mind.

LORD'S-DAY, 28*th September*. Wet weather, yet a tolerably large assembly collected at Carrolton, to whom I preached from Heb. iii. 2: "O Lord, revive thy work." My whole object now is to promote a revival, if possible. For this end I exhort professors in the plainest language to arouse from their supineness, and call upon sinners to repent. Besides public preaching and addresses, I spend much time visiting families, exhorting and counseling individuals. In the evening preached at Thomas Carlin's from the parable of the sower. The people are attentive and solemn. Mrs. Carlin is under deep conviction. (Her husband has already been baptized.) Spent a happy time that night in conversation and prayer. The following day was spent in visiting the sick, and in conversing and praying with families.

Lord's-day, 5*th October*. The Sunday-school met at the house and recited Scripture lessons. I found four or five of the children under serious impressions. I then preached from Philippians i. 21, with some humble confidence that God blessed the word. Religion now flourishes in the settlement.   Here is distinct evidence of the immediate good effect of exertions to promote religion.   Many of the Baptist preachers in this country, in what little doctrine they exhibit, verge towards antinomianism ; or at least while they profess to contend for the doctrines of grace, they say very little about *duty* and practical religion.   They seem not to understand the connection of means with the end, and are not usually inclined to make exertions to promote religion.   Hence, the churches do not increase except by immigration.   Professors live very carelessly, and sinners remain quite stupid.   It has been more the tone of my preaching for some time past to inculcate human obligation and stir up professors to prayer and effort, and to awaken sinners from their dreadful slumberings.   But my dependence for success is alone on God.   Without the special influence of the Holy Spirit, nothing will be done effectually.

The following day, in company with several persons, he rode to the county-seat, and towards evening the court adjourned (Hon. John Reynolds, judge), and he preached in the court-room a spirit-stirring discourse from Rev. iii. 20.

He just notices in his journal that he was about this time strongly urged to settle near Carrolton with the promise of a liberal support, and he merely subjoins : " My chief desire is to be in that place where the Lord would have me." How different the results both on his domestic happiness and the welfare of the cause of Christ at large, had he then planted himself down quietly, and given his chief labors to a single church and the immediate neighborhood, from the results of a very different course to which he actually gave his life ! There is no wisdom in praising the one of these plans at the expense of the other ; for God blesses both ; and every individual ought to ascertain for which he is best fitted, and act accordingly.   It is very certain that if all ministers were to wander as widely and concentrate their efforts as little as did our esteemed brother, there would be little of stability and real permanent progress in our cause.   And on the contrary, if none gave themselves as he did to the general care for the welfare of the churches, the education of the ministry, and the supply of vast destitute regions, where some one must care for procuring the requisite ministrations of gospel truth, a great hindrance in general progress would be the inevitable result. By the stationary policy he would probably have suffered less, and his family would have enjoyed much more. But it is doubtful whether to himself at least the compensations in various ways brought about by his wide range and multifarious labors, were not generally remunerative, so that his gain, intellectual and moral, was as great as his loss. The suggestion of this comparison almost forces itself on one's mind in connection with this overture from the good people in Carrolton and vicinity to monopolize such a man. It was not the will of Providence that he should then and there sit down to luxuriate in the rich spiritual enjoyments, than which God has given no greater, growing out of penning and feeding a spiritual fold, on which the dews and sunshine of fructifying grace are abundantly falling.

The very next day after the events narrated in the above extracts from his journal, he started early in the morning, intending to reach Carrolton to meet an appointment, but his horse, from fright or viciousness, broke away from him while crossing the barrens, and for days, if not weeks, his search for him was fruitless. Even when the horse was ultimately recovered, his loss in saddle, bridle, overcoat, and the valuable contents of his saddle-bags, was a severe one, which it was not easy to repair. Specially some valuable papers and journals he was never able to make good again. But how characteristic it was of the man that when he had done the utmost in his power, that day and the next, to recover the fugitive, in vain, he accidentally fell in company with some small boys gathering nuts; and he entered with such zest into the very spirit of their juvenile enjoyments, as planted him deep in their affections and sympathies ever afterward. One who was intimately acquainted with some of them has thus written of the incident since the death of this venerated man :

In the early years of his missionating in Illinois, he lost his horse, with clothes, valuable papers, and journals. He was passing through a comparatively unsettled portion of the country, and had occasion to dismount, when his horse took very sudden fright at himself or at some other object, and ran very rapidly away through the bushes and woods out of reach and out of sight directly. He followed in pursuit all that afternoon, and at night came to a log-cabin upon the spot where the town of Manchester now is, in Morgan county. He was there made welcome and entertained for the night. The friend in whose cabin he took refuge was afterwards Hon. Judge Marks, of uncommon powers of discernment, who became much interested in his guest from the first, and regarded him with life-lasting affection. In the morning the horse-hunt was renewed with all the help which could be mustered, but it was unsuccessful. Then as jovially as though this had been the very object of his visit, he joined the boys in picking up some fine large nuts, as they returned; and in the evening he was found seated flat on the oroad hearth-stones of the cabin, as one with the boys, cracking and eating nuts, and entertaining the wondering family with lively anecdotes one after another, of which he seemed to them to have a marvelous supply. I have this story from the Judge's own mouth and from the sons also. This kind of buoyancy of spirit and versatility of powers gave him immense influence among the people wherever his lot was cast.

The same individual to whom I am indebted for the record of the above incident (Benjamin F. Lemen, Esq., a lawyer of Salem, Ill.) gives also the following incidents, illustrative of this period of Mr. Peck's life and labors :

I well remember the night when I first heard him preach, and just where he stood in my father's dwelling (there were no meeting-houses then). His missionary life was at that time all before him. Fresh from the exalting society of Dr. Staughton, full of zeal and high with hope, he rose with a smiling countenance, and opening the blessed book, he cast his eyes over the congregation and said : "I am going to preach to the young people, and if there is any-body who doesn't care about the subject, or is too old and sleepy to hear—why it will make no difference to me, I shall preach just the same." This remark was so peculiar and striking as to arrest every one's attention at once. His subject was *the crucifixion.* With affecting simplicity and solemnity he described the cross, and portrayed the darkness and all the horrors of the scene of the Calvary tragedy. He dwelt upon the incalculable value of the soul of man, as evinced by the infinite cost of our salvation.

16

He was then *young*. His full, smiling, open visage, his clear, musical voice and soul-stirring earnestness made his discourses produce a powerful effect upon all; and this first one, as well as several others about that time, by many of us can never be forgotten.

When he first came to Illinois, he was opposed and bitterly persecuted in some of his missionary efforts and other undertakings. But his every-day walk, and general gentlemanly deportment, converted many of the crusty old Baptists, who had tried at first to oppose him, and some of them became his warmest friends. The first show of friendship from one of them was on the occasion of the marriage of one of the family, when Brother Peck was chosen as the *master of ceremonies*. A frank confession was made, and fifty dollars were tendered him, as some offset to past opposition. We all know that for a long series of years his house at Rock Spring was a church and a missionary station—the place of constant resort for great and learned men, and specially for ministers of all denominations on first coming into the country. He was affable and friendly to all, and a remarkably kind neighbor to every new-comer that removed into his vicinity. He was a little eccentric in some of his manners, quite comely in his appearance, and carefully neat in his apparel; but not ostentatious in either the one or the other.

Another illustrative anecdote from the same authentic source, though belonging to a little later period, may rightly enough be introduced here, as it was doubtless characteristic of the man on various similar occasions:

I once saw him, about the time of the founding of the Rock Spring Seminary, in a large company of opposers, who at a big meeting took the opportunity to array themselves in company and oppose him jointly, to show him *his infatuation!* At that period, he was a great smoker; and while they were talking, he lighted his pipe, and got up the smoke! Then when they had about exhausted their stores of opposition, he straitened himself up before them, and laid out his arguments in order to them, as with quickened puffs he sent forth the smoke, and with deliberateness and energy he set forth his whole plan and object, and then awakened their philanthropy and silenced all their cavil by bold and earnest prophesying what would come of it. Thus, on all such occasions, doubts were dissipated and opposition silenced, and so the good work went on and triumphed.

CHAPTER XV.

Bible Societies in Illinois—Domestic Missions—Green, the Mur
derer—First Sunday-school Societies in the West.

THE closing months of the year 1823, with the beginning
of the following year, were filled up actively and usefully in
the various preaching tours which Mr. Peck took, both in
Illinois and Missouri. In the former State, particularly, he
just now witnessed an increased and, as he feared, an implacable opposition, on the part of some of the ministers,
especially, to all missionary endeavors, which much grieved
and perplexed him. We give a few extracts from his journal,
indicating his experiences, both merciful and disquieting :

FRIDAY, *October* 31*st.* This is my birthday : thirty-four years of
my life are fled. It deserves remark that every year seems to fly
away more rapidly as I advance. The last year of my life has been
free from domestic affliction. Praise the Lord for his goodness.

November 1*st.* Rode to St. Louis, and at night attended church-
meeting with the blacks. Each one conversed on the religious
state of their minds, and I gave them advice.

Lord's-day, 2*nd.* Very cold weather. In the morning I preached
from the parable of Dives and Lazarus. Solemn attention. Some
affected. Afternoon, preached again, from "Behold the Lamb of
God," etc. In the evening I addressed the blacks from the Lord's
prayer with much feeling and good effect. My mind is much led
out to God, and I feel resolved to be more circumspect, and more
engaged in private devotion. Oh, for grace and strength !

I have lately learned, much to my disappointment, that the
new association up the Illinois river [the Sangamon, probably]
has made a rule to debar missionaries from a seat. Several of the
friends of missions were prevented by sickness from attending at
its formation, hence this untoward result. Oh, tell it not in Gath.
There is a regular conspiracy formed in the Illinois, to put down
missionaries. The *root* of all this opposition is from the *preachers.*
They fear losing their influence, which must be small indeed.

After writing the above, I searched for and read my "Secret Diary" of 1815 and 1816, in which I solemnly pledged myself in covenant with God to submit to all the trials of a missionary life; and particularly to have my *motives* impeached and my name cast out as evil. It is my sincere desire not to harbor a particle of ill will toward those who oppose and persecute me · but to cherish great desires for their salvation. To the grace of God be all the praise, that I have not felt much irritation of mind at what has taken place, and what my enemies are disposed to do. I grieve, however, to think of the injury they are inflicting on the cause of the dear Redeemer.

November 5th. My mind this evening has been much occupied on the subject of making some more efficient exertions to promote the Bible Society, by ascertaining, in the first place, the exact state of destitution in this county. While reading the Seventh Annual Report of the American Bible Society, my mind has been all aglow with desire for the full accomplishment of the noble work aimed at.

This is the first intimation we have found, in a careful examination of his journals and letters, of special interest in this subject, which afterwards occupied so much of his time and labors. A two-fold motive might very appropriately lead him at just this crisis to entertain with favor some effort of this kind. In the first place, there was palpable evidence of much need of Bibles and Testaments in families and schools; and then again he could readily see that it would be more difficult for the opponents of all those evangelizing efforts with which his mission was identified, to oppose the diffusion of God's word, than any other form of evangelization. Hence the wisdom of beginning on this impregnable ground, and exercising the intelligence and the benevolence of the churches on this branch of evangelical effort, that by exercise it might be strengthened and expanded, and thus be less exposed to be carried away by such anti-mission prejudices as were now artfully excited among the ignorant and the selfish.

Twenty days later the following occurs in his journal :

For some time I have had many thoughts about undertaking an agency to form Bible societies, and thus endeavor to promote the gospel in this country, by a more general circulation of the Scriptures. My greatest desire is to pursue that course which will most speedily and effectually pave the way to more systematic and enlarged efforts to promote the kingdom of a dear Redeemer.

The middle of the following month, on occasion of forming the Greene County Auxiliary Bible Society in Illinois, and the second at Edwardsville for Madison county, he says, " I have no doubt but this will be a death-blow to opposition to missionaries in this quarter."

We have been the more careful to fortify this view from his own recorded statements and convictions at the time ; because it fully redeems the policy he was pursuing from any thing like fickleness. He was a missionary with his whole heart, but when he thought the very cause of missions could for the time be better promoted by his turning to the work of establishing Bible societies, he could not hesitate to become an agent for this object.

Soon after his first successful demonstration in this work—distributing the Scriptures, and awakening interest in behalf of the object, getting individuals of chief standing and influence to pledge him their aid, and preaching frequently on this theme, and forming two county societies and taking measures for a third—he accepted an agency from the American Bible Society to further prosecute this important work. The records of this memorable year may be appropriately closed with his report to the Massachusetts Baptist Missionary Society, setting forth in a summary manner his labors, and the plan on which they were prosecuted.

ROCK SPRING, ST. CLAIR COUNTY, ILL.
December 31st, 1823.

REV. AND DEAR SIR :—In pursuing my labors in the missionary service, it has been an important object with me to enlist as many laborers in the vineyard as circumstances would admit. To effect this I have ranged over a much wider field, and kept my eye upon a greater number of objects than would have been useful had

I aimed merely for the immediate success of my own labors. It affords me satisfaction to state that the advantage of this course is now apparent. A part of my former field in Missouri, and particularly the church in Bon-homme, is now partially supplied by the labors of Brother Holmes, whom I formerly mentioned as a student. By another arrangement, partly effected through my instrumentality, a valuable brother by the name of Lewis Williams is enabled to devote much of his time in Franklin county, and the adjacent settlements. Latterly I have taken some steps to enable a venerable father in the gospel by the name of Sweet to travel some portion of his time in the upper counties of Illinois, and I hope to aid in providing means whereby a Brother Crane, who is soon to be ordained at Carrolton, will be liberated so as to perform some itinerant service. Two or three other preachers have been aided in profitable studies through the medium of correspondence. Still a majority of those called preachers of the Illinois Association may be regarded as opposed to missionaries, missions, and every active systematic measure to promote the gospel amongst the destitute.

Having long known that multitudes of families in this country are destitute of the Scriptures, and having deeply felt the importance of active measures for a wider circulation of the Bible, I provided myself from the Missouri Bible Society with a quantity of Bibles, Testaments, annual reports, and monthly extracts of the American Bible Society, together with a large assortment of missionary pamphlets, tracts, etc., and started for the upper counties in this State on the 8th inst. My chief object was to convey intelligence of the successful efforts now making to promote religion amongst men. At Edwardsville I called on several gentlemen of my acquaintance, made known my object, readily engaged their co-operation, and published a meeting for Christmas day to form a Bible society. Here I found that a few Bibles heretofore deposited by the Missouri Bible Society had served to disclose the wants of the public, and create a thirst for more copies. Leaving ten copies of the Testament on deposit, and distributing two annual reports, and a quantity of tracts, I departed for Carrol ton, where I arrived on the 12th, and the next day attended the meeting of the church, and brought about an appointment for the ordination of Brother Crane, which is to take place in February. I immediately wrote to influential men in different sections of the county, and gave out an appointment to form a Bible society the next night. Accordingly a respectable and crowded audience met in the court-house, to whom I preached from Isaiah lii. 10, and immediately following was organized "The Auxiliary Bible Society of Green County." The officers were duly chosen. A number of Bibles and Testaments were deposited in the hands of the managers, besides selling a number to individuals, and distributing a large number of missionary pamphlets and tracts. Pursuing my route, I visited Morgan county, when I made arrangements to form a Bible society in February. The Sunday-school on Indian creek still progresses, and promises much usefulness. I preached to the children as on former occasions, who assembled for the purpose.

Returning down the country, and explaining the nature and design of Bible societies and other benevolent institutions of the present age wherever I preached, and especially in Apple creek settlement, where I spent the Sabbath and addressed an unusually large congregation. On the 22d instant I met the managers of the Bible society of Green county, and suggested several useful measures to be pursued in their incipient efforts. On the night of the 24th I plead the Bible cause before a respectable assembly in Alton, and the next day (25th) attended the proposed meeting in Edwardsville. After a discourse on the subject, the Auxiliary Bible Society of Madison County was formed under favorable auspices and the Board of Directors chosen. At evening I addressed the public again on the same subject, and deposited with the managers a few Bibles and Testaments I had remaining. By a little seasonable and prudent effort the Testament may become a class-book in most of the schools in this country. I succeeded in introducing it into five schools on my route.

The experiment I have made has fully answered my most sanguine expectations of the important advantages the cause would derive in Bible societies, and the distribution of mission pamphlets, magazines and tracts. A most important service might be rendered to the cause, if the friends in Boston could supply me with an additional quantity of the back numbers of the magazine, missionary reports, old sermons, tracts, and every thing of the like description for gratuitous distribution. These should be packed in a box marked with my name, the freight paid to New Orleans, consigned to some merchant there, and directed to the charge of *A. Skinner*, St. Louis. I have found the most beneficial effects result from the distribution of a few magazines or tracts after preaching; and as the people in all the settlements seldom hear preaching but once in the month, these silent monitors serve to keep alive impressions and feelings till the return of the preacher.

Next week I expect to visit Missouri, and perform the circuit of the Missouri Association to carry into effect the plan for itinerant preaching suggested in the last minutes.

With sincerity of soul I can say there is no pursuit that affords such exquisite satisfaction as activity and success in measures to promote the gospel. I might dwell upon the difficulties attendant on an itinerating life—as absence from home, exposure to sickness, storms, cold, mud, swimming rivers, and not unfrequently rough fare—but these are trifles not worthy of one moment's anxious concern. To live and labor for Him who died for the redemption of man is the highest favor which we need seek after in this transitory life.

May the God of all grace still prosper the efforts of the society, is the prayer of your unworthy missionary,

J. M. PECK.

REV. DANIEL SHARP.

P.S.—I understand there is a paper published by some of the Baptist brethren in Boston called the Christian Watchman. I wish to receive it, commencing January 1st, and hope the Treasurer of the missionary society will pay the subscription and charge the same to me. Direct the numbers to Cherry Grove P.O., St. Clair county, Ill. Yours, etc.,

J. M. PECK.

It was about this time made the painful duty of Mr. Peck to officiate, under very affecting circumstances, at the execution of a murderer. He happened to be in Alton, Ill., the very day of the homicide, December 4th, 1823, and on noticing the excitement produced, he subjoins the following remarks in his journal: "The state of morals is truly deplorable in this State; and this does not so much arise from the general depravity of the inhabitants, as from the dreadful neglect (or connivance, as may be feared) of the judiciary, leading to a non-execution of the laws against crimes. No less than six murders, or homicides in affrays, have been perpetrated in nine months, and as yet not one is convicted."

In this instance, however, the poor culprit was convicted the 14th of the following month, and ordered to be executed the 12th of the next month. He at once applied to Mr. Peck to attend him at the execution ; and before our brother could visit him in his cell, he had professed to be converted, and the rumor was that he desired baptism.   To this Mr. Peck felt the strongest opposition, supposing it would possibly tend to the delusion of the wretched felon, and moreover might lessen the .salutary horror to be produced by the just execution of the laws.   He was also full of suspicion of the murderer's sincerity, and in this unfavorable state of mind had his first interview with Green in his dungeon.   Much time and very thorough examination was devoted to his case, occupying the 4th and 5th of February.   The result was that a very thorough conviction of the genuineness of his conversion was wrought in the mind of Mr. Peck, and he found his former distrust and unbelief entirely removed.   The penitence and humility of the culprit were deep and thorough.   His conviction commenced immediately after he committed the atrocious deed.   The following notice of some of the circumstances of his interviews with the murderer will be interesting :

THURSDAY, 5*th.* Spent most of the day with Green.   Found that the close talk that I had with him yesterday produced much effect upon his mind.   He had spent the whole night in prayer and self-examination.   He was now composed, firm in his hope, deeply penitent, and the fear of death was removed.   The Wood river church, with their pastor, the venerable Father Jones, attended for the purpose of public worship with the culprit in the prison ; and Mr. Peck preached from Luke xxiii. 39–43—the case of the penitent thief.   Green then related his experience, which deeply affected every one in the house.   His replies to very close, heart-searching questions put to him were pertinent and satisfactory, and he was received as a candidate for baptism.   He was then conducted to the water, about two hundred yards from the prison, having a small chain attached to his leg, and a rope around his body and arms which the sheriff held.   The day was cold, and a hole was cut in the ice for the administration of the ordinance.   His baptism excited much solemnity and deep feeling amongst the people.   To baptize a murderer, under sentence of death, and who must inevitably be executed in one week, was a novel thing, and what I should least thought of doing once ; but in this case I became satisfied that it was my duty, and would not shrink from it.

The next two days were spent chiefly in the jail with Green. His Christian character became more fully developed, and Mr. Peck could not but regard him as a monument of grace. By the culprit's desire Mr. Peck wrote a brief account of his life, taken down from his own lips, and carefully corrected by himself.

LORD'S-DAY, 8*th February*. The morning was spent with Green. He is perfectly composed—has no fear of death. His hope seems a solid and firm one, founded on the promises of the gospel. He evinces no ecstacies, no enthusiastic passions. The narrative of his life was read over to him after final revision, which he certified and signed before the three witnesses present for this purpose.

Mr. Peck then left him for three days, and on returning to him the evening before his execution, he found that Green had experienced some trials and temptations, fearing that the Lord would not afford him comfort and support in the trying hour. Still his hope remained unshaken in Christ. At night a prayer-meeting was held in the jail. The poor malefactor prayed, confessed, and exhorted the people, and it was an affecting time. Some present were convicted of sin, and Mr. Peck left him at a late hour, perfectly composed and happy in the prospect of glory. He records in his journal his heartfelt gratitude for the consolations which religion affords.

THURSDAY, *February* 12*th*. The fatal day for Green has arrived. I visited him early in the morning, read the Scriptures and prayed with him, then left him alone for private devotion. At eleven o'clock, he was dressed for the gibbet in a white shroud trimmed with black, with a cap on his head. The guard forming a hollow square around him, he walked on with a firm and steady step, accompanied by the sheriff and chaplain. He surveyed the implements of death, and ascended the scaffold and seated himself on the *drop* with composure. Two thousand spectators in deep and reverent silence were gathered around; two or three prayers were offered, and as many appropriate hymns sung. I then preached the sermon from Ecclesiastes ix. 12 : "As the fishes that are taken in an evil net, and as the birds that are caught in the snare, so are the sons of men snared in an evil time when it falleth suddenly upon them." I also read his narrative and experience, which produced a solemn effect. A great many were in tears. The ministers and the jailer and family ascended the scaffold, shook hands with him, and bade him farewell. The sheriff adjusted the rope and took leave of him. As he did so, Green exhorted him and then the people in a few words, most solemnly and feelingly. He confessed the justice of his sentence, and prayed that he might be a salutary warning to others. I then offered a final prayer and read the hymn I had composed for the occasion. While the last line was sung,

" I make the signal for my flight,"

the drop fell, and the immortal spirit took its flight.

The occasion, the prayers, the eloquent addresses, and perhaps more than all, the behavior of the sufferer, impressed the beholders with solemn awe. Never before did I witness any thing like this. Never did I see such proof of the power and support of Divine grace in the awful hour of dissolution. It appeared convincing to every one that his repentance was real. The effect on the bystanders was solemnity, a consciousness of religion, a deep sense of the heinous crime of murder, and the nature of justice as being but a modification of goodness.

The following Lord's-day Mr. Peck presided at the council, and aided in the ordination of Mr. Crane, a licentiate in the Carrolton church. He then the following evening repeated the execution-sermon, and read part of Green's experience and narrative to a crowded congregation in the court-house at Carrolton. Returning to Edwardsville to put the sermon and narrative to press, he was gratified in finding that some had already been awakened and converted by means of them ; and the same thing is once or twice noticed subsequently in his journal. The pamphlet containing both sermon and narrative was widely circulated at the time, but the writer has not been able to find a copy.

The following month he records having attended by invitation the session of the Presbytery at St. Louis, where one candidate was examined for licensure and another for ordination. He was much edified and instructed during the session. The harmony which prevailed, and the spirit of real religion among the members were most cheering. Near the end of

the month he mentions reading the sermon on the moral dignity of the missionary enterprise by Dr. Wayland. How
widely the aims of its author were now being realized at home
and abroad !

In April, while attending the first anniversary of the Greene
County Bible Society, he availed himself of a favorable opportunity to preach at the county-seat on the importance of
Sunday-schools, and with the aid of a few zealous spirits a
Sunday-school society for the county was also formed. The
following notice of this movement occurs in his journal, and
is noteworthy as one of the first records of what afterwards
engrossed much of his time and energies :

It is my intention to form a number of county societies, and then
concentrate their efforts in a general union of Sabbath-schools.
These with the Bible institutions may be employed to exert a most
powerful influence through this Western country, and will silently
undermine the prejudices against missions more than any thing
else. By the agency appointment which I have lately received, I
shall be enabled (if health and success are allowed) to do more for
the advancement of religion than I ever anticipated."

This, be it remembered, was more than a year before the
formation of the American Sunday-school Union in Philadelphia. Thus early was God opening before him paths of usefulness and honor, which have made his name so familiar and
distinguished. On this very occasion, the court adjourned to
listen to a sermon from him before the Bible society and for
the transaction of its annual business.

The whole of April and May were spent by Mr. Peck,
chiefly in Southern and Central Illinois, the Military Tract,
and the adjacent parts of Missouri, in indefatigable efforts to
awaken and increase an interest in behalf of Sunday-schools
and Bible societies. Frequent mention is found of the apathy,
the misconception and prejudices he had to encounter in his
advocacy of these good objects, and affecting testimonies of
the destitution which he found so prevalent. On the whole
his success was encouraging.

CHAPTER XVI.

Destitution ascertained—Continued Labors—Opposition to Slavery.

Mr. Peck's diary number twenty is contained in a square volume of one hundred and fifty pages, and covers a period of little more than ten months, viz., from 28th of May, 1824, to 5th of March, 1825. On many accounts this was an event ful and useful period of his life, though presenting few salient points of striking interest. He was going on and on with the work described in the last chapter, traversing the old rounds in similar labors to those above recorded, and gradually extending the field of his explorations and labors. While sedulously careful to preach the common salvation in all the little and destitute churches which he could reach, he devoted on an average one Sabbath a month to the Baptist interest in St. Louis, and also made extensive tours through Central and Southern Illinois, and over almost the entire State of Missouri lying south of the Missouri river, and occasionally north of it. These explorations aimed at ascertaining as fully as possible the want of preaching, of Bibles, and of Sabbath-schools, in the several settlements, and the facilities which might be made available for supplying these wants. Some instances of destitution which fell under his personal observation were most affecting. Here is one instance :

19th June, 1824. On my route, twelve miles from Brownsville, I called at the house of a Mr. Butcher to get directions in my journey. The woman I found to be a Baptist, who had lived fourteen years, eight of which were in this wilderness, without any religious privileges. In this time she had heard but four sermons, two from one of her own society, and he a man not in good standing. When I told her my profession, she was too much affected with weeping to speak for some time. She then related her trials and distresses of soul for her forlorn state. She could not read except by slowly

17

spelling out the words in her Testament and hymn-book, and this was all the religious consolation she enjoyed. Her children were growing up in ignorance, and this added greatly to her sorrows. She would give all she possessed, yea, all the world if she had it, to be reinstated in the same privileges she had once enjoyed. It may be asked: "Why did she not return to Carolina, whence she had emigrated, or to some more favored settlement?" She was the wife of a husband who had chosen his residence here for the advantages of stock-raising; had improved a large plantation, and chose to remain. She was the mother of a large family of children, and leaving them and her husband was impossible. Nor is this case a singular one. But could I portray the real feelings, and the simple but energetic cry of this wanderer from Christ's fold; could I lay all her woes and all her secret sighs before an opposer of missions; I would say to him: "Here is an instance of the fruit of your criminal opposition. You would tear from the heart of this forlorn lamb of Christ all the consolation she ever enjoyed in these years of wearisome pilgrimage, in the visit, prayers, and instructions of a missionary. You would tear from her the last hope of her declining age, the hope of benefit to her children from the pious labors of some herald of the Cross, who in his excursions might alight at her cottage, bearing the message of redeeming love." After instruction, and commending her to God, I took my leave of herself and family.

At Kaskaskia he formed a female auxiliary Bible society of some twenty members under circumstances of interest and hopefulness, a pious Quakeress being made President, with whom he formed a pleasant acquaintance. In the end of June he notices seeing in the newspapers an account of the formation of the American Sunday-school Union, Philadelphia, and immediately entered into correspondence with it, giving the facts he had gathered in the vast region over which he was traveling. He notices also the preparation of a sermon in favor of the colonization Society which he preached the 4th of July. Thus early was his heart opening to every good enterprise for the bond and the free. During this year also there are incidental notices in his journal of the great question, then being covertly agitated in Southern Illinois especially, in regard to calling a convention of the State for remodeling the

constitution so as to admit of slavery   There can be no doubt
that a deep-laid plan was formed for securing the consummation of this scheme.   The legislature the preceding winter
had opened the way for the calling of such a convention,
though the real object of it was skilfully veiled.   Governor
Coles, a Virginian, who had emigrated to this free territory,
relying on the inviolability of the ordinance of '87, and had
brought with him the patrimony of slaves from his father's
estate which he inherited, on purpose to settle them eligibly
in freedom, was now fortunately in the executive chair, and
to his commanding and consistent influence it was no doubt
principally owing, that this stealthy movement of the advocates of hereditary bondage was thoroughly circumvented
There can be no doubt that Mr. Peck, who shared the Gov
ernor's intimate acquaintance and confidence, shared with him
also the sentiments above expressed, and in a quiet, unobtrusive manner aided, so far as he properly could, in bringing
about this result.   But it is not true that he traversed the
State, under cover of his commission as a missionary and
a Bible agent, but really as an emissary opposed to the proposed convention.   He seems on the contrary to have prudently guarded his whole deportment, so as not to be obnox-
ious to censure in this respect.   However deeply he may have
felt as a citizen, there is no evidence that he made himself a
partisan.   Against ministers of the gospel doing this he always raised his voice and wielded his pen.   And though, on
the defeat of the above measure, some of its too warm advocates were inclined to censure him, and he notices in a few
instances the unkindness and injustice of their treatment, yet
in the end all the more considerate and trustworthy became
convinced of the erroneousness of their suspicions, and restored to him the full measure of their confidence.   This
result was no doubt all the earlier secured, because, when the
hallucination of the moment had passed away, all parties
seem to have rested satisfied of the fact that the best result
had been secured.   A quarter of a century later, when Mr.
Peck edited the second edition of the "Annals of the West,"

it is correctly stated as the summing-up of this matter: " In six months after the question [of calling a convention] was settled, a politician who was in favor of the introduction of slavery into the State was a rarity."

This is the verdict of an impartial and somewhat remote review of these transactions. But at the time, and when so many causes were conspiring to unite all elements of opposition against our brother, as the staunch advocate of whatever was enlightened, benevolent, and patriotic, it was a comparatively easy thing to load him with obloquy for his sentiments on this subject. Public attacks of a scurrilous and perfectly baseless character were sometimes sent forth against him in the newspapers. To some of these he replied in a temperate but decided and manly denial of the allegations, and a fearless demand for any proof to sustain the assault. He remarks in his diary that to some extent these very attacks, by rendering him more famous, drew towards him more of the attention of the public, and gave him ampler opportunity to advocate with success the great objects to which his heart and life were devoted—missions, the diffusion of the Bible, and the vigorous support of Sunday-schools. In a very few instances, however, he had occasion to lament the alienation of some of his former friends on this account. He mourned over their misconceptions, and, in a kind and fraternal manner, used the best means in his power to disabuse their minds of the prejudices they had entertained. So far as this was merely personal, he seems to have been willing to bear this obloquy and alienation; but where, as in many cases, it affected injuriously the cause of his Divine Master, dearer to him than life, he was deeply grieved with the spirit and the opposition which it stirred up against him.

His growth in grace and in knowledge, as a Christian minister, appears to have fully kept pace with the celebrity which unsought was widely extending his influence. At this period he certainly watched over his heart, his spirit, his entire deportment with scrupulous fidelity He thus expresses himself on hearing of the death of a minister who had injured him :

> Though for three years past he has tried to injure me, I have freely forgiven him ; and I feel thankful that I treated him with the respect due to his age, at the last Missouri Association. Let all that has been unpleasant be buried in the dust and forgotten.

In case of another professed minister, with whom he and his associate, Rev. Mr. Welch, had much difficulty years before, and who had been held up by decisions of churches and associations against the full proofs they had adduced of his unworthiness, when now at length he was demonstrating beyond all question his flagitious character, the journal says, evidently coming from the writer's heart, " Oh, that Divine mercy might reclaim him !"   On detecting in his own mind the frequent and painful recurrence of *doubts* on some of the fundamental principles of spiritual religion, he thus remarks as to what he feared was his culpability as the *cause :*

> My neglect of secret devotion, and failure to cultivate the humility of soul and close walk with God, which ought to be maintained, under all circumstances, is probably the cause of these doubts. Amidst a multiplicity of business, which though not chiefly of a worldly character, yet proves a temptation for relaxation in more spiritual and heavenly engagements, I find myself prone to depart from the living God. In too many instances my pulpit services are destitute of the life of religion. To this I must add the levity of my conversation. There is a constitutional tendency in me to hilarity of spirits which is frequently indulged beyond the bounds of propriety, and on reflection induces me to exclaim, " Who shall deliver me from this dead body ?"

In the same spirit, when he had been obliged by public duties to spend a few days at the seat of government, and mingle very freely with the influential men from different parts of the State, he records his estimate of the influence of such association : " I find them not good for the soul."

As a means of intellectual and spiritual improvement, he

records some experiments which he made in systematic studying of the Divine word, even while traveling. The following notice of such efforts occurs in his diary, and will be read
with interest:

SATURDAY, *9th October*, 1824. Started on my way to Columbia.
For some weeks I have felt a growing attachment to reading the
word of God critically. I have gone through the Epistle to the
Romans in the most careful and minute manner, observing every
expression, and sometimes dwelling for two or three hours upon a
single chapter. This has vastly increased a thirst for a more intimate acquaintance with the sacred volume. I can read while riding
horseback, by the help of sun-glasses which I generally use. My
method is to implore the unction of the Holy Spirit that I may
understand the portion I am about to study; and then commence
and dwell on each verse, observing the connection till I can catch
what appears to be the distinct idea of the writer; often looking back
and examining the part I have gone over, and connecting it with
what follows. If a verse or sentence is not clear at first, I endeavor to
fix my mind on the passage with the utmost intensity, and in a little
time I generally find the obscurity vanish, and clear, definite ideas
present themselves. Passages remaining obscure, on which I can
not satisfy myself, I mark with a pencil, for examination with the
best helps I may afterwards find accessible. This method of study
ing the sacred oracles is both instructive and comforting. I know
a little of what the pious Psalmist means in saying the words of
God were sweet to his taste, yea sweeter than honey or the honey
comb.

In the same connection he laments the indisposition of
some preachers to study the letter of Divine truth, making
extravagant claims to being led by the Spirit.

An old minister named H——, famous for allegorizing, thus
noticed the plagues in Egypt, and the success of her magicians in
imitating some of the miracles of Moses, but could not produce
the lice. "These lice," he said, "signified the grace of God in the
soul. Now," said he, "as you can *feel* these little animals," suiting
the action to the word he here scratched his head, "but cannot
see them, so you cannot see the grace of God, but you can feel it."
Such idle, ridiculous and disgusting comparisons are frequently

made; and such preachers, by ludicrous and antic gestures, and a drawling voice, can often raise a laugh among their hearers. Thus religion becomes ridiculous, and excites contempt among sensible, well-informed men. These too often fly off to deism and atheism, imagining all religion to be folly. The cause of this may be mainly traced to putting ignorant persons into the ministry, and encouraging them to preach without study. O Lord, deliver Zion from such evils!

How incessantly, in all his journeyings, our brother was laying under contribution all his opportunities for learning human nature may be seen by the following item of his journal:

While journeying in settlements where I am not known, I fre quently call at houses, and in a roundabout way introduce the subject of religion, and in this way find out the views which differ ent denominations entertain of each other. They will converse more freely and I can get a better insight into their charac ter than if my calling were suspected. To-day I called on a Cumberland Presbyterian family to inquire the road, and soon fell into conversation with a woman. She represented the Baptists as believing that God had foreordained a certain part of mankind to be saved, and the rest to be damned; and that it would do no good for us to attempt to do any thing till God did all the work. She also said they believed no other society could be saved, because they were not baptized. It is astonishing how much honest, well-meaning people will mistake each other through preju dice and prepossession. I find there is but little difference in the strength and prevalence of their prejudices, however they may differ in other respects. The absurdity of all this is the more striking when it is seen with what eagerness they will receive members from each other's society, and what anxiety is manifested for proselyting.

His Bible and Sunday-school labors especially brought him into close contact with all denominations, and taught him important lessons of true, wide-reaching charity. Entertained as the welcome guest by the good of all denominations, how could he fail to love the good among them all. Speaking of a worthy Methodist family who had cordially received him, he says:

I was received as kindly as I could have been in any Baptist family. Experience has taught me that it is wretched policy for the different sects in religion to oppose each other. As the late excellent Dr. Ward observes, "There is much trash cleaving to us all." Christians can love each other, and provoke to good works without sanctioning a particle of error, or relinquishing a particle of truth. I have good reason to believe that the liberal policy which I have observed for months past has had good effect.

To which we may safely subjoin, it certainly had a good effect on himself, as it always does on every true disciple of Christ. It need not render him indifferent to points of importance held by each family of the Lord's people. That it did not in the present instance is demonstrated by the following account which he gives of a camp-meeting of the Methodists and Cumberland Presbyterians in Missouri which he attended, and of which he furnishes the following account:

At evening of the last day I heard a young Cumberland Presbyterian attempt to preach from 1 Pet. i. 8. He was a young hand and made out but poorly. A Mr. Chamberlain, a Methodist, gave an exhortation, in which he began by lamenting the want of effort on the part of the people, declaring at first that he had no faith to exhort; he reproved the people for sloth and neglect, but soon fell into a strain of the most passionate, powerful appeals to the hopes and fears of all around him. The Methodists were alternately assailed and encouraged, till he wound up by proposing to all who ever did pray, or ever would pray, to engage ten minutes by the watch as the last alternative. Upon this the members and others rushed forward to the stand, and all commenced as if with one voice. Soon a black woman and some others commenced shouting. Two or three appeared in agony for mercy. The preachers would exhort them to have a little more faith, " to struggle a few minutes longer, and God, Christ, and heaven are yours!" They would constantly make appeals to those engaged to prevent the fervor and zeal from expiring. I left them about nine o'clock still engaged, and I could hear them shouting at a great distance.

I remark on this subject generally as follows:

1. Throughout the preaching, the exhortations, and the communion nothing of this kind transpired: hence the people were said to be indolent, lazy, and devoid of faith.

2. The person who now exhorted evidently intended to produce this excitement; and as the assembly was rather small, he first pretended he had no faith to exhort, and that they must depart without a solitary conversion.

3. They all went to work in a way calculated to raise their own and others' passions, and labored at it most determinedly. They appeared to act as if they felt that all depended on human effort "Come forward and help the Lord do it," was a common expres sion

4. The excitement had to be kept up by the same causes which produced it. The moment the preachers stopped, the nerves of the people relaxed and their voices fell.

5. All this excitement and effect, so far as visible, might have been produced without the agency of God, and might be and seemed to be only the effect of human causes.

6. While from the fruits occasionally manifested, I have no doubt that genuine convictions and saving conversions do sometimes follow such confused and disorderly meetings, yet it must be confessed that most of these cases prove false—worse than worthless.

7. The method of talking to and exhorting the persons apparently under conviction is highly improper and injudicious. The whole object of the preachers and leaders appears to be to get them relieved from distress, quite irrespective of the character of the relief. Hence, were it not for the apparent necessity for such meetings, in a thinly populated country, and the fact that sometimes God blesses very imperfect means, I would disapprove of them wholly. As they are congenial to the habits of the people, and may do some good, reaching those not otherwise accessible, they may be tolerated, and as far as practicable regulated.

All sorts of opposition came in his way, and valiantly did he encounter it. In one of his tours for organizing Bible societies, he says :

Instead of persuading the people to unite in circulating the Scriptures, I find it necessary to take higher ground, and support the Bible as the word of God—as a scheme of Divine revelation. There are people of prominent and active influence who reject the gospel of a precious Saviour. I was attacked by two men of this sort, in the public house where I put up.

This led him to review carefully the ground of early and modern skepticism, and to prepare himself thoroughly to defend that Holy Word he was laboring to disseminate.

July 30th, he thus sums up the results of an early and laborious tour as Bible agent:

In this journey in the Bible cause I have rode five hundred miles, preached seventeen regular sermons besides delivering several addresses; have aided in forming eight Bible societies, two of which are branches, the others auxiliaries. The Lord has been exceedingly gracious to me in all my journeyings, granted me an unusual degree of health, prospered me in my labors much beyond any reasonable anticipations, and returned me in safety over several dangerous waters where I had to swim my horse.

Near the close of the following month, as he was preparing to set forth on a still longer tour through Missouri, his wife became very ill, and for several days despaired of recovery. His mind was greatly exercised with distracting emotions in view of this calamity, but at length he found grace to commit himself and family entirely into the Lord's hand, and wait his holy will. Almost immediately God turned the shadow of death into the morning, and she began steadily to recover. One week later, he set forth on this important enterprise. A month later, he thus describes his position and his feelings:

September 28th. I am now at Liberty, Clay county, on the extreme western side of Missouri, north of the Missouri river. Southeast lies the missionary station of Harmony, among the Osages, one hundred miles distant. Northwest are the Council Bluffs, and before me the interminable wilderness, over which the savage Indians roam after the buffalo. Could I but succeed in planting the Bible here, it would greatly rejoice my heart, but prospects at present are not very favorable. The settlement of this remote county in the extremity of the State was begun but four years since, and it now contains about two thousand inhabitants. Baptists, Cumberland Presbyterians, and Methodists, each have societies here. The people who have settled this district are chiefly from Kentucky and Tennessee, sadly destitute of public spirit, and manifest a great degree of apathy towards benevolent institutions, even when they are obviously intended for their own benefit. More than one hundred of these families are believed to be entirely destitute of the Scriptures, yet when I explained—after preaching—the design of an auxiliary Bible society, the need and the benefits of it, and then urged its formation, no one stepped forward and offered to engage in it. In Ray and Clay and Lillard counties, little or nothing could be effected.

On reaching his home (October 20th), he thus recapitulates the labors and successes of the journey :

In this tour I have not been as successful in forming Bible societies as I had fondly anticipated, but I have done what I could. May the blessing of Heaven follow! I have rode on horseback eight hundred and thirty miles, preached twenty-seven times regular discourses, formed five branch Bible societies, attended four Baptist associations, two Methodist camp-meetings, besides making a number of addresses, and preparing the way for other Bible societies hereafter. This has occupied forty-five days.

In November of this year he mentions attending the organization of a society, for the suppression of intemperance, in one of the counties of Central Illinois ; and this is marked in the margin at a much later date as the first temperance society in the State, or possibly he means the first with which he had met or co-operated. Thus we find him sowing beside all waters, and he lived to verify the blessedness which the Divine promise announces. Having sowed bountifully the good seed of all good enterprises—moral, religious, intellectual—it was his privilege afterwards to reap bountifully. Having gone forth, weeping, bearing precious seed, he did return rejoicing bearing the rich sheaves of an abundant harvest. But we may not linger longer in our gleanings of this harvest. Very appropriately might this chapter be closed by the letter of Mr. Peck to the Secretary of the Missionary Society of Massachusetts, with which he still held a connection, but our limits forbid.

CHAPTER XVII.

Revisiting—Circuit-preaching—Perverse Ministers—Infidelity.

THE next ten months were spent in a manner so similar to the preceding as scarcely to require a minute detail of his numerous and multifarious engagements. The same objects aimed at, as described in the last chapter, still engrossed his attention, and were prosecuted on the whole with cheering success. The ordinary amount of discouragement from misconception and prejudice among opponents, and from coolness, indifference, and lack of fidelity in his professed coadjutors, cost him many a severe disappointment: Yet through it all he bated not a particle of heart or hope, but urged his way onward, right onward. When for instance he would make his way through many impediments of bad roads, swollen creeks, and missing bridges, for scores of miles, to meet some Bible society anniversary, and find, on arriving at the appointed place, that no arrangements had been made for the meeting, instead of abandoning such faulty individuals as these officers and managers had proved themselves, he would set about the work which they had neglected with imperturbable patience and vigor, and when after struggling day and night to repair the disaster occasioned solely by their neglect, and when the full tide of success had again been secured, and their coldness was giving place to general gratulations in view of the cheering results, *then*, and not before, would he kindly but faithfully lead these officers to see the bad effects of their lukewarmness, and win from them a hearty pledge of greater fidelity and zeal in future. He came very soon to understand that no auxiliary, Bible, or Sunday-school society was reliably established, until it had been revisited at the end of a year or two of its history, to set in order and re-supply the things which were wanting, and by continuous exercise on the part of its officers and managers, they had formed the habit of earning success by patient and energetic well-doing. This course of reiterated journeying over the same routes where he had passed before gave him much more thorough and complete knowledge of the country and its wants, and the means available for the supply of these wants, than he could have otherwise secured It made him familiar with the men and the means which could be called out, and what was most indispensable to secure them. So that, in reality, great as may have been the immediate benefits from his previous and his present exertions by preaching, and by his systematic formation of Sunday-schools and Bible-distributing organizations, the chief value of these explorations may still be justly reckoned as their preparation for more enlarged and efficient measures in the future. In this light it is certain that he came in the end to regard them. Indeed so little was he satisfied with the amount of permanent and reliable success hitherto secured, that we find him again and again during this period very seriously revolving the question whether he should not break away from the multifarious engagements on which, as he feared, he was frittering away the best of his years, and settling himself down in St. Louis, ministering to a single church, regularly teaching some few hours a day for his reliable support, he should not devote himself to conducting a weekly journal as the principal means of arousing and wisely guiding the Western mind, and heart, and habits, for self-improvement. His correspondence and journals show how nearly he at one time came to yielding himself up to an inviting offer of this kind. But doubtless it was well for the cause that he did not. It was yet too early to trust to the power of the press to set in motion and wisely guide the mass of inert mind on which, for religious and moral improvement, he had to operate. More of the hard, preliminary work had first to be performed, and to that he earnestly and bravely devoted himself.

The necessity of something like a system of circuit-preaching, by the most capable and faithful ministers attainable, seems

18

to have been about this time fully impressed on his mind.
Returning from one of his usual preaching tours through a
pretty wide range of counties, churches, and preaching-
stations, he thus remarks in his journal :

> On this route I have rode three hundred and two miles. This is
> a circuit suitable for an active missionary in this country to ride
> over in one month, and preach thirty times, besides attending to
> keeping alive Bible societies, Sunday-schools, and looking well to
> the discipline of the churches.

The immense mischief done by ignorant, imprudent, and
pretentious preachers, was constantly forcing itself on his
notice; and jottings down in his journals like the following
are of frequent occurrence :

> After much serious reflection I am convinced that much of the
> ignorance, prejudice, and bigotry, which exist among the Baptists
> here, is to be traced to the men who pretend to preach the gospel.

Again, on the following page, he says :

> The Church here is in serious difficulty, and from all appearances
> there will be a division amongst the Baptists through the State. The
> opposers of missions are determined to invade the inherent rights
> and privileges of their brethren, and it really seems as if they were
> given up to violent measures in order to hasten their own defeat. All
> these difficulties originate from the ignorant and selfish preachers."

In the meantime the cheering influence of the Sunday-
schools which he had established, and the willingness of all
classes (with trifling exceptions) to co-operate in maintaining
and extending them, very greatly cheered his heart.   In May,
1825, this record is found on his reaching St. Louis, and looking over the extensive correspondence there received by him
as Secretary of a Western Sunday-school Union which had
there been formed :

> From various quarters I learn that the Sunday-school cause
> prospers. Schools are forming in different parts, and it is to be
> hoped that great good will be the result.

Again, in August following, on occasion of his extending
his tour over the State line into Indiana and there forming

the Knox County Sunday-school Society under auspicious circumstances, he thus remarks :

If circumstances possibly admitted, I could form a complete system of Sunday-schools in Indiana; and I am almost induced at times to forego the objects I have already contemplated, sacrifice domestic enjoyment and family interest, and devote myself to such a work. My lungs are still oppressed with cold and hoarseness, but when I find a number of children and several people assemble in the evening for instruction, I cannot hesitate to address them, relating Sunday-school anecdotes and other things adapted to interest them. In every part of the country is a wide field for exertion. Twenty missionaries might find constant employment in Indiana.

Later in the same month Mr. Peck visited Robert Owen's colony at Harmony—of which he furnishes the following account :

I rode a few miles on purpose to see the community lately formed by Mr. Owen. The town of Harmony is situated on the right bank of the Wabash and was originially founded by a colony of Germans under a Mr. Rapp. There are a number of excellent buildings, fine gardens, with walks, labyrinths, vineyards, etc., but at present much of it lies waste. The town is crowded with population, under somewhat singular police regulations. There is a mixture of every class of people, as to their religious preferences; but a large number, perhaps one-fourth, are deists and atheists. These are the principles taught in the schools. The children are all taught to believe nothing but what the senses can demonstrate. This society is only in the incipient stage of the social community which Mr. Owen contemplates. Here men are to be prepared by a state of probation and discipline, to enter into that rest and happiness which he contemplates will be enjoyed by those who shall be divested of all religious hopes and fears.

At evening, by arrangement of the committee, the meeting of the society for business was postponed, and opportunity given for me to deliver a lecture in the meeting-house. I did not begin in the usual way of public worship, but lectured on MAN, his nature, his character, wants, etc., the necessity of religion to such a being, the character of the gospel; and then enforced the duty of following the guiding light of Scripture. A Mr. Jennings—head teacher, lec-

turer, etc.—proposed to deliver a lecture in defence of his system
some ten days hence. But this did not satisfy the public mind.
Finally it was agreed that he should lecture the next evening, and
give me opportunity to reply. I soon found the whole town in
commotión. Parties were collected at the street corners, debating
Numbers called on me presenting their grateful acknowledgments
for my lecture, and expressing the hope that I would defend the
truth. I cannot but think that God in his providence has sent me
here to stay the devouring flood of infidelity and atheism.

The following evening I heard Mr. Jennings deliver his lecture,
in which he displayed considerable ingenuity, while supporting
his principles of atheism. He did not come out openly and fully to
the understanding of all, but presented the subject in such a way
as could not be mistaken by an observing person. I replied to him
in a short discourse, in which my endeavor was fully to expose his
principles, and publicly declared that I would expose them through
the country. It is now fully evident that Owen's system is based
on atheism; and that every effort will be made to erase from the
minds of its receivers every idea of God.

As a practical demonstration of the bitter fruits of this
system Mr. Peck the next day visited a lady who was a
member of a Baptist church in Cincinnati, and being in
widowhood with several children, she had joined this community of Owen's. Here she was induced to marry one of
the members of it, who turned out very soon to be an atheist
in full, who now laughs at and mocks her, and in every
possible way interferes with her religious duties. She
evinced the utmost distress in regard to her situation and
that of her poor children.

On his return home, a few days later, he found that a son
named John Q. A. Peck had been born in his absence, and
that Mrs. Peck in her accouchement had come near losing her
life. God's goodness in sparing her called for the husband's
warmest and most devout acknowledgments. He thus sums
up the labors of this one journey:

I have been absent from home fifty-three days; have traveled
through eighteen counties in Illinois, and nine in Indiana, rode nine
hundred and twenty-six miles, preached regular sermons thirty-one

times, besides delivering several speeches, addresses, and lectures. I have been enabled to revive three Bible societies, which would never have been recognized but for my visit; to establish seven new societies; to visit and give instruction and encouragement in the management of two societies which had been formed without my aid; and to provide for the formation of four others. I have aided in forming three Sabbath-school societies, and in opening several schools where no societies exist, and improved many important opportunities to aid the great cause in various ways. Now, Lord, give me both gratitude and humility, that I may praise THEE for all my success, and seeing my own weakness and insignificance may sink into the dust of self-abasement, that I may never be proud or vain!

The remaining months of the year 1825 were filled to repletion with incessant engagements and labors of a somewhat multifarious character, in supplying monthly the colored and white churches in St. Louis, which had virtually if not formally separated; in traveling among the associations and churches in Missouri and Illinois, especially in promoting the formation, strengthening and encouragement of Bible and Sunday-school societies in both these States, which threw on him, as their Corresponding Secretary, the laboring oar, and tasked every moment of his time in cares, toils, circulars and letters to prominent individuals. We cannot follow him minutely in these varied and most incessant labors, but will only glean here and there an item from his hurried journal.

In October he attended the annual conference of the "Friends of Humanity," an association of anti-slavery Baptists in Illinois, several of the members of which subsequently became his warmest personal friends. This is his verdict in regard to their sentiments and practices at that period:

I heard several discourses during the meeting. The preaching is rather tinctured with Arminianism. Too much stress is laid on the grace given equally to all men, and the whole result as depending on the improvement which they make of it. This in particular was the fault of a discourse from Father C. At night the communion was observed, but there was far too much confusion and disorder during the observance, too much singing and shaking hands, far too much bodily effort. Still there are valuable things in this society, and, with some improvement, they will be far more useful then the cold Laodicean Baptists around them.

He thus speaks of a Cumberland Presbyterian camp-meeting in Missouri :

More than twenty professed to be converted, but from what I could learn, there was too much of the imagination predominant—such as seeing heaven, seeing hell, shaking hands with Christ, etc. Amongst ignorant people such excesses are frequent, but no doubt a good work is going on here.

On a visit in the same month to St. Charles, Mo., he enters this minute :

I am happy to find among the slaveholders in Missouri a growing disposition to have the blacks educated, and to patronise Sunday-schools for the purpose. I doubt not but by prudent efforts this may be effected extensively.

At the end of the year, and for some three weeks afterwards, he was in and near Vandalia, the seat of government of Illinois at that time, preaching in the legislature halls in behalf of the Bible and Sunday-school cause. By public and personal appeals among those attending the session of the legislature, he was enabled to win many prominent men from all parts of the State to favor these objects. But he was encouraged to aim at securing the funds possessed by a State agricultural society, which was now about to be dissolved, to be transferred to a Sunday-school society for the State. In this he was entirely successful. and together with some individual donations from members of the legislature, he secured about two hundred and sixty dollars for this object.

In February, 1826, while spending a few days in St. Louis he assisted in the ordination of Rev. J. B. Meacham, a colored brother, who then and even to his death was held in high esteem by all who knew him. The General Sunday-school Union also appointed him their agent to solicit funds in New York, Boston, and other eastern cities. The Auxiliary

Colonization Society of St. Louis also appointed him their agent and representative to the American Colonization Society, in whose efforts for the poor blacks he then, and through life, felt the greatest interest.

Having in various ways brought his important work in hand to a state of as much completeness as possible, he was prepared for an absence of several months in an eastern tour, which must be chronicled in the following chapter.

Very appropriate to the close of this are some general reflections written near this time in the beginning of one of his journals, from which the following sentences have been condensed :

I am beginning to fear that my mind is not as susceptible of high religious emotions as formerly. I have less, far less *feeling* about missions, but more firmness, resolution and perseverance to accomplish my objects. In fine, I view an unseen hand guiding me in all my ways, and desire to trust myself entirely to His dis posal. Though my labors have been more arduous, and have more exposed me to the severity of weather and climate for the last two years than before, I have enjoyed better health. After mature deliberation, and ten years experience since I devoted my life as a pioneer in the army of the Redeemer, I am as firm and unshaken in my resolution, as at the first moment I enlisted. I have been sorely tried, my character reproached, and my name cast out as evil, but I do not desire to give up the cause of missions or compromise one of its principles. Though my lot is not what I expected, yet I have hitherto been enabled to act on the great principle I adopted at the first, viz. : that my time, property, talents family, body, soul, and all that I have and am, are sacredly consecrated to the missionary cause, as God's providence may order and direct ; whether in the Bible, Sunday-school or missionary employ, it is all with the same end in view. O Lord, help me to continue faithful and devoted to THEE !

CHAPTER XVIII.

A Nine-months' tour to the Eastern and Middle States.

THE time had at length arrived when imperative duty as well as strong inclination led Mr. Peck for the first time after his removal to the West to set his face towards the scenes and friends of his earlier years. The nine years of his separation from them had in no degree dimmed his perceptions of their worth, or chilled his heart towards them. On the other hand, so free and frequent had been his correspondence, and so vividly was all the past impressed on his mind, that soon as circumstances permitted he yearned to revisit the loved ones he had left so long. But stronger inducements than any mere personal gratification impelled him to this journey. He had borne into the deep mine the explorer's torch, and felt an intense solicitude to rally to his aid the requisite assistance to secure the rich treasures which he had discovered. For six of these years, single-handed and with but little aid from abroad, he had been manfully battling for truth and righteousness, for the enlightenment and evangelization of the mighty West, and he was now constrained to report to the churches of New England and New York what had been done, and what further efforts were immediately demanded. He was the first who, from minute, thorough general knowledge, brought the appeal to the Baptist churches of the East to come up promptly and energetically to the help of their less-favored brethren in the West. While he had felt constrained to correct many extravagant misrepresentations which others had sent forth on this subject, and for this purpose, throughout the previous year, had been writing a series of articles in the " Christian Watchman," Boston, designed to refute many of these misconceptions, he felt equally bound on the other hand not to let the real and pressing religious wants of the great valley of the Mississippi and its tributaries remain unheeded. Very well did he understand also that a personal appeal would be much more efficient than any other.

The record of this tour fills nearly ninety pages of a quarto volume of his journal, besides another folio volume of sixty-seven pages, full of memoranda of various observations in regard to weather, soil, topography, statistics, and whatever he deemed most interesting not falling within the range of his ordinary diary. These materials are superabundant, besides which personal recollections in ample fullness and variety here come to the aid of the biographer. But necessity seems to demand the compression of the most permanently important of all these into the limits of a single chapter.

Mr. Peck left his home and family on the 22d of February, and journeyed on horseback to Cincinnati, a distance of three hundred and forty-eight miles. His health was not good, and the weather and traveling were most wearisome and forbidding, so that with the delays thus occasioned he consumed nearly three weeks in this part of the journey. Over a great part of this route he had traveled before, and here his way was cheered by the society and hospitality of old friends. He did what he could in public and private to strengthen the things which remained—the Bible societies, Sunday-schools, and little half-destitute churches. On reaching the eastern portion of Indiana, he came upon new ground, and formed new and interesting acquaintances. The Hon. Judge Holman, near Aurora was one of these, and a life long intimacy and friendship grew out of it to their mutual satisfaction and the benefit of the cause.

On reaching Cincinnati, which he now visited for the first time, he found a more interesting state of things, both in the city, where he remained five days, and in the State of Ohio, of which he could here learn much more than had before been known to him,—than he had even dared to anticipate. Measures were now set on foot by the personal appeals of one or more of the brethren to the churches, which soon after resulted in the formation of the Ohio Baptist Convention for domestic missions and education purposes. In the city also he found himself surrounded by warm-hearted, intelligent brethren, whose attentions to him and zeal for the cause greatly encouraged his heart. Preaching to the Enon Baptist church then worshiping in Walnut street, he found a larger and more respectable assembly than he had addressed for many years. Religion was flourishing, and additions were made to the church every month. Here, too, a high and increasing missionary spirit was manifest, and for his work's sake he found himself surrounded by warm-hearted, devoted friends, and almost devoured by the demonstrations of their kindness. By special request he preached to them on Lord's-day evening a missionary discourse, and a collection was taken for their own missionary purposes. So wearied had both man and horse been by struggling through rain and mud to this place that he was induced to put both on board a steamer, and in this way accomplished with ease and satisfaction the next four hundred miles to Wheeling. It seems to have been his first experience of traveling any considerable distance in this manner, by which subsequently he was to experience so much of benefit and peril. He remarks on the rattling and crashing of the engines, and the bustle and confusion on board, as rendering it impracticable to have public worship on the Sabbath as he had desired, and as on the large boats was often practicable. In three and a half days he arrived at Wheeling, and thence proceeded on horseback with ease and expedition over the national road towards Washington city.

In Washington, Pa., he mentions an interesting interview which he had with Rev. Charles Wheeler, pastor of the Baptist church in that place (subsequently President of Rector College, Western Virginia), who gave him a pretty clear idea of the continued difficulties in the Redstone Baptist Association, where there was a hyper-Calvinistic party, very rigid and bigoted, and where Alexander Campbell was more and more manifesting his opposition to the above party and their shibboleth, while still a third and more numerous portion of that body maintained a middle ground.

At Cumberland, where he spent a Sabbath, he mentions hearing an excellent sermon from the Lutheran minister; he also visited and promoted the Sunday-schools in the place, and preached in the evening. Rev. Isaac McCoy, having passed through the place recently with several young Indians whom he was taking for education in some of the Northern colleges, had awakened considerable interest in the subject of Indian missions, which the good people desired to have fanned into a flame. They persuaded Mr. Peck to stop on Monday and organize a juvenile society for this purpose. He did so with pleasure, preaching again on this subject, thus wakening anew his own zeal and love for this kindred evangelical enterprise.

By the end of March he reached Washington city, and found himself surrounded, as he said, by every thing grand, pompous, ceremonious, intelligent, and these traits probably counterbalanced by those of the opposite character. His old friends, Rice and Dr. Staughton, welcomed him cordially. But he soon saw the incipient coolness and distrust which was beginning to manifest itself between them and their respective adherents, which, before another month was at an end, blazed out into open rupture. He visited the Capitol, and heard McDuffie, and other of the principal speakers of that era. Considerable of his time was also spent in the Columbian College, into whose affairs, pecuniary and literary, he seems to have looked somewhat closely. He preached both in the city and in the college chapel; and in company with the member of Congress from his district, he waited on President Adams, for whom he had felt so much admiration that he had just named his youngest son after him. The last Lord's day he was here, Dr. Staughton delivered in the chapel a lecture on the wisdom of God in redemption, of which he says: "Though the Doctor has failed in a number of respects, I could see his usual vivacity and eloquence at times during the discourse." The same evening he mentions holding a long and painful conversation with his friend Luther Rice on the various topics connected with the college and missions.

and became more fully impressed with the serious difficulties
which threatened disturbance and the separation of those who
had been warm friends, by coldness, distrust, and jealousy.
With commendable prudence he determined to forbear expressing any judgment on these things till he had been enabled
to judge coolly and understandingly.

After a fortnight spent in the national capital, during a portion of which time he was a housed-sufferer from a severe
influenza, he passed on through Baltimore, where a single day
sufficed him to renew his acquaintance with the Baptist pastors
and other friends, and by the middle of April again reached
Philadelphia, where so many pleasant associations and recollections of the happy months of his student life were awakened.

Lord's-day morning he preached for Rev. Mr. Dagg, pastor
of Sansom street church, and in the evening listened to one, who
had been a fellow-student, in the same pulpit, of whose performance he thus speaks : " He was rather too rapid and violent
in his tones and gestures; otherwise there would have been
many admirable strokes of eloquence in his discourse, which
on the whole was ingenious and instructive.   Several times
he had the attention of the audience roused up to the highest
pitch, but had not the faculty of letting them down again
without too sudden and abrupt a transition."   He rejoiced
also in the evidences of respect and love evinced by this
church and congregation for their new pastor, the successor
of his beloved instructor, Dr. Staughton.

His days and nights were here a continuous round of
welcomes among the friends he had formerly known and
loved.   He mentions dining with a large company of Presbyterian ministers at the hospitable mansion of Alexander
Henry, President of the American Sunday-school Union.   In
this city and its surroundings, among which is prominently
to be mentioned his dear friend and yoke-fellow's home at
Mt. Holly and Burlington, New Jersey, he spent the next ten
days.   Almost every day or night, or both, he was called
out for sermons, lectures, addresses, all bearing more or less
directly on the stores of definite and reliable information

which he could furnish in regard to the mighty West—its wants, its capabilities, and its prospects.

From the 26th of April to the 7th of May he was in attendance on the session of the Triennial Convention in New York, enjoying the hospitality of his old Dutchess county friend Deacon Purser. There *we* met (his biographer and himself), after eleven years separation. In the early part of the session he was ill a day or two, and afterward in the painful collisions so manifest and wide-reaching, between some of his choicest early friends, he was very silent. Indeed, he said little in public during that whole meeting. But he was a keen observer, a good listener, and then and there he learned to read the characteristics of many of those who were more or less directly associated with him through the remainder of his eventful life. There may have been another reason which restrained him from taking a more prominent part in those debates, besides the revering love he felt for the leaders on both sides. He felt that immensely great and sacred interests had been confided to him and his advocacy, and he would not needlessly imperil them by mixing himself with the debates, so engrossing and exciting, which were now transpiring. He was no scheming, selfish trimmer, at this or at any period of his life; but he knew how to reserve himself for an emergency of transcendent interest, compared with which the animosities and collisions, chiefly of a personal character, which now stirred the blood so quickly, were but as the small chaff of the summer threshing-floor.

On both the Sabbaths during the session he preached, and with liveliest interest he visited as many of the best conducted Sabbath-schools as possible. The one in Vandam (now McDougal) street was reckoned at that time one of the largest and best schools in the city, and he made himself thoroughly acquainted with its whole plan, and system of operations. His verdict, after a full, repeated examination of it, was, that it was probably the best conducted Sunday-school in the world. "All the scholars are closely instructed into the meaning of the Scripture." His old fellow-pupil in the

19

Dutchess Academy at Poughkeepsie, Rev. Aaron Perkins, was then pastor of this church, and with him and their former preceptor, Daniel H. Barnes, associate principal with Dr. Griscom of one of the most important high schools of the city, he enjoyed a delightful re-union.

Immediately succeeding the Triennial Convention, the usual May anniversaries of general religious benevolence were held in New York. These he attended with absorbing interest and satisfaction, particularly the assemblage of five or six thousand Sunday-school children in Castle Garden, where Mars with his murderous accompaniments had been turned out to let this lovely throng of Sunday-scholars in, with their sweet faces and peaceful, holy banners, where their hosannahs to the PRINCE OF PEACE went up in blessed harmony, and where prayers and addresses of a most appropriate and spirit-striking character were listened to, and drew forth the exultation of his soul. The American Bible Society, as a special and well-merited token of its favor, made him an honorary life-member, for the important and distinguished favor he had rendered to their cause in the West. This was the first time he had ever been permitted to mingle in their anniversary services. To all of them, the American Tract Society, the American Home Mission, and the Colonization Society, as well as those before mentioned, he gave his attention, as a large-hearted man, loving his whole country and his race, should do. His remarks on the several addresses to which he had listened on this occasion are eminently just and generous, while also they are faithfully discriminating. McIlvaine, then Professor and Chaplain at West Point, and now Bishop of the Episcopal Church in Ohio, received his highest praise in these words : " For sound reasoning, solid eloquence, and brilliancy of thought, I have never heard his address surpassed."

These services all over, he brought his horse from New Jersey, where it had been kept during his sojourn in New York, and hastened to his mother in his native town. The floods of rain which impeded his journey on setting out from home had now been exchanged for drought, and the roads were so dry and dusty as to make his ride very unpleasant. Passing through Stamford and Stratfield on the afternoon of Thursday, the 18th of May, he says:

I drew near to the hills and prospects upon which a thousand times I had gazed in childhood—my native town. How many pleasing and painful associations rush into the mind, on returning to one's native home after an absence of years! Changes have occurred, a new generation has started up, the old people have mostly vanished from the earth; but the hills and valleys, the rocks and rills remain unchanged. Arrived at my mother's house near night; found her alone, and again a widow. Mr. King, whom she had married after my father's death, died in February last. Her health seems tolerably good, but age has silvered even her locks, leaving the heart still unchilled.

The next few days his health was but indifferent, and he felt the weariness and prostration which the journey and the scenes of excitement through which he had passed naturally would produce. He visited among old neighbors and friends with considerable interest. On Lord's-day he went to the house of the Lord where in boyhood he had been accustomed to attend, and heard a young candidate, of whose perform- ances the following characteristic notice occurs in his journal:

He preached both morning and afternoon from Jer. xvii. 9: "The heart is deceitful and desperately wicked." He drew a very horrid picture of the natural heart, by showing what man might do, pro- vided he had opportunity, and was not restrained. It is question- able whether this metaphysical mode of preaching, developing so much from the mental and moral capability, is calculated to do any great good. One thing I remarked, that both discourses did not contain enough of the gospel method of salvation to direct a single inquirer to Christ.

The next week he hastened off by stage through Hartford, where he spent a day or two conferring with brethren in regard to the great errand with which he felt himself charged —help for the West. Then he hurried out to Worcester, and passed the night with Rev. Jonathan Going, and doubtless kindled up those sparks which half a dozen years later burst forth into a genial flame, and led to the formation of the American Baptist Home Mission Society. Then he hastened to Boston, conferred with the pastors there, and on Lord's-day preached for three of them. The following week the religious anniversaries of New England were held in that city, which he attended with lively interest. Wednesday morning in the Baldwin Place Baptist church the anniversary of the Massachusetts Baptist Missionary Society was held. His record is :

> Dr. Sharp read his annual report, and addresses were listened to from Gammel, Dunbar, Benedict, Lynd, Babcock and myself. It was an interesting and most impressive meeting.

Certainly it was so to some of us who heard him for the first time let out without stint the pent-up flames of holy zeal which consumed him. That very afternoon the trustees came together, and he explained to them, in minuteness of detail, the plan of operations which he deemed most suited to the wants of the West. Next day, his plan in its general principles was adopted. He was appointed agent and commissioned to go forth and raise the requisite funds to put the system into operation. "Let me stop," says he, "to acknowledge the Divine goodness in disposing these excellent brethren to enter with so much spirit and life into the business. Oh, for God's blessing to follow !"

This plan of operations as described by himself was threefold. 1. A system of circuit preaching for the States of Missouri, Illinois, and Indiana—giving to each circuit preacher to be employed, under direction of a committee in each of these States, an average sum of one hundred dollars per annum, and the remainder of his support to be secured on his field. 2. An efficient preacher and teacher to be secured for St. Louis, who would be able, it was thought, to one-half sustain himself by the income of a school, and steadily supply the church in that important city. 3. The getting up a theological school in Illinois for all these States, where young men, approved as preachers, might have the intellectual training which they needed, and be aided also in preparing themselves specially for preaching, and the pastorship of the churches.

In regard to this last he says, in a letter written about this time

The theological school has been an object in my mind for years, as a very necessary part of that system of measures which I have attempted to carry forward; but I have never seen the time to accomplish it until now. Friends about Boston and other places have come forward to aid, so that I can now (August 17th) reckon upon about five hundred dollars, as secured, and hope to get the remainder which will be necessary. Of the importance of such an institution in the West there can be no question ; and yet I expect that some of those for whose benefit it is designed will oppose it with all their might, as they now oppose missions, Bible societies, and Sunday-schools. But I cannot bear that our preachers in Illinois and Missouri should continue as ignorant as some of them now are. There are some who wish to improve their minds, and gain useful learning. Young men who commence preaching with very inadequate education will avail themselves of such a school, with immense benefit to themselves and the cause.

When it is considered how much we have sacrificed in removing to the Western country to promote the interests of religion and the welfare of society, I cannot bear the thought of living and dying without an attempt to establish an institution which, by proper measures, may grow into a respectable theological school. I hope to live to see a range of brick buildings put up, adequate to accommodate one hundred students, and where a regular course of instruction can be enjoyed.

To qualify himself to act as a wise pioneer and guide in such an undertaking he managed incidentally to visit all the similar institutions which had been established—Columbian College, Brown University, Hamilton and Newton Institutions—and learned all the interesting facts in regard to their beginning, progress, and present state, thus preparing his own mind fully with all the needed facts, so as to avoid mistakes and secure advantages.

But his chief labors for the summer months of this year were devoted to traveling and awakening an intelligent interest among churches, pastors, and all the more influential members of the community, in regard to means of benefiting the West He aimed indeed to secure contributions to the Baptist Missionary Society of Massachusetts, by which he had been commissioned and sent forth ; but it was obvious to all with whom he came in contact that he aimed less at getting as many dollars as possible at present than at the diffusing of correct information which would lead to permanent benefactions for this work.   Well did he understand that giving a cup of cold water to a weary pilgrim in the desert is not comparable in its abiding good influence to digging a well there, which may remain a blessing for generations to come. During these three months he traveled chiefly in Massachusetts, Connecticut, Rhode Island, and Eastern New York, nearly fourteen hundred miles, and laid adequate foundations, as was believed, for the safe and successful commencement of all parts of his system of operations.

Besides this, we are to remember that he went everywhere with his eyes, and ears, and heart open, to learn and appreciate whatever was excellent and worthy of imitation. Occasional glintings of his convictions—as now a traveled Yankee he returned to investigate more broadly and compare more justly his native New England with fairer and more fertile regions elsewhere—will peep out in his journals and letters of this period. He particularly remarked with some astonishment the littleness and narrowness of views, the hidebound prejudices which here so generally prevailed, as they were now magnified by contrast. But he did full justice, at the same time, to the taste, the moral integrity, the industry and sobriety, as well as the provident carefulness (not to say parsimony), which he here witnessed. Their neat and inviting villages, with the church-edifice and the school-house in central prominence, indicated unmistakably the elements of New England's welfare and happiness. These, too, by a species of social transmission, she was sending abroad and planting and nurturing all over the fertile West   H?·? was the hedged-up nursery, where the seedlings were defended while taking root, and, if need be, receiving the budding or inoculation which insured the excellence of their fruits. " But then," said he, " they need to be transplanted to a broader and more fertile field, where they will have ample space and verge enough to be rooted in our broad, rich prairies, and bring forward under more genial skies their abundant products."

Very pleasant would it be to lead our readers more in detail, to follow him from city to city, from village to village, from the college halls to the workshop and the extensive manufactory, during these months of exploration. What he then and there learned of the intellectual, moral, social, and religious principles and practices of New England was of essential service to him ever afterward. But we dare not dwell longer upon this topic.

While he was gaining information of utmost advantage to himself he was also continually imparting that kind of definite, practical knowledge of the West, its allurements, its capabilities, its wants and its dangers, which was greatly conducive to its prosperity, and was most useful and necessary for those who in their own persons, or their children and friends, were about to transfer themselves or their interests thither. The circulars which he distributed, the addresses, lectures, and various appeals which he delivered, his private intercourse in the families wherever he was domiciled for an hour, a day, or a half-week, made their ineffaceable impression and did much good. The broad catholicity and generous liberalism of his views was also at this time and ever afterward more and more evident. He was not less a Baptist, thorough and decided ; but he learned the wisdom and advantage of heartily uttering one form of apostolical benediction : " Grace be with all them that love our Lord Jesus Christ in sincerity."

It had almost from his first return to his mother been obvious to him that as her only offspring his filial duty made it imperative that he should render her few remaining days as comfortable as possible. She was in comparative poverty,

and he saw no other way open for him to do this, but to pay
her debts and remove her to his home in the West.   To this
proposition she cheerfully consented.   About the middle of
September he had accomplished the details of this troublesome business, had procured an easy two-horse carriage, built
under his special directions, and an additional horse, and set
forth with his mother by easy stages for his distant home.
Crossing the Hudson river at Catskill, he visited his early
home at New Durham, and then proceeded by the way of
Buffalo and the south shore of Lake Erie, and through the
great State of Ohio to Cincinnati, where he spent several
days in soliciting and purchasing such articles as he most
needed for the building of his seminary-edifice, on which his
heart was now so much set.   The cordial approval and aid
of the brethren here very much cheered him.   Setting forth
again he was favored for the most part with fine weather and
roads, and made good progress.   He stopped at one or two
places in Central Indiana to promote the objects of his Bible
society agency, and reached his home Thursday evening the
23d of November, having rode forty-four miles that short day.
He found his family in good health, and overjoyed to see him
once more in their midst.   He had been absent nine months
and one day, and reached home just one day earlier than he
had told them to expect him when he wrote to them of his
time of setting out on his return journey three months before.

Devout, grateful, and humble are the acknowledgments he
records of the Divine goodness to himself and his family
during this period of their separation.   But specially did he
record with overflowing thankfulness his sense of the Divine
favor in so prospering the great objects of his journey that
besides securing aid for the support of many preachers in this
Western field, he had also obtained in money, building-mate-
rials, and books and apparatus for his proposed seminary,
about seven hundred and fifty dollars, or three-fourths of what
he deemed requisite to be raised abroad for setting it in operation.   To effect this he had traveled by land and water in his
whole journey four thousand four hundred miles.

CHAPTER XIX.

Establishment of Rock Spring Seminary.

No sooner was Mr. Peck fairly at home again, and moving in his accustomed circuit among his brethren and neighbors in that region, than he began in earnest to lead their minds to the same conviction which he had long entertained, that one prime essential for the religious welfare of the West was the establishment of a seminary of a comprehensive and somewhat unique character, where the elements of a good, thorough, practical English education should be open to all on very economical principles, and where teachers of common schools could receive better instruction than many of them had enjoyed, but especially (and that was to be its grand peculiarity) where ministers of the gospel, whether young, or farther advanced in years, could come and spend more or less time, according to their several circumstances and exigencies, in learning those things in which their deficiencies were the most painfully felt, pertaining to their great duties in preaching the gospel and building up the churches aright. He saw plainly that to lay down a full ordinary course, embracing two years to fit for college, and four years curriculum, within its walls, and then two or three years of theological training afterwards, would from the outset repel nine-tenths of those whose favor it was so important to conciliate. Abiding cheerfully by the old-fashioned Baptist doctrine that the churches were to be the judges in every case whether any of their members were called of the Lord to preach the gospel, and that those thus called were to give themselves to study, to meditation, to reading, to doctrine [teaching], that their profiting might appear unto all, and they be enabled to make full proof of their ministry, he could not doubt that, in circumstances such as existed in the vast

Western field, where in the little, feeble churches so many of desirable gifts were being raised up to labor in the great spiritual harvest field, many of them would be found, like Apollos, taught of the Lord, *i.e.*, regenerated, and fervent in spirit, *i.e.*, imbued with a noble Christian zeal, who would still need to have some experienced disciples, like Aquila and Priscilla, take them in hand, and teach them the way of the Lord more perfectly. Occasionally such privileges might be secured with some private family, or in traveling with some able and discreet preacher. But such opportunities would be rare.

It was manifestly needful that there should be some place to which such young or inexperienced ones might repair, and receive the aid which they so much needed. Some were called to preach when they could scarce read a chapter or a hymn intelligently. How obviously requisite that they should be taught to read the Divine word, and give the sense, and cause the people to understand the records contained in *the infallible guide-book !* It is scarcely needful, here, to go over this ground more thoroughly, and reproduce the arguments and the answers to objections which required to be so often combatted forty or fifty years ago. More germane to the present purpose will it be to trace with some minuteness the successful methods employed to disarm the hostility of even good men to this enterprise ; to root out the prejudices, and correct the misconceptions which unhappily had taken possession of their minds, and bring them to entertain the idea of, and then co-operate in securing the facilities which such an institution would afford. To this end his correspondence, his visits, his attendance on associations, and the various gatherings where ministers and other brethren of influence came together were mainly directed, for the next few weeks immediately after his return from his eastern tour. True there were other duties, domestic and official, which engrossed a portion of his time. He was obliged to enlarge his dwelling to make a comfortable suit of apartments for his somewhat uneasy mother ; and he had to visit, and plan, and readjust very often the measures for the resuscitation of the White Baptist church in St. Louis, which often seemed nearly extinct ; and he had to superintend the appointment and incipient action of the committees of superintendence, for selecting and locating his circuit preachers in three great States, and moreover he was the secretary and chief functionary relied on for promoting the Bible society and Sunday-school interest in all this field. Nine months absence had accumulated no little labor in all these departments on his hands. Many kinks and entanglements had been accumulating, which awaited his wise, energetic, and loving efforts to smooth out, so that the work might again go forward unimpeded. When with all this you join the care and enterprise devolving on him alone, to provide for and train up a numerous family, with but slender and, as most of us would think, altogether inadequate means, no marvel that he complains of over-work. His now tender hands he had to ply through the day to stone and brick and mortar ; and at night, when other toiling men rested from their fatigue, his sore and stiffened fingers had to grasp the pen and issue as many epistles during the long evening as most leisurely secretaries could think it possible to accomplish in the whole day. It would be easy to demonstrate all this multifarious activity of these important months.

Yet in the midst of it all, he appears to have been blessed with unusual enjoyments. Such acknowledgments as the following occur in his diary at this period :

I have enjoyed a peculiar flow of religious feeling, with only occasional seasons of darkness, when fretted by the vexations of life. Have a growing zeal in the cause of Christ, especially to carry into effect the public measures I have been maturing. I rise early, between five and six o'clock (this was mid-winter), labor on with much toil and fatigue, incessantly, and cannot retire till after eleven o'clock. Yet I burn with zeal to be more laborious and do more good. I never felt so far removed from selfishness, or any personal desires or aims. I am somehow pressed forward in a great work. Vast and important benefits for future generations seem to hang on present efforts. Had I the means I could cheerfully sacrifice thousands for the good of the cause; and such as I have of time, talents, efforts, endurance, I cheerfully offer.

After visiting Vandalia—then the seat of government of Illinois—and conferring with as many brethren, ministers, and public-spirited citizens as possible, as well as writing to as many more, a meeting was called at Rock Spring the first of January, and an organization of trustees effected, with great unanimity. They located the seminary, on land given by Mr. Peck for this purpose. Early in February he contracted with carpenters to put up and cover in the edifice. It was raised by the end of May. Nearly every thing connected with this effort rested on his shoulders, and he was constantly performing the usual work of two or three men besides, in his preaching, his agency for missions, Bible and tract societies, and Sunday-schools. It can scarcely be claimed that all this was *just as well done*, as though he could have given more undivided attention to each sphere of service. Occasionally at the end of a week of unintermitted and harassing over-work, and perplexing care, his journal indicates how unfitted he felt for Sabbath ministrations. But his rule was to do the very best in his power under these infelicitous circumstances. Subscriptions for the seminary had to be gathered, and he was a complete factotum, a servant of all work, in the general organizations he had originated.

In perusing the extensive correspondence which he held with those he was striving to interest in this great work of founding a theological and high school, one cannot but be deeply impressed with the variety and sturdy character of the opposition which he was forced to grapple with and overcome. Far the larger number of *so-called* Baptist ministers at that day, in the two or three States contiguous to this institution, were most decidedly opposed to this movement. In the "Friends of Humanity" or emancipationists, he found more favor for this object, and though he never joined with them in their peculiar organization, he induced a large proportion of them to unite with him in carrying out this and most of his other plans for evangelizing purposes. The anti-mission

Baptists about this period came into an organization by themselves, sundering churches and associations very frequently to
secure themselves against the infection of contact or fellowship with those who were seeking by all lawful means to carry
into effect our Divine Master's great commission—to publish
the gospel to every creature.   Thus was the singular spectacle
presented of a party separating themselves from their brethren,
denouncing and excluding them, on the pretence of greater
piety and more exact conformity to New-Testament order,
whose chief peculiarity consisted in their opposition to the
Saviour's mandate, "Go ye into all the world and preach the
gospel to every creature"—evangelize all nations.   It is vain
to pretend that these ministers and churches were only opposing some (to them) objectionable methods of complying with
the risen Saviour's commission, for they did not prosecute any
other method.   Jealousy, least they in their ignorance should
be cast into the shade—prejudice which shuts itself in and
will not come to the light—and the covetousness which
grudges any expense for educational or evangelizing purposes,
were probably the main elements of this opposition.   Mr. Peck
had full experience of their combined power.   But he had
counted the cost, and now set his face like a flint against this
array of opposition.   Slowly and with difficulty his work was
going on, and the leaven of a quickening light and truth,
most salutary in its effects, was permeating the mass of the
Protestant community.   This whole effort for raising up such
a seminary in such a community, at such a time, reminds one
vividly of Nehemiah's repairing the wall of Jerusalem with
the weapons of defence in one hand, while vigorously building up with the other.   So successful was the effort that early
in September a boarding-house was raised, and 1st November,
1827, a seminary was opened for the admission of pupils.
The venerable Father JOSHUA BRADLEY was made principal,
Mr. Peck Professor of Theology, and other professors and
tutors were secured, so that very soon the number of students
flocking to enter and enjoy its advantages far exceeded their
most sanguine expectations.   This very success embarrassed
20

them. It led probably to some extravagant expectations which could not be realized, and as this mortifying disappointment met them in the face, some of their associates were discouraged and turned back. In these various alternations it is most cheering to witness the steadfast zeal of the chief founder. Never for a moment did he waver ; but in sunshine and storm, when all was hopeful, or when reverses came thick and aggravatingly upon them, he yielded to no discouragement, but held on his vigorous, enterprising, persistent course. To this alone, or almost alone, was it owing that the seminary was made for years successful and eminently useful, until its removal to another locality and its enlargement to a college was its culminating triumph.

The large portion of the pupils at first came together with extravagant ideas of what was to be done for them by a few months instruction. They verily expected to be made very learned, very eloquent, very accomplished, by the influence which the seminary and the professors were to exert on them ; and when, after three or four quarters instruction, they still found themselves, and had to be again and again reminded, sometimes in a way unwelcome to their pride, that they were as yet but mere beginners, it was easy to see they were not satisfied, and that the way to account for their disappointment, most soothing to their self-esteem, was to throw the blame on the management of the institution. No marvel, therefore, that complaints became rife, and changes once and again were made to meet these unreasonable expectations.

When all other resources failed them, the usual resort was to fall back on Brother Peck or his family If no one else could so manage the boarding department of the seminary as to give satisfaction, an appeal was made to Mrs. Peck whether she would not consent, rather than all should fail, to remove into the boarding-house and become stewardess and matron. So when the old veteran in setting academies agoing—Father Bradley—was unable to give the satisfaction which unreasonable expectations demanded, the question came back at last, Will not our professor of theology consent for a while at

least to become principal of the literary and scientific department also ?" Necessity knows no law but the hard one which
it makes, and submission to its requirements here seemed imperative.

All this would have been less intolerable, but for the
multifarious cares and engagements into which already he
had been drawn. There were, first of all, the complications
and embarrassments connected with the church and the un-
finished church-edifice in St. Louis. In the outset, when all
was fair and hopeful, certain brethren who had some little
pecuniary ability were induced to embark it in that most
doubtful and hopeless of all adventures, a loan to build a
meeting-house for a fluctuating and uncertain church. Some
of these generous lenders were now dead, and the widows and
fatherless children became clamorous for repayment. Others
feeling that their claims were larger and just as sacred, insisted on sharing equally in the liquidation attempted. Nor
was there any pecuniary ability now in the church to meet
these demands. Mr. Peck had been a member of it when
the debts had been contracted, and though having no money
to loan, had freely given his name on notes, which were now
presented and pressed for payment. How often, in all these
years and months of his engrossing cares and toils at home,
does the item creep into the diary—" Had to hurry over to St.
Louis and arrange for meeting the claims of the creditors of
the meeting-house," or some words of like import. These
efforts were for the most part temporary palliatives, delays,
not payments. At one time, near the close of 1827, he met
with the trustees of the Baptist church, St. Louis, and they
" agreed to divide the house, pay the interest, and eventually
liquidate the principal of the old debt, and put the rest of the
building in a state of repair." Then, before he left the city,
he learned that all these well-laid plans were likely to fail
from the interference of the municipal government, in passing
a law widening a street, and thus cutting off twelve feet from
the side of the house.

On another occasion he went to St. Louis to attend the

annual meeting of the Western Sunday-school Union, and found to his mortification and grief that the resident managers had made no preparation whatever for the meeting. In about as much impatience as ever escaped from him, he says: "It seems as if they looked to me to go forward and do every thing." Patiently and resolutely he went on and did up their neglected duty and his own together—secured the meeting, though by very great efforts. This could be borne occasionally, but where as now the pressure and strain became habitual, with no relaxation from such severe tension, the healthful vigor and elasticity of mind and body must fail together.

In the meantime God was preparing some alleviation for his over-burthened servant of another kind. Revivals began to appear in several parts of his wide field of labor. In the poor, cold, and long dwindling church at Fefee, northwest of St. Louis, in Missouri, at Edwardsville, and at the seminary itself, in Illinois, and in his own family; when, on returning home from a preaching excursion in the autumn of 1828, he found to his inexpressible satisfaction, that his eldest daughter had experienced the converting grace of God. She had been under conviction for some time, much distressed, and while in her room at prayer Sunday night, she found blessed relief, and broke forth into shouts of praise. Thus while her toiling father, many miles off, was preaching the gospel to others, God was pouring into the heart of his precious child the consolations of that truth which he was proclaiming. [He was preaching at that very hour from 1 John iii. 1–3.] How sweetly was the promise verified, "He that watereth shall be watered."

It was after being permitted to visit and mingle in these scenes of spiritual refreshing once and again, in the different places where he had so often gone forth weeping, bearing the precious seed, that he was forced to turn away, and spend some weeks at Vandalia, endeavoring to secure an act of incorporation for the infant seminary. Nothing gives a truer index of his really spiritual and sanctified nature than the repugnance with which he entered upon the chilling intercourse with these worldlings, and exchanged the blessed scenes of revival for the turmoil and vexation of political associations.   In this legislature he had many worthy friends, and the incorporating act was readily enough carried through the lower house.   In the senate, however, was one anti-mission Baptist minister, who seemed to feel a malevolent delight in leaving no stone unturned to foil his endeavor.   So nearly was this body balanced, and so easy was it for this captious, unscrupulous hater of that which was good to barter away his conscience, his principles, and his manliness, so as to bend a few of his associates to do his bidding in this matter, that the act failed of a passage by his casting vote.   This was enough, surely, to vex a more phlegmatic temperament; but it is delightful to see how Divine grace enabled our brother to triumph even here.   He breathes no maledictions, but prays for his opponent, and hopes God will yet open his eyes to see the evil of his course.

CHAPTER XX.

The Establishment of a Religious Newspaper in the West—Mission-
ary Labors and Successes—Revivals and Candidates for the
Ministry Among their Fruits—Emigrant's Guide—First Visit of
Dr. Going to the West.

LEAVING for a while the progress of the seminary, which
Mr. Peck had successfully gotten under way, we shall next
find him very earnestly engaged in the establishment and
actual conducting both as editor and publisher of the first
religious newspaper in that wide region where so many have
since flourished.   As this was a very important movement,
and moreover as at the time and subsequently serious doubts
of the wisdom of this procedure were entertained among his
friends, it may be well to trace with some care the idea of
originating such a paper to its first inception.   Though some
overtures had been made to him several years before by Duff
Green, Esq., then residing in St. Louis, to occupy a portion
of the columns of the political paper he was there conducting,
of which to a very limited extent Mr. Peck availed himself,
nothing farther in this direction appears to have engaged his
mind till near the close of the year 1827, when a distinct
overture was made to him on this subject from New England.
A Baptist brother, now laid aside from the active duties of
the ministry by failure of his voice, had his mind turned to
the importance of using the religious periodical press for the
purpose of counteracting infidelity, Romanism, and various
forms of error which were spreading with frightful rapidity in
the West.

This brother was now residing in the vicinity of Boston,
where the Christian Watchman, the earliest of Baptist newspapers, had for ten years been augmenting and diffusing its
benign influence ; and no wonder that his mind eagerly seized
on the idea of inducing Mr. Peck, among his other means of

usefulness, to undertake the establishment of such a paper. He was written to on the subject, and the distinct proffer of funds to a considerable extent was made to him, to enable him to secure so important an object. His own mind, ever eager, enterprising, and almost too grasping in its conceptions of the possibilities of success, was ready at once to entertain the idea, and he began casting around him for the means of carrying it into effect. Among his acquaintances at this period there was one individual, Rev. Thomas P. Green, resident on the borders of Missouri and Illinois, who had been educating his sons as practical printers, and who had himself attained some little experience in conducting a weekly journal of very limited circulation. The idea at once suggested itself that this man might be induced to remove to St. Louis or to Rock Spring, bring his printing office along with him, and might be made useful in preaching, partly editing and taking the general oversight of the business transactions of the proposed paper, while himself would give so much time to writing and selecting matter for it, as would multiply his own efficiency, giving a wider extent and more of ubiquitous presence and influence to what he might thus communicate over the vast region where, with much toil and exposure, he had traveled and preached at comparatively remote periods, for so many years. Very naturally we may see how welcome would be such a proposition to his mind. He was, by this time, somewhat wearied with the futile endeavor of keeping things in good order through the two or three large States over which his duties of supervision, and the various kinds of evangelizing labors confided to him, had extended. When by personal intercourse with his brethren he had measurably removed their prejudices, and partially imbued them with his own spirit, and induced their seeming co-operation with him in some of his important missionary or other plans of doing religious good, he would be surprised and mortified to find that before he could again visit them, his opponents would upset his plans and frustrate his begun labors, so that his work would have to be begun over again with increased embarrassment. In the absence of any well-conducted periodical publications, pamphlets—some of them sufficiently low, scurrilous and demoralizing to do immense harm—were circulating to a considerable extent, without any facilities for warning the public against their untruthfulness and perverse tendencies.   He saw, too, the advance which had been made in the Atlantic States, where papers were beginning to be widely circulated, and attributing too much of this effect very likely to this one cause, he the more impatiently desired the same aids, where, from the nature of the case, their availability would be less.

On the other side of the balance sheet, there were also weighty reasons to dissuade from any such attempts.   In the first place, the inadequacy of means.   By all his fervent appeals for supplying the wants of the mighty West, the help requisite for sustaining or half sustaining half a dozen missionaries in half as many States, could scarcely be relied on; and some years it had fallen off to a sad extent.   It was obvious to every considerate mind that besides what the disabled clerical brother had offered to furnish him, quite as much more would be indispensable, even to establish such a paper, and then its current receipts for a year or two would not equal its current expenses.   Next, it was reasonably enough urged, "How can one man, even with hands of Briareus, and eyes of Argus, attempt so many distinct kinds of labor, without the danger of embarrassing or ruining all of them?" The argumentum ad hominem was here plied most vigorously against this new proposition.   "Why does this man, who is crying out under the burdens he now has on his shoulders, seek to accumulate more and heavier still; the result of which will be either to withdraw his needed support from enterprises which even now languish and fall into discouragement for want of his more steady supervision, or to make what he now proposes abortive, by his inadequate time and vigor to give it vitality?"   Even his tried and long-confiding friends, the executive officers of the Massachusetts Baptist Missionary Society, could not but urge him to desist; and some of their letters, after their earlier hints and suggestions had proved unavailing to arrest his course, seemed to him at the time, as they now do on the calm review, very stringent, and almost severe in the demand they made on him to abandon this new and costly, and, as it seemed to the writers, impracticable and unwise enterprise. They remind him that his first endeavor, the establishing of a Baptist church in St. Louis, had become very near a failure, and its church-edifice was about to be sold, after so many appeals had been made to free it from debt. Did he want, on that same spot, to lay another foundation, and not being able to build, to excite the mockery of beholders by another spectacle of miscalculation?

And finally, these opposers ventured to suggest to him that the time for the success of such an enterprise had not yet come. The people of those new States and Territories were most of them very recent settlers, having as yet almost every thing necessary for their existence to secure, and they would not now be likely to patronize such a paper. They had little time to read it, little means to pay for it, and, if possible, less disposition to encourage the effort, for the sake of what good it might do for others. Thirty years ago those removing into the wilderness, even from the Eastern and Middle States, and much less those from other quarters, had not been so accustomed to the weekly visits of a religious newspaper as to miss it, and sigh for it again. Doubtless it would be needed hereafter; but they argued with much plausibility, certainly, that the time had not yet come. Could they have clearly foreseen the future working of this paper, under the editorship of our worthy and self-sacrificing brother, they would have urged another reason, not less potent than these above adduced by them, viz.: that his identification with it, as chief manager, would fill to overflowing the bitter cup of suspicion and jealousy of himself personally, which already he had tasted of repeatedly. Men older than himself, who in this and other countries had been wont to find themselves looked up to as wise and capable, must have found it somewhat humiliating to their self-esteem that this young New Englander managed their missionary, their educational, their Bible and Sunday-

school affairs, and now sought to vault into the editorial chair
also, and thus form public opinion to suit himself, while they
all were obliged to follow in his train. From this cause, as
the sequel showed, he suffered more grief, inconvenience, and
the peril of alienation from choice friends than from almost
all other infelicities combined.

It should occasion no surprise that the above weighty
objections held back the establishment of the paper for more
than a year. True, there were make-weights on the favorable
side. While some of his most valued correspondents dissuaded, as above shown, others with scarcely less ardor
advocated the measure. Among this latter class was the
Hon. Nicholas Brown, of Providence, R.I., who wrote him
frequently, and with a steadiness and zeal characteristic of
that great and good man. He was accustomed to back up his
encouraging words of counsel by acts of liberality, and hints
and provocatives of various kinds made to bear efficiently in
favor of the evangelizing work in different quarters wherever
he learned that these helps were most necessary. This very
wise and far-seeing man, though he never personally visited
the West, had formed a more accurate idea of its ultimate
and not very remote relative importance than hundreds who
had traveled widely, seen much, but thought less on this vast
problem of our whole country's improvement than himself. He
pursued one method which had commended itself to his judgment for interesting those whose co-operation seemed to him
desirable in certain efforts, by making them the almoners of
his bounty. It was not unusual for him, quite unsolicited, to
drop the hint in correspondence or in conversation with some
one in whom he thought it safe to confide. "Will you look
into such or such a case, and if you think it practicable I
authorize you to draw on me for one or two hundred dollars to
promote it." It seemed to the individuals addressed that
Mr. Brown was only saving himself care, and labor, and time,
by using them for his mere convenience to examine such
cases, whereas the real point aimed at was to induce them to
inquire and investigate for the sake of interesting their own

minds more deeply in what he was satisfied was a worthy object and needed their co-operation for its successful prosecution. Probably in this very case he won over the influence of several to aid this plan of a religious paper in the West, who otherwise might have stood aloof, by the judicious division through them of timely aid, which would have been less efficient if given in the lump, and more directly from his own hand.

After considerable delay, and with enough misgivings on the part of many friends to awaken the deepest solicitude in reference to its success, near the close of the year 1828 an engagement was entered into between the Rev. T. P. Green on the one side, and Mr. Peck on the other, for issuing the proposed religious paper. For economy's sake, and to make it more convenient for Mr. Peck to conduct it, they had determined that it should be issued from Rock Spring instead of St. Louis—a great mistake, certainly, so far as the success of the paper was concerned. One-half the funds were furnished by Eastern friends, and Mr. Peck was to be its editor, while the other half was to be put into the concern by Mr. Green, who was to superintend the printing and publication, and for this purpose removed to Rock Spring with his family, some of whom would attend the school. The Eastern donors had stipulated that the share of profits from the printing-establishment and the subscriptions to the paper over and above paying current expenses, which their donation would be entitled to claim, should be given to the seminary. But alas for *the profits!*

The prospectus was issued about the middle of December, 1828, and the 25th of the following April the first number of the paper, called the Pioneer, appeared. The remark was currently made that " it looked well, and it was hoped that it might succeed and do much good." The bona fide subscribers were very few, but then and long afterward it was sent to many whom it was hoped to induce to become its efficient patrons, but who would pay for it or not as suited their convenience. Rather a precarious reliance, surely, for sustaining printers and paper-makers.

In the meantime revivals were appearing to cheer his heart and encourage the supporters of the mission. The details of these were exceedingly interesting at the time, but room cannot be given for their insertion. Summarily it may be stated :

Churches in the Missouri Association are under a reviving influence, for this work is spreading through several churches—St. Louis, Bonhomme, Good Hope, and others. At Rock Spring there was considerable religious excitement, especially among the students, and the seminary was rising in public esteem.

Arrangements were now making to establish a depository at Edwardsville of the Baptist General Tract Society. As a traveling missionary I have been employed at those points where it appeared that most good could be done to promote the general cause, and so far as I can judge from the excitement of the public mind with better success than at any former period.

As the fruits of these revivals, several promising candidates for the Christian ministry were brought into the churches ; and the pleadings of Mr. Peck for aid in sustaining those who were indigent in a shorter or longer course of studies, to increase their usefulness, were heart-moving.

We have thus seen the inception of the various interlinked and co-operative plans of evangelization, progressively set on foot by Mr. Peck and his coadjutors in the vast field of their toil and care for the first dozen years of his residence in it. First, preaching the gospel and establishing churches ; next, promoting the wide and general diffusion of the Word of God · then following up these by Sunday-schools to teach children and adults to some extent to read and appreciate the Scriptures ; then, finally, the seminary to prepare teachers for common schools and aid the ministers of the gospel in their preparation for higher usefulness ; with the religious newspaper to diffuse more equally, and sustain more constantly, and quicken more energetically, and defend resolutely and wisely, all these means of usefulness. Look at him now, as seated in the center of all this diversified plan of operations, watching with deepest solicitude the working of every part, endeavoring to impart strength to what was feeble, a far-seeing wisdom to what was short-sighted, and the vigor and purity of holy love to what was constantly in danger of degenerating into formalism and partyism for the want of it. The years 1829 and 1830, while furnishing little of marked and noticeable peculiarity, were characterized by a steady persistence in the wide round of accustomed duties, evincing variety in the midst of uniformity, and calling for sleepless vigilance on his part to preserve the harmonious action of all the agencies called into operation for the promotion of the common cause. Soon as he could be freed from daily service in the management of or instruction in the seminary, he set forth again in those monthly or quarterly preaching tours throughout Missouri, with Central and Southern Illinois, and occasional extensions into Western Indiana, where though the ostensible object was to meet a line of appointments for churches and congregations almost every day of the week, yet he did incidentally make these tours promotive of all the other parts of the evangelizing process. He watched over and infused vigor and steadiness into Sunday-schools and Bible societies, looked out students for the seminary and subscribers for the Pioneer, while in his private intercourse he was assiduously striving to weed out petty jealousies and misconceptions among ministers and private brethren, and elevate the aims and efforts of all to a worthier appreciation of the dignity and blessedness of laboring and making sacrifices for the cause of the Redeemer and the best welfare of souls.

While thus employed, towards the close of 1829 he received, unsolicited on his part, a pressing request to engage for a portion of his time in the service of the American Bible Society, then very earnestly endeavoring to supply every family accessible with a copy of the Scriptures. What the society asked of him was to superintend this work and select and recommend for appointment suitable agents to canvass the States of Illinois and Indiana, so as *to see to it* **that**

21

this great work was faithfully, promptly, and economically performed. Of course he could not decline such a service, and he gave to it considerable of his time for that and the early part of the following year. Copies of the monthly reports which he made to the Secretary from December, 1829, to May, 1830, are among his correspondence, and they evince his usual vigor and fidelity. Before this work was completed he was again obliged to take the superintendence of the instruction and government of the Rock Spring Seminary, and of course resigned the Bible agency.

Nor were his labors by any means confined to these departments. By his travels and what he had published in the various periodicals in the Eastern and Middle States, the attention of great numbers had been turned to him as more competent than any one else to answer their inquiries; and the large bundles of letters addressed to him by all sorts of persons for all the various purposes which can be conceived, begging him to answer them very fully and promptly, would have required most men to employ a private secretary constantly to give the desired information. As a very large part of this was of a merely secular character, designed to settle the doubts and facilitate the emigration of those revolving the question of a removal to the great West, the idea naturally enough suggested itself to his mind that a printed manual for the answer of such inquiries would be fuller and more satisfactory than he could afford to make each letter answering the questions put to him. This idea originated his " Guide for Emigrants," which was enlarged in its execution to a good-sized volume, and was very popular and useful. In preparing it, along with his labor as principal of the seminary, editor of the Pioneer, and all the other duties of correspondence and domestic care, he was frequently obliged to spend, week after week, sixteen hours a day either teaching in the seminary or writing at his desk. No wonder that this extra labor broke him down. Dyspepsia, instead of being occasional, became chronic, and before the end of the session in 1831 he was obliged to dismiss the school and seek relief from this exhausting toil.

Some of the correspondence of this period, however, was of a character greatly to cheer and encourage his heart. Of this description was that commenced with him by the Missionary Society of Hamilton Theological Institution, New York. Several of the most promising young men of that school of the prophets early caught from his circulars and appeals the spirit of emulous desire to devote themselves to the great valley of the West. They wrote to him, both officially and individually; and such letters as those of H. C. Skinner, Moses Field, and J. L. Moore, students or recent graduates, who were in heart devoted to that field, and were each month and week becoming a quickening leaven to vitalize those with whom they came in contact with the same spirit, are refreshing to read even now. What must they have proved to Mr. Peck himself but as cold water to the thirsty!

At just this period also, and as one result of the labors he was performing and his loud cries for help, the hearts of his Eastern brethren were beginning to warm towards him and his great enterprise in a degree before unprecedented. He had been for ten or more years the missionary, or superintending agent for missionaries, for the Baptist Missionary Society of Massachusetts, and as his reports became more and more cheering, and were widely perused there, and in all the Middle and Eastern States, the conviction was strengthening that Baptists had a work to do in the West, which really required an organized and efficient society for its prosecution more commensurate with its magnitude than any single State. Dr. Jonathan Going of Worcester, Mass., who had been intimately associated with Mr. Peck when the latter visited the East in 1826, and who for the next five or six years had kept up a deeply-interesting correspondence with him on the best ways and means of arousing the evangelized portions of our whole country to care efficiently and adequately for the condition of the destitute, was this year deputed to visit him on his field of labor, and by extensive personal intercourse with him and all others similarly engaged, to devise the best means for promoting home missions.

The following very simple item occurs in our brother's diary under date of June 20th, 1831 : " To-day Elder J. Going, of Massachusetts, sent out to explore the condition of the Baptists in the West, arrived at my house."

Very earnestly did these men of kindred spirit, worthy to be reckoned " true yoke-fellows," devote themselves for the next three months to canvassing the mighty problem : " How can the great work of home-evangelization be most efficiently promoted ?" They traveled together by day and by night, in sunshine and in storm, through large portions of Illinois. Missouri, Indiana, and Kentucky. They conferred with all the more intelligent and pious ministers and laymen ; attended associations, churches, camp-meetings, and all other gatherings of Baptists, as far as practicable ; inquired and consulted, wept and prayed and rejoiced together ; and, finally, just before they parted in September following, at Shelbyville, Ky., there occurs the following note in Mr. Peck's journal : " Here we agreed on the plan of the American Baptist Home Mission Society." The next morning he records : " I parted with Elder Going to proceed homeward." The journal of all this period of the intercourse of these great and good men extends to thirty quarto pages of manuscript. But it is more brief and condensed than usual, plainly indicating how much their minds were absorbed by the great and morally sublime theme which they were now canvassing ; and how much more they thought, and inquired, and weighed the difficulties and capabilities of the proposed organization than were they disposed to give written expression and permanent record to their plans. Nor did they confine themselves to plans for the future, but indefatigably labored, preached, exhorted, instructed inquirers, promoted revivals, and in all practicable ways sought the present benefit of the cause.

The very next day after these brethren parted, and peradventure in part at least in that spirit of sadness which the loss of *such* companionship not rarely induces, occurs the following private entry in the diary of Mr. Peck : " I traveled all day, calling only at taverns for refreshment, and reached a Mr. Osborne's—a Quaker family—four miles west of Paoli. My mind is exceedingly wrong on the subject of religion. Vain, wicked, and foolish thoughts possess me." After much more of the same character, he devoutly prays : "Lord,. revive me, sanctify me wholly, and cause me to be entirely devoted to thee."

In his earlier years such humiliating confessions abound in his journals, and many pages might- be filled with their transcript. But they are less and less seen in all the later portions ; and here they are, in part—at least much more than he was aware—the effect of external causes. For months he had enjoyed the cheering companionship of one of the best and most genial Christian associates. After long, anxious, and intensely prayerful deliberation, they had carefully reached and matured the most feasible plan which they could devise, and having given to it the last finishing revision, and parted company, no marvel that the tensity of mind suddenly relaxing, accompanied as it was by his utter loneliness and listlessness, brought on a mental revulsion, which his morbid sensitiveness records in the above self-condemnatory language. Thus it is physically as well as mentally. The best and wisest physicians, after long experience, do not trust their ability to prescribe for themselves, because of the disturbing influence of disease on their discernment, and on the equableness of their judgment.

Not many days passed before he acknowledges an entire change in all his spiritual convictions. He is as fully imbued with holy zeal and engagedness, and evinces as deep a concern for the glory of his Saviour, and the welfare of perishing souls as ever before ; and God is graciously blessing his labors for the conversion of the perishing. Such alternations from depth to height are characteristic of many, and he who learns to make the proper abatement from both extremes has gained one important point in the rare attainment of self-inspection.

CHAPTER XXI.

The Black Hawk War, its Origin, Battles and Termination—Revivals
—Opposition—State Organizations for Evangelization—Gazetteer
of Illinois.

ABOUT this period also, that is through the summer of 1831,
and 1832, wherever his preaching excursions led him, in
Central and Northern Illinois especially, Mr. Peck found the
public mind much agitated by fears of Indian aggressions,
and still more by the efforts set on foot and prosecuted with
considerable vigor, for the extermination of these poor miserable remains of the aboriginal tribes. He does not seem to
have entered into the spirit of these measures as did many of
his brethren; but their engrossment with these matters very
much hindered his religious efforts for the spiritual welfare of
these new settlements, and the subject in this aspect finds frequent mention in his journals and correspondence.

To make some of these notices intelligible it may be requisite to give, in his own words, a brief outline of what was
popularly known as the Black Hawk war. A condensed
statement only, will be necessary, and this as far as possible
shall be given in his own language.

Black Hawk never was a chief, never was recognized as such either
by Indian authority or by the United States. He was *a brave*, in the
Indian designation, of the Sauk tribe, first heard of in the closing
scenes of the war of 1812–15, who was able to gather around him a
small party of disaffected spirits; refused to attend the negotiations
of 1816; went to Canada, proclaimed himself and his party British
subjects, and received presents from that quarter. When, about the
year 1828, Keokuk was appointed chief of the Sauk nation, and in
accordance with treaties made with the United States, proclamation
was made that the Indians were now bound by their treaty engagements to leave the country east of the Mississippi, and when a
portion of the tribe, under their regular chiefs, with Keokuk at

their head, actually retired across the Mississippi, Black Hawk refused to acknowledge this authority, and gathering around him all the restless spirits he could muster, he set himself up as a chief in opposition to Keokuk. Up to this time he continued his annual visits to Malden, in Canada, and received his annuity for allegiance to the British government.. Though he had not the talent or influence of a Tecumseh to form any general and comprehensive scheme of action, yet he did make an abortive attempt to unite all the Indians of the West, from Rock river to Mexico, in a war against the United States. For this purpose he acknowledges he sent runners to the Arkansas, to Red river, and to Texas, on a secret mission.

The Indians in the spring of 1831, under the guidance of Black Hawk, committed depredations on the frontier settlements. This leader was a cunning, shrewd Indian, and trained his party to commit various depredations on the property of the frontier inhabitants, but not to attack or kill any person. His policy was to provoke the Americans to make war on him, that he might seem to be fighting in defence of Indian rights and the graves of their fathers. Black Hawk had about five hundred Indians in training, with horses, well-provided with arms, and came into the State of Illinois with hostile designs. Consequently the Governor, on the 28th of May, 1831, issued a call for volunteers. The militia to the number of twelve hundred or more turned out, and under the command of General Joseph Duncan, proceeded on horseback to Rock river, while a detachment of regular troops went up the Mississippi river in June. Black Hawk and his men, alarmed by this prompt and formidable array against them, recrossed the Mississippi, sent a white flag, and made a treaty with the United States, in which the latter agreed to furnish the Indians a large amount of corn and other necessaries, on condition of their strict compliance with the treaty stipulations.

In open violation of these treaties, Black Hawk with his party, in the spring of 1832, again crossed the Mississippi, though warned by the commandant of the United States fort at Rock Island not to do so. Troops, both regular and militia, were at once mustered and sent in pursuit. Among these was a party of volunteers under the command of Major Stillman, who, on the 14th of May, was out on a tour of observation, and close in the neighborhood of the savages. On that evening, having discovered a party of the Indians, the whites galloped forward to attack the savage band, but were met with so much energy and determination as to retreat in the utmost consternation. The whites were one hundred and seventy-five in number, the Indians were estimated at five or six hundred. Eleven whites were killed and shockingly mangled, and many wounded. This skirmish occurred at Stillman's run in Ogle county, some twenty-five miles above Dixon.

On the 21st of May a party of Indian warriors, about seventy in number, attacked the Indian Creek settlement in La Salle county, killed fifteen persons, and took two young women prisoners. The following day a scouting party was attacked and four of them slain. Other massacres soon followed. Very soon three thousand of the Illinois militia were ordered out, who rendezvoused by the 20th of June near Peoria. They marched forward to the Rock river, and were there joined by the United States troops, the whole being under the command of General Atkinson. On the 24th of June, two hundred Indian warriors led by Black Hawk himself, were repulsed by Major Demint, with but one hundred and fifty militia, between Rock river and Galena. The Indians were understood to be collected near the head of Rock river, and toward that locality the American army now moved. A detachment under the command of General Henry, on the 21st of July, engaged the Indians near the Blue Mounds, on the Wisconsin river, where, after repeated but fruitless efforts on the part of the savages to break the lines of the Americans, they had to submit to defeat, and fled, leaving fifty or more dead on the field. The loss of the whites was trifling. Black Hawk, with his now dispirited followers, fled westward toward the Mississippi. Upon the bank of that river, near the Upper Iowa, the Indians were overtaken and again defeated on the 2d of August, with the loss of one hundred and fifty men, while of the whites but eighteen fell. This battle entirely broke the power of Black Hawk. He precipitately fled, but was seized by the Winnebagoes, and on the 27th of August was delivered to the United States officers at Prairie du Chien. The following month the Indian troubles were closed by a treaty which relinquished on the part of the red men more than thirty millions of acres, embracing what is now the eastern portion of the State of Iowa—for which adequate annuities were paid the Indians. Black Hawk and his family were sent as hostages to Fortress Monroe, where he remained till June, 1833, when he was allowed to return to his native wilds where he subsequently died. He cannot be ranked with the greatest Indian warriors, since he fought only for revenge; he showed no great intellectual power, but proved him-self a fearless man, and for many months spread consternation through the scattered settlements of Illinois.

Very frequently were Mr. Peck's appointments, even on the Sabbath, broken up by the military *furor* which pervaded the minds of the community. Some of his Christian brethren also, according to the accounts preserved in his journal, became brutalized by the war spirit which this ferocious struggle too naturally promoted. Little as Mr. Peck sympathized with the peace party or the non-resistants at any period of his life, he yet bore his decided testimony, in all proper ways, against the unchristian spirit too frequently evinced even among those of the professed household faith, who with unmixed hate de-clared their settled purpose to shoot down the poor miserable red-skins wherever they might find them, as unscrupulously as they would shoot the wolves which prowled around their dwellings. Our brother's spirit on these occasions was kindred to that of Robinson, pastor of the Puritan church which first came to Plymouth Rock, who on hearing from the pilgrims that they had fought with and killed several Indians, piously re-sponded, " Would to God that you had converted some before you killed any !" Not unlikely the fact that Mr. Peck had originally been sent to the West with special reference to the work of missions among the Indians, and that subsequently he had been directed, on the breaking up of the Mission of the Triennial Convention at St. Louis, to join with McCoy in his labors among the aborigines, though he had never been able to do this, may have wrought a feeling of greater tenderness in his heart toward these rude sons of nature.

It is pleasant to turn from this episode and find our brother's heart greatly engaged in the work of the Lord, as he went his rounds preaching and baptizing in the several churches. Precious revivals began to be more frequent in various parts of his circuit. He seems to have proclaimed the gospel with great unction, and with manifest tokens of the Divine approval, throughout the months and years now pass-ing under review. And though there were some drawbacks of various kinds—sometimes by the prevalence of Campbellism, which he was learning to dread from the experienced ill effects of many of its advocates, whose course he narrowly scrutinized, and partly from the over-zealous and unscriptural course of some of his own associates, as well as from the anti-mission, anti-evangelizing spirit of the party still doing so much around him to keep out the light of Scripture diffusion, Sunday-school influences, and preaching the gospel to sinners—still there was joy in his heart and joy in his countenance, and joy giving renewed vigor to his often wearied frame, when souls by scores were found crying out what shall we do to be saved, and on welcoming the answer which he gave them, to press their way into the kingdom of God. Frequently on these joyous occasions, when he baptized by the half score at a time, he preserves in his diary the names of those who there put on Christ by his hand. And it is instructive to mark the number of notices, appended at a much later period, of the course which these subsequently run. Some fell away and baffled his hopes; others were misled, as he thought, to join with other denominations; while of the far larger part, the testimonies are, "they have worn well, they became pillars in the church;" or, "they early died, giving good evidence that their end was peace."

In such work, as well as in his widely extended correspondence, and in the publications which he chiefly edited, and for which, including his Weekly Pioneer, a religious paper of catholic character, and a monthly journal more decidedly Baptist, and another monthly half-sheet devoted to the advocacy of Sunday-schools, he wrote a great deal—his useful days and nights were more busy, and on the whole more happily spent.

In the meantime it had become evident that the Rock Spring Seminary, for which he had made and called forth so generous offerings, was not in the right situation to secure the extensive patronage, and to concentrate on it the universal favor which he and its other founders and friends desired. True it had done much good—had more than redeemed what he had promised for it : but it had been begun and conducted, as well as was located, on too low and inadequate a scale, and could not *there*—so it was thought—do the important work which they desired to effect. While Dr. Going was with him they had conferred much on this matter, and had together reconnoitered the very spot in Upper Alton subsequently purchased as the *site* for a new and more imposing institution. During the following year that eligible site was purchased, designed for both Illinois and Missouri, and therefore placed opposite to the junction of the Missouri and Mississippi rivers, and measures set on foot for erecting durable edifices, and the transfer of the school to that locality.

In an extensive preaching and exploring tour through the counties of Fulton, McDonough, Hancock, and Warren, Ill., which filled up the month of June, 1832, he had various experiences—some of them by no means cheering—occasioned in part by the war alarms, and the Sunday musters ; in which he complains that even·professors of religion, class-leaders and preachers took a prominent part, very needlessly desecrating the day of holy rest, as he thought ; and partly, too, from the evil influence of anti-mission habits and prejudices. Here is a specimen of some of those latter influences, which his journal records :

SATURDAY, *9th June*. Rode twelve miles to Crooked Creek church. This is a small body, most of the old members inveterately opposed to missions, and of the " do-nothing" class. Brother Logan preached, and they attended to church business. Two candidates for baptism related their experience. A case of discipline came up, and a man was excluded. The business was managed in a bad way, much confusion and contradiction. The family where we stayed, by the name of N——t, live very miserably, while they have ample means of living better. They have large stock of hogs and cattle on the range, and grain, yet for bread they eat mouldy and almost rotten corn, ground in a hand-mill. Most of the people in this settlement seem miserable and stupidly ignorant.

Lord's-day, *10th*. After the people began to assemble, I addressed those in the cabin on Sunday-school instruction. Some of the men, members of the church, were out of doors, and kept on talking, scolding and making a mock of what I was saying, threatening and blustering. One professor of religion was heard to say that I ought to be shot while at prayer. A bitter, malignant, hostile spirit is manifested by this class of persons. This is the temper communicated by a class of preachers here. About one hundred people, old and young, assembled, to whom I preached from Ezekiel xxxiii. 11. Some of the people kept on talking and laughing, encouraged by professors. O Lord, have mercy on them. Brother Logan exhorted : then we went to the water and baptized four young persons Poor things ! No one to instruct them. There is great need of a Sunday-school in this place, but I could find no one capable of giving instruction who would take hold of the business. Some of the converts cannot read, and yet have none to teach them.

In other cases it was his privilege to see and to aid in promoting a better state of things.

LORD'S-DAY, *July 8th.* Brother Bailey and M. Lemer preached in the daytime and I exhorted. At night we assembled again in the meeting-house, when I addressed them. At first many young men behaved very rudely, conversing in groups out of doors ; but before the meeting closed, we had a very solemn time ; many were deeply impressed. Fifteen or twenty came up for prayers under much distress. Professors began to be in earnest, and to agonize for sinners. There were many appearances of a revival. One additional candidate was received for baptism. I am in hopes the good work of the Lord has truly begun in this congregation.

Monday, *9th.* Returned home and spent the week in answering letters, writing for the Pioneer, and other matters of business, all of which press upon me when at home.

Such were the alternations and engrossments of weeks and months as now they bore him along their varied current. He seems at times at least to have been painfully impressed with the multiplicity of his engagements, and with the want of more spirituality of mind ; but for the most part with cheerful equanimity, he was striving to do that first which was of greatest importance ; or perhaps more accurately, to do that first which would involve most disaster if delayed. And as there was always on hand more than he could accomplish, there was no time for ennui or listlessness.

December, 1833, he records his visit to Vandalia, then the seat of government for Illinois, to attend several of those State organizations which he had been largely instrumental in originating ; and as his journal gives a candid statement of their actual condition at this time, it may be interesting to our readers to look over a few pages of it, condensed as much as possible, but left to express in his own words his honest convictions :

MONDAY, *December 2d.* I started for Vandalia, and tarried with Mr. Johnson at Hickory Grove.

3d. Reached Vandalia, and at night attended the annual meeting of the Illinois State Bible Society. Not a single thing has been done the present year. It now appears that there was really no use in forming a *State* society while every county, except on the frontiers, had its own auxiliary. It was found on inquiry that this State society had on hand a large quantity of Bibles, for which they owe in good faith about nine hundred dollars, besides a large stock for which the society is to pay *if able.* On a subsequent day in the Board of Directors I introduced a series of resolutions and marked out a plan to relieve ourselves of this burden and dispose of these debts, which were adopted. The want of energy, system, and correctness in the Secretary and acting portion of the Board, is a serious impediment to operations of any kind.

4th. Most of the day was employed in finishing my report of the Illinois Sunday-school Union. On the evening the anniversary was held in the State-house. A large assembly was present, and much interest excited. Several of the addresses were excellent. The Sunday-school cause has obtained a strong hold upon the affections and confidence of the people. With prudent and energetic management it must succeed.

5th. Very busy through the day in settling and arranging business with the Sunday-school agents present, and attending meetings of the Board, committees, etc.

In the evening the anniversary of the Illinois State Temperance Society was held. Several addresses were delivered, and an impulse given to the cause. The policy of distributing temperance publications largely was adopted.

6th. Still very closely engaged in the objects of the various benevolent institutions. The annual meeting of the Illinois Institute of Education was held to-day, and a committee appointed to ex

22

amine the various documents in my possession, digest and prepare
a summary publication, and then try to arouse the people to the
subject, get up public meetings, have addresses made, and thus
produce general action throughout the State. [He was almost of
course the chairman of this committee.] In the evening the
Colonization Society had a meeting and adjourned.

7th, Saturday. Busily engaged through the day in writing. The
Colonization Society again met, chose officers, and entered upon
business. A series of resolutions opposing anti-slavery societies
and measures, and urging the colonization scheme as the only safe
and effectual expedient to remove slavery, were introduced, and
the discussion on them postponed till Monday.

8th, Lord's-day. In the morning attended the Sunday-school and
addressed it on the subject of temperance. Placed in the library a
copy of the Temperance Recorder. Then I preached to a large
and attentive congregation from 1 Thess. i. 5.

In the evening I gave a lecture on the Burman Mission, which
was heard with great interest, and the next day six dollars and a
half were handed me by Presbyterians for that mission.

9th, Monday. I was induced to stay on account of the adjourned
colonization meeting to be held to-night. The day was occupied
in writing many letters. Evening, the Colonization Society met
and discussed the resolutions, in which I took part, proposing
several amendments, which were adopted. A committee was appointed to digest a document of *facts to be laid before the public.*
Of this committee I am one. Thus I have an amount of business
of various descriptions thrown upon my shoulders, which will, with
my Sunday-school concerns, occupy me very closely the whole
winter.

10th and 11th. Journeyed home and found all well.

12th. Went to St. Louis, chiefly on Sunday-school business, and
returning reached home at a late hour of an exceedingly dark
night.

14th, Saturday. Very busy in preparing the Sunday-school report for the press.

15th, Lord's-day. Very sick with my usual infirmity, sick-headache, and unable to attend meeting which had been appointed
for me.

22d. Preached the funeral discourse for the late Governor Edwards
in the court-house, Edwardsville. Not only was the house crowded,
but a multitude were out of doors, the weather being pleasant.
I took a passage from Ezekiel xix. 12 for a text: "Her strong rods

were broken and withered," in which I portrayed the qualities of an eminent statesman. A call was made next day for the publica-·tion of the discourse with a short memoir of his life and character, which will be complied with.

23*d* and 24*th*. Spent in Belleville, conversing widely as possible on common-school education, and trying to enlist leading persons in this subject.

8*th*, Saturday. For three days I have been closely occupied in arranging my correspondence and other papers, and in preparing articles for the Pioneer on education, temperance, and colonization. I have divers important letters to answer and much other business which will require my utmost efforts to perform.

Lord's-day, 29*th*. Preached at Lebanon from the eighth chapter of Romans. Church business followed, and several cases of diffi-culty occurred. This church has lost considerable in order and piety within a few months. In the afternoon it rained severely, and I rode home in the storm.

The above items furnish a pretty fair sample of the manner in which his time was filled up with urgent duties one day, and one week, and one month after another, for this, and preceding, and following years.

The next February mention is made of the funeral of that veteran, Father John Clarke, of whom he says that " he spent part of a day at James Lemen's looking over the manu-scripts left by Father Clark. The old man commenced writing his life at my suggestion, made considerable progress, but was never able to finish it. It was finally agreed that myself and James Lemen should write and publish his life in a bound volume." This object was accomplished by our brother, but not till nearly twenty years afterward. He purposed doing the same for several friends, as Meacham, Bradley, and others ; and so frequently, and for so long a period were these things before him, and mentioned in his correspondence, that the idea was naturally entertained that he had made con-siderable progress in the preparation of materials for these memoirs. Such, however, does not appear to have been the case. They existed only in his teeming brain. Not a page of either was ever written.

To the preparation of a gazetteer of Illinois, however, with
a new and much fuller and more accurate map than had before
existed, he devoted no small share of the early portions of the
year 1834.   By the end of March he mentions having sold
the first edition of this book to a Mr. Gandy of Jacksonville.

Under date of July 20th, of this year, occurs the following
entry in his journal, showing at how early a period his heart
was greatly stirred in contemplating a work to which ten
years later he gave some of the most important and laborious of his life-efforts :

Yesterday I received a communication from I. M. Allen, general
agent of the Baptist Tract Society, urging me to engage as a superintending agent for the valley of the Mississippi.   This is the *third*
communication made to me with that object in view.   It proposes
an extensive course of operation for the specific purpose of raising
up the condition of the Western Baptists, by addresses, forming
plans and organizations for usefulness, circulating tracts and other
valuable religious books, and endeavoring to bring the great body
of the Baptists to act in harmony and efficiently.   This would be,
indeed, a Herculean enterprise, involving vast responsibility, requiring diversified abilities far beyond what I can ever hope to
possess.   Yet it is a work that MUST *be done.*   Somebody must take
hold of it.   It must be commenced speedily, and followed perseveringly.   I have little reason to think that my circumstances and
deficiencies would justify such an effort on my part, but I feel
bound to give the proposition a prayerful and respectful consideration.

In August he took a somewhat extensive tour into Missouri, traveled and preached in company with his beloved
Brother Vardeman whose house he visited and became for
a little season his welcome guest.   Together they attended a
kind of convention of Baptists to take into consideration the
destitution in that State, and contrive the best means for
supplying it.   Throughout the wide region where he now
traveled in this State, and in considerable part over ground
familiar to him in former preaching tours, he found the state
of religion low indeed just at present, but giving unmis-

takable evidences of progress.   Anti-ism in its various forms was dying out; more regard was felt for Sabbath-schools, missions, and even for the support of preaching in the several churches.   Though in all these respects the progress had been slow, and the present state was far enough from satisfactory, yet, compared with what he had seen eight or ten years previous, it was encouraging.

Early in November following we find him, with several of his brethren in the ministry from his immediate neighborhood, attending a convention of Western Baptists in Cincinnati, Ohio. Among other objects of importance there considered the Western Baptist Education Society was formed, and incipient steps, or at least counsels, taken for the theological institution afterwards established at Covington; in all which, though his health was very poor, he took the deepest interest. Here he met with his endeared Brethren Going, Hill, Allen, and many others, with whom he took counsel on matters of paramount interest to himself and to the welfare of the Baptist cause.

Under date of November 18th, 1834, the following minute occurs in his journal:

Held consultation with several brethren from the East as to my future destiny and course.   All gave as their decided opinion that I should go to the Atlantic States in the spring, spend the summer, and collect funds for Alton Seminary and for the Home Mission. Such a destination would require an entirely new arrangement of business and prospects.   I desire to be submissive to the order of Divine Providence and enter the path of duty; yet such a mission will be on my part a matter of much self-denial, and a most arduous and responsible undertaking.

The following month he was again found, as the preceding year, attending the State anniversaries at Vandalia.   The Sunday-school cause especially seems to have progressed finely, and generally the educational interests were advancing. Subsequently in St. Louis and at Alton, in company with his early assistant, Rev. James E. Welch, they made some humiliating discoveries in regard to the unworthy conduct of a man employed at a generous salary by the American Sunday-school Union to keep their depository. Farming out this service for one-half the sum paid to him for its performance, the other half enabled him to prosecute a sectarian purpose of his own, in direct contravention of the principles of the Union, whose commission he thus dishonored. Our brother's reflections on this mean trickery indicate how sensitive his mind was to every perversion of the noble catholicity of union societies whose very existence depends on the irreproachable fidelity of those intrusted with their agency.

Very poor health nearly prostrated him during the greater part of this winter. He particularly notices his utter inability to endure exposure to the cold as in former years; and during the severer portions of the season he represents himself as only able to hover over a large fire, and strive to keep his torpid liver from an entire cessation of action by vigorous restoratives. The affairs of the seminary (a charter of it as a college was about this time obtained) caused him very frequent visits to its locality at Upper Alton. To secure in an economical and efficient manner the requisite buildings, to harmonize teachers young and old from New England and from Old England, as well as some raised up on the ground, to watch over and procure in tolerable season the scanty finances derived chiefly from small subscriptions, and to give as much efficiency and reputation as possible to the young and unendowed institution, required of him, with all his other cares and toils, much more of effort than he was really able to put forth. At this time, too, he seems to have contemplated a removal of his family, his paper and printing-press to Alton as soon as he could advantageously dispose of his farm at Rock Spring. He even went so far as to purchase eligible lots on which to erect a comfortable dwelling for his family in the vicinity of the college campus; but for some cause the transfer of residence was never made.

In the early meetings of the trustees of the incorporated college, the question primarily claimed their attention, How should funds be secured for the erection of ampler edifices, and for the permanent endowment of at least some of the professorships? After much and earnest discussion of this exigent demand, in every form in which any practicable hope of success seemed to present itself, the conclusion was finally reached that a sum not less than twenty-five thousand dollars must be raised for these important purposes. Two agents were appointed to solicit aid : one in the West, who might raise—so they hoped—one-fifth of this sum, while our care-worn and almost skeleton-looking brother was commissioned to go to the East, with the forlorn hope of getting the other four-fifths of this sum from that quarter.

Soon as. this plan was definitely decided on, and he had accepted the commission for this purpose, he immediately arranged all his affairs with reference to it. He resigned the office of Sunday-school superintendent and active manager in that and other Boards, finished up so far as practicable his correspondence and some special communications for his paper which the exigencies of the times called for, and in all respects endeavored to put his affairs in the best order practicable to be left, whether he should live to return or not.

Among these last services may be reckoned a special com-munication which he mentions having prepared with extra carefulness to expose the pretensions of Mormonism, which just now was making some inroads among the ignorant and vacillating in several parts of the State and in some neighbor-hoods in his own vicinity. His exposé of that bold delusion was in several cases eminently successful. So was probably a similar article, which just about this time he sent forth, exposing the efforts of foreign priests to promote the Romish religion

CHAPTER XXII.

Second Visit to the Eastern States—Triennial Convention at Richmond, Va.—New York Anniversaries—General Operations in Behalf of the College at Alton—Success and Return to Illinois.

SATURDAY, *April 11th*, 1835, Mr. Peck left home, and after spending the Sabbath in St. Louis, where he gave the white Baptist church a brief review of the state of things when he first came there seventeen years and a half before; and then preached to the African Baptist church a kind of farewell discourse, and they by their own arrangement made him a free-will offering of thirty dollars to aid him on his way, though most of them he says were slaves. The next morning, in company with an unusual number of ministers and other professors of religion who had insisted on the boat's not leaving port on Saturday evening, he went on board the steamer Potosi, and proceeded down the river at the rate of twelve miles an hour. The weather was delightful, but the season late, and fires were still needed in the cabins. The red buds were just in blossom, the elm and cottonwood and a few other trees were beginning to show leaves. Passed Fort Massac, now only distinguished as a farm. The boat shook so much that he could not finish his writing as he had intended, and he busied himself in reading the life of Colonel David Crockett, a genuine portraiture of backwood's talent and address. Took on board the celebrated Dr. Caldwell, Professor in Transylvania University, Lexington, Ky., who about this period was making himself conspicuous as the advocate of the views of Gall and Spurzheim in phrenology, who had been on a lecturing tour to Nashville, Tenn., and who afforded much interest and amusement. His semi-infidel notions, not only in regard to phrenology, but to a diversity of original races of mankind, called forth discussion between him and Dr. Ed. Beecher, President Baldwin, and Mr. Peck, which pleasantly filled up their time till the boat reached Louisville. Here they were transferred to another steamer. Stopped for a day or two at Cincinnati, where an opportunity was afforded Mr. Peck of renewing his intercourse with that distinguished promoter of the Western Education Society, E. Robins, and others, then fully engrossed with the plans which ere long resulted in the Covington-purchase of real estate for the founding of the Theological School of the Northwest. Here also he again heard Alexander Campbell, and says: "I have exposed the sophistry of his arguments in the Pioneer." Ascending the Ohio river, which at this season of the year he says is uncommonly pleasant, the banks being both picturesque and romantic, he reached Guyandotte, Va., and thence took stage across that State to Richmond. Spent a Sabbath in Charlottesville, and as this whole route was new to him—up the Guyandotte, across the dividing ridge to the Kanawha, then up that river past the extensive saline works where two million bushels of salt were then annually manufactured, across the Alleghany ridge and the Blue Ridge, near the White Sulphur springs, the hot springs, and the warm springs, and through Louisburg and Staunton to Monticello—the scenes appear to have awakened his highest interest. Passing from Charlottesville to Richmond he found many streams without bridges, and in one instance the water came into the stage. Such, says he, is Old Virginia even now!

Arriving at the capital, Tuesday, 25th April, he found welcome quarters with Rev. I. T. Hinton, the pastor of the First Baptist church, with whom then and long afterward his intercourse was most endearing and mutually satisfactory. That evening he attended the anniversary of the Virginia Baptist Foreign Missionary Society. Among the interesting addresses he remarks on one from Rev. Mr. Sutton, English Baptist missionary to Orissa, India, the seat of Juggernaut's temple, who described the car-festival of that idol, the burning of widows, infanticide, and other abominations which he had witnessed.

The next day the delegates of the general triennial convention assembled and were organized. Twenty-one States were represented by a much larger body of delegates, and from a wider extent of country than ever before. Rev. Dr. Cox and Hoby, from the Baptist Union of England, were most cordially received. They addressed the meeting in a most feeling manner. It was a thrilling scene. In the midst of it, Mr. Peck, still suffering from his former complaint, had a fresh attack of it, which obliged him to retire. In the afternoon the anniversary sermon was preached by Rev. S. H. Cone, of New York, and the next morning the annual report was read, awakening more interest than had ever been called forth before by any similar document. All the remainder of the week was given to the usual business of the convention, which progressed and was closed harmoniously.

On Lord's-day there was preaching by visiting ministers in the third Baptist church and in several others. Mr. Peck heard Rev. Mr. Hoby in the morning—an interesting sermon. In the afternoon Rev. Mr. Sutton, above mentioned, preached and exhibited specimens of the idol gods and other abominations of idolatry to a crowded and deeply-affected audience, after which a collection was taken to aid his mission. In the evening he heard Dr. Cox preach a splendid and powerful discourse from Col. i. 28.

Monday, the Home Mission Society commenced its anniversary. The report was quite interesting, showing an amount of sixty-four years labor performed by the missionaries the past year. The English delegation were here again introduced, when each made a most impressive speech, which was suitably responded to by the President and by Rev. Mr. Cone, as Chairman of the Executive Committee, on behalf of the society.

Tuesday, Mr. Peck introduced a resolution urging the *ground of action* on home missions, and made a speech an hour and a quarter long, specially of the Mississippi valley. At a meeting held with reference to the Baptist General Tract and Publication Society, the position was maintained that the Baptists should co-operate with the great union societies, but at the same time should provide books and tracts such as are specially needed by the denomination. The following evening he preached in the second Baptist church giving a sketch of affairs in the West, particularly some of the good and hopeful things in Illinois.

Thursday, in company with Brethren Hinton and Going, he visited Richmond College, a manual labor seminary with three professors and sixty students, twenty of them Baptist beneficiaries, all of whom labored three hours a day. He found it satisfactory and encouraging.

Early next morning he went on board the steamer Thomas Jefferson for Norfolk, and had an exciting race on the James river with another boat named Patrick Henry, passing the ruins of old Jamestown, and other interesting localities. Saturday noon he took the steam packet David Brown from Norfolk for New York. Passing the Rip Raps, Fortress Monroe and the Cape, they met a violent storm, and he experienced for the first and perhaps the last time, something like *a gale at sea*. Monday morning he saw the sun rise from his ocean bed, off Sandy Hook, and was soon landed in New York, where he found a welcome home with Professor

Abraham Mills of the university, an old and valued friend. It was the week of anniversaries, and the next day he attended that of the Anti-slavery Society, exciting this year more than usual interest, because the English Baptist deputation had been invited to address it. Though they had given encouragement of doing so, yet on fuller consideration they declined, thereby exciting some animadversion. The celebrated George Thompson, of England, however, was present, and Mr. Peck says, "made a *tremendous* speech. Much of his language was intemperate denunciation." The same afternoon he attended the exhibition of the Sabbath-school children in the Park—"a grand and pleasant sight." The two or three following days and evenings were occupied with attendance on the American Tract, Bible and Colonization Society anniversaries, which seem to have exerted on his own mind a powerful and salutary influence. In view of which, he says: "I shall most certainly return to the West with more expansive feelings, and a higher relish for the great object of Christian philanthrophy than I ever felt before. These great national festivals give a wide and powerful impulse to the cause." From New York he repaired to Philadelphia, attending the anniversary of the American Sunday-school Union, which he efficiently addressed, as he had several of the societies in New York. He spent two Sabbaths in this city, visiting some of his old, choice friends, and preaching in most of the Baptist pulpits. He laid his object—securing help for the nascent college at Upper Alton—before the several congregations. As the result of his appeals, private and public, he says: "I find that Philadelphia Baptists will do a little—contribute small donations—but are not yet in the habit of doing things on a liberal scale." Two or three visits he made to the good city of Penn, to Burlington, and Newark, N. J., and in the meantime did what he could in New York and Brooklyn, until the middle of June, when he went up the Hudson and attended at Schenectady the session of the Hudson River Association, which he had assisted to form at Poughkeepsie twenty years before. Then it was a small body, of only four churches. Now he found it numbering forty churches, many of them large and efficient.

Before this association, by its appointment, Mr. Peck preached and pleaded the cause of his Western Institution with so much effect that, previous to the adjournment, a resolution was passed recommending Alton College to the liberality of the churches.

Returning then to New York and vicinity, he spent nearly five weeks more in getting from churches and individuals the donations which they were willing to make for the endowment of a seminary of learning in the West.

About the 20th of July he went to New England : in Providence visited his generous, confiding friend Hon. Nicholas Brown, and attended the examination of some of the classes in Brown University. Thence to Boston, to Dr. Shurtleff's, from whom himself and his object experienced so much generosity. In and all around the city and the vicinity, and even to Portland, Me., he extended his energetic visits and appeals for aid. With various measures of success and failure he became familiarized, and seems to have taken all in good part—or only indicating slight disappointment or displacency when he failed of what he thought reasonable expectations. It was one of the felicities of this good man's nature not to be greatly elated or depressed by success or the want of it. It is almost amusing to one knowing pretty thoroughly and accurately the state of the churches, and the prevalent *animus* of their pastors in a matter of this kind, to follow his course from city to country, and from one church to another, in all these toilsome weeks which so perseveringly he spent in the endeavors to secure the indispensable means for the incipient endowment of the college. Nor was his attention confined to this matter. One day and night he devoted to a visit to Newton Institution, where his endeavor was to imbue the minds of the young brethren—the students—with the purpose to give themselves to self-denying service requisite for success in the noble field to which he belonged.

He attended, too, the anniversaries and lectures of the literary and scientific institutions as far as possible, and in all proper ways both gave and received information. In his journal he remarks, "I find that those who have visited in behalf of the West, and spoke on the state of things there, have almost exclusively confined themselves to the dark side of our moral picture. They have told of our destitution and our danger, without exhibiting those facts which tend to show that great good can be done with comparatively small means. I have endeavored to give both sides —to show our evils and difficulties, and to show also the improvements going forward by a judicious and timely use of such means as are suited to the circumstances of the West. And on the whole I think this course will secure most aid ultimately for the West. At the Worcester Association, meeting that year in Sutton, he spoke in behalf of the Home Mission and the seminary. On again visiting Providence, he conferred at length with Hon. Nicholas Brown on the project of his founding a professorship in the college at Alton. "At first he seemed disinclined, but since has proposed to consider the subject." In that vicinity, too, he called on his frequent correspondent in those and subsequent days, the Rev. David Benedict, historian of the Baptists, and seems to have had much free conference with him on our denominational affairs. In this connection he expresses his regret to see men who have borne the burden and heat of the day cast into the back ground towards evening. "Such," says he, "is human nature. Such may probably be my fate. Well, if those who enter the field, for whom myself and others have *pioneered* out the way, thrust us back as lumber of a past age, be it so, provided they will sustain the cause, and carry forward the great work."

In this vicinity, too, he fell in with one of Barnum's first humbugs, *Joice Heth*, represented as one hundred and sixty-one years old, and that she had been a Baptist one hundred and sixteen years, the nurse of Washington, etc., of whom he correctly remarks : "She was certainly not a Baptist one hundred and sixteen years ago, for no Baptist minister lived in Virginia *then !*" Showing how useful in detecting imposture is some little knowledge of chronology and history.

He attended the first week in September the commencement exercises at Brown University, and remarks discriminately on the day, as pretty uniformly regarded throughout the little State of Rhode Island as a holiday—banks, factories, shops generally closed, and all the people thronging to Providence. The day preceding commencement he heard the oration on Intellectual Philosophy of President Hopkins, of Williams' College, before the United Brothers Society, and in the evening the discourse before the Society of Missionary Inquiry by Rev. R. E. Pattison, and in the afternoon of commencement day, Professor Caswell on Mathematics as a branch of literal education, and Professor Knowles, of Newton Institution, a poem on the Victories of Peace. The evening of the same day Dr. Cox preached a grand sermon from John iii. 30, "He must increase." On the whole he was delighted and profited by the services.

He then made a little tour into his native State, Connecticut. Spent a Sabbath in Hartford, and received one hundred and fifty dollars for his object—attended the Hartford Association at Canton, and records with some feeling his meeting with old friends, naming particularly Elder Rufus Babcock, then seventy-seven years old, Elder Asahel Morse, Deacon John Gurney, and George D. James of the church in Amenia, and others whom he had formerly known.

23

Here, too, Drs. Cox and Hoby were both present and preached, and he parted with them and others expecting never probably to meet in time! Then he returned through Suffield, where he was interested in the Literary Institution, and Springfield, where the armory of the United States called forth the emphatic record, Oh, when will the nations learn war no more?

Returning again to Boston, he found to his high satisfaction that Mr. Lewis Colby, who had been associated with him in his collecting agency, "had done nobly in collecting funds." He then attended the Boston Association, meeting that year with the first Baptist church in that city, where he again plead the cause of the West. The following week he attended in the same way the Salem Association at Lowell, where he and others were solemnly impressed by the very sudden death of the Rev. Mr. Freeman, pastor of the church where the association convened, who preached Sabbath morning, and died the following Tuesday morning, the very day before the association convened.

After visiting sundry other churches and places in the vicinity of Boston, his journal states, under date of October 6th, 1835: "Held a conversation with Dr. Shurtleff on the subject of the college. He proposed to give ten thousand dollars on the following conditions: Five thousand dollars for building purposes, the college to be named Shurtleff College, and the other five thousand dollars to establish a professorship of rhetoric and elocution." Besides this sum, Mr. Peck found that he and his associate had made up in subscriptions, donations, and collections, about ten thousand dollars more, or the entire four-fifths of the sum deemed indispensable by the trustees when he had been sent forth. Visiting once more Hon. N. Brown in Providence, and holding another conversation with him in regard to the endowment of a professorship, he makes this final record: "Though he did not promise expressly, I have strong hopes that he will do it." The following day, October 9th, he took leave of New England.

After a hurried visit to his old friends in Caatskill and Hudson, and to the church in Durham, where he was baptized and licensed to preach twenty-four years before, where he found the same pastor, Elder Hermon Hervey, who had then officiated, and preached again in the same house and from the same text where his first sermon was delivered, he visited several of his wife's and his own relatives, and left New York on his way home the 24th of October. He went by the way of Philadelphia and Pittsburg, and reached, after several detentions, the city of Cincinnati, November 3d. One week he remained here, attending the Baptist convention and holding interesting conversations and conferences with private individuals and larger bodies, which he intended should be promotive of his great object, the evangelization and general improvement of the West.

November 18th he reached his home at Rock Spring, and found his family well. In this tour he had traveled five thousand eight hundred and sixty miles, and secured the object aimed at. Yet there seemed no exultation, only humble gratitude to the favoring Providence which had protected him and the Spirit of God which had inclined so many friends to aid the good cause which he had advocated.

On reaching the site of the college at Upper Alton, he found to his mortification that the buildings and other improvements had not progressed as he expected. But one meeting of the trustees had been held in the seven months of his absence, and the *festina lente* spirit had seemed to characterize all their proceedings. The trustees immediately were called together, and considerable vigor was infused into their counsels and action. His earnest spirit chafed somewhat when, in one department and another, he found a vast amount of business to be done, and yet no one to do it. But he was not the man to sit down despondent. Vigor and efficiency were soon predominant over former listlessness. One day he records himself as engaged in preparing for the boarding-house of the college, and arranging the buildings and improvements ; drew plans for out-buildings, etc. The next he was making out an approximation towards what must be charged for board of the students. The following list of provision and other prices which he put down may interest some readers as indicating a true comparison between that day and this :

Pork, three dollars and a half a hundred ; beef, the same ; common wheat flour, the same ; sugar, eight pounds for a dollar ; coffee, five and a half ditto ; hyson tea, one dollar a pound or eighty-three cents per the chest ; corn, thirty-one cents a bushel ; corn-meal, fifty cents ditto ; boarding at common boarding-houses for mechanics at two dollars to two and a half per week ; iron castings four to five cents a pound ; potatoes, twenty-five cents a bushel ; cows (common) twelve dollars ; new milch, fifteen to eighteen (scarce) ; butter by the firkin, twenty-five cents a pound, and scarce. Property of all kinds has risen from twenty to thirty per cent. in twelve months, or probably money has depreciated at that rate.

To facilitate his labors as factotum, he took up his residence in the college boarding-house ; to regulate which—with forming rules for the preparatory department, and getting with much difficulty a quorum of the trustees to act on matters of most pressing import- ance, as well as an engagement to supply the church in Alton three Sabbaths in the month, and strive to arouse them, and call back a scattered congregation—occupied the chief of his time and efforts during the closing weeks of the year 1835.

Early in January he was in Vandalia, the seat of government, mingling from necessity with politicians and legislators. Part of his object was to complete by the aid of a Mr. Messinger a larger and more accurate map of Illinois with the latest and most reliable accounts of counties, towns, and improvements. While there, by request of the legislature, he officiated at the funeral of one of their number. About this time, also, he was for several weeks very busy in revising, enlarging, and almost making anew his "Guide for Emigrants," a new edition of which was called for, and printed in Boston.

Nearly the whole of this winter and the following spring he seems to have been held in vacillating uncertainty as to his own future course. His health was very infirm, and he was nearly dis- couraged as to the prospect of being able to endure the rough-and- tumble of such traveling preaching tours as he had hitherto fulfilled. The city of Alton (the lower town), was pretty rapidly advancing in population and wealth, and there was a Baptist church very small, but containing some efficient members, which desired him to settle with them as their pastor. He seemed to think he might combine with this a depository of Bibles, Sunday-school and other books, and perhaps the Secretaryship of the Sunday-school operations in the West. This would also bring him near the college, which greatly needed the constant, nursing care of some loving and capable friend.

The Pioneer was also to be removed from Rock Spring to Alton, and a new project was set on foot to raise one thousand dollars in twenty shares to set the paper on a more satisfactory footing, and four-fifths of the shares were taken up. But on the contrary Mr. Peck found unexpected difficulties in disposing of his real estate, his homestead at Rock Spring, without the avails of which he would be embarrassed in the attempt to establish himself else- where. With very poor and infirm health, with responsibilities and virtual pledges to Eastern contributors that their investment for the benefit of the West should not be in vain and should be made widely efficient, it may be well understood his solicitudes were incessant.

CHAPTER XXIII.

Sickness—New Series of Pioneer—Pecuniary Embarrassment—Pioneer Expenses—Excessive Labors—Alton Riots—Death of Lovejoy—Revivals—Missionary Tours—Pastorship at Rock Spring.

THE closing part of May, 1836, and the beginning of the following month Mr. Peck experienced a severe attack of bilious fever, which in a few days brought him apparently to the borders of the grave. This seizure was sudden, and overtook him when away from home, attending at Brown's Prairie the session of the Edwardsville Association. He lay for near three weeks at the dwelling of Elder Elisha Starkweather too weak to be removed. For two or three days his case remained doubtful, but the blessing of God accompanied the use of vigorous means, and at length the fever left him, and very slowly he began to amend. He remarks in regard to this illness that in his extremity he was conscious of the critical situation he was in, but was calm, and his confidence in the Saviour was unshaken, though from the nature of the disease probably he had no joyful emotions. The day after his removal to Upper Alton, he remarks: " I feel now exceedingly grateful to God whose arm alone has sustained me. I am still exceeding weak, and gain but slowly, but am free from fever." He was now in the family of his daughter, Mrs. Smith, which had removed with the printing-office to Upper Alton, and soon as he was able we find him going to the lower town and arranging the Sunday-school depository and bookstore which he there established. The pastorship of that church had in the meantime been confided to the Rev. Dwight Ives, from whose efficient labors much good was expected. The last day of June he records in his diary : " We got out the first number of the Western Pioneer and Baptist Standard Bearer." This of course was but a new name in part, and a new series of the paper before issued at Rock Spring, but hereafter published at Upper Alton for some years, and to editing which he seems to have returned with fresh vigor. In the month of August, this year, he mentions giving a thorough revision and enlargement to his map of Illinois, adding the roads and distances of principal places, also a thorough revision and con rection of his "New Guide for Emigrants," another edition of which his publishers called for.

Then during the same month he arranged to attend a special meeting of the Baptist State Convention of Illinois at Springfield, after which he purposed to accomplish an extensive tour in Missouri. During this meeting at Springfield the Illinois Baptist Education Society was formed under auspicious circumstances. He acted as Secretary of the convention, and remarks that all his time out of the public meetings was taken up in preparing the minutes for the press and reporting the speeches which were delivered. Two or three times during the session he preached in Springfield or the vicinity. Then hurrying on through Jacksonville, where he also preached, he reached, between the Illinois river and the Mississippi, the Blue River Association then in session. Two very interesting subjects engaged their attention; the foreign Bible cause and the Education Society for the State, which had just been formed. In the deeply-interesting discussions on these topics he bore a leading part, and strove, out of the time of the sessions, to report for his paper as fully as possible. The Lord's-day came, but brought no rest to him. He was appointed to preach the first and principal sermon, which he delivered under the trees, where it was very hot and he suffered much. At night the brethren compelled him to preach again in a crowded school-room, where the heat was almost intolerable. He suffered much from heat and fatigue, and the result was great debility, with fever and inflamed sore throat, through the following week. Proceeding on his way he reached Quincy, and stopped at a "sorry tavern," where only the most wretched accommodations could be obtained. Could get no room, or fire, which in his chills he much needed, and his sleeping-apartment was under a broken window, which added to his discomfort and danger. He rested most uncomfortably, and next day crossed the Mississippi and the Fabius (the latter in a canoe to secure his trunk and box of books from wetting); he reached with great difficulty through the muddy bottoms Palmyra, and for two nights and a day rested himself in the hospitable mansion of Brother Wm. Wright. September 1st he left for the residence of Father Vardeman, in Ralls county, where he arrived at night quite ill. This indisposition, which was little else than the result of overdoing and exposure while his system had not yet recovered from the attack before mentioned, confined him for near a fortnight at the house of this revered father in the ministry. It broke up his plans, frustrated his hope of attending the Salt River Association, and then pressing onward to the Boone's Lick Settlement in Missouri, where he had hoped to accomplish considerable for the increased circulation of the Pioneer. Very reluctantly he abandoned this part of his enterprise, and the middle of September turned his face homeward. On the way he mentions getting "stalled" in crossing Bay creek, injured himself in lifting out his trunk, box, and seat, from his wagon, and then had to go three miles to get a man and oxen to haul out his wagon, and through all these difficulties, after crossing the Mississippi and the Illinois rivers, he arrived at his friend Russell's near Beman's ferry, late at night, broken down and ill. Detained in this manner about ten days. Then passing through Alton, where he found many things suffering from his absence, he reached his family the very last day of the month at Rock Spring. After a week or two of lassitude his overtasked frame began to rally again, and by the middle of October he was found at Bethel attending the regular anniversary of the Illinois Baptist convention. Not able yet to be out evenings, he was present at all the day-sessions, and found them interesting and hopeful. Soon after he began to preach again with his usual fervor, and at the end of the month this entry occurs in his diary: "This evening I am forty-eight years old. Still I am a great sinner, relying on a great Saviour. Lord, help me to live more to thy glory!"

Early in November he spent a Sabbath in Alton, preaching twice for his brother Ives, who was ill, and the next Lord's-day he was in St. Louis, where he preached three times, and aided his colored brother Meacham in administering the communion.

Towards the end of January, 1837, he composed two lectures on the early history of Illinois, with a view to deliver them at Vandalia, the seat of government, during the session of the Legislature. February 2d he delivered the first of these lectures, embracing the early exploration of Illinois by the French, from 1673 to 1687, to a large audience, consisting of members of the legislature, officers of government, and other gentlemen interested, assembled in the state-house.

Two evenings afterward he delivered the second lecture, on the early Indian history of Illinois. "At the close, a public meeting was organized, and resolutions passed, one of which requested me to write and publish a Complete History of Illinois." A committee of correspondence was also appointed to aid him in collecting materials. He seems to have seriously entertained this overture for some time, and made considerable preparation for its performance; but his materials were subsequently used in the Western Annals and in other publications.

Three or four weeks were now spent by him in the capital. In some of the debates and other proceedings in regard to the internal improvements in the State, and the fixing its future seat of government, he took some interest, and was present when the measures adopted finally passed. His minute and thorough knowledge of the different localities was also increased by his intercourse with the members of the legislature; and he seems to have given considerable time to going over carefully the whole ground, for the purpose of introducing into his State Gazetteer the most recent and reliable information of every locality. While engaged in this, another project was started. The friends of internal improvement were desirous that a small, cheap monthly periodical should be circulated to advocate their measures, and meet the opposition raised against them. He was offered the editorship of this periodical, and seems to have thought it possible so to connect it with the conducting of the Pioneer at Alton that it might prove a useful auxiliary. He says that should one thousand subscribers be obtained he had consented to undertake it, for without some such appendage he could not sustain the Pioneer. The last day of February he says, "This day, by vote of both houses of the legislature, the seat of government is to be removed to Springfield after the year 1840."

Late in the spring he took a preaching tour through portions of Missouri. Called on a Baptist preacher by the name of Stevens, a determined anti-missionary. Was treated kindly by him, but he said very decidedly that he would have done the same for old friends if we had been gamblers. Such are his notions of all missionaries, and he preaches this boldly. He is a man of talents, and a good speaker.

This year (1837) will be long remembered for the financial troubles which brought so much distress on almost all portions of our country. In various ways it affected our brother very sensibly. In July he mentions having been obliged to labor for several days, as far as his strength would permit, in getting in his rye and hay harvest, because his means had become so exceedingly limited that he could not hire. The expenses of the Pioneer were a continued drain upon his scanty purse, as he was unable to collect from subscribers more than one-half its actual expenses.   Various plans were set on foot to relieve him from this pressure; and on the failure of some of these, from the lukewarmness of a portion of his associates, he became for a time quite discouraged, and wrote a valedictory, which was even put in type, with a view of suspending the publication indefinitely.   But at just this crisis other plans were proposed, which inspired some degree of hope, and he staggered on under the unreasonable load imposed on him.

Just about this time, also, the American and Foreign Bible Society corresponded with him, proposing to give him the general agency for that institution throughout the northwestern States. He entertained the proposition with a degree of favor, and wrote to the Corresponding Secretary very fully as to his plans and hopes for promoting the object, specially the foreign objects of this organization.   Conditionally he proposed to accept of this agency, but before the time arrived when he had expected to enter on these duties, other more pressing demands were urged upon him.   One of these was from the Baptist Home Mission Society, which he and Dr. Going had united in maturing.   The pecuniary pressure of the whole country affected their treasury most seriously, so mnch so as to render it doubtful whether it would be possible for them to pay the small stipends they had promised to the poor, toiling missionaries all over the West.   Many of these men had been appointed on his recommendation; he knew them well, both their worth and their present pressing needs, and he affirmed most truthfully that if the society's sacred engagements were now broken with them, not only would their families be in danger of actual starvation, but the bad faith—as it would be reckoned—of the society itself would bind a millstone around the neck of evangelizing operations in all this region for many years to come.   Under these painfully disheartening circumstances he felt himself obliged to proffer such aid as he could supply in acting as soliciting agent for home missions until present relief could be procured.   Under a special commission for this purpose he hastened among the more able churches of both Missouri and Illinois, and his importunate pleadings for help—*help* in a pressing exigency—were so far responded to that the immediate distress was relieved.

The true character of this man of God shines out very clearly in his efforts in this emergency.   He had other plans

connected with education, periodicals and books, for the promotion of which he now felt the liveliest interest. He had
an amount of pecuniary pressure now resting on him enough to
have turned many a Great-heart into a Mr. Fearing. Besides,
some at least of these missionaries now in debt, and in danger of suffering, had been ungrateful for his past efforts in
their behalf, seemingly more ready to bite than to bless the
hand which fed them. But rising above all this untoward
combination, how nobly did he put forth the most energetic
and persistent efforts to aid those whose past and present
course but too fully proved that the more abundantly he loved
them the less was he loved in return. But this ill-requital
was not true of all. The better and worthier class were becoming more and more thoroughly convinced that his career
was one of noble disinterestedness; and his plans generally wise
and far-seeing. Hence the willingness of this class to come up
to his aid whenever he in earnest uttered the true hailing cry
of distress. Successful as he was in this endeavor, it was
only secured as the result of personal efforts and sacrifices
assumed by him which were quite disproportioned to any one
man's ability long to bear. The hurried entries in his journal
about these days show strikingly how he was driven. Here
is a specimen :

"SEPTEMBER 22d. Reached home [after traveling a great part of
the night] before breakfast. My health is failing from undue
labors and exposures. Spent the day in writing letters, of which
I despatched seventeen, several of them whole sheets full." Next
day he traveled nearly forty miles, so as to reach the South District
Association in time that very day to secure a collection for missions and to get this body to send a committee to visit the
Edwardsville Association next spring for a very important object,
and to induce them to recommend the Pioneer to general patronage. Thus indefatigably he pressed onward in promotion of the
Master's cause. How well that Divine Master knew how to mingle
sweetness in his cup of hard experience! The very next week or
two after the above efforts, he returns home and finds a blessed
revival in progress among his neighbors. Yea, more, two of his
sons were among the subjects of the work which seemed to be
spreading all around him, specially in those places where his own

preaching and praying had been most frequent. For months about this period, it pleased the Lord to give him great enjoyment and also great success in pleading with sinners to be reconciled to God. So emphatically true and surprising was this that he enters a minute of it with adoring thankfulness. "Scarce a sermon have I delivered of late which God has not blessed in the conversion of souls."

In the midst of these pleasant experiences he was called to witness other scenes of most tragic and painful character.

There is preserved in his journal, taken down obviously at the very time, a pretty full account of the Alton riots, and the murder of Bishop by the abolitionists, and of Lovejoy by their opponents. He was induced afterwards to give a very full, and, it may be presumed, a very impartial account of these transactions, which transpired in the very scene of his daily labors, and in the various stages of the progress of which his neighbors and friends were actors and sufferers. Engaged as he was in conducting the Pioneer at Upper Alton, but two or three miles from the seat of the riots, and having daily to mingle with the principal citizens who had endeavored to quench the coals of strife, while some few, and those mainly from a distance, seemed determined to fan them into a flame, it may be presumed he would watch very narrowly, and record cautiously and truthfully, what came under his notice. Accordingly his description of the occurrences of two preliminary meetings of the *Law and Order* citizens of Alton, the appointment of a committee of seven, their names, characters, and propositions, with the tumultuous and excited meeting which failed to adopt their recommendations, is all presented in this private diary with every evidence of candor and impartiality. Mr. Peck evidently thought at the time that there was no necessity for the bloody result; and while blaming with discrimination the faultiness and violent pertinacity on both sides, it is obvious that he foresaw, as others did with equal clearness, that the proposed compromise, not of principles, but of persons, would be sure to gain more, and imperil less for the triumph of truth, of righteousness, of freedom, than the rejection of it. What he regarded as the wrong, the unwise course, however, prevailed, and the fearful loss of life, and of the **very** object for which all this contest was carried on was the result.

Subsequently to these public meetings, at both of which he was present, he was called away to attend a protracted meeting, and engage in the labors of a revival, where God was wondrously pouring out his spirit. At this place— Edwardsville—he was thus engaged when the fearful catastrophe occurred. This is his account of the occurrence :

It appears from the various reports that a new press for the Observer office was landed at Alton on Monday night. On Tuesday night Mr. Lovejoy and some fifteen or twenty associates, with fire-arms, entered the warehouse of Godfry & Gilman, where the press was stored, to defend it. That about ten or eleven o'clock the building was attacked by a mob of some twenty or thirty persons, who demanded the press for destruction. This being refused, they assailed the house with stones. That Mr. Lovejoy (or some other, for the accounts differ) then fired, mortally wounding Mr. Bishop, who was standing alone, neither attempting nor threatening violence. Bishop was carried to the surgeon's office, where he died in two or three hours. The mob then returned more exasperated. The Mayor and civil authorities tried to command the peace, but the cry was "Burn the house! burn them out!" The building was then twice set on fire in the roof; and after much fighting, violence, and disorder, the persons in the house —Mr. W. S. Gilman at the head—proposed to give up the press if they might be allowed to depart in peace. Sometime previous to this, however, Mr. Lovejoy, who is represented as having fought like a hero, stepped out of the house so as to be fully exposed, and while raising his gun to shoot a man on the roof setting fire to it, received the shots of two guns in his breast. He walked into the house, ascended the stairs, fell and expired. Horrible scene truly! A deep and lasting disgrace to the city of Alton!

In the meantime the revival in which our brother was engaged went on with power, and about a score of precious souls put on Christ in the initiatory ordinance of his appointment in Edwardsville, while the good work spread extensively to other places in different directions.

Twice as many soon followed the Saviour at Bethel, still

nearer his residence.   Then followed the regular meeting of the State convention, which appointed him their general agent; and by an agreement with the American Baptist Home Mission Society the supervision of their missionaries jn this field was confided to the Board of the convention, of which by this appointment he became the efficient executive.

In prosecution of these duties he traveled extensively through the central and western portions of Illinois, visiting the missionaries on their fields of labor, advising with, encour aging them, and in some instances gathering information in regard to them and the degree of their acceptableness, which he bore to the Board, thus enabling the latter to make the wisest disposition of those under their direction.

Early the next year he was with unanimity elected to the pastorship of the Baptist church, worshiping at Rock Spring and Zoar.   He accepted with the understanding that he should devote to them immediately one-fourth of his time, and soon as he could terminate other engagements the half was to be given them.   In this service, and specially in religious visiting among the families of this flock, he seems to have felt unusual satisfaction.   To himself this was most welcome after so long having been deprived chiefly of such access; and as a means of increased usefulness to the souls over whom he watched, he had the most satisfactory proof of its efficiency.

As a specimen of his Christian and ministerial fidelity, a letter, to an inebriate, backslidden brother, of the most pungent character, in his journal, is well worthy of being reproduced here, but space cannot be found for it.

He subsequently wrote: " This and other letters had the desired effect, and completely reclaimed him."   How blessed the consciousness of having been thus made the honored instrument of reclaiming the sinner from the error of his ways, and saving a soul from death!   This man, too, was one of high standing and wide influence, thereby enabled to do extensive good.

24

CHAPTER XXIV.

Transfer of the Pioneer—Mission Tours—Extent of Correspondence
—Return of Illness—Fifty Years Old—Pastorship at Belleville.

NEAR the close of the year,1838 sundry communications
were received by Mr. Peck from the publisher and editor of
the Baptist Banner, Louisville, Ky., proposing a union of the
two papers. So great had been his embarrassment in sustaining almost alone, with only casual and trifling contributions from a few public-spirited brethren, this whole enterprise
that he felt constrained to regard such an overture favorably.

Earlier in the year, about the last of May and June, he had taken
an extensive tour throughout the whole of Northeastern Missouri
from St. Louis and Columbia, in which latter place he had attended
the "central meeting" of Missouri Baptists, where some twenty
ministers and many private brethren convened, counseled, and in
fused new vigor into their plans for domestic missions; thence
onward to the northern corner, and even into Iowa across the
Des Moines river. He was performing in all this journey the work
of an exploring missionary agent, and made full report of the
result of his investigation to the Secretary of the American Baptist
Home Mission Society in New York. He found much to be done
in counseling with missionaries and churches on this field, and tried
to settle difficulties, remove misconceptions and prejudices, and
arrest the tendency to schism which he found prevalent in several
localities.

For this purpose he had some important advantages. A
native of New England himself, and fully acquainted with
the views and practices prevalent among his Eastern brethren,
he had also the experience of many years residence in the
free West, had mingled much with the in-comers from every
section of our own country and from other lands, had learned
that all possible excellencies were not found among any one

class, but that the free mingling and blending of all, and the eclectic spirit which culls the good from every quarter was the true wisdom and the solemn duty of these new settlers. How earnestly and perseveringly he labored to diffuse this spirit, wherever most needed, his journals bear frequent witness. In preaching and prayer, and specially in all his private intercourse with the "one-sided" brethren whom he met, his endeavor was to soften their hearts, and to lessen, if he could not entirely remove, their mutual prejudices and antipathies. In these efforts he was measurably successful, and great good was the result.

On his return home a notice occurs, under date of July 22d, of his preaching with great earnestness in behalf of the better observance of the Sabbath. As is too common in the new settlements, and where but a portion of the Lord's-days have religious services, the young persons get into lax and lawless habits of desecrating the holy day. To his great grief he learned that some of his own children along with many of their neighbors had done this, and his spirit was deeply stirred within him to attempt a thorough reformation. His earnest and solemn remonstrance on this subject, with a lucid illustration of the great Sabbath law, as made for man universal, seems to have done much good; and in various circles, at associations and elsewhere, he discoursed on this important practical measure with happy effect.

Late in this month he set forth again for another similar tour of nearly six weeks in Central and Western Illinois, and extending into Iowa. He mentions, as one encouraging feature of what he found, that "Baptist churches in every direction were building meeting-houses." Some of these were indeed very humble and of primitive simplicity; others were more pretentious and commodious as well as tasteful; while in both classes there was a common disposition to begin and not finish, and hence many inceptive and hitherto abortive efforts of this character stood forth only in their incomplete and repellant condition to mock the inefficiency of their projectors. His efforts had to be often turned to awakening and directing public spirit and endeavors to the finishing of such enterprises, or at least to bringing them to such a condition that they could be used and preserved from ruinous waste or dilapidation. **The** territory of Iowa was just now attracting considerable interest, and was drawing into it a worthy class of emigrants from different quarters. His efforts and counsels here in the several counties which he visited, chiefly in the southeastern section of the territory, were timely and useful in an uncommon degree. He managed, too, to attend as many associations and protracted meetings as possible throughout his whole tour. The Military Tract of Illinois, as that inviting portion of the State between the Illinois and Mississippi rivers is called, often drew him within its borders, and the blessed fruits of his footprints, his early labors and counsels, yet remain indelible there.

Immediately on his return home from this tour he was again seized with congestive bilious fever, which brought him to the brink of the grave. After lingering a while in apparent equipoise between life and death he at length slowly recovered, but was for eight weeks unable to preach. During this confinement the State convention of Baptists in Illinois held its anniversary, and knowing with what difficulty he had for months struggled to maintain his paper, the Pioneer, they proposed to raise a fund adequate to purchase it, and help him hereafter to conduct it more efficiently as their editor. The convention committee, charged with the execution of the enterprise, entered upon the attempt with considerable zeal, and raised in pledges about the half of what was requisite. So sanguine were they of being able to complete the whole sum that it for a while arrested the progress of the negotiation mentioned in the beginning of this chapter for uniting this paper with the one in Louisville.

Mr. Peck did not share in these cheering expectations of success. He had seen more efforts of the same kind, after beginning hopefully, end in disappointment, than the younger brethren who were making this attempt. However, he waited patiently till the end of the year, giving all the time asked to test the practicability of the endeavor. He used this intervening period also most wisely in writing to the more influential brethren in Illinois and Missouri, especially those who had done most in aiding the circulation of the paper, telling them frankly that in the years of his conducting it, besides all his own time, labor, and risk, he had actually sunk between three and four thousand dollars in cash in the endeavor to carry it on, and that he could do no more, asking them, at the same time, whether under these circumstances they would not advise the transfer of its subscription-list to the Kentucky Banner. Almost unanimously they responded in the affirmative, so that with cordial assent and approval this transfer was made in January, 1839. The understanding was that he should continue to collect the outstanding dues of the concern until he had paid himself for his current advances, and then all the future pecuniary interest was to become vested in the publisher of the Banner, who obligated himself to pay Mr. Peck a small amount for each subscriber who might continue to take the paper after this union. The name of the Pioneer was also to be combined with the Banner so as to make the union as perfect as possible. He was desired to continue his own services as assistant-editor, but wisely declined at such a distance as his residence from the place of publication being more than a contributor, though afterward by the earnest entreaty of Illinois brethren he did for a time assent to the former arrangement. His son-in-law, Mr. Smith, who had been the printer, and greatly aided in selecting articles for the Pioneer, was thus thrown out of employ, and the poor, meager printing-office was left on Mr. Peck's hands as well as the house and office in Upper Alton, where it had been published. Soon as practicable these were disposed of, and thus a great burden was cleared from his shoulders.

This gave him more time for pastoral and missionary work. It also allowed him more opportunity to read and enrich his mind, by a survey of the best thoughts of the most nobly endowed and cultivated intellects, which he was always ready to do, but often lacked the time for it. The brief and summary notes and critiques which appear in his journal, in regard to books thus read by him, are often interesting. Here is a specimen. He had much admired many of the writings of John Harris, D.D., his Great Commission, Mammon, and some others, and he now fell upon his volume on Christian Union. After reading which, he thus discriminately analyzes:

Many good thoughts and suggestions are here, but also some sophistry. Union among all Christians is certainly desirable, but it never can be gained by compromise with any part of scriptural obedience or duty. Harris lays down the following as the "kind" of union to be sought: *"Union, to be permanent, must be based on the sole authority of the word of God, and the inalienable right of private judgment."* And yet there runs through this treatise the assumption that Christians must surrender minor matters. Afterwards he urges, "A rejection of all terms of communion, which are not terms of salvation." Now, as in exercising the "inalienable right of private judgment," I verily believe this to be an unscriptural doctrine, therefore, on this very point, Dr. Harris and J. M. Peck are as wide apart as before.

Here is another specimen, in quite another range of literature. "Read FAULKLAND by Bulwer. Its tendencies are certainly licentious. The impression made by reading the book would be that the passion of unlawful love is uncontrollable, and that all attempts at self-government are useless. Walter Scott's novels have a contrary tendency. They leave the impression of *blame* adhering to criminal acts and desires, as well as their destructive tendencies."

Early in the year 1839 he wrote a third lecture on the early history of Illinois, embracing the conquest of that territory by General G. R. Clark, which he also delivered at Vandalia by request of members of the legislature and others, with much acceptance.

How intensely busy he must have been during all this period is obvious, for I find the record of two hundred and twenty-five letters written by him in the first two months of this year, besides transacting an unusual amount of business connected with the transfer of his paper, the removal and settlement of his son-in-law in a new location, and preaching almost every Sabbath, as well as numerous journeys, which even at that inclement season of hard traveling he was obliged to undertake. Copies of some of these letters are preserved, and they are by no means brief, but extend to a dozen foolscap pages, written out and copied by no machine process, but by the slow and careful labor of forming one letter at a time by the pen. The matter of some of these epistles is as elaborate and carefully constructed as any thing which he ever wrote. Take for an example his defence of the right and the wisdom of a Baptist presbytery to proceed to the fellowship of a minister coming over to us from another evangelical denomination without anew laying on hands upon him, as an entire re-ordination. The ground he assumes is, that Baptist independency of churches demands this freedom in judgment on the part of each church, and each ordaining council assembled by their desire, and hence, while the practice in such cases is various, neither the one course nor the other is to be condemned—for which judgment he certainly furnishes very cogent reasons, in answer to a ministering brother who had somewhat violently assailed him, both as a pastor and an editor, for taking the part which his conscience, in a particular case, approved.

It is doubtful whether an abler argument is extant than this long letter contains on that side of the question. It would seem that he had made himself familiar with all the views and practices on this subject of Baptists, early and modern, in this country and abroad, as well as the reasons they assigned for them. One cannot but marvel at the extent and accuracy of his research. At the same time he evinces no pertinacity for the prevalence of his views in regard to this practice of re-ordination; but says candidly, on the very threshold, that he regards it as one of those difficult and delicate questions about which sound and orthodox Baptists differ, and that a controversy on it would do no good, and might do harm. Hence he forebore to publish these views, and contented himself with presenting them to the brother referred to, in a private letter. This was his more common practice in all similar cases, and in after years he was wont to speak of this course as in his judgment much happier than to publish abroad more freely, in doubtful cases.

When his year of pastorship at Rock Spring terminated, he was unanimously re-elected, and consented to serve the church as before, viz.: to visit each family (they were not very numerous) once a quarter, and to preach three or four sermons to them every month, ordinarily occupying, however, but one Sabbath of the month, as his other Sabbaths were claimed elsewhere, in St. Louis frequently, and in other important parts of his great field.

In the latter part of April, 1839, he was urged by brethren in Kentucky to visit them, as an important meeting was to be held in Lexington for the organization of a State auxiliary to the American and Foreign Bible Society, and it was desired that the same occasion should be improved, when the brethren were generally together, to consider other questions of common and important interest to the welfare of the denomination, not only in Kentucky, but also in other Western States. Thursday, April 25th, he left St. Louis for this purpose in a splendid steamer—the Western, Captain Price—making twelve miles an hour. How unlike the facilities of locomotion twenty-two years before, when he first traversed those waters! He reached Louisville Sunday noon, and was cordially welcomed by his yoke-fellows Elliott and Waller, the publisher and editor of the Banner and Pioneer, and by other brethren. After remaining three or four days there he took the stage for Lexington, and was an active participant in the councils and proceedings of the convention, which was in session a number of days. He preached the opening sermon, and preached again on the Sabbath.

In regard to Bible operations, he records: " Find a concurrence among the brethren on leading principles. None are friendly to a new version of the English Scriptures. All agree that the first and paramount object should be, the *foreign* field, and that very little ought to be expended for *home* work, stereotype plates, etc. During this meeting, Rev. Dr. Noel, pastor of the Lexington Baptist church, a great and good man, died, and his funeral sermon was preached by Elder Buck, pastor of the first Baptist church in Louisville."

Before the close of the meeting other subjects were discussed, such as the union of the Banner and Pioneer, which was much approved, ministerial education, but more especially the desirableness of a Western organization for home missions. Mr. Peck spoke at large on this subject, and thought it could be effected so as to move in entire harmony with the American Baptist Home Mission Society by a sort of partnership; and that it would give much energy and system to the cause in the Western and specially the Southwestern States, where much more extensive efforts are needed.

While in Lexington, he was waited on by a committee to inquire if he would consent to receive an invitation to a pastorship in that city. He records his conviction of the importance and desirableness of the position, among wealthy, spirited, and liberal brethren. No doubt he felt some influence from these attractions; but he remembered the destitution and greater need of his services in the field he had left behind him, and like a scripture worthy who was tempted by the proffer of elevation, he responded, "I dwell among my own people."

He advocated the cause of temperance and of colonization while there, and subsequently returned by the way of Georgetown, where he preached, and then, in Louisville and the adjacent towns in Indiana, he spent a Sabbath or two more, pleading the cause of Christ and of souls, and aiding in the incipient measures for the formation of a new Baptist church. During all this period he was much in consultation and co-operation with J. L. Waller, the editor of the paper, in which, as the successor of his own "pet" which had engrossed for years so much of his time, care, and money, he felt a paternal interest. He reached home the 18th of May, in imperfect health, having suffered considerable during his whole journey from congestion of the liver, which was in danger of becoming chronic. Near the end of May the Edwardsville Association held its annual session with the church at Rock Spring, his residence. The business occupied but little of the time, so that ample opportunity was gained for preaching, which was continued day and night with happy effect. A considerable revival was the direct result, in which two of his children and the hired girl were deeply impressed, and one or more of the number cherished hope of having passed from death to life. This was joy indeed to a loving and devoted father. He baptized on two occasions twenty-two in all, one of whom was his son William.

On the 4th of July he delivered in Belleville an oration on *the principles and tendencies of democracy*, meeting entirely the approbation of both political parties. He endeavored to show that gospel morality lies at the foundation of true democratic principles. A committee from each party requested its publication, with which he complied. One week later he set off with his old fellow-laborer, Rev. J. E. Welch, on a preaching tour in Missouri, which occupied a fortnight, and the following month, August, he rode one hundred and thirty-seven miles to attend the Clear Creek Association in Missouri. Was hospitably entertained during its session by an intelligent and liberal-minded man, Mr. A., who kept a small distillery to make whisky for his own use. He acknowledged that he loved it, and sometimes got drunk. His guest, availing himself of the man's frankness, gave him repeated and earnest admonitions during his sojourn ; the result was that he soon became an active, praying Christian, and of course put away his strange gods. Yea, much more than this was effected : the holy flame of converting grace becoming thus kindled, spread in different directions. In a foot-note, subsequently added to this part of his journal, it is stated that "This revival spread through the country, and many professed Christ and were baptized. The churches took quite a different course in regard to practical religion from this time, said to be caused principally by my very plain preaching. I preached under a peculiar impulse, as for my life, to both saint and sinner, and God blessed the word—his own word—abundantly. To him be all the praise !"

On the 5th of September himself and wife started for a long tour through Central and Northern Illinois and a corner of Northern Indiana into Michigan, partly for missionary labor and supervision and to visit his wife's relatives. First reached and attended the North District Association, held with the Salem church, Hamilton settlement, at a camp-ground, where during the night they were thoroughly drenched with rain. By special appointment, and at the instance of a number of the Methodist neighbors, Mr. Peck preached a long discourse on baptism. These Methodists said that they had heard repeated representations from their own ministers as to what the Baptists believed and practiced, and they now desired to have the statement from themselves. This resulted in the sermon of two and a half hours above mentioned, which he preached from Acts ii. 37 to the end of the chapter. Six or eight of the Methodist members left their society and were baptized before the end of the meeting. The whole journey above indicated was accomplished not without the usual accompaniment of such tours, sundry breakdowns, the loss of the right way in the woods and on the prairies, and specially many thorough wettings in the rains which were more than usually abundant for this season of the year. As often as possible he called on missionary and other ministering brethren, aided them in labors, counsels, and sympathy, and learned all he could of the existing and prospective religious condition of that extensive country. On this tour he made his first visit to Chicago, reaching that incipient city the end of September, and spending a Sabbath and several days with Brethren Hinton, the pastor, Dr. Boon, and others, and preaching several times.

At Elgin, on Fox river, he attended another association (name not given) where by appointment he preached, giving a historical sketch of the origin, rise, and progress of the Baptists in Illinois. Then hurrying on his way by Ottawa towards

Bloomington, where the Illinois Baptist State convention was about to meet, he was arrested by sickness, and confined for ten days, so that he failed entirely of reaching the convention, though having all the records and papers, so essential for their use, in his trunk. Then, soon as he was able to ride a little, he slowly moved on his weary way towards home through Newark, Ottawa, Vermillionville, Washington, Tremont, Delavan, to Springfield, where he stopped for a short time, and reached home near the end of October. The following two days' entries in his journals are copied entire, as indicating the convictions he had reached in regard to himself, and the feelings with which life's survey was accompanied.

October 29th. Reached home and found all well. Quite fatigued. Learned the afflicting news that Charles Darrow (a valued neighbor) died yesterday, and was buried to-day. This is a heavy loss to our church and the neighborhood. After much serious reflection I have come to the conclusion that I must give up traveling and all missionary agency. I have now made trials for four seasons, and *cannot* sustain the fatigue, labor, and exposure. My liver is permanently affected, my constitution seriously impaired, and I must retire to a more quiet and sedentary life. There is field enough for me to occupy around me, and Divine Providence will in some way provide for me.

October 31st. This day I am fifty years old—turned half a century. When I look back, how short and frail a thing is life! Not only my years are gone, but my physical powers have failed greatly within a few years past. I am now an old man, and ought to regard myself as such, and be looking every day for my great change. O Lord, help me to consecrate myself to thy work and cause. Help me to live the rest of my feeble life to thy glory.

Near the end of the following month a pleasant incident occurred, which illustrates very strikingly his Christian character, and its results. A neighbor who had been an anti-mission Baptist minister, and both in that relation and as a politician had done Mr. Peck all the injury in his power, but towards whom our brother seems to have exercised the true Christian return of rendering good for evil to an uncommon extent, now summoned him to officiate at the marriage of his youngest daughter, and at the end of the ceremony handed him the unusual fee of fifty dollars, saying in the hearing of all the guests that it was because of his special respect for him. How blessed the privilege of thus overcoming evil with good !

In furtherance of his plans to change somewhat the course of his hitherto very active life, he endeavored to put off some of his official cares and get others into harness for bearing a portion of his public burdens. After exerting himself to the utmost to wind up his relations as general agent of the State convention and of the Home Mission Society, he made a somewhat detailed report of his last year's labors in these appointments, of which the summary shows that he had written two hundred and ninety-four letters on missionary affairs, visited and labored continuously in seventeen different churches, attended four associations, preached (on his mission field) sixty-four sermons, delivered thirty-eight lectures and addresses, baptized twenty-one converts, and traveled three thousand five hundred and twenty-eight miles, of which one thousand one hundred and eighteen were by steamboat and stage, and two thousand four hundred and ten by his horse.

Looking forward to some other disposal of his time, he yielded to the solicitations of his neighbors in Belleville, and accepted the pastorship of that church in addition to the one at his residence, Rock Spring and Zoar. In this way he expected to have more than half his time disposed of in his own immediate neighborhood.

The Belleville interest had sunk very low, though embracing valuable materials, and he set himself immediately to work for resuscitating it. For this purpose, in part, he announced a series of lectures on sacred history, thus striving to call out and interest the young men. The introductory of this course he delivered on Saturday evening, January 18th, 1840, " to as crowded an assembly as could get into the house, and many went away disappointed. It seemed to produce an excellent effect." In this and other feasible ways he was trying his utmost to prepare the way of the Lord, and gain the ear that he might win the heart of a worldly-minded community. He immediately set about the systematic religious visiting of the families of his flock, and with these labors for Belleville, and somewhat similar efforts in the church at his residence, which had fallen into some disorder and coldness in his long and frequent absences, the early weeks of the year 1840 were fully occupied.

CHAPTER XXV.

Various Labors and Trials—Transfer to Louisville, Ky.

IT may be recollected that the illness of Mr. Peck prevented his reaching the place of meeting for the Illinois convention of Baptists in the autumn of 1839. Those who assembled on that occasion, without the aid and the records of the Secretary, proceeded to make some rather radical changes in the constitution of the convention and in the general operations of an evangelizing character which it was seeking to carry forward. Proceeding, too, without the requisite caution and wisdom, what they attempted to accomplish was, in some cases at least, irregular and abnormal. When the minutes of their proceedings came into the hands of the Secretary for the usual revision and publication, he at once perceived these unconstitutional proceedings, and so far as practicable corrected what he was sure was wrong in the hasty proceedings of the body. This gave offence in certain quarters, and at the meeting of the Board in the early spring, which also the Secretary failed to reach by reason of ill-health and bad traveling, a vote of censure was passed upon his action, and a communication forwarded to the Banner and Pioneer for insertion, reflecting rather harshly on his proceedings. No wonder that he, as principal founder of the convention, and the man who had been throughout the right-hand of its operations, felt aggrieved by these proceedings, and earnestly remonstrated against them. This led to some unpleasant correspondence between the parties, in which, however, he appears to have preserved a happy degree of equanimity, and the meekness and gentleness of Christ. Eventually, the proceedings which he complained of were all rescinded, and their record ordered to be struck from the minutes by a nearly or

25

quite unanimous vote. In reviewing these proceedings at this distance of time from their transaction, it may not be easy to say who was most in fault. But this incident shows most clearly how possible it is for very good brethren, aiming at the good of the same cause, to see things differently and how much allowance is due for human infirmity and mutual misconception.

In the latter part of May, 1840, we find Mr. Peck setting forth for a month's absence from home for the double purpose of attending first the regular session of the Edwardsville Association, meeting that year at Carlinville, and next proceeding across the country by land-route to Louisville, Ky., to meet the convention of Western Baptists. The association, though not very numerously attended, was a pleasant and satisfactory session. On the Lord's-day, the great day of the feast, Elder Hinton preached in the morning on the signs of Christ's coming. He enumerated seven distinct signs, which seem to have deeply interested our brother, and they are preserved with considerable fulness in his diary. Very instructive and somewhat humiliating, too, is the review of these speculations now after twenty-four years have passed away. How impressively does it reiterate the wise and pithy sentiment of Sir Isaac Newton on this subject, that "the prophecies were not given to make us prophets, but the predictions were written down by inspiration of the Divine Omniscience that when they come to pass we may see and believe." There is, however, something very captivating to most minds in the startling and bold announcements put forth by writers and speakers on the prophecies yet to be fulfilled; and when they bring, as the ingenious and enthusiastic always do, very plausible and apparently Scriptural reasons for their credence that some events of absorbing and transcendent interest and importance are on the eve of fulfilment, how easily may they attract attention and deepen to profoundest deference a regard for their startling vaticinations. In not a few instances, within the last fifty or sixty years, have grave and learned doctors, as well as some bold empyrics of less respectable attainments, ventured most dogmatically to set the times and seasons for the events which are to be hereafter. And how mortifying generally have been their failures! It is easy to see that Mr. Peck, from about this period for several of the following years, was an enamored student of the prophecies. He prepared and delivered in several places a course of lectures on this subject, and his study of what pertains to it doubtless rendered him more familiar with prophetic symbols for the remainder of his life.

Soon as the meetings of the association were concluded, in company with some others who had been in attendance with him, Mr. Peck set out for Kentucky. They traveled through Vandalia, and stayed over the Sabbath in Washington, Ind., where they heard a political speech from Robert Dale Owen, and in course of their journey met with a large procession, in wagons and on horseback, going to a Harrison political gathering. On the 3d of June they reached Louisville, and found many brethren already assembled from the Eastern as well as from the Western States.

Dr. Going was made President of the convention, and Dr. Lynd preached the opening sermon. The plan of a more efficient organization coming up, a committee was raised to report on the subject, of which Mr. Peck was chairman. After much deliberation this committee agreed to recommend the outlines of a constitution, to be published and referred for consideration to the conventions and general associations of the Western States, and hold another general convention the next year, to act on the adoption of the proposed constitution as guided by the wishes of those appointing them. Foreign and home missions, the American and Foreign Bible Society interest, and a Western historical society, successively engaged the attention of the brethren assembled. The Lord's Supper was administered at the close of the services on the Sabbath in the second Baptist church, at which Drs. Going, Malcom, and others officiated. In subsequent conferences Mr. Peck was solicited to revise the Social Hymn Book, most in use at the West and South, called Dupuy's Hymn Book, by removing the doggerel and inserting good hymns in their places. To this proposition he acceded, and subsequently spent considerable time in their revision.

He mentions securing a valuable collection of papers, minutes, manuscripts, and various materials for the Western Historical Society, of which he had been made Secretary; and on Wednesday, the 10th of June, he left Louisville on his return home. Spent the Sabbath in Black's settlement, Indiana, where he officiated, and aided in setting in order a new and promising Baptist church, ordaining deacons, etc. Tuesday following he preached by request in the court-house in Salem, Illinois, and two days after reached his home, after an absence of four weeks and one day. The 4th of July he delivered an oration in Belleville, embracing the history of the conquest of Illinois by General G. R. Clark in 1778.

In August and the early part of September we find him engaged in promoting a revival at Bethel with his beloved brethren, the Lemens. A new house for religious worship had been completed there. He preached at its dedication, and again soon after a funeral discourse for old Mother Lemen, in which he gave at much length a sketch of the early religious efforts in Illinois, and of the Lemen family. A blessed work of grace commenced and progressed with much power. He witnessed the baptism of nine on one occasion, and a few days afterward of eight more, and still the work went on. At Silver Creek, also, where the Southern District Association was that year held, the church had erected a brick meeting-house, so far completed that it could be used, and after the business of the association was over, religious services were continued with happy effect for several days and seven or eight were here baptized. Returning from the meeting, several cases of discipline of a rather painful character demanded attention in the church at Rock Spring. He mentions with evident feeling that three of the professed converts whom he baptized there turned out badly. "They had been examined with carefulness, and all reasonable pains taken in their instruction, and yet how soon have they turned away to a course of profligacy!" He adds, "I learn from this, that persons who have been trained to bad habits, and who have a peculiarly vicious mental organization, are not easily reclaimed."

In October he attended the regular session of the Illinois Baptist

Convention at Alton, where the adjustment of the difficulties growing out of the action of the previous year was happily consummated, as mentioned in the beginning of this chapter. The affairs of the college and of education of ministers engrossed considerable attention, and was very fully considered. Rev. Mr. Hinton, of Chicago, had been elected President of the college, and measures were now set on foot to liquidate its debts, and provide for the support of its faculty and its general efficiency hereafter. For the consummation of such an object Mr. Peck was induced to pledge a liberal sum. He says that though he was greatly embarrassed, he felt that there was a necessity for this special effort and sacrifice, as the movement now made was regarded as a turning point. On hearing a Brother Coles, a former pupil of his at Catskill, speak with great efficiency, he records his satisfaction that the disciple is much beyond his master.

During the summer and autumn of this year he was also engaged for many days in taking the United States census of St. Clair county. This brought him into minute, personal intercourse with every family, and furnished some amusement, especially among the French settlers about Cahokia, as well as many instructive incidents. It was while engaged in this service that he mentions hearing a Mormon preach in the court-house, and try to prove the truth of the Mormon book. He afterwards held considerable conversation with one of this community, whom he found very wild in his notions. He adds this general remark: "The worst evil from Mormonism is its influence in strengthening the sceptical notions of unbelievers, by their ludicrous interpretations of Scripture."

Early in January, 1841, we find him in Springfield, near the seat of government; and while detained there for several days on public business, the following items are found in his journal.

SATURDAY, *January 2d.* I am preparing to preach to-morrow three times; in the afternoon in the state-house on a peculiar and somewhat hazardous subject, viz.: to apply some of the principles and methods of action in the late Presidential contest, to moral and religious uses.

Lord's-day, *3d.* P.M. Preached my projected discourse to a large congregation in the state-house. Text, Luke xvi. 8. Had tolerable liberty, and the people gave solemn attention. I inquired, 1. Who are the children of light? 2. Who are the children of this world? 3. In what sense are the children of this world the wiser?

The principles and modes of action during the late Presidential contest furnished a principle illustrative of this third part.

1. Look at the efforts made to enlighten the public mind. Political discussions, newspapers, handbills, pamphlets, and preaching or proclaiming, were all laid under contribution for this end. They took the right way, in harmony with God's appointed method in His kingdom.

2. Notice the continuity of their efforts, meeting after meeting, at all seasons, in all places—protracted meetings truly.

3. The parties selected times, places, seasons, and instruments *wisely*. Exchanged their orators in the most skillful manner, so as to excite and deepen the interest.

4. By their untiring zeal they produced a great excitement through the nation.

5. Their *perseverance* was unintermitted till the election was decided.

In all the above respects they went far ahead of Christians in their endeavors to promote Christ's kingdom.

II. Showed that the men of this world were wise ONLY in their generation. How indifferent and neglectful they are to the things of another world. For that, too, they had an election to make. Showed how they reproved themselves in their inactivity about eternal things. Applied the subject also to professors, and offered reproof for their supineness and inactivity.

On the way as he was returning home, at Bunker Hill, in the southern part of Macoupen county, he preached at the constitution of a new Baptist church. In his own immediate neighborhood, in the churches of which he was pastor, he was indefatigable in his efforts to promote a genuine revival, and with some success, as the instances of baptism bore witness—seventeen on one occasion, March 6th. About this time also, the St. Louis church having become destitute by the resignation of their late pastor, Rev. Dr. Pattison, he was induced to promise to take the oversight of them, and supply their pulpit the second Sabbath in each month at least. Himself and Father Rogers soon held a protracted meeting there, with some happy effects. During all this period he continued an extensive correspondence, wrote editorials for the Banner and Pioneer, and made himself widely useful by his pen in other enterprises for the public good.

In April, only a month after his accession to power, President Harrison died, the first instance of the death of an incumbent of his office since the organization of our national government. The sensation produced by this event was deep and universal, and he endeavored, in all the churches where he officiated, to improve it in the most efficient and salutary manner. In St. Louis especially, the municipal authorities set apart a day for public solemnities, on account of this national bereavement. The stores and offices were closed; and a vast civic procession, consisting of all the various associations, religious, mechanic, literary, military, masonic, with a large concourse of citizens, marched through the streets, while bells were tolling, and minute guns were firing. At three o'clock all the churches were generally opened. Mr. Peck officiated in the Baptist church, delivering a discourse from Psalm xc. 3–12 to a crowded and very solemn assembly.

Early in May he was enabled to sell, though at very considerable sacrifice, lots of land which he owned in Upper Alton, and thus pay off his most pressing debts. He regarded this as a most welcome Providential relief, and records his gratitude for this favor at a time of great scarcity of money, and when his pecuniary involvements were most embarrassing.

From the 2d to the 5th of June he was on board the steamer Ion, on his way from St. Louis to Louisville to attend the meeting of the convention of Western Baptists, which had been provided for in the arrangements of the preceding year. From the 9th to the 14th of the month this meeting continued its sessions, evincing at times considerable want of harmony from the earnest desires evinced on the part of some to sunder the ties between Western and Eastern Baptists in their benevolent organizations. After much discussion and the grave consideration of reports submitted on various topics, the result was that a Western Baptist publication and Sunday-school society was formed in strict co-operation with that in Philadelphia. Mr. Peck was mainly instrumental in securing this result, and his journal contains abundant evidence that he introduced and carried through this proposition, not because he deemed it really the wisest and best course, but because he found it was the only way in which a degree of harmony and co-operation could be secured, and the utter breaking off of a portion of the West from the East could be prevented. Having thus thrown himself into the threatened breach for the purpose of closing it, many of the better and more influential of the brethren immediately turned their eyes to him as the needed executive functionary of the new society. Accordingly its general agency was tendered to him by the Board elected for the purpose of setting it in operation, and before he left Louisville he had agreed to take into serious consideration the question of dropping his other engagements and giving himself chiefly to this service. His diary contains abundant evidence of the deep concern with which this proposal was weighed by him. Two principal objections seem to have had much influence with him. He could not but feel sad in view of turning away from the field and the labors which for so many years had engrossed him, where, though he had many trials and impediments, he also had enjoyed encouraging success, and now began to see the fruit of his manifold sacrifices and efforts in the wider and more inviting facilities opening before him for doing good through these instrumentalities—the churches, the college, and the convention, and education societies, which he had been mainly instrumental in originating. But the chief difficulty in accepting the appointment to the new post was his health, and the fear that he should soon break down in attempting so much travel as would be indispensable. True, he would be able to go more by comfortable public conveyances than he had done hitherto, yet the whole business would be of the most laborious description. In view of all these difficulties, and with the urgent importunity of his brethren whom he had just met that he would not decline, he resolved on going home that he " would take time to weigh the subject well, and would also consult our leading brethren, both East and West, and endeavor finally to decide as may appear best for all concerned."

The surprising versatility of his pen is manifested by his

writing a dramatic exercise about this time, called "Te-cumthe," which was elaborated by him with considerable care, and was actually presented in a college exhibition at Alton in July of this year.* The composition required very considerable knowledge of the astute Indian character, as well as that of the other personages introduced—the scheming British agent, and his subordinate, and the exposed pioneer settlers whose safety was so deeply involved in the questions then at issue. In all these respects the drama was a decided success, though from want of more experience in this kind of writing, it lacked the liveliness, and vivacious, life-like interest so indispensable to successful exhibitions on the stage. The marvel certainly is that with all his multifarious engagements, preaching every Sabbath and frequently in the week, writing for some half a dozen periodicals—some of his articles very elaborate and extensive, such, for instance, as his contributions about this time to the American Quarterly Register of Boston on the history and statistics of the Baptist denomination in each of the Western States—with many other cares and labors, domestic and pastoral, that he could have found time to contribute to the drama at all. His facility of com-position, and the readiness with which he could turn from one thing to another so widely dissimilar, was truly won-derful.

On the 24th of September he wrote to the Secretary of the Western Publication Society, Louisville, accepting the gen-eral agency. This decisive step involves so much of responsi-bility that it seems but just to him to give the reasons he assigned at the time for taking it. He says :

After a pretty extensive correspondence East, West, North and South, I have arrived at this conclusion : that unless I do take hold of the general agency of this organization, the American Baptist Publication Society will do very little. The field in the

---

* Mr. Peck was present at the exhibition, and says it was well spoken, though it must have suffered much from lack of appro-priate costumes and scenery on which the real drama, as distinct from the mere dialogue, so much depends.

West and South is the main place of operation, because its wants are here more directly felt and its necessity appreciated. Here, also, a very large part of the labor has to be performed. Our Western society will do nothing efficiently unless I take hold of it. Moreover, all to whom I have written, and who have answered my inquiries, say in substance that I am the man, and ought to engage in this work. The condition of the denomination in the West and South now calls for the free and extensive circulation of religious books. Various indications of Providence in opening my way and removing difficulties seem to point out the pathway of duty in this direction. Whether I can endure the exposure and fatigue necessarily involved, and sustain health, is to be tested by experience. My hopes are that by steamboat and stage traveling, by spending the winters South, and the summers North, and having comfortable houses to lodge in, I may keep up a few years longer. This certainly is the greatest and most responsible business I have ever undertaken. May the Good One direct and keep me, and allow me to fill up the balance of my life with usefulness.

Immediately he tendered his resignation as pastor of the churches he had served, and was happily instrumental in leading some of them to the choice of his successor.

Early in October he attended the Illinois Baptist convention, meeting that year at Payson. He was chosen President, and every honor which affection and fraternal confidence and gratitude prompted was tendered him. He preached during the session, and took occasion to contrast the present flourishing aspects of their affairs with what he had witnessed on the same field in former years. Especially did he strive— and successfully too—to enlist them in the new enterprise in which he was engaging. Many life-memberships were subscribed, and the object was embraced cordially with the prospect that it would be prosecuted with vigor. About the same time he mentions having written to the general associations of Kentucky and Tennessee and the convention of Indiana to enlist them in this enterprise.

Returning from the convention he spent some few days in Quincy and its neighborhood, visiting with special interest a number of mission institutes, or manual-labor schools, there established by Rev.

David Nelson. He found about sixty students, male and female, in the two which he examined. The men were designed for mission-aries, and many of them sustained themselves or nearly so by work, He could not but condemn the fanaticism which he thought preva-lent, while at the same time he found much to commend. He says: "Nearly every species of ultraism springs up here as from a hotbed. The practice of what is called *free discussion* keeps the students in a continual excitement which forbids calm and deliber-ate investigation, and prevents the formation of a sound mind." He formed the acquaintance of a few Baptist students among them who had apparently been injured in this way.

·With different feelings he visited his old friend, Governor Carlin, and held with him a long and interesting conversation on personal religion. The Governor manifested much devotedness and deep feeling, declaring, among other things, that no man can be a par-tisan politician and maintain a Christian character.

On his way to Kentucky he aided in the ordination of a worthy colored brother, Anderson, belonging to the African Baptist church in St. Louis, and preached the sermon, and remarks of this brother that he passed a very good examination. It was near the middle of November before he reached Louisville, and took his head-quar-ters there for the purpose of carrying on with the utmost vigor the plans of the new society. For a while he lodged, by his own desire and preference, in the editorial office of the Banner and Pioneer, of which paper he continued to be a kind of assistant-editor. He also preached very often both on the Sabbaths and on week even-ings in the Baptist churches in Louisville. Soon as arrangements for this purpose could be completed, he visited Cincinnati and Covington in furtherance of his agency; and on returning, after spending a few days more in Louisville, putting in order and sup-plying as well as he could the things which were wanting, he set forth on a tour through the Southwest. In the Green river country he lingered some days, laboring for the diffusion of information on his agency, and securing the first fruits of the bounty of both churches and individuals. By the close of the year he had reached Nashville, Tenn., which he now visited for the first time, and found a most cordial welcome at the City Hotel, then kept by the excellent and lamented Colonel Marshall

CHAPTER XXVI.

Slave Sale—Visit to New Orleans and Mississippi, and again goes to Eastern States.

THE first half of 1842 was indeed crowded with events of stirring and, some of them, permanent interest in the life of this active man. Some of the more important of them will be gleaned from his journals and letters, so as to furnish the outlines of his eventful history. In Nashville, on New-Year's day, the following item occurs :

To-day I attended for a few moments a sale in the market-place. A negro boy was sold, who appeared about twelve years old. He stood by the auctioneer on the market-bench, with his hat off, crying and sobbing, his countenance a picture of woe. I know not the circumstances ; but it was the first human being I ever saw set up for sale, and it filled me with indescribable emotions. Slavery in Tennessee is certainly not as oppressive, inhuman and depressing, as the state of the poorer classes of society in England, Ireland, and many parts of Continental Europe ; yet slavery in its best state is a violation of man's nature and of the Christian law of love. I mean as a state or condition of society ;, for doubtless there are individual cases where the slaves are truly better off than if they were set free, and remained in this country.

For the next three weeks he remained in Nashville, or its immediate vicinity, his health some of the time rather imperfect, but he was able to preach, or otherwise address churches and congregations very frequently, averaging nearly one sermon or address each day, promotive of the revival of religion or of his benevolent object. He was also a laborious writer, sending forth from his chamber at the hotel almost every day, letters, circulars, reports, or communications for the press, enough to fill up the entire time of an ordinary man. He then made an excursion into Wilson county, visiting as many churches and prominent individuals as possible, to enlist their convictions, and call forth their contributions for the Publication Society. On his return, February 1st, he called on General Jackson at the Hermitage, and was welcomed with warm favor and interest by this distinguished man. The General was in feeble health, warm and excited on political subjects, but evincing a calm, intelligent, and considerate concern for the religious welfare of himself and his countrymen, and hence entering with cordiality into the object of Mr. Peck's mission among the churches, and at the close of the interview wishing him God-speed. With emphasis and iteration he thanked his visitor for calling on him, and on parting said, "The Lord go with you."

The legislature of Tennessee was in session while he was in Nash-ville, and occasionally he looked in upon their deliberations With several of the members, too, he formed an interesting acquaintance. This body adjourned just about the time he was leaving the State, the 7th of February, and several whom he names were his travel-ing companions on board the steamer on which he embarked on his way to New Orleans. He had opportunity further to cultivate their acquaintance as his fellow-passengers; and also as the steamer touched and sometimes laid by for several hours, he landed at Clarksville, and made a speech at a temperance meeting; at Ashport in West Tennessee, and again at Vicksburg in Mississippi. Below this point Mr. Peck became greatly interested in the great river, its "coasts," as the high levee banks are here called; in the milder climate and earlier foliage and bloom of the trees, which, in his rapid passage to the south at that season of the year, very strik-ingly impressed him. The plantations lining the river on both sides like a continued village, with occasionally a Catholic church lifting its spire and cross, were all features of novel interest to him.

The 14th of February he, for the first time, set foot in New Orleans. He spent now but two or three days in the city, finding the Baptist cause there lamentably low, and that very little could be done in furtherance of the object he was laboring to promote. He called upon the Baptist minister who was then officiating there, and upon Cornelius Paulding, an eccentric and wealthy Baptist professor, of whose peculiarities he seems to have formed a toler-ably correct estimate.

Returning up the river, the steamer in which he was a passenger had a race with a competitor, and a collision too, but without much injury except the severe fright of the lady passengers. He landed at Port Hudson and took the railroad to Clinton, La., where, and in the vicinity, he spent the next two weeks, preaching, lecturing, and conferring with influential friends, several of whom became warmly interested in his object. He preached to whites and to slaves, visited some of the latter in their quarters, especially the

26

sick, attended some funerals among them, and evinced an earnest desire to make himself as thoroughly acquainted with plantation affairs as possible.

The masters and proprietors were his guides, and he, as their privileged guest, saw just as much and through such a medium as they desired. He makes no comments at the time; and it is not strange that his subsequent recollections are largely tinged with the favorable aspect in which the peculiar institution was presented to his notice.

Returning to the river, he found passage, after some delay, to Vicksburg, and thence by railroad to Jackson, the seat of government of Mississippi. Here, and in several Baptist churches in the vicinity, he spent some days profitably and wisely. Brethren of intelligence and liberality were found, who appreciated the noble object he was soliciting for, and generously aided his enterprise. The names of Lea, Granbury, Denson, Balfour, Whitfield, and ex-Governor Runnells, with others, appear in his journal as those whose sympathies and co-operation he had secured. Others in Vicksburg of the same character were also mentioned: such as Ranney, Sparkes, and Bond, whom he saw and loved for the truth's sake, both as he went and returned. It was also agreed to raise two hundred dollars to establish a depository of the books and tracts of the Publication Society in Jackson for the accommodation of the State of Mississippi.

On the evening of the 21st of March he got on board a steamer for St. Louis, and after a rapid and pleasant passage reached that city on the 25th. Here he rejoiced to find the Baptist cause flourishing, and the following evening he reached his home at Rock Spring, finding his family well and prospering after an absence on his part of three and a half months. He found to his great joy that the work of the Lord had cheeringly progressed in the churches which he used to serve. In the Belleville church thirty had been hopefully converted, and twenty of them baptized. Here and at Rock Spring and at Bethel with his beloved brethren, the Lemens, he spent a few days most delightfully and profitably, and seemed much refreshed by the pious and fraternal sympathy which was manifested towards him, and the object to which he was now devoting his labors. At Upper and Lower Alton also he met with the like favor; and having adjusted his most important business, domestic and public, on the 9th of April, he set forth for another long Eastern tour. Spent a Sabbath in St. Louis, preaching for the white Baptist church in the morning, for the colored in the afternoon (recounting with much tender feeling on both sides the way the Lord had led them for more than twenty years), and in the evening he officiated in the second Presbyterian church, whose pastor was absent, and he mentions incidentally that the first and second Presbyterian churches—the New and Old school—like the Jews and Samaritans of old, have no religious intercourse with each other, though both are clamorous for "open communion."

The following morning he took passage by steamer for Pittsburg, paying only twelve dollars for the trip—one cent per mile, with excellent fare. The cheapest traveling, he says, which he had ever known. The same day, before the boat left, he and Rev. Mr. Hinton called on Charles Dickens, then in St. Louis, on his tour through the United States. He appeared to be a remarkably good-natured, amiable, benevolent man, very much like the spirit of his stories. He stated that he had been educated by a Baptist clergyman. Mr. Peck afterward sent him two of his books, "Guide for Emigrants," and "Traveler's Directory." The trip, per steamer, seems to have been unusually pleasant, affording him a few hours time for calls on his brethren both at Louisville and at Cincinnati, which he gladly embraced. Reached Pittsburg on the 19th, and found a good hotel near the landing, at which for dinner, supper, room with fire, and attendance, the charge was only seventy-five cents. Hence to Philadelphia, by canal and railroad, stopping over the Sabbath in Harrisburg, where he preached twice, and Monday afternoon reached Philadelphia. The following day he went to New York, where the Baptist anniversaries were then commencing. During the meeting he mentions having made a long address before the Publication Society, setting forth its claims on ministers and churches, which was listened to with interest, and produced, as he thought, a good effect. He also alludes to his having served on a committee in reference to Indian missions, and particularly the relations of Rev. Isaac McCoy to the Board, which involved matters which were not a little perplexing. This meeting with so many of the loved associates of former years was not a small item in the gratification which he now experienced. Particularly one evening which he spent with Rev. A. Perkins, then a pastor in New York city, in company with Rev. Lewis Leonard, he says, "Much of the old times when we three were associated in Dutchess county in 1814–15 was vividly revived in our recollection." The various meetings, both denominational and general, which he attended seem to have afforded him considerable satisfaction, and early in May he left

New York on his return to Philadelphia, stopping as usual a night in Burlington with his old and dear friend, J. E. Welch, and family. He preached here also in behalf of his object, and endeavored to awaken the liberality of the church to make their pastor a life-member of the Publication Society. The next day he met the Board of this society in Philadelphia, and by their request gave them, at full length, his impressions of what ought to be done by them, and how to do it. His whole plan laid before them was looked into by a special committee and subsequently adopted. The following is his record of what he found, and what he recommended:

"I find that the brethren in Philadelphia have done but little comparatively in this cause. There has not been quite enough of harmony and mutual concert. Petty jealousies and rivalships about officers and little matters have retarded the business. Yet, with sufficient effort and patient perseverance, the society can be made to live. I suggested a delegation to Boston to enter into arrangements with the New England Sunday-school Union to raise a sum of two thousand dollars to circulate Sunday-school books in the valley of the Mississippi through the Publication Society and its agency. Another suggestion was to negotiate with the Baptist Library and the Baptist Memorial to secure a co-operation with those who are interested in those publications." A delegation to New England, of which he was one, was accordingly appointed.

On his way East he spent a Lord's-day in New York, and came in contact with the celebrated MILLER (who gave name to the Millerites, or Adventists), and heard him deliver one of his lectures. "He believes that Jesus Christ is to descend from heaven, and reign personally on this earth, and that the saints are to be raised and the judgment to set in 1843—next year. This calculation he bases upon his interpretation of the prophetical period of one thousand two hundred and sixty days. This morning his lecture was concerning the two witnesses (Rev. xi. 3, 4), which he supposes, and with much ingenuity seemed to prove, were the Old and the New Testament, the Word of God. There is plausibility in this as the right interpretation. Much of his discourse was solemn and impressive. He is undoubtedly sincere; but like other men whose whole physical and mental system has become excited, he is very sensitive, very positive, and will not bear to be contradicted or argued against. Evidently to my mind there is a degree of *monomania* about him, as there is about every one who dwells so intensely and exclusively on one idea. I introduced myself, and conversed with him a short time. He and his associate Adventists are now holding a series of meetings in this city."

He preached in two Baptist churches on the Sabbath, and the following week gave himself up to attending the general anniversaries. The Old or Garrison Abolitionists, he thought were monomaniacs; for if their principles were fully carried out, all government, authority, and rule, would be broken up. The Sunday-school anniversary was delightful. The American Tract Society gave him an opportunity to plead fifteen minutes for the great West. Here also he heard and was introduced to Mar Yohannan, Bishop of the Nestorians in Persia, whose address in Syriac was translated to the audience by the Rev. J. Perkins, who also gave many interesting facts in relation to the Nestorians. The following day at the anniversary of the American Bible Society, Mar Yohannan appeared again, presenting a Syriac New Testament written on parchment more than six hundred years old. In like manner he witnessed with interest the exhibition of the deaf mutes and temperance and colonization meetings. In a more private way he visited the rooms of the American and Foreign Bible and the Baptist Home Mission Societies, conferring with their executive officers, and contriving ways and means for their enlarged usefulness and efficiency. Another Sabbath he spent in Brooklyn, pleading his cause before several churches there.

In Boston, whither he went the next week, he was welcomed by his old friend, Dr. Shurtleff, the generous patron of the college at Alton, Ill., and for two or three days gave himself up to attending on an anti-slavery Baptist convention, against many of whose doings and speeches he in vain remonstrated. May 21st he attended a meeting of the Board of the New England Sunday-school Union, and laid before the brethren the project of aiding by a special fund our Western operations. The plan was referred to a special committee.

On Lord's-day, after officiating in one of the Baptist churches, he had an appointment in another (Baldwin Place), and had entered the pulpit for its fulfillment, when he was suddenly seized with a severe spasm, which made it impossible for him to preach. By timely and vigorous treatment he soon recovered. Next day he met again the Board of the New England Sunday-school Union, who declined his overture, on the ground that they could not get the requisite funds. Though this was a grievous disappointment to him, yet it is pleasant to notice the equanimity of spirit with which he received the announcement, and the undiminished love with which he still clung to his brethren and labored and coun-seled with them for the promotion of *their objects*, while they declined co-operating to secure *his*. Particularly it may be no-ticed that he was invited to address the anniversary audience of the New England Sunday-school Union, and there urged that they needed a fund of ten thousand dollars, to be raised and used in New England for issuing books, which were now very necessary in all parts of our country. In like manner he addressed the anni-versary meeting of the Northern Baptist Education Society, and spoke on their theme, particularly with reference to the mighty West, giving facts in regard to their ministerial education, the states of colleges and schools, all of which was listened to with much interest. At the ministerial tea-party in the lecture-room of one of the churches, he gave by request some account of two of the deceased pioneers of the West—Elder John Clarke and J. L. Holman.

One evening he went as a listener to the advent-meeting, and heard one of their lectures, on which he makes this comment: "A chart was used containing a representation of the prophetic sym-bols, in the Book of Daniel, in painting. Most of what the lecturer said in his definitions was correct, but the application was wholly incorrect. The grand error of the Miller system is, that it employs symbolical language correctly as to past prophecy, and then inter-prets the symbols which relate to the conquests of Christ and the setting up of his Kingdom literally. It is this confusion of the *symbolical* and the *literal* which produces the wrong and mislead-ing results."

His great effort for the week, however, was the closing address before the Massachusetts Baptist Convention—the successor of the old Massachusetts Missionary Society, under whose commis-sion he had so many years labored. His principal design was to show *the effect of missionary operations on the Western valley for seventeen years past, as follows:*

1. In giving great encouragement to missionary friends there.

2. In calling out ministers from the influence of the world, en-abling them to acquire correct views and habits, and by employing, to enlarge their talents.

3. In raising up, and sustaining, while feeble, churches in the important towns and cities of Cincinnati, Cleveland, Marietta, and Columbus, in Ohio; Covington, Louisville, and other places, in Kentucky; Nashville, in Tennessee; St. Louis, Alton, Springfield, Chicago, Detroit, in the farther West and Northwest.

4. In waking up the churches and people throughout the whole valley, to provide for, and sustain their own ministry.

5. In raising up ministers, and sustaining all other benevolent measures.

6. In producing organization and system in benevolent operations generally.

7. In promoting revivals extensively, and numerous conversions, so that Baptists had doubled in the West within eight years.

8. In the advancement, very generally, of religion, morals, education, colleges and schools.

9. In uncovering the still great destitution, and making it more widely known. The resident population doubles, in ten years, so that one hundred missionaries were now wanted, and a very great work yet remained to be done.

In conclusion, gave two reasons why this work has increased so greatly:

1. The rapid increase of population and extension of occupied territory; and this, on the whole, best for our country and the world.

2. An increasing appetite or desire thus formed for missionary service, even among Germans, Catholics, and others.

After the close of these Boston anniversaries, he thus sums up the state of things and the prospects, so far as his own immediate objects were concerned. Owing to the plans and arrangements of the New England Sunday-school Union, the prospect of raising funds for publication purposes is but meager. I must direct my labors to New York and the Middle States chiefly.

He preached, however, in several pulpits in Boston, Lynn, Malden, and then in Hartford, after which he attended the Connecticut Baptist State Convention, at Middletown, where he explained and pleaded his publication objects with happy effect.

Then he hastened through New York city to Poughkeepsie, to attend the Hudson River Association, which, he remarks, had become an immense body of forty-five churches, and nearly ten thousand communicants. What a change had twenty-seven years wrought, since its formation at the same place! He was much pleased with the aspect of things which he witnessed. Most of the churches had been largely increased the preceding year, the aggregate of additions by baptism being more than eleven hundred. The evening of the second day he addressed his brethren on his publication cause, and there appeared to be much interest excited.

The following day he listened to the closing sermon before the association by Dr. William R. Williams, reviewing the Baptist history for the last fifty years, and contemplating particularly the influences, internal and external, which had so rapidly increased their numbers and effectiveness. He well characterizes it as a splendid sermon, by a masterly hand. It has been widely published, and the analysis of it contained in his journal need not here be reproduced.

The day following he attended an ordination in the interior of Dutchess county, and remarked on the sermon—by one of the pastors in that county—that it was exactly a Kentucky or Western sermon in style, spirit, language, and mode of illustration. The preacher had certainly never been at the West, and this similarity therefore was the more pleasing, showing as it did how certain it is that earnest minds, in their original and untrained manifestations, will be found nearly assimilated. On this occasion, also, he improved a favorable opportunity to address the large congregation assembled, in behalf of the Western Publication Society.

The next few days and Sabbaths he devoted to New York city, conferring with the pastors and preaching in as many churches as possible, on the subject so near his heart, and with which he was now officially charged. In the intervals of public service and private conference he was writing extensively on the same subject to influential brethren, throughout the Middle and Western States especially. The confidence reposed in him and his judgment by the Board of the American Baptist Publication Society, Philadelphia, and specially by its excellent secretary, Rev. Morgan J. Rhees, drew forth from him long and carefully considered letters to them, in which all the possibilities of ways and means for carrying forward their enterprise were fully discussed. Indeed, his mission to New England at this time had that object chiefly in view, to settle the question whether both East and West could not be induced cordially to co-operate in one national society for the promotion of the object, which, as it seemed to him, ought to be dear to every intelligent Baptist, viz.: the diffusion of Bible or gospel truth widely as possible among all our churches and their surroundings, for the double purpose, first, of making all our membership more intelligent, united and harmonious in faith and practice; and next, to disabuse the minds of the uninformed masses in regard to our real views, removing those monstrous perversions which have been so industriously circulated to our disadvantage, and in derogation of our just claims to be reckoned an important integral portion of the great evangelical brotherhood.

CHAPTER XXVII.

Testing the Churches in regard to Publication Society—Ministers'
Meeting in his own House.

THE next eight months, from the closing days of June, 1842,
till April of the following year, he was most of the time
busily engaged, traveling much of the earlier part of this
period among the churches, with a view of sounding their
sentiments, and inciting their more systematic action on this
publication subject. Having no doubt himself that such a
denominational organization was needful, he quietly moved
among his brethren and the churches, determined to test their
convictions on this subject. It was no easy matter to induce
many of these to give sufficient heed to a great practical measure of this kind to enable them to settle it satisfactorily. So
many local interests were demanding aid, and so slow of heart
were the majority of the churches to co-operate in the other general societies for foreign and home missions and the diffusion
of God's word, that it is no wonder he was sometimes led to
doubt whether another general object of denominational benevolence would secure a sufficient amount or degree of
favor to make it worth his while to leave other spheres of
labor which were inviting his acceptance, and give himself to
the promotion of this.

His Western and Southwestern tour had fully satisfied him
that a Western publication society by itself would be too meager in resources to accomplish the desired object. It only
remained to test the question whether such a combination of
East and West, of North and South, in what would be sub-
stantially one Baptist Publication Society, would unite the
suffrages and call forth the liberality of the churches to such
an extent as to measurably insure success. He knew of no
other way of testing this than by actually visiting as widely

as possible among the churches and associations, and learning whether they would be willing, in view of the facts which he spread before them, to take hold of this work systematically, making this one of the cherished objects of their benevolent endeavors, and giving it year after year a regularly assigned place among their charities.

To test this matter as practicably and reliably as possible, he spent about four months continuously in the Middle States, and chiefly in New York.

Before setting out on this mission he met, while yet in New York city, with one of those rebuffs which so often and injuriously affect the course of public men. Taking up one morning the Banner and Pioneer, the religious paper of the West, which still kept his name on it as one of its editors, he there saw a series of resolutions directly and somewhat severely censuring him for leaving the Western agency with which he had been commissioned, to labor in the publication cause of the East. This he regarded as the more cruel, because the very man who was the mainspring and organ of this attack upon him was his *professed* friend and co-adjutor. He sat down at once and wrote him a *feeling* letter, setting forth the unkind and unchristian course which he had thus pursued against him. Confident, as he says, that his own course had been right, and that the Board of the Western society through this man's influence had been wrong, he determined to continue his labors as though this unpleasant transaction had not occurred, and on his return West have it adjusted correctly. Meekly enough he subjoins, " Most men in my circumstances would resign at once, thus producing *a family quarrel*, but I do not think it is expedient." It is very gratifying to know that Mr. Peck's favorable anticipations in this case were fully realized. In October following, the same Board which now had censured him reversed their action, and thus this storm blew over innocuous. Something is to be learned from this case, however, both by general agents and directing boards; and very happy will it be for both when they so adjust all matters of mutual conference and control as to spare one another such damaging manifestations of antagonism.

Cheerfully as though nothing had occurred to dampen his ardor, he set forth the very next week to meet the associations, whose annual sessions continued week after week for most of the remainder of the summer and early autumn. He had prepared and printed a little tract of eight pages, by distributing which among the pastors and delegates at their anniversaries, he was enabled to present many important facts in a more consecutive and permanent form than by an oral address, and leave him at liberty, when preaching or speaking in behalf of his object, to give more space to the utterance of truths connected with the common salvation, and the very marrow of the gospel of Christ. In these visits to associations throughout his whole circuit, reaching almost to the west and south of New York, and quite through the centre, the east and north of the State, he was accompanied by Rev. Lewis Leonard, his old friend of former years, who pleaded the cause of the State Convention, and part of the time by the veteran Dr. Kendrick, who earnestly solicited the aid of the churches for the education cause. With these men and their objects he most cordially co-operated; and it is pleasant to notice in his journal with what interest he listened to the good and grave doctor, and how many of his different sermons (all brought to the same practical point however) Mr. Peck preserved an analysis of, and seems to have treasured up with the highest satisfaction.

His remarks on the state of the churches and ministers as compared with those in the West, together with some incidents which he met with, developing matters of a more general character, might give some variety and additional interest to this part of the chapter, but space cannot be allowed for them.

He witnessed the anniversary exercises at Hamilton, where eighteen young men, who had finished their course of studies, were sent forth, with the benedictions of their professors and the prayers of the churches, to engage in their great work. Intensely interesting was the scene to him, for

several were going to the West for which he had pleaded so
long.   Two to western Pennsylvania, one to Tennessee, and
another to Wisconsin.

In the same neighborhood, a few days later, he listened to
a lecture by a Rev. Mr. Storrs, now a zealous Millerite, and,
as Mr. Peck says :

" Quite enthusiastic in the belief that Jesus Christ is coming next
year to raise the saints and burn the world, and that he will dwell
on earth one thousand years.   He was severe on *the clergy*, as he
called all those ministers who will not receive fully and *examine*
his dogmata.   He represented them and their members who
adhered to them as foolish virgins, not willing to see their Lord.
Now I regard this doctrine of a personal reign of Christ on earth,
after the present inhabitants are destroyed and all generations of
men cease, as exceedingly dishonorable to the Son of God in his
mediatorial kingdom.   The fair representation in regard to these
men is, that finding the impossibility of converting or reforming
the world with all their intense and alarming messages, they
therefore conclude that it must be destroyed!   This lecturer is
quite sincere, probably, and he has fully converted to his theory
the pastor of the Welch Baptist church in Utica."

Incidentally Mr. Peck mentions the cheapness and comfort he
found in traveling on the canal from Utica to Rochester, two hundred miles, for two dollars, good board included.   In the latter city
he devoted an evening to listening to the notorious Abby Kelly.
Her speech and the others which he then heard, he says, " Were
characterized by violent gesticulation, rant, denunciation, and
especially the abuse of ministers and all organized churches.   There
was a singular mixture of fanaticism, Quakerism, Unitarianism, and
infidelity, with ultraism of various hues, in all their speeches.   Such
measures as they advocate can never free the poor slaves; and their
tendency to unhinge society is obvious and appalling."   Occasioned
probably by what was now passing around him, he wrote, while on
his journey, a series of editorial articles for the Banner and
Pioneer on " Ultraism."   He seems to have found the associations
which he was able to attend generally harmonious, and imbued
with a good spirit.   For the most part they very cordially welcomed the object for which he was now pleading.   Many of the
dear old friends whom he had known twenty-five or thirty years
before, now welcomed him to their hearts and houses with grateful

cordiality. Among these he specially mentions Elder Harvey, by whose hand he put on Christ in baptism, more than thirty years before.

Near the end of September he found it practicable to gratify his desire of once more visiting his birthplace in Connecticut, and calling on a large number of old neighbors and friends, by whom he seems to have been welcomed with the utmost cordiality. After three or four days delightfully spent in their society, each recounting the way the Lord had led them for so many years, he took what he then expected, and indeed proved to be, his final farewell both of the place and people. The following Sabbath he spent in Amenia with the church which he left a third of a century before, to prepare for his mission labors. A new generation had arisen; but he found a few of the families of his former flock delighted to see and hear him once more. All of the congregation, indeed, knew him well by the report of their fathers and mothers, if not in person; and to them, by their common desire, he recounted with deep interest the way his Lord had led him so many "years in the wilderness, to humble him, and prove him, and to see whether he would follow the Lord or not." The state of the West he also portrayed before them in a kind of living imagery, which seemed to set all the objects of greatest interest in a clear and satisfactory light.

In the middle of October he attended in New York city the celebration of the completion of the *Croton Water Works*, the most Herculean enterprise, he thinks, ever attempted in this country. As a temperance man and advocate, one of the most delightful and noticeable characteristics of that immense gathering was the almost universal prevalence of the temperance reformation. Of all the miles of procession, and the acres of people who were mere spectators, scarcely one could be seen intoxicated. In the evening of the same day he attended a temperance meeting, and heard Hawkins and Anderson of the original Washingtonians give some of their "experience." In this way, he says, more than one thousand dram shops in New York city had been shut up effectually, and an untold amount of misery and ruin had been prevented.

Soon after, he repaired to Philadelphia, and spent considerable time in free and earnest conferences with the Board and executive officers of the Publication Society. Their corresponding secretary talked of resigning his official connection with the society. What should be done if he did, and what if he did not? were questions of serious magnitude which the more active and responsible men

27

bers of the Board found it difficult to answer satisfactorily. T**.** him they looked as one better qualified to aid them than any othe one, both from his long and intimate acquaintance with their wants the necessities of our widely-spread denomination in all parts of the country, and also from his having recently felt the pulse and tested the willingness of the churches to entertain this society as one of their regular objects of religious benevolence. His opinion was frankly expressed, that the secretary had better resign. He also pointed out what he thought requisite to be done in order to give the society a firmer hold on the confidence and liberal support of the churches. But he declined giving any encouragement that he could come to their aid, though many of the brethren entreated him to consider the question, and expressed their conviction that he was the only man who could successfully carry forward the enterprise at that period.

The 20th of October he bade adieu to Philadelphia, and with as much expedition as the low water in the Ohio river would allow, pushed forward to meet the Western Association at Cincinnati. He reached that city the 27th, after the meetings had commenced. Here he participated in all the important deliberations. The formation of the Indian Mission Association was one of the chief of these; and though he did not expect much benefit from it, further than to gratify and sustain the veteran McCoy and his family, and to gratify some local feeling in the West, which was scarcely satisfied with having a mission so peculiarly Western in its scope, managed exclusively by an Eastern Board, he thought it better on the whole to gratify this demand than to resist it. For the same reasons the Board of this Indian Mission Association was located in Louisville. The educational interest, and specially the Theological Institution in Covington, then rising into some notice, engrossed considerable attention. He looked to this most hopefully, and spent much time with Brother E. Robbins, its enterprising founder, in counselling for its future course, and in endeavoring so to promote its success as should least interfere with the prosperity of the infant colleges in the Western States, which so much needed the fostering care and united support of their several localities.

Monday, the 31st of October, was his birthday; he had finished his fifty-third year, and seems astonished at the rapid flight of time and years. But another aspect of the case still more deeply impressed his mind, and he cries out, Bless the Lord, O my soul, for his abundant goodness!

He took leave of Cincinnati, and the next day spent some time in Louisville looking into the state of things, which he found, so far as the interests of the denominational paper of the West, the Banner and Pioneer—of which he had continued one of the editors to this time—were concerned, somewhat confused and unsatisfactory. An informal meeting of the Board of the Western Baptist Publication Society was also held, to whom he communicated his general views of this subject, as they have above been stated.

The next day he pursued his rather slow course—owing to the low stage of water—towards home. A Sabbath was spent on the steamer ascending the Mississippi, and he and an English Brother May, both preached on board the boat. They reached St. Louis in safety on Monday, the 7th of November, and the following day, in company with Dr. Huxtable, an English Baptist brother, who went West to spend some weeks with Mr. Peck, he reached home, finding his beloved family well and happy, which called forth his praise and grateful acknowledgments. He had been absent seven months.

With more time and undisturbed quiet than he had hitherto been able to command, he now sat down and made a full written report to the Baptist Publication Society at Philadelphia; accompanying it, by their desire, with suggestions as to the wisest course to be subsequently pursued. He wrote, also, to some of the brethren of the Board personally, explaining more minutely the difficulties which had become known to him, as growing out of their past action or want of action, and suggesting the appropriate remedies. The tenor of his journal at this period, and such copies of his letters as he preserved, indicate very decidedly how deep a hold of his convictions this publication work had taken, and how anxiously solicitous he had become that just the right measures should be pursued to give it a firmer, broader hold on the regards of the churches.

The remainder of this month and the following one Mr. Peck was engaged mainly in an extensive and laborious correspondence with brethren in all parts of the country, writing sometimes a dozen long letters a day, and on a variety of subjects, some. private and personal, but far the larger part with reference to various aspects of the Redeemer's kingdom, and the ways and means of its advancement. He seems to have favorably entertained a proposition about this time to engage as a Western assistant to the Rev. David Benedict, in helping to prepare the new edition of his History of American Baptists. His plan was for Mr. Peck to undertake the Western portion, and secure recent and reliable information in regard to the rise and progress of all the Baptist associations in

the West, and sketches of the history of the more important
churches, and of prominent individuals, ministers and others. To
prepare himself for such a work, he spread the net of his inquiries
over this whole region, and called forth many responses and much
aid, both in letters written to him particularly on this subject, and
in minutes and other documents which he procured.

But his labors in correspondence did not prevent his preaching
or lecturing on prophecies or on temperance, or some other useful
topic, nearly every Sabbath, and frequently on week-days and evenings. Among the rest, a protracted meeting at Bethel was held for
a week or more, and he was desired to do all the preaching, while
other ministers helped in prayer and exhortation. He did preach
once or twice each day, and by giving something like systematic
order and coherence to the range of topics which he discussed, much
more religious instruction was communicated than usual, and a
high degree of satisfaction was expressed with the results of the
meeting. If less were professedly converted than at some former
meetings of the kind, the ministers thought that more permanent
good was done, as the mind was much more fed, and the character
of the converts evinced more solidity and Scriptural knowledge
than usual.

A ministers' meeting was appointed at his house for the end of the
year, and to secure a large attendance, he wrote scores of letters.
The last day but one of the year 1842, a goodly number of the
brethren assembled. They had preaching once or twice a-day, and
held a private conference among themselves in the intervals, dis
cussing some of the more important practical questions, relating
to Shurtleff College and ministerial education in the West: how
both might be carried forward with vigor and success. His own
case, and what might be his duty in present circumstances, seems
also to have occupied considerable attention; and he mentions how
deeply all were affected, when one of the Lemens, by request of his
brethren, engaged in special prayer for him; thanking God for preserving his life so long, and for his continued usefulness to the cause
of Christ at large, and begging for Divine direction for him in
future.

The meeting continued for more than a week, and seems to have
been a season of much spiritual refreshment to them all. The
last question on which they deliberated was: "Has a parent, from
the authority vested in his hands by God and the laws of our
country, any right to *coerce* his child in matters *strictly religious?*"
This question, he says was brought up by a decision of Judge

Lewis, of Pennsylvania, against a Baptist minister (Rev. William S. Hall), for baptizing a minor daughter of a Dr. Armstrong. After full discussion, this ministers' meeting decided this question in the negative. A distinguished doctor of divinity and a Baptist, at nearly the same time, however, wrote to this judge, approving his decision. Who, alas! shall decide where the doctors thus disagree?

The middle of January, Mr. Peck visited St. Louis by request, and found, to his great joy, a pleasant revival in the white and colored Baptist churches. The immediate object in his invitation was for him to preach at the dedication of a new house of worship, just erected by the African church—a substantial brick edifice, thirty-five by sixty-five feet, with galleries, and costing four thousand dollars. Their church then consisted of more than three hundred members, and they maintained good discipline. They had already raised among themselves the larger part of the cost of the house which that day they solemnly gave to the Lord. He gave a sketch of the origin and history of this church, and its several places of worship, all of which was listened to with deep interest.

Once and again he also preached for his esteemed Brother Hinton, then pastor of the other Baptist church, where several conversions had lately been witnessed, and more were anxious. At the same time he was getting from the surveyor-general's office in St. Louis, such sketches as would enable him to correct and perfect his new map for his Gazetteer of Illinois.

For the same purpose, a few weeks later, he visited Springfield, the seat of government of Illinois, and while there, engaged in doing good, lecturing, preaching, and counselling with all the wise and good whom he found assembled from different parts of the State. The governor solicited him to accept the office of State Superintendent of Instruction, then, as was supposed, about to be permanently created. So much was this in harmony with some of the important objects of his life, ever since he had been in the West, and so wide a field would it open for his usefulness, that it is no wonder he felt strongly tempted to engage in it. It shows, moreover, the high estimation in which he was held by his fellow-citizens, and those most competent to appreciate his worth. But the Lord had other designs for him.

CHAPTER XXVIII.

Secretaryship of the American Baptist Publication Society—His Ac
ceptance and its Conditions.

On the 27th of February, 1843, Mr. Peck received, from a
private source, intelligence that he had been unanimously
elected to the Secretaryship of the Baptist Publication Society, Philadelphia. Four days later he had the official announcement from the hand of his predecessor, who still held
the office *ad interim.* This was a fair specimen of the efficiency with which the most important business of the society
had been conducted. He was in some degree prepared for
this announcement, as by previous correspondence he had
known the wishes of a large number of the Board. To an
inquiry addressed to him some weeks earlier, whether he
would consent to accept this place, if elected, he had very
freely responded, stating at considerable length the conditions
precedent on which alone he could consent to serve, and
closing with the assurance that if any other brother could be
found able and willing to assume the arduous and difficult
duties of this office, he sincerely desired that he might be appointed ; since in his own case there were other doors of usefulness opened before him, more congenial with his health
and former habits, and also more remunerative.

It may be well, in this place, to give, in a condensed form,
from his own statement, the conditions on which he would
feel at liberty to entertain the proposition of accepting this
appointment. They were as follows :

1. Measures must be promptly adopted to inspire the denomination with confidence in the management and efficiency of the society. He had found, the preceding year, great want of confidence
in the energy, efficiency, and economy of its management, which
proved one of the most serious obstacles in his path. . He then did

all in his power to produce confidence, and thinks he succeeded in some degree.

2. Economy in the incidental expenditures must be carried to the lowest point possible, without impairing the efficiency of the society. The salaries of all employed in Philadelphia to be reduced twenty per cent., beginning with his own office.

3. A thorough, searching examination to be at once instituted into every department of the society, so as to ascertain the exact value of the stock on hand, whether at the depository, or in the hands of agents and colporteurs, or in branch depositories, with the losses incurred by bad debts, depreciation of books, tracts, plates, etc.

4. Make the corresponding secretary the general agent, with the understanding that he shall be relieved from editing the Record— a small monthly paper—and, also, that he spend not less than two-thirds, and perhaps three-fourths of his time in agency works, getting funds and superintending the sales and the colporteur system. Make it the duty of the depository agent to conduct the appropriate business correspondence of the depository and sales, as well as the ordinary correspondence of the society, in his absence ; having, if need be, associated with him an advisory committee of the Board, to counsel him in important matters. The secretary, even on his tours of agency, to be still a diligent correspondent, endeavoring to address every association, and every principal church once a year, unless he paid them a personal visit. To facilitate his operations, he should be provided with two forms of circulars : one for associations, churches, and auxiliaries ; and the other for ministers and other individuals. In all cases, when sending one of the circulars, he should write a short letter on the blank side of the sheet; since people do not notice a mere printed circular, as they do a written letter.

The secretary should also visit all our colleges and theological institutions, address the students on the objects of the society, and keep up a correspondence with the officers, and with every society of missionary inquiry. Should correspond, also, with all our home missionaries, and with the secretaries of all general associations and State conventions, inducing mutual co-operation, and opening channels for the circulation of the society's publications. Though this double duty of corresponding secretary and general agent must be arduous, self-denying, and responsible, it *all **must** be done;* and since the society has not means, at present, to support two men for this work it must be done by one.

Now, in view of this outline of both the comprehension and distribution of duties,

5. Will the acting members of the Board stand pledged mutually and efficiently to co-operate in any feasible measure to make the society what the denomination needs and expects?

"Probably it would be requisite for me, if I accept the office, to reserve one or two months, to be with my family and attend to my personal affairs, with a proportionate reduction of salary. One thing more in reference to *my health:* I cannot expose myself to travel in the severe weather of winter in a northern climate, and, consequently, any agency service I may perform in winter must be in a southern field."

With this full outline of his views, which the Board, by pressing his acceptance of the office, and the assurance that he was the only man they could find capable of carrying out their designs, did expressly indorse and approve, the way was fully opened for his entrance on this enlarged sphere of labor. He had counted the cost, and with deliberation and resoluteness put his hand to the plough.

March and the first part of April he remained at home, and in its immediate neighborhood, putting the finishing hand to some of his begun labors and enterprises, and preparing himself and family as well as possible for a long separation. He continued, moreover, the extensive correspondence in which he had been engaged, making it a preparation for the work in which he was so soon to be fully engrossed, and calling forth the counsels and pledges of co-operation from those whom he addressed in all parts of the country. He seems, also, very fervently to have sought the Divine blessing on this devotement of himself to a new, wide, and very responsible sphere of service; and he also sought very earnestly the prayers of his brethren, that the sacrifice he was now willing to make might not be in vain. The weather, for these two months, was remarkably severe; storm after storm of the most terrific character occurred; and when it was the time of year for the genial return of spring, the rigid frosts and deep snows held undisputed sway. On the 5th of April, he writes, not a green thing has yet started from the frost-bound earth. The following day he engaged his passage by steamer from St. Louis, and taking leave of his family and other friends, he set forth on his way to Philadelphia. A young man, an entire stranger, occupied the same state-room with him, and improved the opportunity, while Mr. Peck was asleep, of abstracting from his pantaloons' pocket two little packages of gold coin, amounting to sixty-two and a half dollars—nearly all the money he had. It was done so stealthily—though his nether garments had carefully been placed behind him in his berth —that he was not awakened, and the thief went on shore, probably at Smithland, without exciting any suspicion. On his explaining to the officers of the boat, in the morning, the robbery, they promised to use their best endeavors, by the aid of their agent at Smithland, to detect the perpetrator of this villainy. But he remained undiscovered, and the loss was final. Our brother, with characteristic equanimity, enters in his journal: "Though it is nearly all of my ready money, yet I am not disturbed. Providence will provide! I can only say, in regard to this wicked young man, 'Lord have mercy on him.'"

Stopping for a few hours at Louisville, he called on Mr. Buck at his office, and about this time demanded to have his name taken from the head of the Banner and Pioneer as one of its editors. This semi-official connection had continued from the time when his own paper, the Pioneer, was transferred to Louisville and united with the Banner, and he had written a great deal for it; but in the new and official relations which he was henceforth to sustain, he seems to have felt, and justly, that there would be an incongruity in his appearing as one of the editors of a paper some of whose contents might prove embarrassing to him and to the society he was to serve.

His good-will to the paper and its conductors was not by this step diminished. He wrote for it frequently and ably, as a contributor, but without editorial responsibility. While on the steamer, passing up the Ohio river, his journal shows that he was busy in writing out some numbers of a series of articles on the prophecies, under the head of "Millerism," which was now making considerable headway in the West. In Cincinnati, he found that the Episcopalians were lecturing and writing on the prophecies, especially on the second advent of Christ to live on earth one thousand years—the old Millenarian doctrine.

He was cheered by the companionship of a Brother Potts, a missionary to the Indians, and they reached Wheeling on the night of the 14th April. In getting his baggage from the steamer, Mr. Peck fell down the stairway, cut his head, which bled profusely, but undeterred by this and his want of rest, which it occasioned, he took the early mail-stage the next morning and hastened on his

journey. The next night, very weary and worn out, he reached
Baltimore. But after resting a few hours, he felt obliged to hasten
on to Philadelphia, which he reached the afternoon of the 17th,
and for about a week devoted himself early and late to the investigation of the affairs of the Publication Society.

The investigation which he then made showed that some
things were better and some worse than he had expected
On the whole, he determined to press onward, right onward,
and endeavor to earn and deserve success. In company with
several Philadelphia brethren, he hurried onward to Albany,
where the Baptist anniversaries were that year held. He
reached there in time for the earliest of them, and with deep
interest attended them all. This, indeed, was always characteristic of him; and to this trait he owed in no small degree
his success. He was too good and too great a man to narrow
down his sympathies and ardent good-will to that branch of
benevolence with which he was officially connected, and never
evinced the slightest jealousy lest others should secure more
than their share of the attentions and the benefactions of the
public.

The annual report of the Publication Society had been
drawn up by his predecessor, but he read it, and took at once
the official position to which he was entitled. The arrangements for resolutions, addresses, etc., had been but imperfectly
made, and the audience at this anniversary was neither large
nor enthusiastic. However, the new secretary seemed to feel
that he must familiarize himself to reverses.

It appeared that the contributions to the society of the entire year only reached the meager sum of fifteen hundred and
fifty dollars, for the general purposes of its organization, and
the receipts from all sources, exclusive of a small amount
towards a building fund, were eight thousand, five hundred
and fifty-three dollars. True, there had been some public reverses in the pecuniary affairs of the country. There had
been an opportunity for the penurious to excuse themselves
on the complaint of hard times; but the report very justly remarked, that this excuse would not suffice to account for this

beggarly deficiency: for, "The very superfluities of Baptist living would have been ample to furnish a working capital for the denominational Publication Society."

As soon as the anniversaries closed, he hastened back to Philadelphia, and applied himself with vigor to preparing the annual report and accompanying documents for the press, and to examining still more minutely and thoroughly into the general state of the society's affairs. This was only inter· mitted for a few days the second week in May, to enable him to attend the general anniversaries in New York.

The anniversaries proper which Mr. Peck attended in New York, were the Seamen's Friend Society, the New York Sunday-school Society (where he made one of the addresses), the American Tract Society, where Kincaid was very happy in delineating tract operations among the Burmans and Karens, and Dr. Nevin, very truthful in describing the German character in the West; a convention called by a Mr. Bingham, a missionary from the Sandwich Islands, for a conference on the evangelization of the world—a new organization proposed for this end being opposed by Rev. Dr. Anderson, Secretary of the American Board, for fear it would clash with other organizations; the American, *Pedobaptist*, Home Mission Society, where he heard some good and sensible speaking ; the American Bible Society, where he thought the tirades uttered against sectarianism, against Puseyism, and against Romanism, by several of the speakers, were in exceedingly bad taste at a Bible anniversary. In the end, he attended the anniversary of the American Temperance Union, where some of the Washingtonians held forth.

The venerable Lyman Beecher, his old neighbor and friend, also gave the following account of the origin of temperance efforts in America :—He stated that in 1811 he attended two ordinations in Connecticut, where rum, brandy, and all sorts of intoxicating liquors were profusely drank, even by the clergy; that at the General Association of Congregationalists in 1812, a committee on this subject reported that nothing could be done to arrest the evil of intemperance, when he (Dr. Beecher) moved a recommitment of the report and was added to the committee, who thereupon brought in a reso lution recommending the disuse of *ardent spirits* at ordinations and like occasions: that this led on to his six sermons, preached and since published, and that here, and in this way, originated the great temperance movement.

At the close of the week he returned to Philadelphia, and resumed the work on which he was before engaged. Soon he arranged to lodge in the depository building, thus saving both time and expense, and also securing what he seems to have much prized, more undisturbed opportunity for private devotion. He was not a little embarrassed by the connection of the Record with the Publication Society. It was objected to by many, as really little else than the local religious paper of the Baptists in Philadelphia, while at the same time the funds of the Society were used to sustain it. The desire of the secretary, after looking into the matter, was to secure the Baptist Memorial and unite it with the Record, the Almanac and Annual Report, making the publication monthly, and pretty closely identified with the interests of the society. But he found a difficulty in securing the concurrence of the Board, some of whose members were tenacious for having it a weekly paper.

Under date of May 20th he mentions that Brethren C. and H., formerly Baptist ministers, beloved and confided in, but now carried away by Millerism, called on him in passing through Philadelphia on their way to the West, to propagate the delusion of Christ's personal coming in 1843–44. "They conversed with me for an hour, and I tried to show them that the judgment announced in Dan. vii. was not the last great day of judgment, but rather the providential judgment of God on the monster, in which he would break down the anti-christian hierarchies and open the way for Christ to come by his gospel and Spirit to convert the world. These good men are deluded. The devil is certainly very busy with good men to spoil their usefulness."

Mr. Peck's free and generous spirit led him often to overdo in order to comply with the wishes, and lighten the burden of his ministering brethren, the pastors of the city churches. Once and again his journal notices the pressure thus brought on him by being persuaded to supply for one and another, so that very often he preached three times on the Sabbath, and walked half a dozen miles from one remote part of the city to another. The consequence was that at a late hour Sabbath night he would reach his solitary lodgings in the depository quite worn out. On the 19th of May he took part in the anniversaries of the American Sunday-school Union. Drs. Tyng, Leland, and Higgins spoke before him, the two latter quite long. He spoke twenty minutes, giving statistical facts of the Western valley, and Dr. L. Beecher spoke as much longer on general principles. Though quite unwell, he went home from these exercises and was engaged several hours in preparing a large amount of appropriate matter for an extra Record which the Board now wished to issue. Such are fair specimens of what occurred in the history of almost every week and day.

MONDAY, MAY 29*th*. Though quite unwell, set forth on a tour to meet the New England anniversaries in Boston. Tuesday attended the anniversary of the New England Sunday-school Union, where he had been announced to speak, but those preceding him were so intolerably long, that he declined. Next day the Northern Baptist Education Society was held, and at the end a sort of conference on education occurred, at which he spoke a short time on "the state of our ministry in the Western valley." At the social tea-party that evening. he gave, by request, some account of the late Jeremiah Vardeman. Then followed the meetings promotive of foreign and home missions; before the latter, Dr. Wayland preaching from Rev. xiv. 15 with his usual ability. The following Sabbath evening, at the united Baptist lecture, he preached in behalf of the Publication Society and the West. The house was full and the impression was favorable; but just as he was about to clinch the nail he had driven, and call out the liberality of the brethren in a collection for the object, there was an alarm of fire, which broke up the assembly abruptly. Thus were his hopes prostrated. He stayed another week, visited some churches at their week-night lecture, and twice preached on his object, the following Lord's-day, but it proved rainy. Then he hastened away from Boston to attend the Connecticut anniversaries, meeting that year at Norwich, where the pastor, Brother M. G. Clark, received him most cordially. The Baptists in Connecticut number about one hundred and twenty churches, and some fifteen thousand communicants, with one hundred ministers. On home missions Mr. Peck made an address, designed to show the encouragement there was to labor for the evangelization of the Western valley. On Thursday the Publication and Sunday-school cause came up. He

28

spoke again on this subject, and notices that considerable feeling was manifested. Prospects of co-operation in his object of the brethren and churches in his native State he thought very favorable. Near the close of the session, a celebrated revivalist preacher and pastor of that neighborhood preached, producing as usual great effect. Mr. Peck records his doubts, however, whether such spasmodic influence is the best and most permanently useful. He notices that "a number of Baptists under this revivalist's ministrations have become as noisy as any of our frontier people. They cry out 'Hallelujah!' 'Amen!' 'Glory to God!' and other like expletives, very frequently and vociferously, and such habits, in these regions, I cannot but regard as decidedly injurious, as their natural tendency is to ultraism and disorder." Friday he went to New Londor and lectured at night on the Publication Society and its influence on the West. The following day and the Sabbath ensuing he spent with the second and third Baptist churches in Groton, where a life-membership was also secured. On Sabbath evening he went to Stonington borough and preached. The two following days, in company with beloved brethren who desired to promote his health and happiness, he took several water excursions—boarded a noble whaler just ready to sail for the Indian Ocean—took a few blue fish and crossed over to Watch House Point, and obtained a fine view of the three States, Rhode Island, Connecticut, and New York, as well as of Block Island and the Atlantic Ocean. In the evening attended a temperance meeting and made an address. He notices with great satisfaction the benign effect of the temperance reformation, having reclaimed hundreds of sailors from inebriety.

Next he attended the Stonington Union Association, meeting that year at Voluntown. He notices a characteristic sermon preached during the session by the revivalist, and another on the Bible Society question, in the close of which it was stated that *all* the persecutions, corruptions and evils of the ecclesiastical hierarchies of Europe, were the result of infant sprinkling; which wholesale denunciation our brother thought wrong and injurious. He advocated the cause of his society the second day, and then hurried back to Philadelphia, to resume his routine of duty there. In the end of June the Board transacted some important business which he had prepared. In July he wrote and began sending out his circular appeals to the churches. In August he attended a camp-meeting of the church of God, or Winebrennarians, near Harrisburg, and so the summer passed away.

CHAPTER XXIX.

Secretaryship—Wreck of the Shepherdess Steamer—Tours and Labors.

THE position of the Baptist Publication Society in the year 1843, and that point at which it is found twenty years later, are so dissimilar that it may be difficult fully to appreciate the embarrassments of the chief functionary at the former period. One prime object of Mr. Peck in his discourses, and the written and printed appeals which he sent forth to the churches, was to awaken a livelier interest in *good reading*, for the purpose of promoting the higher intelligence of the membership and the community. "Give attendance to reading" was a favorite and pertinent theme on which he often discoursed to conventions, associations, and churches. They began to wake up to the importance of it; and as the result, they sent to the society, not the means to provide the requisite books, but clamorous demands for publications on credit—for more books, and in greater variety, but not the funds for producing them. The demand was for bricks in more extended tale than ever, but little straw was furnished for their manufacture. This was one of the embarrassments of the secretary. Could but a few generous-hearted, enterprising friends of this cause then have come forward—as they have at a later period—with endowments by thousands of dollars at once, how it would have lifted the cloud before him, and smoothed his way to earlier, larger success! A public sentiment had not yet been formed of sufficient power to draw forth such gifts, and the society had to feel its way with a degree of timid caution which hard necessity imposed.

Repeated, short excursions were made into New England and the Middle States, where some little help was obtained, and more promised; but it came very slowly. From May to December he preached seventy-eight times, delivered thirty other addresses, visited forty-five churches officially, four associations, five State conventions, six ministers' meetings, one camp-meeting, and one college commencement, and traveled three thousand three hundred and ten miles, besides office-work enough to have fully engrossed an ordinary man. Such were his common experiences and efforts, for the whole period of his official connection with the society, varied and somewhat relieved by his annual visit to Rock Spring. The first of these visits was marked by fearful peril. He was hoping to reach his family by New-Year's day, but the boat proved a slow one, and the low stage of the water retarded their progress. On the last Sabbath of the year, by invitation of the captain and passengers, he preached from the text of 1 Peter iv. 7, *The end of all things is at hand*, etc. How solemnly appropriate to the captain and others of that company! On entering the Mississippi river from the Ohio, the "White Cloud," from New Orleans, passed them, and some half a dozen passengers got on board of her, because she was so much faster than the "Shepherdess," on which he was traveling. His journal is as follows:

JAN. 3*d*. Our boat lay by for some hours this morning before light, as the navigation was deemed dangerous. At sunset we were a few miles above Herculaneum. At nine o'clock the cabin passengers signed a testimonial of thanks to the captain for his carefulness and prudence in navigating the boat amid the dangers of the Mississippi at this low stage of water, as snags abound in the channel. Retired to my berth at about half-past nine, with my clothes on except my coat, the night being very cold. After considerable time I fell asleep. Near eleven o'clock I was awakened by a dreadful crash: the boat struck a large snag, scarcely above the surface of the water. This occurred a little below the mouth of Cahokia creek. I heard nearly at the same instant screams of distress, and sprang from my berth, put on my coat, seized one boot, but before I could put it on the water was rushing into my state-room, which was forward of the wheel-house. Without boots or hat I rushed on to the guard, seized the projecting portion of the hurricane (or upper) deck, where, after considerable difficulty, I succeeded in getting on to that deck. A number of persons were already there, and many more got on from the stern afterward. The bow was so far under water as to cover the guards, but the stern held up some time longer.

Hearing cries in the ladies' cabin I got the pole of a wagon on the deck, and thrusting it in at the sky-light tried to pry off the roof, but found it impossible. The ladies, however, succeeded in getting on the hurricane deck, as did most of the steerage passengers. The boat was then floating sideways down the current, and soon ran on another snag and careened partly over. This threw off the boilers, and the bow thus lightened, brought the guards to the surface. The hull of the boat then separated and floated alongside the cabin and upper works. Next the smoke stacks, or chimneys fell, which tore off the end of the hurricane deck. Captain Howell, with several other persons, was killed or knocked overboard by the fall of the chimneys. The wheel-houses were soon separated from the deck, and floated off or sunk.

Finding myself exposed to the piercing atmosphere, I got down on the guards. But before this I had prayed repeatedly with the people around me. At first there was much confusion, and many screams and howlings to God for mercy. Some professors of religion prayed consistently. While I was on the guard, and the hull of the boat was floating alongside, I got on the bow, and stood for some minutes, but not liking its movements I was induced to return to the guard again. Soon the hull struck a bluff-bar and turned nearly over. Several were on it, and were drowned. Persons now gathered planks, doors, and pieces of the wreck to swim on. I looked about for something of the kind, but finally concluded to stick by the wreck while it floated.

The hurricane deck fell after a while, caused I suppose by the weight of the people upon it. We were now on a sort of raft, formed by the cabin-floor and guards, which continued floating as the current bore us, first on one side, then in the middle, and then on the other side of the river. Some were entirely wet—men, women and children, with very little clothing on. They suffered intensely. A steamer lay at the shot-tower, just above *Videpoche*, and as we passed near, we aroused the men on board, who came off in their yawl. As it neared the wreck, I directed them to pass around to the stern, and first relieve the women and children, who were perishing. They took on board their boat most of the ladies and children, and put them on shore. The next time the yawl came near the stern on my side. I had made up my mind—since I did not suffer as severely as some others—to give them the preference; but seeing a little girl quite helpless, I caught her up and leaped into the boat. By this time we had floated a long distance down the current, and were landed a full mile below Vide-poche, so that I had to walk without boots or shoes. My stockings were soon worn through. The ground was frozen hard, and its sharpness hurt me at every step. One foot was frozen about the ball, and very much cut. I carried, too, one of the babes of Mrs. Snell, a passenger. On reaching the first house they would not let us in. At the next we obtained shelter and refreshment. Soon after a little girl was brought in by some men, entirely cold, speech-less, senseless. I got a blanket, removed her wet and frozen gar-ments, and rubbed her with flannels and vinegar. It was about an hour before she began to moan, and more than four hours before any warmth appeared, except about the heart. She so far recovered before I left the place as to speak. [Her name was *Maria Pool*, and some days after, in St. Louis, Mr. Peck received the grateful acknowledgments of her parents.] A boy was brought in alive and I prescribed the same course for him, but he was suffered to die. Another girl was brought in dead. The yawl went four times to the wreck, and the ferry-boat Icelander helped to complete the work. Soon as daylight dawned I went to the store and bought a cap and shoes. Went also to the wreck in a steam tug sent down by the Mayor of St. Louis, found my large trunk with manuscripts and other materials, with overcoat, so that the pecuniary loss was but about thirty dollars. At an early period, and when the boat was breaking up, I fully expected death, as I could not swim, but felt calm and resigned, no ecstasy and no fear, but perfect self-possession, with ability to think of, and care and pray for others. Eternity will never seem nearer till I enter it.

Though dreadfully lamed by the disaster, Mr. Peck, with characteristic energy, rode home the next day, before his beloved family had heard of his wreck. Far and near his friends were greatly moved by his great peril, and their sympathies and congratulations poured in upon him from every side. Thus briefly he records his sense of obligation to the DIVINE HAND which rescued him : " Blessed be God for his goodness to me. I consider myself under additional

cbligation, anew to devote myself unreservedly to his service."

Through the following week he was confined to his room,
obliged to poultice his frozen, lacerated, and badly swollen
feet, but nevertheless vigorously engaged in writing. A full
sketch of the disaster he sent off to several periodicals ; and
by the earnest desire of many friends he immediately set
himself to work collecting the proper facts to be embodied in
a memorial to Congress, urging an appropriation for the
removal of snags and obstructions to navigation in the
Western rivers. This was soon completed and forwarded,
and was so favorably regarded that a generous appropriation
was made for this important purpose. Thus promptly
assiduous did he prove himself in turning all the events of
his varied life to good, for the welfare of his country, and the
safety of his fellow-men

For about ten weeks, or till the middle of March he remained about his home at Rock Spring, though the larger part
even of this period was given, directly or indirectly, to promoting the interests of the Publication Society. Besides
abundant correspondence in its behalf with friends all over
the country, he appealed personally to as many churches as
he could visit both in Illinois and Missouri. His prime
object was to raise two hundred dollars, and establish with it
a depository in St. Louis, and a somewhat smaller depository
of their publications at Alton, hoping that these examples
would provoke other communities to a worthy emulation.
The quotas of books and tracts which the life-members were
entitled to he also delivered or sent to them as far as possible,
so that zeal for this good work might grow by what it fed on.

In his return journey East, he contrived to plead his
cause in Kentucky and Ohio ; and early in April, found himself again in Philadelphia, where, after a brief survey, he
writes : " Prospects of the society far more encouraging than
when I entered the depository a year ago. In this respect
my success has fully equalled my expectations ; not by
collecting ample funds, but by inducing economy and system,

and especially by making a general impression on the denomination, and rousing up a spirit of practical and mutual co-operation."

The next work was to gather materials, then prepare, write and re-write the annual report of the society. On a review of his own labors for the society he found that during the year he had traveled seven thousand and ninety miles, preached one hundred and twenty-four sermons, written eight hundred and fifty letters of official correspondence, besides sending out many hundreds of religious circulars.

In the report he advocated with earnestness setting about raising a publishing fund of fifty thousand dollars in five years. So favorably was this regarded, that at the anniversary, held that year in Philadelphia, the project was approved, and nearly one thousand dollars in cash and pledges were secured on the spot, which the secretary hoped "might prove an indication of what will generally be done."

In May and in July of this year, he notices with deep sorrow and mortification the riots in Philadelphia, aimed mainly against the Catholics. These were not the means he approved for securing or defending Protestant ascendency. The truth in love he thought better than bludgeons or incendiary torches for this purpose.

His time till near the middle of September was nearly equally divided between office work, the selection and superintendence of publications, correspondence and the like, and going among the churches and associations of the States of New York, New Jersey, Pennsylvania, Maryland, Virginia, calling forth interest and aid, and specially pressing the fifty thousand dollar effort. Carson's works on Baptism, Fuller's works, and some of Booth's works, were then edited and their publication commenced

Early in the autumn he set his face to the West again, spending some time in western Pennsylvania, and then hurrying on as fast as the low stage of water in the Ohio would allow, he just reached Illinois in time to meet their State Convention in Belleville, near his family home, the first week in October. Failing to meet the Kentucky General Association the middle of that month, he met with that of Tennessee at the end of it, and gave several weeks afterward to the prosecution of the society's interests in middle Tennessee. This was in the midst of the exciting political canvass of 1844, which nowhere raged with more violence and intensity of interest than in the native State of Mr. Polk, the successful candidate. His own State was carried by a very small majority against him, while he prevailed in the Union at large.

Three or four days immediately preceding the election Mr. Peck was in Nashville, where he says, " Meetings, mobs, speeches, songs, processions and fights were the order of the day." The week before, in company with a few Baptist preachers on their way to Wilson county, where the Baptist anniversaries were that year held, Mr. Peck had called again on General Jackson, at the Hermitage. He was not well that day and had refused himself to other company, but learning who they were now desiring to pay their respects to the Ex-President, he at once required their admission. He was evidently quite feeble—sitting near his bed—but not emaciated, and preserving still the same genial urbanity of deportment of which he was a consummate master. He had that very morning been publishing some political paper of considerable severity, but which contained, in the close, a few sentences from Washington's farewell address, exhorting all portions of the country to seek its continued Union. One of the preachers adverted to this with commendation, which fired up the patriotism of the old veteran. For a few moments he quite forgot his infirmity, and poured out a well-digested apostrophe to the spirit of union, and mutual concession on the part of all his countrymen. His eye kindled, his tall frame dilated to its full proportions, and he showed himself again the great patriot captain which he was, especially whenever the designs of traitorous Catalines were to be thwarted.

With the venerable Colonel William Martin also, a worthy

Baptist brother, then seventy-nine years old, but hale and vigorous, Mr. Peck formed a pleasing intimacy, accompanying him to his home in a romantic vale in Smith county, Tenn., and spending a few days, pen in hand, taking down from the Christian veteran's lips many of the remarkable incidents connected with his own and his associates' endurances and successes, both in their civil and religious history.

This visit to Tennessee the secretary was wont to speak of afterward as one of the pleasantest of his official labors; not largely remunerative in pecuniary results, but helping, as he thought, the fraternal union and permanent co-operation of the widely-extended brotherhood for whose general welfare he was always solicitous. Who can say how much the prayers and labors, the spirit and deportment of such a man are even now doing to bring back that noble State to the cordial union and fellowship aimed at by the loyal adherents to the Constitution and Government which our fathers have bequeathed to us?

November 11th Mr. Peck set out, on his return from Nashville, to St. Louis, on board a small, stern-wheel steamer, which proved a slow one, and consumed a whole week in the trip, which ordinarily occupies only half this time. He suffered somewhat from illness, but prompt remedies and cheerful friends soon put him in good spirits again; and when wearied with his writing, to which, whenever able, he gave some of the best hours of each day, he beguiled the weariness of the long passage by recapitulating, to willing listeners, his varied experiences on these western waters for nearly thirty years, from his first ascent in a little boat with oars, sails, and setting-poles, in 1817, down to his fearfully-disastrous shipwreck on board the Shepherdess the winter previous. As he passed the very spot which had so nearly proved fatal to him, he looked through some dimming tears of tender, sad remembrances, on the scene of such deeply tragic interest.

On reaching St. Louis, he learned two things of significant interest and importance: first, that Rev. Mr. Hinton, pastor of that Baptist church which he had regarded with so much love, and cared for and labored with so earnestly, had given notice the day preceding of his determination to leave them the following month, in order to raise a Baptist church in New Orleans; next, the news had just reached the place, that New York had cast her electoral vote for Mr. Polk, instead of Mr. Clay, thus deciding the contest in favor of the former. On the result Mr. Peck remarks in his journal: "Thus, after the most exciting contest ever waged, and the most ludicrous, reckless, unprincipled means ever employed in an election, the result has turned out precisely as it would, had no such efforts been made."

Early the following month, a considerable gathering of ministers occurred at his house. He had lamed himself badly, and could not go to them, and invited some twenty of these bretnren to meet him and a brother secretary, most of whom came at the appointed time. One of the number thus describes the scene, which, as it seems to have been no unusual occurrence, and helps to a more accurate conception of his home and his neighbors, is here inserted:

"Rock Spring is the home, and for so many years has been the center of influence of the veritable author of the Emigrant's Guide and the Gazetteer of Illinois; the man whose publications and correspondence have led more settlers into this State than any other ten men. Who needs to be told that this is the Rev. J. M. Peck! We should love to draw aside the veil, just a little, from this domestic scene. It proves that he who has shared the hospitality of so many families, in all parts of our country, is as willing to exercise as to accept it. See his cheerful helpmate, contenting herself as best she may to abide at home and assiduously care for the welfare of the family and guests, having never re-visited her native New England since her first departure in 1817. Nor can you fail to notice that daughter Mary, with the father's energy, and the mother's quietness: how steady, noiseless, and efficient are all her movements! and to her, in no small degree, are owing the comfort and happiness which always smile around that dwelling. We need say nothing of the sons, for the older ones were now absent, and of younger, half-grown men it is not quite fair to speak; for they are not yet what they soon will be, or ought to be: but as their good, considerate mother said: 'They do so much need their father

with them.' Still, we can truthfully testify to the kind-hearted
ingenuousness which they uniformly evinced. May they one day
prove their parents' crown of rejoicing!

"A good farm, lying around this Rock Spring (you should remember that neither *rocks* nor *springs* are frequent hereabouts,)
and a comfortable, pleasant house, larger in its capacity to furnish
good accommodations for the family and numerous guests, by day
and by night, than any of its size we ever saw, is the home of this
brother. He had expected our coming, and knowing how very
limited our stay must be, had arranged every thing in the best
order possible to fill up the day. Most of the morning was spent
with him alone, in his study. What accumulations of laborious
carefulness and orderly accretions, during a long lifetime, here surround you! Near noon the neighboring ministers, for a dozen or
twenty miles around, begin to arrive. After some time spent in
introductions and mutual greetings, dinner being over, a goodly-
sized congregation met in the Rock Spring Seminary building, of
former years, now only used as a chapel. After praise and prayer
and preaching, some of us strolled over the more interesting localities, bathed in the effluents of *the spring*, and drank of its pure
waters. After tea, all assembled in the largest room, our host acting as moderator of the meeting; and from each in turn, beginning
with the eldest, some recital was given of the way in which the
Lord had led them in the wilderness, lo, these many years! Thus
we heard in succession from *Darrow* and *Ross* and the *Lemens*
(who witnessed the first baptism in this territory in 1794, and the
first Baptist Association formed in 1807), from *Pulliam* and *Taylor*,
from *Rogers* and *Dawson* and the younger *Ross*, and some others.
Most of these were inadequately-sustained ministers, but loved the
cause apparently in proportion to the sacrifices they had made for
it. In private, and in various incidental ways, it was gratifying to
see the high regard which they all felt for Brother Peck. "He
has been faithful to us in helping to correct our faults, and to improve our minds and hearts, and we thank him for it," was the
common sentiment. At a late hour that evening, we prayed and
sang and wept and rejoiced together; near midnight, retired to rest.
And when all were comfortably sleeping around, we long lay in
wakeful musings, thinking over the scene which we shall never witness again. Before daylight, next morning, we were hurried away."

With no little regret, the secretary gave up his well-
arranged plan of a southern tour for the promotion of his so

ciety interests, that winter.   Family cares, in part, rendered
this imperative ; and his concern for the Baptist cause in St.
Louis, and his hope by remaining at home to do something
more efficient by his pen, all conspired to the same result.
For nine successive Sabbaths he filled the pulpit left vacant
by his Brother Hinton, and succeeded, in some good degree,
in animating that church with fresh courage.   His labors
were constant and efficient in other localities also.   Dedication and ordination sermons, in city and country, were called
for, and he performed an immense amount of acceptable and
useful service, both sacred and secular, during the winter.

Early in March he was again at his post in Philadelphia.
Finding that the society had been obliged to embarrass itself
by temporary loans to the extent of twenty-four hundred
dollars, his first endeavors were to provide means for their
liquidation.   But he found the minds of pastors and churches
so much engrossed by the new and disturbing influence of the
response given by the Boston Board of Foreign Missions to
the Alabama Resolutions, that it much impeded his success.
March 18th the pastors in and around Philadelphia met to
confer on this agitating matter.   A wide difference of views
was found to prevail, and some ultra utterances on both sides
were listened to ; and Mr. Peck's journal says, that, after much
" FREE" discussion, a resolution was passed, avowing the adherence of these pastors to the platform agreed on at the last
convention.   This was reaching "point-no-point," so far as
the recent agitating action was concerned.

At just this juncture, also, missionary meetings were held
successively in several of the Baptist churches in Philadelphia,
to listen to appeals for the Foreign Mission Board, already
forty thousand dollars in debt, and the current contributions
(by the withdrawment of the South) were steadily and largely
diminishing.   The embarrassments thus thrown in the way
of the operations of his own society were greatly perplexing
to the secretary.   He had been planning for a strong appeal
to these churches, for the relief of the Publication Board,
when this overshadowing and more urgent distress of another
29

body, in whose prosperity they were deeply interested, inter-
vened to postpone, or thwart altogether, their own hopes of
relief.   It only remained for him to do the best in his power
now, and hope for better times. He gathered some encouraging
contributions from a few churches, and with a brave and
trustful heart went on to arrange the materials for the annual
report.

At Providence, R. I., where the Baptist anniversaries were
that year held, he says:

The Bible and Publications Societies passed off with much harmony and success.   But both the Home and Foreign Mission Societies were greatly perplexed and worried by discussions growing
out of the slavery aspect, in the bearings which this subject now
assumed.   Both of these organizations were plied with the practical question, "Will you appoint slaveholders your agents and your
missionaries?"   It became evident, before these anniversaries were
over, that all hope of harmonious reconciliation on these points was
futile.   The Boards were placed in the midst of communities pretty
thoroughly anti-slavery, and becoming more and more so every
day; and though many of the members, so far as they were indi
vidually concerned, would not have hesitated to go on as they had
commenced, disregarding any distinctions between North and South
on this matter, and striving only to preach the gospel to all accessible to them, by any competent instrumentality, yet even these
were forced to a stand by the surrounding pressure.

Mr. Peck's journal is very full and minute on all the questions then debated.   He was no partisan in these distracting
deliberations ; his voice was rarely heard, and whatever utterances fell from him, were characterized by the good sense,
the practical element of sound judgment, consistency, and adherence to the golden rule, which were his daily guides
through life.   It was now his happiness to disagree only with
extreme men and measures on either side; while his views,
his feelings, his action harmonized entirely with nine-tenths
of the whole mass, the candid and moderate men of all portions of the country.

In June he attended the Baptist conventions in Connecticut,
New Hampshire, and Maine.   The interior of this last named

State he had not before visited, and was now much pleased with it, especially the Kennebec valley, Waterville College, and the indomitable enterprise and industry which he saw on every side.   In like manner, during the summer and autumn, he did his utmost, under the existing circumstances, to increase the efficiency of the society, whose chief executive officer he was—traveling into Virginia and North Carolina, to attend the associations, State conventions, and any meetings where he could reach the public ear and heart.

As early as the end of September, he arranged with the Board for his permanent retirement from the position he now held, at the end of the current year of the society's operations, and the appointment of his successor, for which cause he assigns these two reasons : " I think the society can now be made to prosper, with such a secretary as Rev. T. S. Malcom would make ; and my presence is very necessary in Illinois, both for my family and the churches."

His description is graphic of the special meeting of the Old Triennial Convention, the last ever held, in November, 1845, where he was one of the committee on framing the constitution of the Missionary Union, and active in the subsequent debates on its adoption ; where, also, he met the venerated missionary JUDSON for the first time ; where, also, he acted an important part as chairman of the committee on Indian missions, and also led off, by arrangement, in the one hundred dollar subscriptions, which completed the extinction of the forty thousand dollar debt of the Foreign Mission Board—are all of deepest interest, but room for their reproduction here cannot be allowed.

By the 1st of December he reached Charleston, S. C., on a brief visit to that State and Georgia.   The hope and effort was earnestly, persistently made to retain the connection of North and South in the Publication Society enterprise ; and for this purpose, every concession and guarantee desired, were cheerfully proffered, but not with much final success. The spirit of secession was then as rife in the bosoms of many southern leaders in the churches, as it has later become in the

States. The majority of southern men of intelligence and principle did not in heart approve of it; but for the sake of union among themselves, as they said, consented to what was neither wise nor right. They and others are now reaping the bitter fruits of such concessions.

The remainder of the winter was passed chiefly in and about Philadelphia, in much labor, care, and enterprise for the furtherance of the society's interests, and to facilitate the labors of his successor. His annual report argued, at considerable length, the demand, the economy, and efficiency of the colporteur system. In summing up his own labors for the year, he recounts his travels seven thousand, one hundred and sixty-nine miles; has been absent from the office one hundred and seventy-one days; had preached ninety-eight times, and made forty-five addresses; had visited five Eastern, four Middle, and five Southern States, in promotion of the Publication Society objects.

Wednesday, May 6th, he took a final leave of the scenes and duties which for three or four years had engrossed his thoughts, and tasked all his powers, and turned his face towards his western home. How joyously he leaped up from the removal of the heavy burdens he had so long borne, and how, like the carrier-bird, long sundered, and by a wide interval, from its rest and its young, he now sped on with an impatience of delight to greet those from whom he had so unwillingly been sundered, he found no language adequate to express.

CHAPTER XXX.

Authorship—Boone's Life—Western Annals—Characteristics—Dr. Jeter's Testimony—Burning of Seminary Building—Final Tour in Eastern States.

GRACEFULLY to retire from a prominent public station to a narrower, humbler sphere, is at once difficult, and yet indispensable to one in Mr. Peck's situation. He achieved this transition with entire success, and reciprocating the cordial welcome of all his friends and neighbors in Illinois and Missouri, he seemed to enter without an hour's delay on the discharge of the multifarious duties, public and private which had accumulated in his long absence. These will hereafter be narrated only in the most summary manner, because they are generally quite similar in character and influence to those which have already been described.

One son was just now determining, against the father's remonstrances, to enlist as a subaltern officer in the Mexican army. Another, now a student in college, and under age, could scarcely be restrained from following his example; and though finally yielding to parental remonstrances, had become so inoculated with the desire of roving as to unfit him for study, and thus disappointed the hope of a literary career. Beyond the bounds of his immediate family-circle Mr. Peck's deepest solicitudes were awakened for the welfare of the Baptist churches in southern Illinois; and with great effort and much correspondence he set on foot measures for their improvement. This year, too, 1845, he wrote for Dr. Spark's American Biography, the Life of Daniel Boone. Much of the material for it he had long possessed, but he now took a long journey among the old hunter's descendants, to glean something more in reference to his later days. Rejecting the many romantic stories in regard to him, Mr. Peck sifted

every thing, and by the venerable man's own statements was
able to give, in less than two hundred duodecimo pages, the
reliable record of his life, which afforded the public the highest
satisfaction.

At the New Englanders' celebration of Forefathers'-day in
St. Louis, he was called on for a speech and a sentiment, and
gave " The North, the South, and the West, a right-angled
triangle, the hypothenuse resting on the Mississippi valley."
His remarks were much admired.   From his multifarious
correspondence at this period, two letters of superior interest
and importance should here be given but for want of room.
One to the Secretary of the Cincinnati Historical Society, on
occasion of his being elected a corresponding member, gives,
at great length, a summary of his own historical studies and
accumulation of materials.   The other to the Home Secretary
of the Baptist Missionary Union, discusses very fully the
hindrances, specially in the West, to the more successful
prosecution of that great and good enterprise, with suggestions as to the best method for their removal.   He wrote also
in favor of African colonization ; on Biblical interpretation ;
on pulmonary diseases as affected by the Western climate :
lectured ably on both home and foreign missions ; prepared a
new and improved course of sermons for revival meetings,
and delivered them, in series, at different places ; corresponded with Baptist ministers and others in Ireland, on the
facilities and advantages of transferring their then starving
population to the fertile prairies of the West; prepared and
delivered a course of lectures on Aboriginal Missions in
North America; drew up an elaborate report on the better
observance of the Lord's-day, and secured its adoption by a
convention of all denominations in southern Illinois.   At the
college commencement at Alton in 1847, he delivered a commemorative discourse, embalming the memory, character,
liberality and worth of Dr. Shurtleff, whose noble donation
had given name to that institution.   The same year he failed,
by political trickery, to be elected to the convention called for
revising the Constitution of Illinois, after having been

earnestly invited by both parties to allow himself to be a candidate ; this induced him to forswear politics entirely for the future.

In the meantime he was pastor or stated supply of several churches comparatively near his home, as Troy, Edwardsville, Belleville, and Bethel. His zeal, system, fidelity, and the versatility of his powers for reanimating a despondent church were, in most of these cases, demonstrated in a way to inspire fresh confidence in him as a wise and good under-shepherd of the flock. Nor did he intermit at all, but rather increased his contributions for different periodicals. A series on the Pioneers of the West for the St. Louis Republican ; Notes on Illinois for the National Era ; Incidents of Illinois for the Illinois Journal, were each a series of articles begun about this period, and some of them continued till the year of his death. Other compositions of a higher order, on which he bestowed much labor, were often coming from his hand. Such were his discourse on the anniversary of the battle of Buena Vista ; a commemorative discourse on John Quincy Adams ; and the Literary Address at the commencement of Georgetown College, Ky., on Elements of Western character.

From the first of the year 1849 he officiated as pastor of the St. Louis Baptist church, between the leaving of Dr. Lynd, and the coming of Dr. Jeter, for about nine months, editing also the Western Watchman, and giving much time to the African Baptist churches and all other evangelizing operations in the city. During this period he was the efficient instrument in leading a large number of Germans and Hollanders who had been pedobaptists, but now embraced more scriptural views, to be baptized and organized into a church. Some of them had gifts for usefulness in the ministry. He guided their studies and reading, and one of them formed the nucleus of the German Baptist Mission of the West, which at one time promised large results. He successfully also set on foot measures for paying off a debt of twelve thousand dollars on the church he was serving : by dint of his own persevering efforts chiefly, this good work was accomplished, **just** before a most disastrous and extensive conflagration laid waste a large portion of the best of St. Louis, and its fleet of steamboats, burning up several millions of wealth in a few hours. The Western Watchman office was consumed among the rest. It had been owned by a poor brother in the church, and there seemed no way to recommence the publication, but to raise one thousand dollars at least, in small sums, in that State and the proximate portions of Illinois.

Added to all the rest, the cholera made fearful ravages during a portion of this summer, sweeping off many of his personal friends, and clothing others in mourning. Nor was the college at Alton—that fond child of his affections—without its serious difficulties in these busy weeks. Once and again he was summoned to meet with its trustees, to adjust difficulties with agents or others, who had added to its embarrassments. The autumn of this year, 1849, brought him also the visit of the veteran Dr. Maclay, who seems to have spent some days at Rock Spring, to their mutual satisfaction. Still later Mr. Peck visited Iowa, where four of his children were then settled, and seems to have taken much pleasure in the rapid advances of that young State.

The year 1850 opened auspiciously. Dr. Jeter as pastor of the second Baptist church, St. Louis, required Mr. Peck's assistance very frequently, some protracted religious services being now held. The German church was flourishing, and both the African churches were doing better, and their valued friend, the Pioneer, was helping them all. Meantime the Western Watchman was resting almost entirely on his energy, for editorship and the means of its publication. Editing and greatly enlarging a new edition of the Annals of the West, was also thrown upon him. As it came from his hand, it is a noble octavo volume of over eight hundred pages, full of materials tolerably well digested, for the use of future historians.

Soon after Dr. Jeter assumed the pastorship of the St. Louis church, relieving Mr. Peck of that labor, his old friends, the Lemens and others of the Bethel church Illinois, arged him to accept its pastorship, which he did, and labored with them in that relation for two or three years. Before the close of 1851, Conrad Witter, a German, entered into a contract with Mr. Peck to write a description of the scenery of the Mississippi river, from its rise to its estuary, to accompany a series of splendid engraved plates. He entered promptly into its execution, and sent off his first number of eight pages, beginning with Itasca lake, within a week, and by the end of the month had brought his descriptive sketches down the river as far as the Falls of St. Anthony. Witter finally failed, and the plan was only partially carried out.

This was a fair specimen of his promptness. That was one of his leading characteristics. Rarely did he hold any matter under consideration a very long time, in order to gain more evidence; the best within his reach was grasped with vigor, and then he acted on it without much delay. Because his decisions were thus prompt, it would sometimes subsequently appear that they were less safe and reliable than could be wished. But the celerity of his mental processes made up, in a great degree, for this incidental disadvantage.

The first Sabbath in the year 1852 he gave this summary of his labors with the Bethel church for the preceding nine months:—Preached fifty-four sermons, besides thirty-two addresses and extended exhortations; made one hundred and nine family visits; attended nine monthly and five special church meetings, and rode seven hundred and six miles; he had been present and officiated thirty-four Sabbaths; absent by approval of the church, attending associations and the like, five Sabbaths; unable to attend by reason of sickness, three Sabbaths.

June 13th he mentions having all his sons, with two of their wives and two grandchildren, at home, and surrounding the supper-table together. He says they were five strong, hardy men, from twenty-one to thirty-eight years of age. Two days later he was in St. Louis, and officiated at the Baptist church, when their esteemed pastor, Dr. Jeter, very decidedly, though kindly, tendered his resignation, having been called back to Virginia. As a competent and impartial witness, the testimony of Dr. Jeter to the habits, standing, and character of Dr. Peck, may appropriately here be given.*

---

* " I had known Dr. Peck several years before I went to St. Louis in 1849, but not intimately,'and my estimate of his worth was considerably increased by my intimacy with him for nearly three years. He was a true, earnest, laborious, faithful servant of the Lord Jesus. I was particularly struck with his *disinterestedness.* He was willing to labor anywhere, in any department, and with anybody, if he might be useful. He engaged with equal readiness in the labors of a pastorate, an agency, an editorship, or authorship, with little regard to the exposure and fatigue involved in the enterprise, or the meagerness of its pecuniary reward. He was not a man to wait for important and honored posts of usefulness to be opened to him; but he entered promptly the fields of service before him, and cultivated them diligently, with the assurance that he would not fail of his reward. Though he was a man of strong will, and loved, as earnest and energetic men are apt to do, to have his own way, yet I never discovered in him the signs of envy or of mortified ambition. He thought, of course, his own plans right, and struggled manfully to carry them out; but accorded to brethren differing from him sincerity and worthy motives. In all his plans for extending the kingdom of Christ—and they were numerous—and in all his warm controversies in supporting them, there was an almost perfect self-abnegation.

The most remarkable trait in the character of Dr. Peck, that arrested my attention, was *volubility.* Brother Peck was both a full and ready man. He was well informed on almost all subjects; and on matters relating to the West, his knowledge was various, general, and minute. He might be called a Western Gazetteer, and poured forth an incessant stream of conversation on any subject— religious, scientific or political, grave or ludicrous—that might be broached in his presence. His resources in conversation were perfectly inexhaustible. When once he was fairly enlisted in conversation, the most resolute hearer could do nothing more than ask a question, suggest a doubt or difficulty, or give some direction to the current of discourse. Being somewhat fond of talking myself, when I first became acquainted with him I made frequent attempts to participate in the conversation; but soon I resigned myself, as did others, a mute auditor of his ceaseless and interesting remarks. Let it not be supposed that he was rude or overbearing in his manner. He was a courteous man His manners, however, were emi-

In the autumn of this year he prepared a special report on the finances of Shurtleff College, and, in attending the meetings of the committee and Board, devoted in all twelve days hard work to this object. So, too, at the association, not a

nently Western. In most social circles he was the acknowledged autocrat. He talked because all wished him to talk, and all chose to be silent in his presence. When he associated with those whose age, culture, and position gave them a title to a full share in conversation, he still engrossed it, partly from habit, and partly from the gushing fulness of his thoughts which would admit of no restraint. You might as well roll a ball down the mountain side, and attempt to stop it in its mid-career, as to arrest, or hold in check the impetuous thought and bounding words of the old pioneer.

Much has been said, and foolishly said, of Western character. Most people in the West formed their characters before they emigrated thither; and they have been slightly or not at all modified by their change of residence. But Mr. Peck was a *Western man*. He removed to the West while young; and his tastes, manners, habits, and modes of thinking and speaking were formed there. No intelligent and observant man could be in his presence five minutes without perceiving unmistakable evidence of this truth. The pioneers were a hardy, self-denying, courageous, and independent class of men. For forms, etiquette, and pretensions they had no respect. They were practical, not theoretic. Mr. Peck was not only a pioneer, but a master-spirit among the pioneers. Perhaps no man of the class did more than he to guide the thoughts, mould the manners, and form the institutions of the West. He was an embodiment of Western character—plain, frank, self-reliant, fearless, indomitable, with all his powers, physical and intellectual, subordinated by grace to the service of Christ.

I will mention an anecdote as illustrative of the peculiar character of Dr. Peck. When he resided in Philadelphia—so the story runs—as Secretary of the American Baptist Publication Society, after having been absent some months, he reached home by the stage in the morning, and, unobserved by any of his family, went into his study, and finding a great accumulation of letters and papers during his absence, soon became absorbed in the examination of them. Late in the afternoon some member of his family, to his great surprise, found him in his study, peering over his papers. I do not vouch for the accuracy of the story—indeed, I do not wholly believe it; but it is significant that such a story should be circulated concerning him. Of all the men I have ever known,

little extra labor fell on him.   In preparing the minutes for
printing, carrying them through the press, and other connected
services, eight days labor, besides the Sabbath, was required.
He subjoins, with earnest positiveness: " This extra labor is
too pressing on me, and I am resolved hereafter to throw it
all off :" the practical comment on which was that, a few
weeks after, he attended the General Association of Illinois,
and in the absence of some to whom it more properly belonged,
he prepared reports, and laboriously advocated important
measures in repeated speeches, very much the same as though
he had not so firmly resolved to the contrary.   The same was
the case at the Pastors' Conference, later in the season.   He
also wrote an elaborate article in the Christian Review, on
the History of the Baptists in the Mississippi Valley, and
several papers of importance for the Christian Repository, as
well as carried on vigorously his numbers of the " Mississippi
River Illustrated."   His old neighbor and friend, Governor
Reynolds, was importuning him to write a report and review
of the school laws of Illinois.   Revolving this matter, he thus
jots down in his journal : " If I had time, I could at least prepare a report on a more perfect system of common school,
academic, and college education.   *I will think of it.*"

In the meantime a heavy calamity befell him, which must
be recorded in his own words :

---

it was most likely to be true of him.   He was not without social
affections—had, no doubt, a fair measure of them.   His wife held
him in the highest reverence.   He was never charged with the
slightest neglect of his family.   But so completely had he subordinated all his social affections, and all his habits, to duty and usefulness, that if any man could have been innocently oblivious of
his family under the circumstances indicated in the anecdote, that
man was John M. Peck.

In a high sense of the terms, I did not consider Dr. Peck either
a great or a learned man, or an eminent preacher ; but a man of
sound sense—of various attainments—of earnest piety—of good
preaching gifts—of extensive labors—of much usefulness, and as
deserving a name among the benefactors of his race, and the lasting gratitude of the inhabitants of the Mississippi Valley, and of
the Baptist denomination."

NOVEMBER 18*th*, Thursday. What I have sometimes feared, but tried to guard against, has to-day happened. *Rock Spring Seminary has been burnt!* My son, working in the lower story, had a fire in the fireplace. Leaving for a few moments, he found on returning that the wind had scattered fire among the combustibles around his work-bench, and the flames soon reached the ceiling above. He gave the alarm, but it was too late to put out the fire. Some of the books of most value were saved, partly in a damaged state. But an important branch of my labor for more than thirty years is wholly lost. My collection of files of papers, periodicals, and other pamphlets, amounting to several thousand volumes, mostly unbound, but carefully filed, and my mineralogical collection from every part of the country where I have traveled, thoroughly arranged and labeled, together with much other matter which I had intended for some public institution, to be preserved for generations to come—these can never be replaced. Well, it seems to me to be providential. I have done what I could, and failed! I am afraid my materials are so destroyed that I cannot obtain means to prepare my projected work on the Moral Progress of the Great Central Valley of the Western World. I can only say, the will of the Lord be done.

It must be very difficult for any one not acquainted with the character of the man to appreciate the afflictive circumstances of this calamity—the loss of just what, of all material things he most prized, and, as many thought, almost idolized, the collection and preservation of which had, next to his Christian duties, been the great absorbing passion of his life—or to conceive aright of the composure with which he accepted it, as the indication of his Heavenly Father's will. Though it broke up his life-plans and hopes in a moment, yet it is doubtful whether any one half an hour afterward would have noted any disturbance of his accustomed equanimity.

The middle of January, 1853, found him gathering his scattered and charred books, some fifteen hundred volumes, into the largest room in his dwelling-house, which became henceforth his library and study. Later in the month he spent some days in Springfield, where the legislature was in session, by which he was supplied with all their published laws, journals

30

etc., a unanimous resolution for this purpose having been passed.

No little sympathy for his loss by this fire was expressed to him by his correspondents, and also in the notices of the papers east and west. Encouraged by numerous assurances of loving friends, that they desired to supply in part, at least, and in kind, what had been consumed, he set forth, April 21st, for one more eastern tour, intending to be absent several months. At Covington, Ky., he witnessed with sorrow the failure of that theological institution which he and his friend Robins had hoped would prove a blessing to the whole Northwest—one of the early sacrifices at the shrine of slavery.

At Philadelphia, with what delight he spent a Sabbath with his friend, Dr. Kennard, "the model pastor," as he calls him, witnessing the baptism of half a score of candidates, and aiding in the sacramental services! At the annual meeting of the Publication Society, in company with a young friend, H. G. Jones, Esq., appointed a committee for this purpose, he brought in a plan for a Baptist Historical Society, to form a kind of adjunct of the Publication Society, and successfully advocated its adoption, dwelling with satisfaction on the progress of Baptist principles. With his old friend, Dr. Malcom, he visited the ecclesiastical patriarch of that vicinity, the venerable Dr. Jones, at Roxborough, finding him, at the age of seventy-six, still pastor of his beloved church in Lower Merion. The American Sunday-school Union, which he had so early and efficiently served, and the Presbyterian Publication Board, tendered him such of their publications as would help to supply his loss, as did also several private publishers both here and in the other principal cities which he visited. In Troy and Albany he attended the Baptist anniversaries of that year, noticing much to approve, and some things which he could not approve. In Boston, too, he attended the May meetings; and at Harvard University, Cambridge (which the preceding year had honored him with a Doctorate) he was the guest of President Sparks, and witnessed the inauguration of his successor, Dr. Walker. The younger Dr. Shurtleff, and others, vied with each other in tendering him hospitality and merited honors. Dr. Anderson, senior Secretary of the American Board of Foreign Missions, invited him to their rooms, to supply, from their reports and other publications, his losses as far as practicable; he preached, also, in as many of the principal churches as his time and strength would allow. Visiting all the public libraries of most importance in this vicinity, he copied whatever was most important for his purposes, and sent home two boxes of books and pamphlets towards supplying his losses. Returning to New York and Philadelphia, the next two months were spent in a similar manner. At Poughkeepsie, where an esteemed friend had proffered him any fifty volumes he might choose from his library, he secured many rare and valuable works not elsewhere procurable; and by the end of July set out on his return West via Albany, Buffalo and Chicago, reaching his home the 12th of August. He had been absent three and a half months, visited for the last time many of his early Eastern friends; and had traveled by railroads, stages, and other methods, a total of four thousand nine hundred and fourteen miles.

He immediately recommenced his pastoral duties with the Bethel church. Death had taken away some of its loved members, but he was joyfully welcomed by the survivors. In September he was surprised by the reception of a unanimous call to the pastorship of the Covington Baptist church, opposite Cincinnati. It occasioned him much solicitude. He wrote to several friends for advice, and finally concluded to visit them the following month to reconnoiter. Ere he did so, the second Sabbath in October he terminated his official labors with the Bethel church, satisfied that he could not continue them through the ensuing winter with safety to his health. They parted in love and with mutual respect and confidence, his labors having been very useful to the church.

CHAPTER XXXI.

LAST THINGS.

A Last Pastorship—Last Volume Prepared for the Press—Last Loss
of a Child—Last Hours of His Wife—Last Tour Through His
Wide Field—Last Illness—Death and Burial.

SOME of Dr. Peck's correspondents, whom he consulted
in regard to the propriety of his accepting the call to the
pastorship of the Covington church, earnestly remonstrated
against it, as likely to involve both himself and the church in
great embarrassment.   But it was always difficult for him,
with his buoyant, hopeful impulses, calmly to weigh the pro-
babilities of failure in his own case.   He found the church
somewhat disheartened by repeated failures to secure as their
pastor some man of standing and influence.   It consisted
of some two hundred members, resident in Covington and
vicinity, some of them most excellent persons; but the
ordinary attendance of the whole congregation was scarcely
as large as this, even in favorable weather.

Scarcely six weeks had elapsed ere, in an attempt to hold
extra religious services, with preaching every evening, he
broke down utterly.   He thought it, at the time, an attack
of his old foe, congestion of the liver ; but after his partial
recovery, his kind physician, Dr. Wise, informed him that his
lungs had been more diseased than his liver.   Finally the
physician told him with candor, that he had never known a
case of a man at his age, and with his enfeebled constitution,
recovering entirely from so severe an attack of lung disease.
Hence the attempt to resume his pastoral duties was out of
the question, as it would involve the certainty of soon breaking
down.   This decision, so unwelcome both to him and the loving
people whose hearts and hopes more and more clung to him
as their beloved pastor, was received by both with humble

Christian submission. In his private diary Dr. Peck says, "I have prayed most earnestly for Providence to show me my duty in the present exigency, and am bound to regard the affliction sent as the decision. I have been over forty-two years in the ministry, and with all I have done in secular labor, I have made *that* the paramount business of life, and every thing else subordinate."

He resigned the 19th of March, 1854, scarcely three and a half months after entering on the duties of his pastorship—determining henceforth to devote himself to such work with the pen, in finishing the books on hand, as he might be able, and to be in readiness for his departure. The church, a week later, by his earnest desire, accepted his resignation, and passed resolutions, indicating their enhanced estimate of his worth, and their continued confidence and esteem. The testimony of one of their number is subjoined in a note, written after his death.*

His leave-taking of his dear church and Sunday-school and many personal friends, was very tender and affecting. April

---

* Covington, Ky., *July 7th*, 1860.

Brother Peck was one of the most original and remarkable men I have ever met with : he appeared to be guided and determined by a stronger sense of duty and a more unwavering faith than any individual I have had the pleasure of observing.

When called to the pastoral charge of the first Baptist church in Covington, he was told that the congregation could probably pay him one thousand dollars per annum. His immediate reply was, that eight hundred dollars was all he intended to receive ; that two hundred dollars could be kept to help other ministers who might be called in to assist him ; that his health might give way and he might fail in any protracted effort. This soon proved to be true, and brought on his severe illness.

When his physician, attendants and friends came to the conclusion that his days were few and numbered, I asked him to let me telegraph his wife (left at her home in Illinois) to come to see him. He consented, with the instruction that nothing should be communicated that would alarm her, and declared that he would not die then ; and for several days, when at his lowest, and all believ-

20th, in company with his invalid friend Dr. Sherwood, he left by steamer for St. Louis, recording his testimony : "Were I twenty years younger, and able to perform the duties of pastor, I know of no church I would prefer to this, no city I would more desire to live in than Covington."

On getting home, he set himself down very diligently to arrange materials and compose articles for reviews and other periodicals, and wrote with care a life of Vardeman for Dr. Sprague's Annals. The last volume he wrote was the Life of Father Clark.

April 25th, 1855, the following entry was made in his journal : "It is one year to-day since I got home from Covington. Now I am far more feeble than then." Nor till June was he able to attend church, even as a hearer. Then he enjoyed a visit at Bethel church, where a revival had occurred, and sixty or more, many of them his old, dear friends, for whose salvation he had long prayed, and wept, and labored, were rejoicing in obedience to the Saviour. Near the end of the month, at the commencement at Shurtleff College, he was drawn into extra efforts to settle difficulties. A special committee was raised for this purpose of which he was chairman, and says, "I accepted the post with greatest reluctance, but with the determination to risk health, or even life, to save the college." Alternating between sickness and partial recovery, he passed the next three or four months.

---

ing that he could not live, his faith that he should recover never wavered, although he was scarcely able to speak.

Dr. H. Malcom once said in my presence, that his greatest difficulties in life were to know his duties—that knowing them he could always do them. Dr. Peck seemed to have graduated in that knowledge. He appeared always to know and equally to do his duty under all circumstances. He was like an angel in the wilderness : he could rise above every thing, and soar where and when he pleased.

With wonted esteem, your friend and brother,

P. S BUSH.

DR. RUFUS BABCOCK.

OCTOBER 31*st*. My birthday has come round once more, and finds me an infirm old man sixty-six years old, but as frail and feeble as some men are at eighty-six. Still I have abundant reason to be thankful to the good providence of God that I have been thus far preserved on the journey of life; and desire to trust in futuro for all things to the same merciful and gracious Providence.

November 11th. Ventured to preach a short discourse, sitting in his chair to avoid the fatigue of standing. Returning home, conversed too much with a beloved friend, and was injured by it. Until Christmas continued in much the same state of health, getting out to meetings in the neighborhood, when the weather was fine, and occasionally speaking a few words, by request, after the sermon, not more than once or twice attempting to preach, sitting in a chair.

At the end of the year he received the tidings of the death of his son, Harvey Jenks Peck, who departed this life at his residence in Iowa, December 17th, a little over forty-one years old.

January 17th, 1856, he thus wrote: At the moment when your letter came to me I was giving a familiar lecture to our young pastor, on sermonizing. He expressed a desire to come to my house once each week, and get me to instruct him. He came to-day with the skeleton of a sermon for the Sabbath, and so I gave him a familiar lecture on sermonizing, loaned him some books, and pointed out in them several portions to be carefully examined. So, you see, I am at the head of a theological school, with one student, whom I most cordially regard as my pastor. I am working out practically what Dr. Wayland—as "Roger Williams" in the Examiner—commends theoretically.

My life and health are exceedingly precarious; and I know not how soon I may break down entirely. Many have urged me to prepare something like an Autobiography. I have thought of "Reminiscences," and keeping person and self behind as much as possible, draw sketches of what I have seen and heard; the "Times" in which I have lived, and the events which have occurred, in which I have had some small part. This is the leading idea, and I have actually commenced such a series of reminiscences, in the Western Watchman.

In the same letter he solicited me to take charge of what he should thus write, and of the manuscripts, journals and correspondence which he might leave behind him, and prepare them for the press. A few of the reminiscences, in full, or abridged, have been reproduced in the earlier portions of this volume.

Again, October 11th, he wrote me : My health and strength are continually failing, of which I have conviction in the want of ability to write which I possessed two years since. I cannot write as much in three days as I then could in one. I cannot walk more than one hundred yards without extreme fatigue. I cannot stand ten minutes. I am literally *worn out*.

But another and altogether new ingredient was now to be mingled in the cup which his heavenly Father prepared for him. Hitherto his help-mate had vigorously sustained him ; henceforth he was to finish his pilgrimage alone. It seems proper to give the letter announcing this bereavement.

ROCK SPRING, ILL., *November* 11th, 1856.

MY DEAR BROTHER :—Before this reaches your office, you will have seen in the Western Watchman, and perhaps other papers, the weighty and crushing affliction that has befallen me.

The wife I have loved was an extraordinary *wife and mother*, and I think, in justice to her memory, and as an illustration of my poor labors, I ought to devote one *reminiscence* to her, as a remarkable *help-mate* in all my labors and efforts. I have never thought it expedient and proper to write or speak in praise of my late dear wife while living; but now she has finished her course, it ought to be known in *what sense*, and to *what extent* she was the *help-mate*, pre-eminently, in every department of labor her husband undertook. I now assure all my friends that had not that woman possessed the principles, and been the wise, prudent, self-denying HEAD, and *government* of my family she was, I could not have made half the sacrifices, and performed half the services my kind friends have attributed to me. She was destitute of all sentimentality, never manifested the nervous emotion of many females, while her mind and feelings were under perfect self-control. She professed conversion in the great revival in Litchfield, Ct., in 1807, and joined the Congregational Church in 1808. We were married May 8th, 1809. * * * * Two years since about this time both of us broke down by a little exposure and fatigue in attending a series of meetings ; both had the same complaints—congestion of the liver primarily—attended with a bronchial affection.

There was so much affinity in our temperaments and constitutions, that not only were we afflicted with similar diseases but the same medical treatment answered for either. My wife went with me to St. Louis and Alton the last week in June to commencement. As twice in nine months I had broken down by effort and fatigue, in endeavoring to resuscitate the college, she seemed unwilling for me to go alone without her watchful eye. This was the last time my wife went from home. About the middle of July she was attacked with an irregular intermittent fever. The usual remedies for intermittents were employed, but without permanent effect. Two days after she was growing worse and could take neither medicine or nourishment, and her prospects of recovery became hopeless. Her fever had subsided, but on the 14th it returned, and become continuous with remissions till the 20th, when her fever left her, never to return. On the 15th October I saw there was no hope of her recovery, and held a special conversation and prayed with her. She stated that she had always had doubts about her interest in Christ, and many misgivings lest she should rest on a false foundation; but since her illness she had gained clearer views of the all-perfect righteousness of Christ, and all doubts were gone. She evinced no uncommon emotions, no raptures, but perfect calmness and resignation, strong faith, and an unclouded hope of future and immediate salvation. For three or four days (I think) she was kept alive by the skill and palliative medicines of her physican.

Three of our six children now living were here. After giving her granddaughter Mary one of the most pertinent and effective addresses from a dying person I ever heard, she then addressed. all present, declared to them her assurance that before another day she should be in that state where pain, sorrow, sickness, and death can never enter. At a quarter before six P.M. on Friday the 24th she was lying quite over on her side, when some of the women noticed a struggle and change. I approached the bed where she lay, turned her over, found no pulse in her wrists, and only a slight pulsation at her heart. I held her hand, but not the least consciousness remained. I felt no disposition to resist the impulse to kneel by the bedside and offer prayer and thanks for such a triumphant victory over death.

On Sabbath I was quite ill, and could not leave my house. At ten A.M. the company assembled, and our pastor read and sung Hymn 1072 of the Psalmist, and prayed. The procession formed and moved to Oakhill church-house, where Elder James Lemen preached from Ps. lxxxviii. 10: "Shall the dead arise and praise thee?" The coffin was opened, and several hundred friends saw her face for the last time. The procession again formed, came past my house, and passed on northeast three-quarters of a mile to Rock Spring cemetery, where she will remain till the resurrection. Yours fraternally,

J. M. PECK.

Very shortly after the burial of Mrs. Peck, that early, constant friend of their hearts, Rev. James E. Welch, arrived from Missouri. His presence and sympathy were a timely consolation to the bereaved one; and the invitation, cordial and earnest, which he tendered to Dr. Peck, to return with him to his home that they might pass the winter together, was fully appreciated, though it could not be accepted.

Near the end of June he was once more able to attend the commencement at Alton, and took an important part in the deliberations of the Board of Trustees of the college.

About the 20th of July he set forth on one more somewhat extensive tour through the northern portion of the wide field, which he had so often traversed. With an old and valued friend, Colonel Shook, he took passage in an up-river Mississippi steamer at St. Louis, and reached Smith's Ferry, nearly opposite Galena, the 1st of August. Children and grandchildren here welcomed him most cordially; and after four or five days he went to Madison, Wis., where he was the guest of a dear friend, L. C. Draper, Esq. Thence he went to Chicago, where he spent a Sabbath, and found troops of old friends gathering round him, and much enjoyed their society. Dr. Boon, the Mayor, made him his welcome guest, and in his carriage took him to the several localities of greatest importance. Returning to Galena he spent a Sabbath there, and reached home early in September.

During the autumn and winter Dr. Peck had frequent alternations of illness and partial recovery. October 21st, his journal says: "Find myself very feeble; unable to do much; and think I shall be compelled to quit writing for the papers and periodicals and confine myself to such manuscripts as are indispensable to my reminiscences." Ten days later he says: "This is my birth-day, and I am sixty-eight years old. It is hardly possible for me to live to see another anniversary. My sole dependence is on the mercy and grace of God. O Lord, into thy hands I commit my spirit!" The following are among the last entries in his journal:

November 17*th*. At one o'clock my old friend, Welch, came to see me, and I talked and talked till quite fatigued. I forget to refrain from talking, a sure sign that my mind and judgment are failing with my body.

20*th*. To-day my friend Russell arrived from Bluffdale. Of course he was joyfully received. We conversed till I was tired out.

26*th*. Thanksgiving: Governor Reynolds, Deacon Simmons, Elders Storrs, Ross, and Ely, with neighbors Crosby, Colver and wife, dined with me.

Feb. 16*th*, 1857. President Read and my old friend Cyrus Edwards came here to see me, and we met most cordially. Discussed college matters very fully. The conversation was cheerful and exhilarating, and we enjoyed ourselves greatly.

This was about the last of his social enjoyments which he had health really to relish. For some days afterward he kept about as before; but on the 25th of February he made the last entry in his journal, and that a brief one, chiefly in regard to the weather. Next day, and several following ones, he seemed to have no appetite, kept his bed most of the time, merely rising to conduct morning family-worship, but not remaining for breakfast, and saying very distinctly, but with much cheerfulness, to his son Henry, that his time was short.

Sunday, 28th February, he came into the dining-room in the morning, took the Bible as usual, read three verses only, and then kneeled with the family and with great difficulty offered a short prayer. It was *the last reading, the last prayer with the family.*

But why repeat here the struggling endurances of the last few days? His mind remained most of the time serene and unclouded to the last. Lord's-day, March 7th, his pastor, Elder Storrs, called after preaching; had some very solemn conversation with him; asked particularly how he felt in view of dying. He replied: "I feel as I always have felt since relying on Christ. If I was not ready for death, this would be a poor time to prepare. But I have no fear of death at all. I assure you I am a stranger to any such feeling as fear in reference to dying. Tell this to all these kind friends" —many were then in the room—" and pray for them and the family."

Sunday, March 14th, he had an interview with his friend, Rev. W. F. Boyakin. He said to him with emphasis : " I have never done any thing that can save me. All my works could never rescue me from destruction. Only Christ is my Saviour, my whole dependence !" His pastor and L. Sleeper of St Louis were with him in the evening. The latter, on coming in, was recognized and addressed with the calm testimony of the dying man : " I am almost gone." He had before given his parting words and blessing to each of his family, and a quarter before nine in the evening he expired. In imitation of his example at the deathbed of his wife, a few months before, the company all kneeled and joined with Mr. Storrs in fervent prayer and thanksgiving. For thirty-six hours from that time the rain came down profusely and incessantly. But when the hour for the funeral arrived, the rain ceased and the sun shone out beautifully. Rev. James Lemen preached a funeral sermon from the emphatic words of the apostle : " *I have fought a good fight, I have finished my course, I have kept the faith.*" Very touching was the scene when the venerable preacher descended from the pulpit and, approaching the cold remains, laid his trembling hand on the brow of the deceased, and with a choked utterance sung three stanzas of the hymn beginning : " The languishing head is at rest. Its thinking and aching are o'er."

Twenty-nine days later, by the special desire of many friends, his remains were removed to the Bellefontaine cemetery, St. Louis, where another funeral service was attended, Rev. Dr. Crowell delivering a commemorative discourse, embracing a well-merited eulogy of his character and labors. In that central position of the wide field which he had watched over, and labored so long and well to cultivate, his remains repose. " Si monumentum quæris circumspice."

NOTES
INDEX

NOTES TO INTRODUCTION

1. E. W. Hicks, in *The Standard*, Chicago, June 14, 1913. Quoted by Coe Hayne, *Vanguard of the Caravans* (Philadelphia: Judson Press, 1931), pp. 147–48.

2. Helen Louise Jennings has compiled the most complete, but not exhaustive, bibliography of Peck's published and unpublished writings. She identified ninety-one published articles and eight books by Peck. "John Mason Peck and the Impact of New England on the Old Northwest" (Doctoral dissertation, University of Southern California, 1961).

3. John Peck and John Lawton, *An Historical Sketch of the Baptist Missionary Convention of the State of New York* (Utica: Bennett and Bright, 1837), pp. 22–23.

4. Cf., William Warren Sweet, *Religion on the American Frontier: The Baptists, 1783–1830* (New York: Henry Holt and Company, 1931), pp. 41–42.

5. Theodore C. Pease, *The Frontier State, 1818–1848. The Centennial History of Illinois* (Chicago: A. C. McClurg and Co., 1922), II, 364.

6. Alice Felt Tyler, *Freedom's Ferment* (Minneapolis: The University of Minnesota Press, 1944), p. 35.

7. Lyman Beecher, *Plea for the West* (New York: Leavitt, Lord & Co., 1835), pp. 60–71.

8. *Life of Daniel Boone,* in *The Library of American Biography,* ed. Jared Sparks (Boston: Little, Brown, and Co., 1847), XIII, 15.

9. John Mason Peck, *A New Guide for Emigrants to the West* (Boston: Gould, Kendall & Lincoln, 1836), pp. 147 f.

10. *Ibid.,* p. 149.

11. Cf., pp. 293–294, *infra; also* Reinhold Niebuhr, *The Children of Light and the Children of Darkness* (New York: Charles Scribner's Sons, 1944).

12. Cf., *also* Jennings, *op. cit.,* p. 244, who quotes an assessment of J. M. Peck by another contemporary, Mason Brayman.

13. George H. Williams, *Wilderness and Paradise in Christian Thought: The Biblical Experience of the Desert in the History of Christianity & the Paradise Theme in the Theological Idea of the University* (New York: Harper & Brothers, 1962), pp. 3 f.

14. *Ibid.,* pp. 5 f.

15. H. Shelton Smith, Robert T. Handy, and Lefferts A. Loetscher, *American Christianity* (New York: Charles Scribner's Sons), II, 5.

16. Philip Schaff, *America,* ed. Perry Miller (New York: Charles Scribner's Sons, 1955), p. 47.

17. *Infra.,* p. lxxvii; also J. M. Peck, *Life of Daniel Boone,* in *The Library of American Biography,* ed. Jared Sparks (Boston: Little, Brown, and Co., 1847), Vol. XIII.

18. *Infra,* p. 227.

19. *New Guide for Emigrants* (1836), pp. vi f.

20. *Ibid.,* pp. v f.

21. *From Barbarism, the First Danger,* quoted in Winthrop S. Hudson, *American Protestantism* (Chicago: University of Chicago Press, 1961), p. 77.

22. *New Guide for Emigrants,* pp. 14, 49–50.

23. Quoted by Coe Hayne, *op. cit.,* p. 126.

24. Matthew Lawrence, *John Mason Peck, the Missionary Pioneer* (New York: Fortuny's, 1940), p. 89.

25. Clarence W. Alford (ed.), *Governor Edward Coles,* in *Collections of the Illinois Historical Society* (Springfield, Illinois, 1920), XV, 323–24, 328.

26. *New Guide for Emigrants,* p. 127.

27. *A Guide for Emigrants,* 1831, pp. 291 ff., quoted by Austen K. De Blois, *The Pioneer School: A History of Shurtleff College, the Oldest Educational Institution in the West* (New York: Fleming H. Revell Co., 1900), p. 25.

28. This is excerpted from a letter written to an eastern businessman who requested the information. "The Future of Chicago— in 1834," ed. Douglas C. McMurtrie, *Bulletin of the Chicago Historical Society,* March, 1936.

29. *New Guide for Emigrants,* p. viii.

30. J. H. Perkins and John Mason Peck, *Annals of the West* (Pittsburgh: W. S. Haven, 1856), pp. 1001 f.

31. Hayne, *op. cit.,* p. 127.

32. Charles I. Foster, *Errand of Mercy: The Evangelical United Front, 1790–1837* (Chapel Hill: University of North Carolina Press, 1960), pp. 182 f.

33. Edward A. Tiryakian, "Introduction to a Bibliographical Focus on Emile Durkheim," *Journal for the Scientific Study of Religion,* III, No. 2 (Spring, 1964), 248.

34. Sweet, *op. cit.,* p. 37. Sweet reports that the ministers were paid in small cash, groceries, and whiskey.

35. Pease, *op. cit.,* p. 23.

36. Sweet, *op. cit.,* p. 52.

37. Perkins and Peck, *op. cit.,* p. 989. Peck was quoting *Ford's History of Illinois.*

38. *Ibid.,* p. 990.

39. *New Guide for Emigrants,* pp. 125 f.

40. John Mason Peck, *"Father Clark" or The Pioneer's Preacher* (New York: Sheldon, Lamport, and Blakeman, 1855), pp. 209 f.

41. *Daniel Boone,* pp. 158 f.

42. Cf., *New Guide for Emigrants,* pp. 114 ff. Quoted in full in Turner's essay "The Significance of the Frontier in American History,"*The Frontier in American History* (New York: Henry Holt and Co., 1921), pp. 19–21.

43. For a survey of the debate and an excellent assessment of the literature, cf., Earl Pomeroy, "The Changing West," and John William Ward, "The Age of the Common Man," in John Higham (ed.), *The Reconstruction of American History* (New York: Harper Torchbooks, 1962).

44. *New Guide for Emigrants,* p. 114.

45. Turner, *op. cit.,* pp. 1, 2–3, 30.

46. *Ibid.,* p. 23.

47. *New Guide for Emigrants,* pp. 102, 104 f., 110 f.

48. *Ibid.,* pp. 116–21. It is unfortunate that contemporary social historians have proceeded little beyond Peck in their analysis of the religion and society of the frontier and their mutual effects. H. Richard Niebuhr, however, did utilize the advantage that the perspective of time offered to him in his description of the transition of frontier life from the pioneer to the agricultural to the urban stages, including the impact of these changes upon religion. Cf., *The Social Sources of Denominationalism* (Hamden, Conn.: The Shoe String Press, 1954), pp. 181 f., *passim.*

49. Turner, *op. cit.,* pp. 273, 274 f.

50. Foster, *op. cit.,* p. 138.

51. *Ibid.,* p. 133.

52. *Ibid.,* p. 133.

53. *Ibid.,* p. 166.

54. *Ibid.,* p. 209.

55. William Stringfellow, *My People is the Enemy* (New York: Holt, Rinehart and Winston, 1964), pp. 86 f.

56. Foster, *op. cit.,* p. 190.

57. Smith, Handy and Loetscher, *op. cit.,* pp. 49–52.

58. Peck and Lawton, *op. cit.,* p. 23.

59. Cf. Sweet, *op. cit.,* 48 ff., and *passim.*

60. Peck and Lawton, *op. cit.,* pp. 18–28.

61. H. H. Gerth and C. Wright Mills (ed.), *From Max Weber: Essays in Sociology* (New York: Oxford University Press, 1946), pp. 304 ff. Cf., also Pease, *op. cit.,* p. 23.

62. *"Father Clark,"* pp. 140 f.

63. "Their emigration is of a very serious utility to the ancient settlements. All countries contain restless inhabitants; men impatient of labor; men who will contract debts without intending to pay them; who had rather talk than work; whose vanity persuades them that they are wise and prevents them from knowing that they are fools; who are delighted with innovations. . . . Under despotic governments they are awed into quiet; but in every free community they create, to a greater or less extent, continual turmoil; and have often overturned the peace, liberty, and happiness of their fellow citizens." Quoted in Hudson, *op. cit.,* pp. 76 f.

64. *"Father Clark,"* pp. 122 f.

65. *Ibid.,* pp. 119 ff.

66. For those who are unfamiliar with the history of Baptists, see Nelson R. Burr, *A Critical Bibliography of Religion in America,* IV, 258 ff., *passim,* in J. W. Smith and A. L. Jamison (eds.), Religion in American Life (4 vols.; Princeton: Princeton University Press, 1961). A more recent bibliography is offered by Edwin S. Gaustad, "Themes for Research in American Baptist History," *Foundations,* April, 1963, 1100 S. Goodman St., Rochester 20, N.Y.

67. H. R. Niebuhr, *op. cit.,* p. 230.

68. Cf., Robert Lee, "The Organizational Dilemma in American Protestantism," *Cities and Churches,* ed., Robert Lee (Philadelphia: Westminster Press, 1962); *also* Paul M. Harrison, *Authority and Power in the Free Church Tradition* (Princeton: Princeton University Press, 1959).

69. Pease, *op. cit.,* pp. 24 f.; *also* H. R. Niebuhr, *op. cit.,* pp. 171–73.

70. Peck and Lawton, *op. cit.,* p. 101.

71. *"Father Clark,"* pp. 143 f.

72. A. H. Newman, *A History of the Baptist Churches in the*

United States, The American Church History Series, ed., Philip Schaff (New York: The Christian Literature Co., 1894), II, 437 f.

73. Yearbook of the American Churches for 1961.

74. Sweet, *op. cit.,* p. 71.

75. Newman, *op. cit.,* p. 439; *also* H. R. Niebuhr, *op. cit.,* p. 230.

76. Sweet, *op. cit.,* p. 74.

77. *Ibid.,* p. 65.

78. John William Ward, *op. cit.,* p. 86.

79. *"Father Clark,"* pp. 201 f.

80. Sweet, *op. cit.,* p. 76.

81. H. R. Niebuhr, *op. cit.,* p. 4.

82. Peck and Lawton, *op. cit.,* pp. 92 ff.

83. *Ibid.,* pp. 102–4.

84. Robert G. Torbert, *A History of the Baptists* (Philadelphia: Judson Press, 1950), p. 350. Cf., *infra,* pp. 215 f, 304.

85. Foster, *op. cit.,* pp. 146, 154 f. Whitney R. Cross, *The Burned-Over District: the Social and Intellectual History of Enthusiastic Religion in Western New York, 1800–1850* (Ithaca, N.Y.: Cornell University Press, 1950 , pp. 23–29.

86. *Infra,* p. 340. H. R. Niebuhr would have considered this a characteristic sectarian statement. He says, "in general it may be said that the sects divided on the slavery issue and the churches divided on the political issue. . . . While the Baptists and Methodists divided into Northern and Southern branches many years before the outbreak of the Civil War the Presbyterians, Lutherans, and Episcopalians did not separate until secession had taen place." *Op. cit.,* p. 191.

87. *"Father Clark,"* pp. 257 f.

88. Quoted in Lawrence, *op. cit.,* p. 28.

89. *New Guide for Emigrants,* pp. 105–7.

90. Perkins and Peck, *op. cit.,* p. 951.

91. Alford, *op. cit.,* p. 139.

92. Pease, *op. cit.,* p. 82.

93. *Infra,* pp. 194–96.

94. Perkins and Peck, *op. cit.,* pp. 953 f. The actual vote was 6640 to 4952; cf., Jennings, *op. cit.,* p. 92, and Pease, *op. cit.,* p. 89.

95. Alford, *op. cit.,* pp. 138 f.

96. "A Discouse in Reference to the Decease of the Late Governor of Illinois, Ninian Edwards," delivered in the Court House, Belleville, Ill., December 22, 1833. (Rock Spring, Ill., 1934), p. 10.

97. *Ibid.*, p. 5.

98. "The Principles and Tendencies of Democracy," an address made at Belleville, Ill., July 4, 1839. (Belleville: J. R. Cannon, 1839), pp. 4–8.

99. *Ibid.*, pp. 9–11.

100. Sidney E. Mead, *The Lively Experiment: The Shaping of Christianity in America* (New York: Harper & Row, 1963), p. 61.

101. *Ibid.*, p. 62.

102. Cf., Gordon Harland, "The American Protestant Heritage and the Theological Task," *The Drew Gateway*, XXXII, 2 (Winter, 1962 , 77.

103. Lincoln once wrote an effective criticism of a public address Peck made favoring American action in the Mexican War. There is no record of a reply by Peck, but he later observed that Lincoln was "a very profound thinker" and said that he thought he would become a national leader. Cf., Jennings, *op. cit.*, pp. 194–97. Roy P. Basler (ed.), *The Collected Works of Abraham Lincoln* (New Brunswick: Rutgers University Press, 1953), I, 472–73.

104. "The Principles and Tendencies of Democracy," p. 7.

INDEX